ROMAN RELIGION AND ROMAN EMPIRE

The Fifteenth Publication in

THE HANEY FOUNDATION SERIES

University of Pennsylvania

Roman Religion and Roman Empire

Five Essays

ROBERT E.A. PALMER

UNIVERSITY OF PENNSYLVANIA PRESS
PHILADELPHIA

TO
LLOYD W. DALY

Acknowledgements

The essays in this book have been severally read by friends whose kind help has improved their presentation. In this regard thanks are tendered to R. Brilliant, L. W. Daly, J. A. Fitzmyer, S.J., H. M. Hoenigswald, M. H. Jameson, R. M. Ogilvie, and M. Ostwald. For other help I am grateful to M. Fowler and S. Panciera.

The cost of reproducing the photographs (except for that of Figure 8) was borne by the Department of Classical Studies, University of Pennsylvania. The photographs of Figures 1-7 and 11-16 come from the American Numismatics Society, courtesy Dr. J. Fagerlie; of Figure 8, from the German Archaeological Institute, Rome, Inst. Neg. 70.210, courtesy Dr. H. -G. Kolbe; of Figure 10, from a negative of Dr. W. Hermann, German Archaeological Institute; of Figures 17, 18, 20, from the Fototeca Unione, Rome, negs. 235, 5203, 6411, courtesy Dr. E. Nash; and of Figure 19, from the German Archaeological Institute, Inst. Neg. 39.565.

The Committee of the Haney Foundation Series of the Graduate School of Arts and Sciences, University of Pennsylvania, has made generous contribution toward the publication of this book. To the committee, and especially to two of its chairmen, M. H. Jameson and R. Hirsch, I acknowledge my great debt.

Swarthmore
January 1973

Foreword

In a justly famous discussion of the Roman constitution written after the last Punic War, the historian Polybius includes a brief notice on the Romans' solemn and constant religious observances. The degree to which religion pervaded all levels of Roman society was so alien to Polybius' way of thinking that he undertook to explain the extravagance as a manifestation of aristocratic policy aimed at the preservation of social stability. No religious activity, the Greek observed, was too base for a Roman, high or low.[1] More than a century after Polybius, another knowledgeable Greek, Dionysius of Halicarnassus, bore witness to the Romans' constancy in observing the oldest state rites and to their avoidance of modern luxury.[2] From the glorious pageantry of Roman festivals and the simplicity of its old-fashioned cult, the two Greeks drew different conclusions, one that the Romans were moved by political design, the other that they acted out of conservative piety.

Only for a brief period in the fourth century after Christ was the Roman empire guided by a policy approximating state neutrality with respect to the gods. In the following century, Augustine of Hippo would articulate in his *City of God* a denunciation of Roman religious practices that the pagans had mistaken for the right path to imperial greatness. The Roman people had tenaciously and consistently kept their religious observances for nearly a millennium of empire. As the sovereignty of Rome spread outward from central Italy to borders marked by stout walls, rivers of strange names, hot desert, and the boundless Ocean, and the greatness of the Roman people, a people of name and not of race, came to be acknowledged by all known men, Romans from high to low, low to high, held to their own cults and gods at the same time that with equal tenacity they sought to embrace the cults and gods of other states and peoples who had withstood them or aided them. The Roman clan, the household, the Roman city-state, and the imperial state seldom let a day or an hour pass without asking of their gods some boon, and gratefully acknowledging the success of their prayers. Rome's empire began before her history was first written. By the time that a coherent story of the empire was composed for us to read, the empire was already centuries old and rested upon lasting modes of governance. The lack of a thoroughly reliable political and imperial history of Rome for the early period frustrates our efforts to obtain a certain understanding of its development. Among the few historically worthwhile data from this archaic time are some very meager notices on Roman religious institutions and observances. The normal historian in antiquity could not ignore these snippets of information even if he depreciated their historical worth.[3] When we confront the discursive literature of a truly learned Roman culture, we are asked to accept the "rationalist" attitudes of a Cicero and the systematic "theology" of a Varro as the norm of a Roman's thought and feeling about his religion. As if this wrongheaded view were not sufficient to suppress modern interest in the subject, we are further required by some well-meaning men to look upon the "rationalism" of Latin literature and the advent of oriental mystery religion as the signs of a general yearning for a savior destined to buy man's security beyond the grave. The wealth of actual religious dedications and Augustus' remarkable success in religious revival and innovation speak louder than all the Ciceros and Varros, and than all the more modern Christians, of the abiding strength of Roman religious beliefs.

The five studies that appear together in this volume undertake to examine several aspects of Roman imperial religion before the foundation of Augustus' principate. The impetus that informs them is a desire to explain quite elementary religious urges in terms of Roman concern for the greatness of the Roman people. This *maiestas*, as the Romans called it, did not admit scepticism or disbelief. Much of the matter introduced here requires a suspension of our incredulity and an acceptance of primitive but persistent Roman attitudes.

The five chapters deal with five subjects, all of which verge on the general topic of Roman empire. None lends itself to our easy understanding, for the Roman concept of religion has little in common with our own. The details of the five subjects are culled from many sources of several kinds. The most familiar treatment of the Roman gods, that found in Latin literature, and especially the poets, is also the least informative, being as distant from the realities as is Augustine's critical scrutiny of Roman paganism. Latin writers adhered to a long-established Greek literary tradition, to which they undertook the adaptation of their religious heritage. Yet the Romans also wrote for a Roman public that was anything but unaffected by the spirit of their people, a spirit that was inseparable from Roman religion and was destined to find a place in the literature. Roman religion embraced not just a few, but many religious cults of other peoples who in victory and defeat taught the Romans how and to whom to pray. Although Roman receptiveness to other gods and other cults opened paths to religious observances that had taken root at the lowest level, the sovereign state recognized some of them as efficacious for all the Roman people by raising them to the level of state function. Sometimes, however, the process seems to have been initiated by the ruling class.

Whether polytheist or monotheist, a society tends to see each new god in terms of a god already known to it. The first chapter deals in part with syncretism as a means of eradicating an enemy people's independence through the importation to Rome of its chief deity; in this case, a goddess was believed to control the sovereignty of the vanquished people. The study goes beyond this problem to include an account of the Etrusco-Phoenician documents brought to light at Pyrgi within this decade.

The second chapter also depends upon inscribed documents. Indeed, the existence of a religious canon as an aspect of imperialism comes to light mostly from a few inscriptions scattered over the Roman empire. The inscription on which our attention is focused throughout the greater part of the chapter has been known only for some twenty years, and has not received the attention it deserves.

In the third chapter, new epigraphic finds—Latin, but perhaps not, strictly speaking, Roman—also occupy a special place. Although they were published less than thirty years ago, the four short dedications to divinities now rank among the oldest religious documents in the Latin language. The knowledge of where they were found throws light on otherwise little-known native incubation rites. The second half of the chapter treats again of the matter of syncretism of an enemy people's god, and closes with a study of some rather unsavory practices promoted for the purpose of gaining the favor of Gaulish gods and with allusions to the Christian hagiography that borrowed from this set of Gallo-Roman divinities. Beliefs in incubatory rites and a certain kind of goat-god are surveyed.

The penultimate essay draws on no new-found evidence, but discusses a very old problem in the history of archaic Latin song and letters, set in terms of the learned religious antiquarianism of the last republican century. Quickened interest in their own clouded past induced the Romans to take up a new Greek genre of "antiquities" and to follow a method of linguistic and literary research promulgated in Hellenistic centers of culture.

The last chapter was begun more *ioco* than *serio*, although its inception was an attempt to heal a mutilated lexical entry on a god. What appeared at first a study in religion and topography acquired a more serious aspect as it became clear that the cult concerned not merely phallus worship, but also the phenomena of the Roman triumph and Roman monuments of victory.

This last combination of religious manifestations, the cult phallus and the triumph of military conquest, can be said to exemplify the several incongruities inherent in Roman religion. Learned Romans skirted these incongruities, and the Christian Fathers scorned them, while the people, who continued many primitive practices, appear to have lost sight of their original intent and function. This appearance of forgetfulness may have been created by the ancient authors who played the "rationalist" when they selected the less unintelligent, and unintelligible, religious observances for their literary disquisitions. Roman religion was not cast in a dogmatic mould. It seldom acquired a theological articulation (and thus found no ancient exponent among learned men). But the Romans themselves saw no wrong in coupling a really profound belief with the ceremonial formalism that modern students condemn as a sign of religious atrophy. The laws of Roman religion admitted every sort of religious expression so long as it conduced to amplify the greatness of the Roman people and likewise conformed with a Roman mental habit of religious law and order.

Roman religious history contains a sense of the wonderful that will perhaps always defy our own sense of what religion and its gods *must* be. Most of us bring to a study of Roman cult the prejudices of our own contemporary outlook and insight, and we usually dwell upon the subject only long enough to reinforce another prejudice, one that arises from a conviction that the Romans took lightly the gods whom they had recreated in literary and mythological settings. Since the Roman mythology was borrowed, we have no right to expect that the Romans ever venerated the divine characters they put in their literature. Their literary view of the gods, with its mythological ramifications, also represents in its own way the Roman's attitude toward his religion: all that he avowed was susceptible of foreign influence, even the literary influence of Greek *mythos* upon his native gods.

Without congregations and without edifying principles of personal conduct, the officers of the Roman state performed the regular ceremonial functions, which the people believed made the city and the empire thrive. In rare instances, a proper clergy was attached to some specially imported god; otherwise, the worthies of Rome and her subject towns met the cult needs of prayer and sacrifice on behalf of the community at large. Although personal involvement was not needed while the state machinery operated in the interest of the common religion, it was not interdicted on the many occasions when personal concerns were expressed in religious terms.

Rome's want of a recognized clergy or priestly caste worked to advance many personal or popular religious beliefs. The public priests and state officers charged with cult duties did not consciously keep common religion at a distance. The enthusiasms conducive to religious strife or civil sedition are very rarely met in Roman history. When we do witness religious encounters, we also witness pacific resolutions through compromise. To explain this situation by a lack of conviction among the Romans would, in my view, be wrong. The explanation would seem rather to lie in the Roman sense of religious acquisitiveness, adaptation, and accommodation.

Although the Romans could be both generous and conservative in their worship of gods familiar and strange, they wished to give these gods no other return. Here, in part, are the words of a prayer recited as early as the mid-fourth-century B.C., and still uttered more than 550 years later: "I beg and beseech you that you may increase the empire and greatness of the Roman people at war and at home, and that the Latin peoples may ever obey us, and may you bestow upon the Roman people and upon their legions everlasting safety, victory and bodily strength, and may you keep sound the government of the Roman people. . . ."[4] In the third chapter we shall see that these prayers were made to oracular goddesses addressed by their Greek names and normally thought of in regard to childbirth. The Roman priests did not reserve such words for magnificent gods with Roman names.

Contents

ROMAN RELIGION AND ROMAN EMPIRE

CHAPTER ONE

JUNO IN ARCHAIC ITALY

According to their own tradition, the Romans had no goddess older than Juno. In comparison with other deities, Juno enjoys great renown through the survival of many epithets and a discernible history of her cult at Rome, the only Italian city whose history accords us the confidence to trace hers. Although we can date relatively her many Roman manifestations, little attention has been paid to her prominent role in politics and diplomacy. The fact remains that Juno played a very important part in the civil life of Romans and their neighbors. This chapter will discuss what role Juno played in the civil religion and the political life of archaic Italy, and will seek to demonstrate how the Romans, and thereby we, lost sight of her origin and early function through a shift of emphasis that ought perhaps to be dated to the beginning of the fourth century B.C., and to be attributed to Etruscan influence.

At the end of the last century Roscher culminated his research on Juno, whom he bound very closely to her Greek counterpart Hera, with a canonical entry in his *Lexicon*. Of the thirty-one columns of print, some sixteen are devoted to Juno as goddess of menstruation, marriage, and birth.[1] Roscher dogmatically asserted that Juno's name comes from the root *diou* + *on* and is thus derived from *Diou-* > Jupiter, and that her cult epithet Lucina "doubtless" comes from *lux* "light."[2] The first etymology has been untenable on religious grounds since 1905, and is today, as we shall see, equally untenable on linguistic grounds. The second etymology is now highly doubtful; the shadow of doubt was first cast as early as the first century A.D.

W. Otto attempted to reconcile the inconsistencies in Roscher's theories in his own study, published in 1905, that connected *iuno* with L. *iuven-* and suggested that *iuno* means "young woman."[3] This interpretation found favor with Wissowa in the second edition of his monumental survey of Roman religion.[4] Nevertheless, occasional attempts have been made to restore the older supposed linguistic relation with *Diovis*. At the same time as Roscher's encyclopedia was issued, W.W. Fowler published an examination of the evidence for the contention that the wife of Jupiter's flamen was a priestess of Juno; he determined that the flaminica was not so charged.[5]

In the English-speaking world, H.J. Rose recently championed the priority and pre-eminence of Juno as a goddess of female functions.[6] For him she "became" what, in point of fact, is her oldest attested function, a divinity of the state: when we can put her story in relative chronological order, it is clear that Juno is a political goddess. Although we intend to bring out this aspect of her cult, we do not deny that she oversaw female functions. Noailles, however, convincingly argues that her protection of marriage is much later than her other functions.[7] But we need not, and ought not, so to separate the phenomena of Juno that we, too, arrive at a portrait divided into compartments that seem mutually and dogmatically exclusive. There would be no gain in that method. If we devote more attention to Juno's role in diplomacy and statecraft in the following pages, we are merely attempting to restore a balance and to order the priority of functions. For Juno's cult by women has been so amply treated that we have lost sight of the lady in the war chariot brandishing a spear and holding a shield.

Furthermore, we must never forget that Juno, like all else Roman and Italian, was susceptible to foreign influence, and was remolded and viewed differently by the common people, the politicians, and finally the poets, whose contribution to her development was made quite late.

Beginning at the beginning, we treat the name *iuno*. Any relation to **diovin-* or *diov-on* must be rejected because the Etruscan form of her name *uni* betrays an initial *y-*, not *di-*, lost in Etruscan.[8] On the other hand, the acceptance of Otto's and Wissowa's semantics of *iuveno "junge Frau"[9] puts us, willy-nilly, in a prejudiced position. First of all, Otto is wrong in stating that Juno is the only deity whose name is so formed. There is the oft-attested Semo, but his name evidently comes from a verb. The best linguistic parallels are *homo, -inis* and *hemo, -onis* (> *hemona*, Festus 89 L.), and *homo, -onis* whose long ō is assured by Ennius *Ann.* 138 V. Just as *homo* is "person of the earth," (< *humus*), so *iuno* can be construed the "deity of youth." Although *homo, semo*, many Latin cognomens (e.g. Labeo, Fronto), and occupational names (e.g. *fullo, praedo*) are masculine, while Juno's gender is feminine, this usage does not deter us at all because irrefutable analogies are found in *cerus/ceres* and *venus*, both neuter nouns whose gender has changed with their recognition as the goddesses *Ceres* and *Venus*. Therefore, we shall proceed on the assumption that Juno, a *iuveno, meant merely deity of youth(fulness), without assigning that physical state to men or women.

The essence of Juno can be ascertained from her cult names and cult attributes, to which proximate times of appearance can be assigned. Since we will insist on the importance of cult names and cult practices, drawing no comfort or confidence from epithets that we do not find in cult, we can draw a definite line between ourselves and the one chief ancient source of Junonian religion, M. Terentius Varro. When a modern student wishes to pursue the story of Juno, he confronts evidence for the most part from Arnobius, Tertullian, Augustine, Martianus Capella, and the like; he sees Juno, like many other gods, through the eyes of men who had not the slightest sympathy with heathen ways. Secondly, at least in the case of Juno, such men directly or indirectly owed to Varro[10] the anti-pagan weapons of their armory. Varro was no fool, but equally no keen student of religion.

What was Varro's Juno? She was the earth (*terra*), the goddess of light first seen by new-born babes (*Lucina*), the moon (*Luna*), the air (*aer*) and a star.[11] Of her names, *Iuno* comes from the verb "to help" (*iuvare*), and *Lucina* from the noun "light" (*lux*).[12] For Varro she was the earth because, as wife of Jupiter who is the sky, she is his opposite; she was the moon because of the real linguistic relation of *lux* to *luna*. She was the air because her Greek counterpart Hera was etymologized from *aer* (see below, n. 150). Varro associated with her a deity of menstruation, Mena, and gave Juno the province of menstrual flux.[13] The monthly duties of Juno in the matter of menstruation are mentioned no earlier than Varro. The folk etymology of *Lucina* > *lux* is older,[14] but it remains a folk etymology. Varro's hodge-podge cannot be considered *prima facie* evidence of Junonian cult. In fact, it is far from being valuable in assigning priority to Juno's female supervision. Varro's contribution to our ignorance does not end here but begins with the oldest Juno at Rome, Juno Quiritis.

1. JUNO QUIRITIS/CUR(R)ITIS

According to Varro, Titus Tatius, the Sabine king of Rome and colleague of Romulus, introduced the cult of Lucina and the Moon.[15] On that account Dionysius of Halicarnassus, who relied heavily on Varro's *Antiquities*, attributes to Tatius the worship of thirty Junones Quirites in each of the thirty military and political units (*curiae*) that Romulus organized. Furthermore, instead of acknowledging the proper derivation of the name from the thirty *curiae* and the relation to the Romans as Quirites, Varro connected the epithet with the Sabine word for spear *(curis)*, which he also put abroad as the etymon of the Sabine town Cures and the god Quirinus.[16] Juno Quiritis was worshipped also in Falerii,[17] and by the local consul in the colony of Beneventum.[18] From Tiburtine religion survived the prayer, "Juno Curitis, protect my fellow natives of the curia with your chariot and shield."[19] The shield and chariot, not unique to Tibur, are strange equipment for a sexual deity of females. At Rome, the rites of Juno Quiritis were observed in all thirty curias, political units of the primitive state. In the curias Juno Quiritis was worshipped by means of very simple sacral suppers consisting of first fruits, barley and spelt cakes served on earthen plates and baskets, set on old-fashioned wooden tables called curial or sitting tables (*curiales* and *adsidelae mensae*) used by the curial flamens. The suppers were washed down with wine poured from earthen pitchers into similar cups. Dionysius witnessed these repasts and admired the curias for maintaining archaic simplicity in the splendor of Augustan Rome.[20] Juno is the only deity known to be universal in the curias, the oldest divisions of the Roman state. The Tiburtine prayer and her Roman cult in no way suggest a deity concerned with women. On the contrary, this Juno has the accoutrements of war with which she protects the members of the curias, and at Rome she receives her cult from political divisions. Another Juno who can be dated to royal Rome not only shares Quiritis' kind of cult but bears a name incontestably military.

2. JUNO POPULONA

Populona is formed from *populus* as Bellona (OLat. Duellona) from *bellum*, Pomona from *pomum*, etc. Although on this score no doubt arises, the sense of archaic *populus* is beclouded by the word's later meaning of "people." In old Latin the word *populus* has the sense of "infantry," arrived at indirectly from the verb *populari* "to plunder" and the notion of the *populus Romanus* as the centuriate army which became the centuriate popular assembly.[21]

The oldest and only certain reference to the Romans' Juno Populona comes from the Jus Papirianum, a republican collection of royal laws that concerns mostly religious matters, evidently because the sacral law of the kings remained valid in the Roman republic.[22] The context of the statement is worth examining:

> For when Tertius also discussed religious rites at length, he said that this passage [*Aen.* 1.736] came into his discussion. Nevertheless, he does not remove his own hesitation with the necessary source. For in the Jus Papirianum it is clearly reported that a dedicated table can take the place of an altar. It says: "Just as in the precinct of Juno Populona there is a table consecrated by the augurs."[23] For in shrines some things are called vessels and holy furnishings and others, ornaments. Those vessels have the appearance of utensils with which sacrifices are made. The table on which dinners, libations and donations are placed has the greatest importance among these utensils. Indeed there are decorations such as shields, garlands and like gifts. But they were not dedicated with the shrine while the table and altars are usually dedicated with the temple. On that account a table duly dedicated in a temple functions as an altar and enjoys the veneration of a pulvinar.[24]

The table of Juno Populona belongs to the royal age. On it would have been placed the dinners (*epulae*) mentioned by Macrobius. This Juno, who by her name is connected with the fighting men, also enjoyed a Roman cult of suppers. Seneca alone designates Populona a spinster goddess without other name.[25]

Martianus Capella, relying on some of the Varronian material cited above, composes this lengthy prayer to Juno, which puts before the reader a kind of distilled summary of Varronian thought:

> Oh lovely Juno, although another name assigns you a heavenly partnership, let us name you Iuno from helping [*a iuvando*] as we also name Jupiter. Or it is meet to hail you as Lucina and Lucetia because you give light to those aborning. For it is not necessary for me to call on Fluvonia, Februalis, and Februa, since I have suffered no bodily contact being yet undefiled. Human maids ought to call on Domiduca, Unxia, and Cinctia at their weddings so that you might protect their route, lead them to desired homes and, when the door posts are anointed, you might yield a favorable omen and not abandon them who place their girdles in the bridal chamber. Those whom you will protect in the hour of their confinement will pray to you as Opigena and peoples ought to call on the warriors Curitis and Populona. Now I invoke you called Hera named from the realm of air. Give to one who wants to know knowledge of what this aerial latitude and fields alight with the clashing atoms of beings bear and why here it is said the atoms of deities fly upwards. I seek not knowledge of the lower atmosphere which is filled with birds and which the height of Mt. Olympus overtops although it scarcely reach ten stades in height, but I seek the highest heights . . . .[26]

No religious tradition yields this prayer. The words belong to the sophisticated litterateur. Of all the Junonian epithets only Lucina, Populona, and Curitis are founded in cult, although the others are attested elsewhere in literature after Varro (see below).

Dedications to Juno Populona are also found in Aesernia,[27] Teanum of the Sidicines,[28] and Apulum of Dacia. In the last, a legionary legate of Commodus' reign and his wife set up three dedications to each of the Romans' Capitoline triad: Jupiter Optimus Maximus, Juno Regina Populonia (*sic*) "goddess of the fatherland" (*deae patriae*) and Minerva.[29] At Teanum the oldest dedication was made by a man, the two later ones by a *ministra* and a public priestess. The Dacian epigraph is our only explicit statement that Juno of the Capitol bore the epithet Populona as well as Regina. We shall examine this conjunction of epithets in the discussion of Juno Regina.

Neither the Jus Papirianum, which contained mention of the table in the precinct of Juno Populona, nor Martianus Capella, who names the warrior Populona of the people's prayer, tells us where the shrine of Roman Populona stood.

3. JUNO CAPROTINA OF FIDENAE AND JUNO RUMINA OF ROME

Because Quiritis is connected with curial religion and Populona is cited by the Jus Papirianum, we can safely assume these two Junos date back to the royal age. Juno Caprotina, however, is related by aetiological tales either to Romulus' demise or to a concerted attack on Rome by the Latin League. Her rites, which were held on the nones of the month Quinctilis (therefore called the Caprotine Nones), were anciently connected directly with the festival of the Poplifugia and indirectly with a victory celebration. Both these ceremonies must be referred to the *populus* as an army, so that we treat Juno Caprotina closely with Juno Populona although, at first blush, the warrior goddess seems to have little in common with the former, whose history is told only in connection with the *populus* of the Poplifugia.

In his survey of the calendar Varro gives us the oldest surviving account of the Poplifugia and Nonae Caprotinae:

> The day Poplifugia seems so named because on that day the people [*populus*] suddenly fled in an uproar. The Gauls' withdrawal from the city [took place] not much later than this day [Poplifugia], when the peoples [*populi*] around the city such as the Fidenates, Ficuleates and other peoples on our frontiers swore an oath against us. Some traces of the flight on this day appear in the ritual which I have discussed in greater detail in my *Antiquities.* The Caprotine nones are so called because on that day women sacrifice in Latium to Juno Caprotina and conduct the rites under the goat-fig, from which they apply a branch. Garbed in the *toga praetexta* she taught them at the Ludi Apollinares why this [is done].[30]

Before turning to other accounts, we can emphasize these facts. Varro does not necessarily treat the Poplifugia and Nonae Caprotinae as the same day. However we do not obtain much information from the inscribed calendars. Despite the contrary statement in some modern authors, the nones of Quinctilis (7 July) are never marked Caprotine, nor is a feast of Juno noted; we find either the unique *Palibus II* in Fasti Antiates Maiores or the first day of the Ludi Apollinares (instituted in 212 B.C.) marked on the calendars for 7 July.[31] On the other hand, Poplifugia is marked only at 5 July, the only day between the calends (always the first day) and the nones (either the fifth or seventh day) of any month that has a state festival in the old calendars. Although the Fasti Amiternini alone have in small letters feast of Jupiter (*feriae Iovi*) with *Poplifugia*, the only deity connected by the authors with the Poplifugia is Juno Caprotina.[32] The Juno garbed with the *toga praetexta* at the Ludi Apollinares is very strange indeed, even if the first day of the games had coincided with Caprotine nones. As a young man Caesar Commodus still gave largesse and held court in his boy's *praetexta*. "Moreover, he wore the *toga* [*praetexta*] on the nones of July when Romulus ceased to exist on earth . . . ."[33] It would appear that Commodus, who otherwise liked to dress up as Hercules at Omphale's court,[34] also liked to wear the *praetexta* as did Juno on 7 July. The day on which Romulus died is the crux of the relation between Poplifugia and Nonae Caprotinae.

According to Livy (1.16.1), Romulus was holding a public meeting for a military review at Goat's Marsh (*Caprae Palus*) when he ascended into heaven during a violent storm. Ovid says that he was dispensing justice at the same place (*F.* 2.491-92). Plutarch's three accounts contribute in part to our confusion. Romulus disappeared on the day called Poplifugia and Nonae Capratinae (*sic*) at Goat's Marsh, where he was addressing the people, whereupon the people rushed to Goat's Marsh calling out praenomens (Gaius, Marcus, and Lucius) and offered sacrifice there.[35] Plutarch was not consistent; elsewhere he reports that Romulus was at Goat's Marsh sacrificing with the people and senate on the Capratine Nones, the fifth day of July.[36] But the fifth day is Poplifugia (so only on the calendars), the nones the seventh.

Plutarch knows another version of how the rites of early July began. Although he tells it twice (*Rom.* 29, *Cam.* 33), it does not clarify the situation. Macrobius (*Sat.* 1.11.35-40) knows only the second aetiological tale, wherein he omits mention of Romulus, Camillus, and Goat's Marsh, but adds that the enemy commander was dictator of the Fidenates, a detail recalling Varro's remarks on their oath at Poplifugia, which Macrobius also omits. If we compound Plutarch's two tales and that of Macrobius', we have the following story. Once upon a time when Camillus was alive, the Latins, Aequi and Volsci banded together under Livius Postumius, dictator of Fidenae, and threatened the Romans with destruction unless they consented to give the finest flower of Roman maidenhood to be their brides. The Romans despaired until a plucky slave girl Tutula or Tutela (Macrobius' name), who was also called Philotis, persuaded the Romans to have her dress up her fellow slave girls in noble garments and go off to the Latin camp. The Romans, quick to see the value in such a plan, willingly gave them the clothing. Off they went to make their Latin bridegrooms drunk. Then Philotis signalled the Romans from a goat-fig with a torch shielded by her garment, and they rushed from the city and slew the besotted Latins. Recognizing the generosity of their female slaves, the Romans freed and dowered Philotis and her friends and ever afterward allowed them to celebrate the festival of Caprotine Nones. On that day men go rushing to Goat's Marsh to sacrifice and shout, "Marcus, Lucius, Gaius" in commemoration of their flight from, or assault on, the enemy. In commemoration of their own part, freeborn ladies and their mistresses let the slave girls dress up like ladies. Then the slave girls stone each other, fight, and feast under arbors made of goat-fig branches. The "milk" from the goat-fig (*caprificus*) is used in this festival for Juno Caprotina.

Plutarch adds one detail that leads us to the third day (*Rom.* 29.9) when the Roman men kept a victory celebration which marked their defeat of the Latins. The shouting of names and the victory celebration refer to a ceremony following the nones and known only from Macrobius (*Sat.* 3.2.11-15):

> In the first book of Pictor's *Pontifical Law* the word *vitulari* is found. Titius reports as follows on its meaning; *vitulari* is to rejoice by voice. Also Varro in the sixteenth book of his *Antiquities of Divine Matters* reports that in certain ceremonies the pontiff is supposed to *vitulari*, which the Greeks call *paianizein* . . . . According to Hyllus' book on the gods the goddess who presides over rejoicing is called Vitula. Piso says the heifer is called the victor's heifer (*vitula victoria*). On this matter he adduces the argument that on the day after the nones of July, when things had turned out well because the *populus* had been put to flight by Etruscans, a ceremony of *vitulatio* is held at fixed sacrifices after the victory. The Poplifugia are named after the flight.

Then follows in Macrobius an etymology of *vitulatio* from *vitam tolerare*! Degrassi, p. 481, draws attention to the fact that the "vitulation" took place a day after the nones, which was an unlucky day (*dies religiosus*), regularly avoided for public holidays (as were almost all even-numbered days of the month). Hyllus' goddess *Vitula* existed only in the imagination (see Varro *LL* 7.107). The *vitula victoria* was offered for a victory Calpurnius Piso had connected with Poplifugia, which he dated in the second century B.C. to the nones of July, the same date as Plutarch's. The verb *vitulare* "to sacrifice with a heifer" resembles *libare* "to sacrifice with a cake."

We sum up our evidence before discussing it. The inscribed calendars mark the Poplifugia at 5 July, and have no festival on the nones, 7 July (except *Palibus II* in one calendar), or 8 July, except references to the Ludi Apollinares. Varro does not date the Poplifugia but explains them. He discusses the rites held on the Caprotine nones, which he alone relates to an occurrence at the Ludi Apollinares when Juno Caprotina wore a *toga praetexta*. Plutarch speaks of the Poplifugia and Nonae Capratinae as identical. On that day Romulus disappeared at Goat's Marsh while either addressing the people or offering such sacrifice as the men who shout names offer at the Poplifugia or on Nonae Capratinae. On the same day, Roman slave girls observe rites for Juno Capratina in commemoration of a victory over the Latins led by a man of Fidenae (so Macrobius). On the next day, 8 July, the day after the Poplifugia of the nones, the Romans held a victory celebration, which Calpurnius Piso and Varro had once treated. Macrobius reports this sacrifice of the victor's heifer without connection with the festival of Juno Caprotina, which he treats in another book of the *Saturnalia.*

Now we turn to an interpretation of this baffling series of three rites.[37] First of all, Calpurnius Piso wrote almost a century before the surviving inscribed calendars. He, followed by Plutarch, dates the Poplifugia to 7 July, the nones. Yet the inscribed calendars have the Poplifugia on 5 July, and Varro discusses the festival before that of 7 July. However, *Poplifugia* is plural and refers to at least two flights or routs. Accordingly, one *poplifugium* should be referred to 5 July and another to 7 July. To the question how one is absent from the calendar, we propose the answer that Poplifugium II, already shared with the two Pales, was overshadowed by the rites of Juno Caprotina, more especially by the ever-expanding Ludi Apollinares, founded during the Hannibalic War.

Secondly, the Poplifugia were not the flights of the Roman *populus.* In the calendar we encounter the similar compounds Regifugium (24 February), Equirria (27 February and 14 March), Tubilustrium (23 March and May), Fordicidia (15 April), and Armilustrium (19 October). The nature and interpretation of the name Regifugium is still a matter of dispute. However we can paraphrase with certainty the rest: *equi currunt*; *tubae lustrantur*; *fordae caeduntur*; *arma lustrantur.* Did the army or armies flee, or was it (or were they) put to flight? Varro says neighboring peoples, including the Fidenates and Ficuleates, took a common oath against the Romans at the Poplifugia. In recording the vowing of another Juno's temple, Livy (32.30.10) apparently represents the language of the vow: "consul principio pugnae vovit aedem Sospitae Iunonis si eo die hostes fusi fugatique fuissent; a militibus clamor sublatus compotem voti consulem se facturos, et in hostes est factus." Without unreasonable belief we may imagine similar circumstances surrounding the flight of the Latins and a similar vow to Juno Caprotina. In any event, the Roman pontiff celebrated the victory over the Latins with a heifer on 8 July, so that we are compelled to conclude that the Romans must have put to flight and the neighbors have taken to flight at the Poplifugia. Such business, a longish ritual at first, might later have been reduced to a single day, although memory of its observance on 7 July, two days after the day marked Poplifugia in the calendars, lived on. This interpretation is supported by the fact that the victory celebration fell on 8 July, a kind of day otherwise devoid of worship because it fell after the nones. Otherwise, victory ought to have been celebrated on 6 July, the day after the day that bears the calendar notation of the Poplifugia.

Before turning to the combination of Poplifugia and the feast of Juno Caprotina, let us sum up what we have said about Poplifugia. The Poplifugia were the ritual routs of at least two Latin armies (*populi*). Some of the ceremonies took place at Goat's Marsh in the Campus Martius, where the centuriate *populus* usually gathered. There Romulus had ascended into heaven while sacrificing as did the Romans after him (Plutarch *Rom.*), or while addressing the people (Plutarch *Num.*), or while reviewing the army (Livy). At the Poplifugia men presumably shouted, "Gaius, Lucius, and Marcus." Now the outspoken cursing and expulsion of foreigners is recorded in the Iguvine Tables. The Iguvine cursing and banishment are preceded by auspices taken with special care to the bird *parra*, and belong to a lustration of the Iguvine *populus*. Not only are foreigners cursed and expelled by three shouts, but the cursing is followed by a chasing of heifers, three of which were sacrificed to Tursa Cerfia or Tursa Jovia; their enemies were cursed in the language of the cursers. The resemblance right down to the heifer victim is too close te be ignored, although there is no rout recorded at Iguvium.[38] Yet more than one people were involved, as were the several Latin neighbors of Rome. Roman name-calling at the Poplifugia parallels the Iguvine practice and can explain the legal definition of *vitulari*, "to rejoice by words."

At the Roman *poplifugia* the presiding magistrate performed a lustration of the Roman *populus* appropriate to the Campus Martius, where the centuriate army regularly foregathered. Thereupon the Roman army engaged in expelling and driving off Fidenates, Ficuleates, and other Latin neighbors who had solemnly banded together to participate in the ceremonies. On many occasions the Romans held personal or proper names to be ominous (Cic. *Scaur.* 29-30); they contrived to draft first men with ominous names (Valerius, Salvius, Statorius) and to let public contracts by first leasing the fisheries of Lacus Lucrinus as if its name meant "profit" (Fest. *Epit.* p. 108 L). In matters of marriage and fertility the Romans applied the name of two birds, Gaius and Titus, also borne as personal praenomens (see below, ch. 5). In this vein should be interpreted Plutarch's report of the praenomens shouted to commemorate the Roman victory through the ruse of the slavegirls. Such names comport with the sexual aspects of Juno Caprotina's rites (see below), as well as with the ominous power to ward off or exclude those who do not belong at the rites or within Roman territory. In Festus' *Epitome* (p. 72 L) survives the formula: "exesto, extra esto. sic enim lictor in quibusdam sacris clamitabat: 'hostis, vinctus, mulier, virgo exesto,' scilicet interesse prohibebatur." ("Begone! be outside. At certain rites the lictor shouted so, 'Begone stranger, prisoner, woman, maid.' This means they were kept from participating.") At the Poplifugia and the rites of Juno Caprotina, Roman men shouted personal names to accomplish the same effect.

To Poplifugia the notation *feriae Iovi* was added in one calendar; if the words are to be understood as a "gloss" and not as another rite, Iguvium's Tursa Jovia offers an analogy. Furthermore, Tursa Jovia, the "Terror of Jupiter," has a parallel in legendary Roman history in king Tullus Hostilius' vow of shrines to Pallor and Pavor in his battle against Veientes and Fidenates! Of course, the enemy was filled with Homeric terror and fright and was put to flight.[39] Against an identification of the Poplifugia as a festival of Jupiter is the fact that at Iguvium sacrifice was also made to Cerfus Martius, to Prestota Cerfia of Cerfus Martius, and to Tursa Cerfia of Cerfus Martius, just as Tullus Hostilius vowed twelve Salian priests along with the shrines to Pallor and Pavor. The Roman Salians comprised a sodality for worship of Mars. Second, there are Juno Caprotina and her festivals' purported commemoration of a victory over the Latins led by a man of Fidenae, one of the towns that swore a solemn oath against Rome at the Poplifugia and one of the towns that opposed Tullus Hostilius in a battle that echoes the ceremonies of Poplifugia.

In order to understand how the Nones of Caprotina and Poplifugia were treated together before Plutarch wrote his lives of Romulus, Numa, and Camillus, we must ascertain Plutarch's source. Fortunately our task is quite easy. Before Macrobius quotes Calpurnius Piso on the heifer of victory and his dating of the Poplifugia on the nones of July, he cites Varro's *Antiquities of Divine Matters* Book XV (*Sat.* 3.2.11-14).[40] Varro himself says that he has discussed the Poplifugia at length in his *Antiquities* (*LL* 6.18). Macrobius used a book of the *Antiquities of Human Matters* on days[41] and often cites Varro on subjects related to the calendar.[42] In his discussion of the month of May, Macrobius also cites Calpurnius Piso in the company of the antiquarian Cincius and Cornelius Labeo;[43] furthermore, he has just remarked Varro's agreement with Cincius on an April matter.[44] I thus assume that Macrobius directly or indirectly obtained his quotation of Calpurnius Piso's *Annales* from Varro's *Antiquities*, since Varro cited the *Annales* on the Lacus Curtius and on a law of Numa Pompilius for keeping the gate of Janus open.[45] However there is the remote possibility that Cincius may have been responsible for Plutarch's account, although there is no evidence that the latter knew the former's work. Macrobius' account of the Caprotine Nones (*Sat.* 1.11.35-40) ought also to be referred to Varro's *Antiquities* because it parallels Plutarch's accounts, which can be shown to have been derived from the *Antiquities*.

Varro had a friend cast a horoscope of Romulus in order to obtain knowledge of early Rome. Plutarch reports that he took his horoscope of Romulus from Varro, "a philosopher most learned in history" (*Rom.* 12), and dates the disappearance of Romulus to the nones of July at Goat's Marsh (*Rom.* 27, 29 etc.). Solinus (1.16-20) reports the same horoscope from Varro and dates the disappearance of Romulus to the nones of July at Goat's Marsh. Varro the adept in history can only be Varro the author of the *Antiquities*. But Varro's interest in Romulus' horoscope did not end there; he also wanted a horoscope of *Roma Quadrata*, founded on Parilia, the April feast of Pales.[46] Since the festival of the two Pales occurred on the nones of July,[47] Varro had another reason to notice the date of Romulus' death. Rome was born on a feast of Pales, and Romulus died on a feast of two Pales. Furthermore, Varro knew of the pair of Pales: in his dialogue on agriculture during the discussion at the election of aediles under the hot sun,[48] one of the interlocutors, Q. Lucienus, says, "Murrius, be my representative while I pay *asses* to the Pales, so that if they should want something from me, you can offer testimony."[49] Although the season of the year and the time of the elections fit July, this reference to the Pales cannot be applied to activities of the nones, for there was no comitial day in the month until 10 July. Nevertheless, the passage demonstrates Varro's knowledge of the twin Pales and perhaps of some aspect of their cult. Since the interlocutor Lucienus who had left to pay *asses* to the Pales returns just a few minutes later,[50] the place where he paid the *asses* must have been quite close to the scene of the dialogue, the Villa Publica in the Campus Martius.[51] This vicinity may or may not be significant, inasmuch as Goat's Marsh (*Caprae Palus*), where Romulus disappeared and the Poplifugia and Nonae Caprotinae were celebrated, was also in the Campus.[52]

Although Varro seems to treat Poplifugia and Nonae Caprotinae as distinct festivals (*LL* 6.18), he must be held responsible for their coincidence in Plutarch. Somehow Varro connected the two ceremonies with the day of Romulus' disappearance. The coincidence of the festivals Varro himself owed to Calpurnius Piso. If Livy may be taken to represent the annalistic tradition, the annalists situated Romulus' disappearance at *Caprae Palus* during a public meeting before a military review. Livy, however, gives no date (1.16.1). It seems clear enough that, even if a *Poplifugium* did not also occur on Caprotine nones, the connection was made through the place called *Caprae Palus* where part of the Poplifugia was held, as is reflected in Romulus' activity there, and where the rites for Juno Caprotina were held. Furthermore, in the aetiological tale of Tutula (Tutela), alias Philotis, the entire narrative is held together by the belief that the festival of Juno originated with a Roman victory over Latin neighbors. In her part Philotis uses her *himation* to conceal from the Latins the light with which she signalled the Romans.[53] The Greek *himation* is Plutarch's word for *toga*.[54] Not only is the toga a man's garment, but the *toga praetexta* was donned by Juno Caprotina of the Ludi Apollinares.[55] The *toga praetexta* was usually worn either by Roman boys or by Roman curule magistrates and priests, but not by Roman ladies.[56] Juno Caprotina's garb may have been that of the magistrate or priest who historically performed the rites attributed to Romulus at Goat's Marsh. If this is the case, the activity was not strictly military, for a magistrate went to war *paludatus*. Under these circumstances the festival of Juno Caprotina would seem not to have been an integral part of the Poplifugia. According to Pliny (*NH* 8.197) the statue of Fortuna dedicated by king Servius Tullius wore an ancient *praetexta*, which lasted until his own time. The *praetexta* of goddesses reflects an archaic robing in the trappings of the chief magistrates.

However, the *toga praetexta* can also be related to the character of the rites of Caprotine nones by the facts that the freedmen mayors of the neighborhoods (*vici magistri*) wore it at the *Ludi Compitalicii*, and that the participants in Nonae Caprotinae were slave-girls whose predecessors had been freed and dowered after their generous conduct on behalf of Rome. Again Festus' lexicon comes to our aid:

> "Sards for sale!," someone is more worthless than another. Hence the proverb seems to have arisen because at the Capitoline games, which are given by the neighbors wearing the *praetexta*, an auction of Veientines is held, at which the most outlandish and weak old man wearing the *praetexta* and a golden pendant is brought forth by the auctioneer. The Etruscan kings, who are called Sards because the Etruscan race originates at Lydian Sardis, were costumed in this manner. With a great band Tyrrhenus set out from Lydia and seized that part of Italy which today is called Etruria. But Sinnius Capito claims that Tiberius Gracchus, the consular colleague of P. Valerius Falto, reduced Sardinia and Corsica, and that no good booty was taken except for the slaves, of which there was a very cheap lot.

From this lexical entry we can clearly see that the Romans had little certain knowledge about the *toga praetexta*. To all appearances the *praetexta* was a foreign garment imported to Rome under varying circumstances, and in the case of Juno

Caprotina came with the goddess from elsewhere. The town of Fidenae was normally allied with Etruscan Veii.[57] Having seen that Juno Caprotina was dressed in
men's clothing, which was appropriate to Roman freedmen as well as boys, curule
magistrates, a certain goddess, and Etruscan kings, we turn to the Juno whose
festival is not marked on extant calendars at the nones of July.

We have already remarked that the Poplifugia of 5 July is the only old festival
marked on the calendars between calends and nones, and that the "vitulation" of
8 July is the exception to the rule that makes the days following calends, nones,
and ides unlucky and devoid of ceremony. According to Ovid Juno watches over
calends and ides, while the nones have no patron deity.[58]

On the calends of July the notation [*Iun*]*oni* is marked in small red letters,
whereas the so-called oldest calendar feasts are written in large black letters in the
Fasti Antiates Maiores. We know nothing else about this Juno.[59] Her rank in the
Antiate calendar is the same as that of *Palibus II* at 7 July, the nones elsewhere
called Caprotine.

The following pattern is evidenced by a variety of calendars and notices:

	February	*March*	*July*	*October*
Calends	Juno Sospita	Juno Lucina	[Jun]o	tigillum sororium
Nones	*dies februatus*	Junonalia	Caprotinae	Juno Quiritis in
	proclaimed			Campo

Attestation of these ceremonies, all of which concern Juno, depends on sources of
diverse quality.[60] We shall discuss these Junos in turn. Just as Juno Caprotina and
the Nonae Caprotinae are not marked in the inscribed calendars, the proclamation
of *dies februatus* and Junonalia of other nones are omitted from the inscribed
calendars. Knowledge of the former and its connection with Juno comes directly
and indirectly from Varro (see below). The Junonalia is noted on the calendar
called after Furius Filocalus and dated to 354 A.D. Only Juno Quiritis, who was
situated in the Campus Martius, can be found in the inscribed calendars. However,
her origin is disputed.[61]

When Ovid wrote his *Fasti*, Juno was already certainly connected with the nones
of February, July, October, and perhaps March. This connection ought not to be
overlooked in discussions of the absence of Juno Caprotina from the inscribed
calendars.

Because Varro (*LL* 6.18) says that women celebrate the Nonae Caprotinae in
Latium, it can be urged that the festival did not have a peculiarly Roman origin. In
support of the Latinity of her cult is adduced this Praenestine inscription:

```
       C. Saufeio(s)   C.f
   •   Sabini
       C. Orcevio(s)   M.f.
       ————————ị
       censores
       hasce aras
       probaveront
       Iuno(ne) Palostca
       —————————riạ⁶²
```

Lommatzsch in editing this inscription for the *CIL* believed the inscription ended with the one word *palostcaria*. He suggested the word *palost(i)caria*, likened it to *palustris*, and thought of a connection with the Pomptine Marshes which he could not elucidate. Vetter read the inscription again and saw that *-ria* stands at the end of the next line after mention of Juno. Degrassi concurs in this reading. After examining a photograph of the stone [63] I believe it possible to read lines 8-9:

```
       Iuno(ne) Palost(ri) Ca-
       [prot(inae)————]ria
```

The epithet *palostris* might refer to a site like the *Caprae Palus* outside Rome. For similar divine names, compare the Dii Campestres [64] and Nemestrinus (Arn. 4.7). The latter is a double compound, *nemus* > **nemes-tris* > *nemestr + inus*. The inscription's last word might be restored *dona]ria* or *Iunona]ria.* [65]

Varro's belief in a Latian festival of Juno Caprotina can also be related to the Latin League, which opposed Rome under Livius Postumius of Fidenae. Plutarch and Macrobius attribute an aetiology of the festival to this purported war. Nor can Varro's description of the Poplifugia go unconsidered. According to him the Fidenates, Ficuleates, and others on Rome's frontiers (*finitimi*) swore an oath against Rome. Another piece of the puzzle is the participation of slave girls in the festival and the robing of Caprotina in the *toga praetexta*, a garment worn by freedmen on certain religious occasions. If we put the pieces together, we obtain a picture of a festival of Juno evoked from a conquered town and transported with all her rites to Rome, where the foreign women perform the rites. This picture closely resembles the history of Juno Regina (see below). Not only do the Fidenates figure in the Poplifugia and a Fidenate dictator appear in the aetiology of Caprotine nones, but the incident of Tullus Hostilius' vowing shrines to Pallor and Pavor also involves the city of Fidenae. Fidenae was apparently destroyed by the Romans in 426 B.C. [66] Although no witness to the evocation of Fidenae's tutelary deity has survived, we do know that the city of Fidenae suffered a *devotio*, the sacral cursing that usually followed an evocation. [67]

The cumulative evidence on the ceremonies of the Poplifugia and Nonae Caprotinae points to Juno Caprotina as the Juno of Fidenae who was evoked, brought to Rome, and worshipped by slave girls on 7 July.

The ceremonies of Roman Juno Caprotina involved fertility rites [68] whose character in no way militates against the proposal that Juno was the tutelary goddess of Fidenae. The ladies of Rome also worshipped the tutelary Juno of Veii brought to Rome. However her garment is interpreted, Juno Caprotina wore a man's toga and was connected with a war and a ritual rout. For the sake of chronological order she is discussed here after Juno Populona. Her festival in conjunction with the Poplifugia suggests that her protection had formerly extended to the *populus* of Fidenae. However, this Juno bears a different epithet to which we now turn.

Two forms of her epithet are known. Besides Caprotina, Plutarch and one Latin inscription have Capratina.[69] If the latter is the correct form, it has a parallel in the goddess Collatina which Otto derives from the town Collatia,[70] and in Tifatina from *tifata* (n. pl.).[71] Capratina might also represent a double toponymous name such as Ardeatinus (Sen. *Ep.* 105.1). The Etruscans used *kapra* for goat,[72] and apparently named one of the mouths of the Po River Caprasia.[73] The site conforms somewhat with the sense of Rome's *Caprae Palus*. At Perugia we meet an apparent personal name Caprti.[74]

The form *Caprotina* presents problems both of the vocalization and the semantics of the *caprōt-*. To all appearances its stem is that of *capr-*"goat." The goat figures in the name of Roman *Caprae Palus* and the wild goat-fig (*caprificus*). In addition to these items in her cult, the goatskin employed at Lupercalia was called "Juno's cloak," and Juno Sispes at Lanuvium wore a goatskin as a cloak (see below). Caprotina did not wear a goatskin. In the second half of the second century she is represented on a coin, riding in a chariot drawn by two goats which she is whipping. In her other hand she holds a scepter (see Figure 1).[75] None of her cult attributes precisely explains the formation of her name.

Caprotina is found in three Latin authors.[76] Neither **caprotus* as "caped with goatskin" nor **caprotus* as goat-fig has a parallel.[77] The name Fagutalis, applied to Jupiter after the beech tree, presupposes a **fagutus < fagus*. However, we must then assume that *caper* or *capra* alone could have signified the *caprificus*.[78] The suggestion of Radke that Caprotina and Capratina are derived from a word for phallus depends mostly on his interpretation of Tutula, Philotis' other name in Plutarch, which he holds also means phallus.[79] Weinstock, however, refers the name to Tutilina, a goddess who protects.[80] Macrobius, the only Latin author who mentions the other name of Philotis, calls her Tutela. Although this is no personal name, the common noun was spoken in the formula of evocation, and I would refer that name to the aetiology that knew such a formula.[81] Names meaning Protectorate and Friendship have their own charm.[82] Although Radke calls the rites of Juno Caprotina obscene and finds a phallus appropriate, they were fertility rites which are not obscene as they are described for us; slave girls stoning each other are rather more appalling than obscene.

Since the formation of Caprotina has not been satisfactorily explained, I offer another explanation: that the two forms Capratina and Caprotina are toponymous, derived from a place named after a goat. Capratina has the parallels from Collatia, Tifata, etc., mentioned above, while Caprotina remains without a parallel.[83]

One practice at the rites of Caprotina deserves close attention today because of a change in the interpretation of its analogue. The descriptions of the cult mention a branch from the *caprificus* which the celebrants employed. Macrobius alone (*Sat.* 1.11.40) notices the application of milk, which dripped from a goat-fig. This practice was thought to have an analogue in the cult of Rumina, a goddess whose name was interpreted by the ancients as derived from *rumis* etc., "breast." In his work on agriculture Varro describes the addition of fig-tree milk and vinegar to animal milk so that it would coagulate into cheese. He goes on to remark that at the shrine of Diva Rumina, where shepherds had planted a fig tree, the sacrifices are of milk instead of wine or of sucklings (*lactentes*), because of the origin of her name. [84] Although Wissowa accepts the ancient etymology, Latte correctly analyzes the name as *Romana.* [85] Schulze had held that certain Etruscan names with the root *rum-* were not related to *Roma*, but Rix has demonstrated the opposite. [86] The name of Rome ought not to be separated from the archaic local name of the Tiber River, *Rumo*, and the existence of a gate called Romana or Romanula in the Palatine wall. [87] In the same passage in which he calls Populona a spinster, Seneca calls Rumina the same. [88]

Augustine claims that Diva Rumina was in fact Juno. [89] Moreover, Augustine also records the existence of a Jupiter Ruminus, [90] who can be nothing but Jupiter Romanus, for breasts have no place in his cult; his existence would render Augustine's inference plausible. Offerings of milk to Rumina hardly bear an interpretation of a fertility cult *per se*, since milk was also offered to Jupiter Latiaris, the pan-Latin deity on the Alban Mount, [91] and to the water spirits Camenae. [92] The *ficus Rumina* or *Ruminalis* which is introduced into the cult has undergone linguistic violence. [93]

The Ruminal fig stood by the Lupercal, the center of rites [94] which we may perhaps connect with Juno (see below). Livy (1.4.5) says the fig tree used to be called Romularis in some quarters, and Ovid (*F.* 2.412) that it used to be called Romula. It matters little whether the toponymous adjectives refer to the Rumo River or to the original Roma. [95] The process of distortion of Rumina and related words can be referred to the year 296, when the aediles Ogulnii set up a sculptural group of the she-wolf and twins at the Ficus Ruminalis. [96] From that moment on Rumina and her relatives were connected with the suckling Romulus and Remus, or Remulus, as the latter was sometimes called; Rem(ul)us, too, is a toponymous name. In this connection we cite the Ager Remurinus, the Aventine site Remoria (or Remuria), the place called Remoria thirty stades from Rome, and Remora and Remona. [97] The Palatine dedication to Remureina, who is the analogue to Rumina, indicates the local cult. [98]

The names of Jupiter Ruminus, Diva (Juno?) Rumina, and Remurina ought to be reckoned as toponymous, like Jupiter Capitolinus and Juno Lucina (see below). Although fertility rites might be attached to such cults, they do not impose an exclusive interpretation that the deities were originally and principally gods of (female) sexuality and procreation. On the contrary, in Juno Caprotina we have an example of the prominence of war and diplomacy in her origins.

4. JUNO OF FEBRUARY

Although Juno's cult in February nowhere appears explicitly in the inscribed calendars, Juno is variously called Februa, Februalis, Februlis, Februtis, and Februata by ancient authors and is connected with Flu(ui)onia, a purported goddess of menstrual flux, and with the month of February or its feast Lupercalia. The Lupercalia must have been observed partly at the Lupercal, where the Ruminal fig of Rumina grew. The root of these words seems to be *febru-*, a Sabino-Latin word for the refuse collected in ritual cleansing.[99] However, cleansing (*februare*) could be done to anyone, even the *populus.* So Varro (*LL* 6.34) calls the Lupercalia a *dies februatus*, a "cleansed day," when the *populus* is cleansed and the Palatine town purified by the naked Luperci. Thus Juno Februata can and should mean nothing more than a cleansed Juno. To my mind this means that her statue was given a bath. It follows that after the bath the statue should have been oiled. Here, I propose, belongs her name Unxia.[100]

The Roman priest king announced the monthly festivals of February on the nones and referred to Lupercalia as a *dies februatus.*[101] We have seen that the Ficus Ruminalis was said to be near the Lupercal. Varro believed that the Palatine town and the *populus* were cleansed on that day. Censorinus in reporting Varro's discussion in the *Antiquities* says that Rome was purified with hot salt called *februus.*[102] This purification may have included Diva (Juno?) Rumina, although we only infer from the fig tree and the notion of a shepherds' cult (like Parilia?) where her shrine was situated. At the end of his discussion of Rumina and breasts, Varro (*RR* 2.11.6) writes: qui aspargi solent sales, melior fossilis quam marinus. Is he referring to salt in cheese production, the subject under discussion, or to the cult of Rumina? We know that Juno could be purified with salt water.[103] Lupercalia was one of three days on which the Vestal Virgins made sacral salt meal of spelt and a special salt (*muries*).[104]

The details of the famous fertility rites on Lupercalia are too many and too diffuse for any close examination of arguments thereon.[105] Much of the month was given over to cleansing before the new year (old style) commenced on 1 March.[106] The part of the ceremony of Lupercalia that included the purification of women was made famous by the career of Julius Caesar. In a garbled notice from Festus, Paulus (pp. 75-76 L) has: mulieres februabantur a lupercis amiculo Iunonis, id est pelle caprina. The only Juno who we know wore a goatskin cloak is Juno Sispes (Sospita) Mater Regina of Lanuvium. Our oldest inscribed calendar notes sacrifice to a Roman Juno Sospita on February 1.[107] As we shall see below, there were at least two Roman shrines of this Juno, one of which was on the Palatine. Palatine Sispes probably wore the cloak which the Luperci employed. Although the purification was intended to cleanse barrenness for the sake of fertility, this purificatory act was just one of many, since the *populus*, the Palatine, Rome, and, I have suggested, Juno were also cleansed on that day. It therefore obfuscates the character of the day to maintain that the Juno involved in Lupercalia was closely connected by the ancient authors with the Junonian epithet Fluonia or Fluvionia or Fluvonia. This relation is no older than Varro.[108] As the name is reported, it is best interpreted as the goddess of a river or running water, *fluvius*. Analogous are Vallonia, goddess of valleys,[109] and Populona, Bellona, etc. Close at hand for Lupercalia were four large sources of running water: the rivers Tiber (formerly the Rumo), Spino, Nodinus, and Almo, all of which the augurs mentioned in their rites.[110] The waters of the Almo were suited for washing *sacra*.[111] The name Rumo, however, is mentioned only in association with religious matters,[112] so that I would connect Flu(ui)onia with the Tiber. Holy articles ought to be washed in running water, in order to be thoroughly cleansed; if the name *fluvionia* belonged to Juno at all,[113] it should be understood as the result of Juno's cleansing with river water. All ancient notices on this putative goddess of menstrual flux go back to Varro, whose interpretation cannot be controlled for the simple reason that there survives not one reference to a cult of a Juno so named. In light of the story of Juno Lucina, it appears to me very likely that Roman women devised the explanation of the epithet as they assumed greater and greater interest in the cult of all Junos.

The Juno whose cloak was employed in the Lupercalia, and upon whom were imposed epithets derived from the religious term for cleansing, can be either the Palatine Sispes or Diva Rumina. The former Juno had a Lanuvian counterpart whose cult statue wore a goatskin. The latter had a shrine with a fig tree presumably identical with the Ficus Ruminalis by the Lupercal. The topographical association of the tree and Lupercal led the aediles of 296 to dedicate a statue of a she-wolf (*lupa*) with the twins at her breast at the site. Regardless of her identity, the Juno of February emerges from a series of purifications which were by no means exclusively concerned with female sexuality.

5. JUNO LUCINA AND THE TUSCULAN RITE

On 1 March, 375 B.C., a temple which stood in a grove (*lucus*) was dedicated to Juno Lucina. Pliny (*NH* 16.235) supplies us not only with the year but also with the information that the grove, in which stood an aged persimmon, named the goddess. The Vestals regularly hung their hair upon that tree.[114] Although Pliny was not the first to derive her name from the grove,[115] he belonged then to a minority which today prevails. For many years the Romans held that Juno was the bringer of light to the eyes of the new born. However, Pliny was right.[116] All indications of the cult point to an old grove. Varro (*LL* 5.49) writes as if the Esquiline region had originally been demarcated by the groves of Jupiter of the Beech Tree, of Mefitis, and of Juno Lucina, and the shrine of the Lares of Oakgrove. But Varro believed that Lucina, "goddess of light," was the Moon, and that Tatius introduced both Lucina and Luna into Roman religion.[117]

According to Verrius Flaccus' notice in the Praesnestine Calendar at 1 March, the temple of Juno Lucina was dedicated by married women after the wife or daughter of Albinius vowed it if Juno would vouchsafe the birth of her child. The notice is intended to explain the observance of Matronalia, a festival held by mothers at the temple on 1 March. This festival is not marked on the calendars that contain the ceremony for Mars and the anniversary rites of the temple built in 375 B.C.[118]

The temple was public and maintained by state officers. [119] Its grove was one of many where there were stations called Argei, which were visited by state priests twice a year, and which are to be related to all the Roman curias where Juno was worshipped. [120] The grove and the temple were not the preserve solely of women; it is quite doubtful that women were ever empowered to dedicate a state temple (see note 118). A Junonian cult in a grove is not an isolated occurrence. Since Juno Moneta and Juno Sispes of Lanuvium, among others, had their temples in groves (see below), Juno could have been associated with the grove long before 375. The arrival of Juno Regina and Caprotina quickened the interest of Roman ladies in the cult of Juno Lucina.

Two dedicatory inscriptions, one Roman and the other Norban, record the fast of Jupiter in connection with Juno Lucina:

> Iunone Loucinai Diovis castud facitud, [121]
> P. Rutilius M.f. Iunonei Loucina dedit meretod Diovos castud. [122]

The word *castus* is a religious term for abstinence, generally abstinence from food, [123] and nothing compels us to assume that men abstained from their wives, as Jupiter from Juno, after childbirth. [124] The banquets given Jupiter are well known. [125] Jupiter's Fast seems to be no more than abstinence from eating certain foods, or from eating anything. Jupiter's priest, the flamen Dialis, could never name or touch a goat, uncooked meat, beans, or flour with yeast; if his priest did not eat these foods, Jupiter himself was presumably not offered such a menu. [126] Roman husbands may have waited to make an offering to Juno Lucina for the safe delivery of a child until they had served out their own Fast of Jupiter. But since we are acquainted with the fast only from the two inscriptions, the dedications may have nothing to do with Roman men's interest in Juno Lucina. In Ode 3.8, Horace draws attention to his celebrating the Matronalia although he is a bachelor. The scholia on the first line of the poem attribute his allusion to the fact that husbands prayed for the preservation of their marriages. Horace himself attributes his own celebration to his preservation from the notorious tree that almost fell on him. Whether he was aware of the tree's relevance to Lucina is not known.

At least by the early second century B.C., Juno Lucina was invoked by women in childbed. Calpurnius Piso has Servius Tullius ordain the practice of depositing a coin in the treasury of Juno Lucina for each new-born child. [127] The donation would have been impossible without coinage, and was imputed to Tullius as a part of his institution of the census, which, of course, operated in an entirely different manner; the custom was thus not archaic.

Lucina's home was a grove on the Esquiline. In 375 B.C., a temple was built for her and was reportedly dedicated by Roman married women on account of a vow for safe delivery. On every calends of March, a day officially set aside for the cult of Mars, the women held their own festival of Matronalia in her precinct.

By the traditional date of 381, the Latin town of Tusculum was incorporated into the budding Roman empire and received Roman citizenship. Theretofore similar political mergers had been celebrated by an invitation to the people's Juno to join the Romans as the tutelary Juno of a new curia. Centuries after the incorporation of Tusculum, Juno Lucina and Hercules received offerings in the vicinity of Capua. The cippi were inscribed with the deity's name and the character of the rite under which the offering was made:

> [Herc]ole [Tusc]olana sacra.
> Iunone Loucina Tusculana sacra.

The Tusculan rite had been assumed by Roman *sacerdotes Tusculani*, while the Tusculans enjoyed the local services of a *monitor sacrorum*. It follows from the Capuan dedication that Juno Lucina had special ties with the Tusculan rites even when she was worshipped beyond the confines of Latium. The annexation of Tusculum in 381 and the dedication of a Roman temple to Juno Lucina in 375 should be related to each other. [128] Therefore, the neatest explanation of the Tusculan rite of Juno Lucina can be had from the assumption that Juno Lucina received her Roman temple in a grove long sacred to the goddess because she was inported from Tusculum between 381 and 375 B.C. This Juno was apparently the last to be taken from a people that adhered to Rome. In subsequent instances, only hostile Junos were brought to Rome, and the Romans sent their own officers to annexed citizen communities to sacrifice to the annexed gods. From the legend of Juno Lucina's shrine, we see that the grove alone had once sufficed her and that she subsequently received a foreign Juno, who took on the epithet of the place but retained her original rite.

Contemporary illustration of the introduction of hostile gods is to be found in the case of Jupiter Imperator. In 380 the dictator T. Quinctius Cincinnatus reduced Praeneste and brought thence a statue of Jupiter Imperator, which he installed on the podium of the Capitoline temple. In contrast with Juno of Tusculum, who was brought to Rome at the same time, Jupiter Imperator received no temple of his own and, apparently, no special cult. [129] This Jupiter was kept in captivity, like Faliscan Minerva Capta, at Rome (see below, sect. 13). Tusculan Juno adhered to the Roman people by her own people's will, Praenestine Jupiter was detained at Rome a prisoner, and Juno Regina consented to abduction from the fallen town of Veii, where she had been worshipped before its conquest.

6. JUNO REGINA

In the Roman annals no foreign deity has enjoyed such romantic luster as the goddess whom M. Furius Camillus brought to Rome from conquered Veii and established on the Aventine Hill in the early fourth century. Her Veientine temple had stood on the citadel, where the king of Veii is represented sacrificing to her at the moment of conquest. [130] Juno Regina was invited to come to Rome by the process of evocation. The cult which came with her has certain rather non-Roman elements, which lend the appearance of preserving what she had enjoyed at Veii (see below).

Before 400 B.C., the Veientines still lived under a kingly constitution, while most Etruscan and Italic communities had adopted republican governments of varying hues. Juno Regina remains closely tied to the religion of Veii and of Veii's king. Although doubt can be cast on the tradition that Veientine kingship persisted until 400, it is well enough attested in the previous generation. Furthermore, we cannot rule out the possibility that Veii's king at the time of the Roman war was a sacrificial king, since in the story he plays his role as priest as well as king. [131] It would be natural to assume that the deity whom the king held in special regard would have preserved him first and foremost. The word *regina* is an adjective meaning "of the king." which has undergone specialization and in classical Latin denotes "the king's woman." [132] In the classical period *regalis* and *regius* meant royal. Analogous forms are *augurius/auguralis, pontificius/pontificalis, flaminius/ flaminalis.* In addition to these derivatives there are the cognomens Augurinus, Flamininus, Censorinus (cf. *censorius*). When it is applied to Juno, *regina* differs not at all from these honorific cognomens. Although all authorities attribute the adaptation of this surname to the existence of Hera Basileia, one can argue that the name is just one of many that could have been used to describe Juno's patronage, and one that happened to coincide with a Greek name. The Curias had their Quirites, the *populus* their Populona, a grove its Lucina, and Roma its Rumina. Although it eludes precise analysis, Caprotina belongs to the same group. (We have already met Nemestrinus, Remureina, Tiberinus, and Tifatina in other connections.) The Junos of king, curias, and *populus* seem a most natural series of attributions. The king and the curias and the *populus* have each their own deities of "youth."

It follows that the kings of Rome, who tradition held came from disparate stocks, would have had their Junos, and that some trace of them survives. Indeed, late accounts refer to the Juno of the Capitolium as Regina. [133] The Old Capitol on the Quirinal was a *sacellum*, not a temple, which contained Jupiter, Juno, and Minerva, [134] but the Quirinal Juno may have been a Juno of a Roman king. The new Capitol containing the same famous triad was partly built by the last king and dedicated in the new Republic. [135] When we treated Juno Populona, we did not attempt to locate her precinct (*templum*) in which stood the consecrated altar table. [136] At the Roman colony of Aesernia one Juno is called both Regina and Populona. [137] During Commodus' reign, one of his legionary legates stationed in Dacia made a dedication to each of the triad: *I(ovi) O(ptimo) M(aximo)*; *Iunoni Reginae Populoniae deae patriae*; *Minervae Iovis consiliorum participi.* [138] Although the second dedication is extraordinary in calling this double Juno "goddess of the fatherland" such an appellation conforms with all Roman political attitudes of Juno. [139] The *templum* of Populona could have been any kind of precinct. The Jus

Papirianum is not explicit. A *templum* need not be a temple *(aedis)*, but may be any area consecrated and defined, such as an open-air precinct or a separate room of a temple. Thus the *cella* on the Capitol complies with the sense of Latin *templum.* Livy (7.3) calls the Capitoline shrines of Minerva and Jupiter *templa.* The consuls, captains of the *populus*, made their vows in the *templum I.O.M.* (Livy 21.63.7-10), but Livy (42.49.1-6) implies that the two other Capitoline deities were involved in the consul's attention. Certainly the name *populona* can have nothing at all to do with females; she is a political and military goddess, pure and simple. Livy (6.4.2-3) reports that Camillus dedicated three golden cups *(paterae)* inscribed with his name in the *cella* of Capitoline Jupiter at the feet of Juno; evidently they remained in the *cella* until the fire of 83 B.C. Likewise the Capitoline *cella* of Minerva had a cult statue and altar to Iuventas. [140] Further, the temple of Jupiter Stator, built *ca.*146, held a statue of Juno Regina, while her companion temple held his statue; Pliny (*NH* 36.40-43) suggests that the workmen had made a mistake(!). Manifestly, a deity, too, had his *iuno.* [141] As the result of prodigies in 218, two of which took place in the Lanuvian temple of Juno, the Romans cleansed their city and gave forty pounds of gold to Lanuvian Juno, a bronze statue to Aventine Juno, a *lectisternium* to Iuventas, and five larger victims to Genius (Livy 21.62). The connection between *iuvenis* and Juno will become clearer in a moment. Now it is clear that political persons, entities and deities, too, had a *iuno.*

The *templum* of Juno Populona seems to me best situated in the Capitolinᵣ temple, where she was installed instead of the intended Regina of the king. On the single republican coin that has the Capitoline triad are represented both Juno and Minerva holding the scepters of power. The problem of proper identification of the Capitoline Jupiter and Juno is vexed by the fact that the former is sometimes king *(rex)* rather than *optimus maximus*, and his wifely consort then queen *(regina)*. [142] From this it follows that Jupiter at least was viewed as the divine paragon of his dedicant, the Roman king, just as Jupiter Imperator held another mortal title (see above). Juno Regina can be reckoned as, first, Hera Basileia, or second, Juno of the king's queen, or third, Jupiter Rex's *iuno*, or fourth, the king's *iuno*. The second construction finds support in the function of the *regina sacrorum* (see below), the third in the fact that an image of Juno was given to Jupiter (see above). The fourth can be paralleled by the Veientine Juno taken to Rome, if an interpretation of her close relationship to Veii's king is valid. The Dacian dedication accords to Juno, "goddess of the fatherland," both titles of Regina and Populonia, and distantly reflects a double patronage; the former belongs to the era of monarchy and the latter to the era of the centuriate constitution of the military *populus*. Moreover, Juno could have been hailed Regina at second hand after her identification with either the Greek goddess or the consort of Jupiter Rex. Thus the identity of Juno Populona with Juno of the Capitol seems much more secure. The cause and date of Capitoline Juno's assumption of the epithet Regina remain uncertain, for after Veientine Juno arrived at Rome and after the Romans learned of Hera Basileia— whenever that occurred—the epithet was accepted in several instances.

The Roman king's *iuno* did not suffer neglect; during the Republic the sacral king's queen (*regina sacrorum*) offered sacrifice to Juno on the first of every month in the king's house (*regia*) in the Forum. [143] This confirms two facts: first, the king's queen was a priestess of Juno, indeed the only known priest of the goddess besides the curial flamens, and second, the cult of the Roman king's *iuno* had been degraded to worship in the king's former residence, which left the Capitoline temple free for the worship of Juno Populona. Related to the Juno of the king and thereafter the priest king are the rites on the calends of every month when the pontiffs said either five or seven times *calo Iuno covella*, to fix the nones of the month. [144] Although called on the calends, the nones meant the ninth day before the variable ides, which Varro (*LL* 6.28) thought to be an Etruscan or Sabine word. Varro considers the custom, on the basis of its terms a foreign borrowing; the fact that *calo Iuno covella* is grammatical nonsense may thus not have bothered Varro, who is our only ultimate source of the custom in at least two works. Modern students simply say that Covella is Juno's epithet of unknown meaning, spoken when invoking her control over menstruation. [145] What does the rest of the phrase tell us? Nothing. *Calo* has no predicate object, which according to this explanation must be *te*, and *Iuno* a vocative. How, then, is the minor pontiff calling the nones, and what have the variable nones (from the variable ides) to do with menstruation? Variable regularity of the menstrual cycle was surely not dictated by the state for all Roman women. Varro does not explain *covella*, which in any case stands in a corrupt passage. Macrobius, however, details a great deal more information on the custom, which he derives from another (lost) work of Varro; [146] what follows comes from his report. Before Cn. Flavius, a scribe (i.e., *pontifex minor*; cf. Livy 22.57.3), published the *fasti*, the minor pontiff used to announce the new moon to the sacral king. [147] He used a "Greek" word *kalo*, for the custom, as well as the ides themselves, came to Rome from Greece and Etruria. Furthermore, *nonae* comes from *nonus* or from *nova luna*. Clearly, Varro only inferred the latter (erroneous) etymology from the pontifical archives he cited (*Sat.* 1.15.18), and himself never heard the "calling," because when Cn. Flavius compiled and published the regular calendar, *ca.* 304 B.C., [148] the practice ceased forever. What is more, the archives in archaic Latin would have been subject to Varronian conjecture, since he obviously believed the custom was non-Roman.

What the minor pontiff had once called on the first day of every month was the new moon: *calo lunam novellam*. It is very unlikely that Varro saw *covella*, since in two places he etymologizes *nonae* from *nova*; *covella* is a manuscript error, [149] but *Iuno* for *lunam* is owed to Varro alone, who believed that all calends were sacred to Juno, and also sometimes believed that she was the moon itself. [150] The calends were evidently sacred to Juno, for before Varro many Roman temples were dedicated to her on the first of the month. [151] The Laurentes, however, held that only the calends of March to December, the period of growth, were sacred to her. [152] Despite the Junonian character of the calends and nones in the Roman mind, no marriage took place on those days. [153] Much more telling is the monthly sacrifice on the calends of a female lamb or pig to Juno by the sacral king's queen in the king's house (*regia*). [154] The sex of the victim reflects neither the sex of the deity nor the sex of the sacrificant, the king's queen. Sacrifice must have been made to the king's *iuno* (not the queen's) since he had charge of the day's business. [155] The queen's sacrifice to her husband's *iuno* makes (primitive) sense as an offering for the king's continuing youth with the passing of each month; a *iuno*, surnamed *iuga* or *iugis*, may contain the notion of "everlasting" and "constant." [156] The sacrifice by the king's queen every calends had suggested to the Romans the consecration of the day to her. This suggestion in turn influenced the Romans in choosing a date for dedicating temples to Juno, until, finally, Varro and others came to believe that Iuno was *luna* and so understood the pontifical archives, in which the two words would not have resembled each other in archaic Latin.

We have remarked the cult practice of spreading a simple banquet before the thirty Junos of the curias. The consecrated altar table of Juno Populona implies a sacrificial dinner. The celebration of Caprotine nones was partly observed by feasting participants, and the Capitoline cult exhibits the same custom. On 13 September a banquet was set out for Jupiter, Juno, and Minerva. [157] After the fire for which the Christians were blamed, the married women *(matronae)* of Rome sprinkled the Capitoline *cella* and cult statue of Juno with sea-water, and "women who had husbands" gave her a supper upon consultation of the Sibylline Books. [158] The requirement that the women have husbands (which excluded widowed *matronae*) stresses the prominence of women even in the cult of a Juno whose function is the protection of the state.

This female prominence can be indirectly attributed to Etruscan influence at an early date. While the names Quiritis, Populona, and Lucina do not betray the prevalence of women in the Junonian cult, the ceremonies of Caprotina, who, we argue, was brought from Fidenae, seem to characterize a political Juno with a cult of female sexuality. Fidenae fell to Rome because of its persistent alliance with Etruscan Veii. Even more pronounced in their Etruscan influence are the rites for Juno Regina, who came to Rome from Veii itself about twenty years before the dedication of the temple of Juno Lucina. Although, as we shall see, Juno Regina was transported for political reasons, this fact in no way prevented the practical usurpation of her cult by Roman women.

At the outset of the second Punic War, some horrendous prodigies prompted the Decemviri Sacris Faciundis, who had charge of alien cults at Rome, to decree the gifts of a golden thunderbolt to Jupiter and silver thunderbolts to Juno and Minerva. At Lanuvium, Juno Sospita was to receive a sacrifice with full-grown victims, and at Rome Juno Regina on the Aventine Hill was to receive the same sacrifice. In addition, Roman mothers were to collect money which they would offer with a banquet (*lectisternium*) to Juno Regina on the Aventine. [159]

An account of how freedmen won the right to wear the *toga praetexta* ought to be referred either to these ceremonies in 217, or to the institution of the Ludi Apollinares in 212, or to the ceremonies of 207:

> By no right whatsoever did freedmen wear the *praetexta*, and even less so aliens who had no ties with Romans. Later, however, the *praetexta* was also granted the sons of freedmen for the reason which M. Laelius, the augur, reports. During the Second Punic

War, he says, the Decemvirs approached the Sibylline Books at the senate's discretion on account of many prodigies. After reading them they announced that a supplication on the Capitol and a banquet from collected donations had to be performed in such a way that freedwomen who wore long gowns might also contribute money for that business. Therefore the performance of the entreaties was entrusted to the sons of freeborn men and freedmen, while the singing of the hymn was entrusted to girls both whose parents lived. Consequently, the sons of freedmen who were born of a legitimate *mater familias* were permitted to wear the *toga praetexta.* . .[160]

We have already remarked that Juno Caprotina wore the *toga praetexta* at the Ludi Apollinares, although her cult is much older than their institution. In the account just rendered the grant of the *praetexta* was made to the sons of the freedmen, whereas we have suggested that Juno Caprotina wore the *praetexta* because the toga originated with foreigners and because the freedmen mayors of the *vici* had the same right. [161] The participation of freedmen's sons in the ceremonies that may be referred to Juno Regina reflects the foreign origin of the deity and the character of a cult subject to considerable foreign influence.

Whenever the Decemvirs and Sibylline Books are involved, the cult is bound to be tinged by foreign practices. Thus the religious activities in 207 also serve to confirm that Juno Regina's female cult was inspired by non-Romans. In that year a number of prodigies occurred when the danger from Hannibal in concert with his brother was imminent:

Haruspices were summoned from Etruria and they declared the prodigy [an androgynous child] foul and vile. They ordered it to be taken far away from Roman territory and from the land and be drowned in the deep. They shut it alive in a box and carried it out to sea, where they threw it overboard. Also the pontiffs decreed that twenty-seven girls should go through the city singing a hymn. When they were learning the hymn composed by the poet Livius[162] in the temple of Jupiter Stator, the temple of Juno Regina on the Aventine was struck by lightning. After the haruspices responded that this prodigy pertained to the married women and that the goddess would have to be appeased with a gift, the curule aediles issued an edict that all married women who lived in the city or within ten miles of Rome were to assemble on the Capitol and to select twenty-five of their number to collect a donation from their dowries. From the collection a golden bowl was made and carried to the Aventine, where the married women sacrificed *pure et caste*. Immediately the Decemvirs declared a day for another sacrifice to the same goddess. Its schedule was as follows. From the temple of Apollo two white cows were led through the Carmental Gate into the city; behind them were carried two statues of Juno Regina carved in cypress;[163] then came twenty-seven maidens, dressed in long gowns, singing the hymn to Juno Regina (for its age a fine piece because of its simple talent, but today uncouth and crude if I were to repeat it); the Decemvirs, wearing bay-leaf crowns and *praetextae*, followed the chorus of maidens. They came from the Vicus Jugarius into the Forum. In the Forum the procession halted and the maidens took a rope in their hands and proceeded while keeping time to the words with the beat of their feet. Thence, by way of the Vicus Tuscus and the Velabrum through the Forum Boarium, they ascended the street of Publicius and reached the temple of Juno Regina. There the Decemvirs immolated the two victims and the statues of cypress were carried into the temple.[164]

Seven years later the same ceremony took place under similar circumstances. Only a new hymn, by P. Licinius Tegula, made it different.[165]

In his revival of the Secular Games in 17 B.C., Augustus, reckoning the *saeculum* at 110 years, staged rites evidently new to what had originally been a centennial celebration for underworld deities held at night at the Tarentum of the Campus Martius. [166] The earlier games had been instituted under Etruscan influence, with the involvement of the Decemvirs and Etruscan haruspices, [167] while Augustus' games were sponsored by a Sibylline oracle. Horace composed a secular hymn. The new rites, which were held in broad daylight, did not concern Dis and Proserpina. We are not interested in this Hellenistic affair, nor in the fact that Capitoline Juno is called Regina in the official transactions of the Quindecemvirs who participated. The prayers, which came from the Romans' Sibylline Books, included entreaties for the supremacy of the Roman people at war and at home and for everlasting victory. One hundred and ten married *matres familias* participated by praying to Juno Regina on the Capitol and laying a banquet for her and Diana. Instead of a processional hymn, twenty-seven boys and twenty-seven girls sang Horace's *Carmen Saeculare* on the Capitol after the religious business had been completed. [168] Some elements of the Etruscan secular games may have been transferred to Augustus' daytime celebration. For instance, the cup (*atalla*) by which the major priests stood seems to be Etruscan, [169] and the choruses of twenty-seven that were employed in 200, 207, and perhaps also in 217 B.C. bear the mark of Etruscan influence mediated both by the Sibylline Books and by the haruspices from Etruria. The *acta* of the secular games of 17 B.C. demonstrate how Juno of the Capitoline triad, who was only one of the deities invoked on this occasion, could be subjected to a non-Roman cult.

We have taken pains to elaborate the character of the cult for Juno Regina of the Aventine because the manner of her arrival at Rome in no wise portended the introduction of a deity for the sake of female sexuality.

The ritual by which the king's *iuno* was brought to Rome from Veii finely illustrates the original sense of *iuno*. Picked youths (*iuvenes*) from Camillus' army, after cleansing themselves and their clothes, approached the goddess' statue and asked "Do you wish to come to Rome, Juno?" She nodded assent. Livy says the young man who put the question was affected either by divine inspiration or by "youthful raillery." [170] Livy seems mistaken. The *iuvenalis iocus* could have meant a sacred formula (*iocus*) used by men of military age (*iuvenes* or *iuniores*). The Iguvines use the Umbrian cognate of *iocus* as sacred formula. In the most recent edition of the Tables, Ernout renders the Iguvine into L. *preces* and reiterates its specialization in Latin from the IE "solemn declaration" to "raillery." Such specialization points to the form of the Latin ritual that involved badinage. Another vestige of this sense of *iocus* may survive in a queer pontifical notice which Livy preserves with some latter-day embellishment. In 420 B.C., one of the Vestals was tried and acquitted of unchastity. The chief pontiff delivered his college's acquittal and cautioned her "to refrain from frivolity and to conduct herself in a manner befitting her priesthood rather than with chic (*abstinere iocis colique sancte potius quam scite iussit*)." Although convictions and suicides of the Vestals were recorded in the pontifical annals, only two early cases of acquittal are noted. The first is the notorious folktale of the virgin who proved her innocence by carrying water in a sieve. The second acquittal was a political *cause célèbre* in 114. The charge and acquittal of the Vestal in 420 and its resultant reprimand are so unusual a pontifical notice as to make further doubtful the annalistic interpretation. Rather, it seems likely that the Vestal was charged and found guilty of some misdeed less serious than unchastity or, more likely, of some omission of a duty; in this case, that she failed in saying her prayers. The provisions for such lesser crimes in the sacral law required scourging of the guilty. A consequence might have been an exclusion from the prayer rites and an injunction to behave in a manner befitting the priesthood. Livy's statement that the Vestal was forbidden to indulge in *ioci* hardly makes sense as the outcome of a trial. [171] Juno would have been induced to quit Veii by the recitation of a proper prayer.

After the young men's ceremony of enticement, to which the goddess assented, Juno's statue was transported by no mean vehicle, but by chariot, to her new home on the Aventine Hill. (Juno Quiritis of Tibur was expected to protect members of the curia with her shield and chariot.)

Still in 396 B.C., the Romans performed their evocation of a conquered town's chief deity through the offices of the *iuvenes*. Habit or syncretism perhaps induced the Romans to believe the chief deity was the equivalent of their own Juno (see below on Juno of Carthage). Such a belief was a political and military necessity. On the other hand, the goddess may have been an Etruscan Uni. A town deprived of its Juno would not rise again, for it had lost the foundation of its citizen body and its army; had the Romans lost their Juno Populona in a like manner, they would have considered their position hopeless. When the Juno of the Veientine king went into an honorable captivity, the Romans annexed all of Veii's extensive territory, and Veii's sovereignty ceased. Thirty years earlier Fidenae had surrendered its land, independence, and perhaps its Juno Caprotina.

If the Romans knew that they were taking the king's Juno in 396 B.C., as we argue, the theory that Regina is a cognomen inspired by knowledge of Hera Basileia appears untenable; for the syncretism of Juno with Hera had presumably already taken place through Etruscan intermediaries. In all accounts of the rite of evocation the deity is specifically asked whether it consents to its removal. Without context, an archaic Latin word for willingness has survived in a disquisition on odd religious terminology: *heries Iunonis.* [172] In Livy's account of Juno Regina's evocation the formula was already modernized: visne Romam ire, Iuno? [173] Hence we propose that Juno's "will" (*heries*), which originally belonged to the formula of evocation and referred to her consent, was explained as her identification with the Greek Hera at a time when the Romans had forgotten the meaning of the word. Finally, we argue that the epithet Regina came with Veientine Juno to Rome. The evidence on Juno Caprotina's origins and cult points to a like conclusion. Juno who was evoked from Carthage seems to have brought with her the title *Caelestis* (see below). This Latin name, which renders a Semitic title, doubtless contributed to the view that Juno had a heavenly domain, which ancient scholars anachronistically applied to Lucina.

The origin and cult of this Juno Regina can be sought only in Etruscan Veii. While it may be true that Greeks directly influenced the Romans to introduce the custom of a supper party (*lectisternium*) for certain gods in 399 B.C. (see Livy 5.13.6 and Ogilvie's commentary), Hera or Juno was absent on that occasion. The foregoing discussion of Juno Regina points from all directions to the Etruscans and to Veii. Indeed, at the time of the third sacred supper party in 364 B.C., the Romans instituted stage plays to gain the gods' help and imported Etruscan players (Livy 7.2), just as Etruscan haruspices were to advise the Roman magistrates how to treat the prodigious lightning bolt that struck Juno Regina's temple in 207 B.C. I have assumed that the cult title is a Latin rendition of the Etruscan. Etruscan Junos certainly had epithets (see below, sect. 14). Moreover, Regina could have been continuously applied to a Juno at Rome other than to Juno of the Aventine, for the Roman priest-king and his queen were responsible for a monthly sacrifice to Juno. Finally, the pre-republican Junos could have been royal (see below on the old Roman Juno Sispes).

7. JUNO MONETA

On the Roman acropolis (*arx*) stood the temple of Juno Moneta, vowed in a war probably with the Gauls, and dedicated for the grandeur of the Roman people, in 345/44 (Livy 7.28.4-6). Romans explained her name as "warner," and pointed to different historical occasions on which the warning took place. The variety and dubious historicity of the occasions deprive the Romans' accounts of credence, although it should be noted that all are related to war-time hostilities. [174] Moneta had some connection with war. Another etymon of *moneta*, we suggest, may be that of Latin *mons, e-mineo* and *monile*, in reference to the hill, or hills, where this Juno's worship was centered. In the case of Moneta, Juno may have been the deity of the *arx* and Capitolium, two eminences of the same hill. A prodigy of 196 B.C. was the combustion of the two spear points in her temple, which may have belonged to the cult of the twin peaks. [175] Although the suffix of the noun remains troublesome, the most likely explanation is that **monētus* is an adjective of a form whose neuter substantives have yielded *argiletum, saxetum, sepulcretum*, and many groves, e.g. *aesculetum*. Vitruvius (8.3.17) tells us of a Campus Cornetus, lying in Faliscan country, which contained a grove and spring and was evidently named after the hill Corne (Pliny *NH* 16.242). The word Cornetus will support the adjectival character of *moneta* derived from a noun. [176]

A lack of precision in the analysis of the word *moneta* may result from the possibility that it is a Gaulish word taken after the victory in 349. The goddess herself could have inspired young Furius Camillus to vow the temple, through the appearance of the bird that gave M. Valerius the cognomen Corvus or Corvinus. The *corvus* is attested in connection with the goddess. [177]

After the temple of Juno Moneta was dedicated in 344, the Romans stored the

Linen Books there. These documents can be related to the abolition of the so-called military tribunes with consular power, which occurred some twenty years before the temple was founded. The goddess' record-keeping suggests another interpretation of her epithet: *moneta* is derivable from *monere* in the sense of "recorder" (cf. *monumentum* "record"), not "warner." On this interpretation, *moneta* would have been applied to the goddess after she began to keep the documents stored in her temple. Later she was anachronistically assumed to have uttered a warning during the Gaulish occupation of 390. At the beginning of Latin literature, Livius Andronicus believed that Moneta betokened Memory rather than Warning.[178]

Although Juno Moneta is represented and named on Roman coins by the simple bust of a lady without military accoutrements, [179] nevertheless both Moneta of Rome and she of the Alban Mount received their temples according to vows made in wartime. Both these temples stood on hills. At Rome, the temple of Juno Moneta was presumably in two groves, [180] just as Juno Lucina's temple stood in a grove from which she took her epithet. Both Monetas had temples on heights.

8.   JUNO SISPES

After the dissolution of the Latin League, the Lanuvians exchanged citizenship and cults with the Romans in 338 B.C. The chief goddess of Lanuvium, Juno Sispes Mater Regina, became the object of Roman worship. Before the Latin War the Romans dealt differently with cults. When Tusculum had joined with Rome to make one state, all Romans assumed responsibility for the religion of Tusculum and the state created special priesthoods which oversaw the Tusculan rite of Roman religion. Juno Lucina received offerings in accordance with this rite. In discussing Lucina, we proposed that her temple was built in Rome in consequence of the transfer of Juno from Tusculum to Rome that betokened the new arrangement. In 338, however, the Romans and Lanuvians exchanged rites, and the Roman consuls went to Lanuvium once a year for the sacrifice to Juno Sispes.[181]

Sispes is the proper cognomen attested by the epigraphic dedications. The classical variant Sospita is a more or less learned man's attempt at recovering a goddess of rescue through an etymology that would conform to the Hellenistic concept of the *Sōter*. [182]   At Lanuvium her cult temple stood in a grove on the slope of the town's acropolis. [183]   In her Lanuvian precinct Juno received food offerings of legumes, at least, which archaeologists have unearthed in notable and carbonized abundance. [184] Part of her temple was a dining room (*cenaculum*), which had the normal cushioned couch for reclining at table (*pulvinar*). [185]   No doubt, this Juno was also worshipped by sacrificial meals just as the political Junos of the curias and infantry were venerated at Rome. What is equally remarkable is the Lanuvian Juno's third epithet, *regina*, because Lanuvium is one of the few Latian communities that we know retained a sacral king to perform what must have been the religious function of the defunct political kingship. We are even so fortunate as to have a dedication by a

Lanuvian king to Juno Sispes Mater Regina. [186] Furthermore, Lanuvium is one of the few towns in Italy for which we have certain and indisputable evidence of the archaic curiate constitution, [187] so that we may safely assume it was possible to distinguish between the king's and the curias' *iunones* there as well as in Rome.

The Romans had at least two temples to Juno Sispes. At the beginning of the second century B.C. they built a temple to her in accordance with a war vow made in northern Italy. [188] Clear and unequivocal reference to another shrine (*delubrum*) of Sospita on the Palatine hill near a grove is made at the beginning of the Christian era; [189] this probably does not refer to the temple of the second century, which was restored in 90 B.C., [190] because Ovid describes the Palatine shrine in ruins. Furthermore, the restoration of the year 90 had been prompted by the vision of a Roman lady of very good family, who reported that Juno Sispes had told her she was leaving town because her precincts were disgustingly filthy (*quod immunde sua templa foedarentur*). [191] At least one other of these trashy precincts must have been that on the Palatine Hill, the site of archaic Rome. Since the Palatine was the civic center only in the royal period, the Juno Sispes of the hill could have been another *regina* whose cult and shrine had long, long ago fallen into neglect when the last king had sited worship of his *iuno* on the Capitoline and the cult of Juno Regina was transferred to the Regia. The suffix of the name *sispes* may be identical with that of the borrowed Latin words *miles, velites,* and *satelles,* all of which have military connotations. [192]

When the Roman consuls assumed responsibility for the annual ceremonies of Lanuvian Juno, [193] the Romans were in fact asserting their hegemony over Lanuvium; the religious act was but an extension of Roman sovereignty despite the tactful manner in which Rome made the Lanuvians, with their gods, into Romans. The Roman republican coinage amply illustrates the garb of Juno Sispes, which Cicero also describes: "cum pelle caprina cum hasta cum scutulo cum calceolis repandis." [194] When only her head is shown, she is portrayed on coins with the top of her goat-skin cloak (see Figure 2). [195] At full length Juno Sispes stands outfitted with her goat skin, a spear, the turned-up slippers, and an old-fashioned figure-eight shield, and she rides in a chariot (see Figures 4 and 5). [196] Sometimes the serpent belonging to her cult is pictured with her (see Figures 5-7). [197] The best representations of Juno Sispes brought into relation to alien gods can be seen on the coins of Q. Cornificius, a Roman augur and proconsul of the province of Africa from 44 to 42 B.C., [198] who issued four coins portraying her. On an aureus and a denarius he had represented Jupiter Ammon with his horned ram's-head cap on the observe, and on the reverse Juno Sispes crowning Q. Cornificius, who held his augural wand. [199] The third and fourth coins are denarii that show Juno Sispes with her spear and shield, on which sits a crow or raven (*cornix* or *corvus*); on the obverse is Ceres or a personified Africa wearing an elephant headdress and holding two spears over her shoulder. [200] By this one series Cornificius has called to mind Alexander, the elephants of Hannibal, and an old warrior goddess of Latium whom the Romans had appropriated in the fourth century; as well, I dare say, as doubly the *corn-* of his own gentilicial name.

The crow or raven on Juno Sispes' shield has brought to the attention of many the association of Juno with these birds. [201] In 218 were reported the Lanuvian prodigies of a spear moving and a crow flying into Juno's temple, where it sat on the cushioned couch. [202] Among the prodigies of 215 was a nest of crows in the same temple. [203] Across the Tiber from Rome a grove was dedicated to *cornices* because they were thought to be under Juno's protection; its deities were *Divae Corniscae*. Both the raven and the crow figure prominently in Roman augury and as omens. They were renowned for long and many lives, and the raven's call was in certain cases reckoned a harbinger of death. Although they may thus have been associated with the notion of a life force such as *iuno*, [204] we have no indication from the ancients of the way these birds were first considered in religious beliefs.

9. JUNO MARTIALIS PERUSINA

In 40 B.C., Caesar Octavian invested Perugia, which was held by Lucius Antonius and Fulvia. When the besieged held out in the face of excruciating hunger, the besieger took to prayer and sacrifice. But a quick sally of gladiators carried off his religious paraphernalia, and his haruspices could only solace him with the prediction that upon Perusine heads would come disaster. The tale is reminiscent of the religious prelude to the fall of Veii, whence Juno Regina came to the Aventine. The haruspices told Octavian true, for the city was fired; only the temple of Vulcan and a statue of Juno were spared the flames. The young general had a dream which bade him bring the statue of Juno to Rome and to permit the restoration of the town by any settler desiring to live within a one-mile limit of the previous site. Caesar did as he was bidden. Although the old Perusines had honored Juno as their chief deity, the new Perusines accorded that role to Vulcan.

No specific record of Juno Perusina at Rome is preserved. She disappeared from sight until the brief principate of C. Vibius Trebonianus Gallus, which lasted from A.D. 251 to 253. Both the emperor's father and his son bore the name Veldumnianus, whose Etruscan appearance is confirmed by the name of the person to whom Vegoia delivered her prophecy, Arruns Veltumnus. Trebonianus honored his hometown with colonial status and the full name Colonia Vibia Augusta Perusia. His imperial coinage figures Juno Martialis, either simply seated on a throne or on a throne in a round, domed temple with a peacock (raven?), and jars at her side. In two instances she holds a scepter, and in a third an orb. However, her ladylike garment prevents us from assuming that the cognomen Martialis refers to warfare. The title in another connection is very old at Rome, for a flamen of Mars bore it.

Martialis also refers to the month of March; the epigrammatist was so named because he was born on 1 March, and Juno Martialis had a festival in March. The calends of March was occupied by Lucina, and on 7 March was celebrated Junonalia. The rites, however, are attested only by the calendar of Furius Filocalus published in 354 A.D. A long interval occurs in our knowledge of the inscribed Fasti, and Filocalus' calendar marks the end of the pagan liturgical feast days.

In 40 B.C., Octavian brought Juno Perusina to Rome; on 7 March in some later year, he founded a temple for her. Nearly three centuries later a Perusine princeps rebuilt the shrine of the goddess from his native town and surely figured her on his coins. By 251, she had acquired an epithet from the month of her worship. This revival of the cult of Juno Martialis is evidenced by record of her feast only in a calendar published 100 years after the minting of her coins. [205] Despite the lack of congruity with known ceremonies of evocation, the manner of Juno Perusina's transfer to Rome and her subsequent absence in Perusine cult leave no doubt that she must be numbered among those goddesses made to quit their native places to serve Rome's majesty in Rome, and so to deprive their former worshippers of their protection. She was the last of the foreign Junos to reach Rome in this style.

10.   SUMMARY ON ATTRIBUTES AND CULTS

Before quitting the Roman cults and turning to Juno in syncretism and to the Carthaginian goddess who was destined to be Juno Caelestis, we shall examine a few details in the Junonian religion at Rome. We begin with a list extracted from material in the Roman liturgical calendar:

1 February. Juno Sospita at her temple in the Forum Holitorium, dedicated in 194. (Degrassi, pp. 405-406)

5 February (nones). Priest-king proclaims the *dies februatus* of Lupercalia.

15 February. Lupercalia, when the *populus*, Palatine, Rome and women are cleansed. The latter are lashed with "Juno's cloak," a goatskin. (Degrassi, pp. 409-11)

1 March. Juno Lucina at her temple, dedicated in 375, in her grove where the married women kept the Matronalia (Degrassi, pp. 418-19). This temple was given after Tusculum became Roman. Lucina enjoyed the Tusculan rite.

7 March (nones). An obscure Iunonalia (Degrassi, p. 421), here attributed to Juno Martialis of Perugia.

1 June. At the temple of Juno Moneta, built on the Arx in 344 B.C. (Degrassi, p. 463; see October 10)

1 July. At the temple of a Juno whose name is restored in the oldest inscribed calendar. (Degrassi, p. 475)

7 July (nones). Festival of Juno Caprotina at Caprae Palus in the Campus Martius. We have argued that her cult was brought from Fidenae to Rome in 426. Perhaps, she had the shrine noted at 1 July. (Degrassi, pp. 479-81)

1 September. At Juno Regina's temple on the Aventine. Regina came to Rome ca. 396. (Degrassi, pp. 504-505)

13 September. All members of the Capitoline triad receive *epula*. (Degrassi, p. 509)

23 September. At Juno Regina's temple in the Circus Flaminius. It was built perhaps in 146. (Degrassi, p. 512; see December 23)

1 October. A sacrifice to the *tigillum sororium* by altars of Juno Sororia and Janus Curiatius. (Degrassi, pp. 515-16)

7 October (nones). At the temple of Juno Quiritis in the Campus Martius. Her origin and the date of the temple's foundation are uncertain. (Degrassi, p. 518) This is the third nones on which Juno was worshipped (see 7 March and 7 July), and the fourth related to her cult (see 5 February).

10 October. At the temple of Juno Moneta, a second ceremony (see 1 June), which is unusual. Perhaps the two spears in her temple, the two groves near it, and two festivals for her indicate twin Junones Monetae who are not attested. (Degrassi, p. 519)

23 December. At Juno Regina's temple in the Campus Martius, dedicated in 179. See 23 September. (Degrassi, pp. 544-45)

Except for the temple of Jupiter, Juno, and Minerva (13 September), all the Junonian shrines are republican foundations—if we can date them at all. The altar of Juno Sororia is probably very old. The annual ceremonies for the Junones Quirites and Juno Populona, who were the oldest forms of the goddess, are not marked on the calendars. Perhaps two other Junos, Sispes of the Palatine and Diva Rumina near the Lupercal, reach back to high antiquity. The festivals of Juno on 7 March and 1 July are open to assignment to the several Junos whose ceremonies are not specifically dated in the calendars or the authors. Although the absence of a clear pattern in the day of the month on which Juno was worshipped prevents formulation of a theory of her monthly protection, she occupies in all six calends and four nones.

Second, we summarize the cult practice and cult attributes of Roman Junos. The priestess queen is the only sacrificant known to have sacrificed regularly to Roman Juno. Her monthly sacrifice in the Regia on the calends belonged to a ritual series over which her husband, the priest-king, presided until ca. 304. Her role seems to differ not at all from that of the lesser pontiff, whom the priest king directed to call the new moon in a manner calculated to proclaim the number of days before the nones—the "ninth" day before the ides. In the rites to Juno Regina of the Aventine, the Decemvirs participated, since supervision of a cult of alien origin was incumbent on that priestly college.

In the curias thirty Junos received an old-fashioned supper on old-fashioned wooden tables. The precinct of Juno Populona, which we argue can be the *cella* of Capitoline Juno, had a consecrated table that took the place of her altar, and at Lanuvium a part of Juno Sispes' temple was a dining room in which was spread the goddess' cushioned couch.

Juno's accoutrements make manifest a goddess of war and power. The Capitoline Juno and Juno Caprotina hold scepters when represented on coins. [206] We are told that Juno had a king's scepter; [207] otherwise, Juno's outfits betoken the warrior: shield, spear, and even the *corona civica.* [208] With such armor she rode in a war chariot. [209]

Juno's temples were often situated in or by groves. During the Cimbrian War, an elm in Juno's grove at Nuceria was topped because it bent over onto her altar. When it immediately grew back to its former height, the grandeur of the Roman people revived from its recent low mark of defeat.[210] The place was sometimes chosen for its natural height;[211] both groves and high places commonly received cults throughout the Mediterranean world. The ancients held that gods situated on the hills were their civil protectors.[212]

The peculiarly female cult of Juno, however, remains to be explained. Is it the oldest worship of the goddess whose name would mean "young woman"? How does such a priority give way to the goddess of curias and *populus*, ready for battle? The word *iuno* "young woman" is quite a specialization, if it is derived from *iuvenis.* Slave women participated in the cult of Caprotina, and freedmen's sons in the cult of Aventine Juno Regina. The former goddess wore the *praetexta*, which we propose was the sign of her captivity. The women who cleansed the *cella* and statue of Capitoline Juno after the fire of 64 A.D., those who gave the supper and prayed to Juno at the secular games in 17 B.C., those who were the mothers of the freedmen's sons wearing the *praetextae*, and those who celebrated Matronalia in Juno Lucina's temple after 375 B.C. must all be duly married *matres familias.*

Besides the details given above, two other old indications of Juno, goddess of marriage, are cited as early evidences. Charisius alone attests an archaic oath *eiuno* which, with *ecastor* and *edepol*, he attributes to womankind. Yet both the deities referred to in the latter, Castor and Pollux, are male deities, albeit of Greek provenience– and moreover, divine patrons of the cavalry. The oath of Juno probably had a political origin;[213] Roman women would naturally have sworn by such deities when praying for their men at war. Protection of husbands, besought by wives, need not imply an exclusively female function of the divinities to whom women pray or make promises. Oaths *per Iunonem* are attested as early as Plautus, who has Alcmene swear by the kingship of her almighty ruler and by Juno, mother of the household.[214] The division of the *genius* and the *iuno* between men and women, respectively, is artificial. We saw that male deities had *iunones* just as the curias and the *populus*; so, too, the *genius* could be invoked. The *genius* of an entity comprised its procreative force, while its *iuno* implied the temporal period of that procreative force. Without "youth" there is no procreative force.

The second piece of evidence is a royal law, ascribed to Numa Pompilius: paelex aram Iunonis ne tangito; si tanget, Iunoni crinibus demissis agnum feminam caedito.[215] A *paelex*, so we are told, was the mistress of a married man. Presumably Juno guarded regular marriage so early as the Roman kings. Given the legal status of women at the time, it is with the greatest difficulty that we believe a Roman king provided for a religious protection of wives. Rather, the contamination of the touch of a *paelex* must not have been related especially to Juno but have been felt in the case of many a deity.[216] After all, the women sacrificed *pure et caste* at the ceremonies for Juno Regina in 207 B.C.; this means more than having bathed.[217] When one contemplates the ancient customs of adultery, any interpretation of Numa's law that conceives of a wife's being religiously protected by the humiliation of a prostitute will forever want confirmation. The violation of Juno's altar, which perhaps refers to a cult table, demands expiation. But the source and nature of the pollution matters. If Juno had indeed been the goddess of marriage, as Gellius himself asserts, and if this royal law had been formulated to protect Roman marriages around 700 B.C., why and how does the *paelex* get off with an expiatory sacrifice to the goddess whom she has just insulted, whereas a Vestal Virgin would have been buried alive or hurled from a precipice for doing once what a *paelex* daily did? Of course, the Vestal was a state priestess. But her chores make the difference: a Vestal was perpetually observing religious ceremonies. If she had enjoyed a day's vacation, the rules would have been different.

The oldest instances of *paelex* are to be found in Plautus, where the word signifies no more than a hired prostitute.[218] The later professional opinions do not yield a unanimous definition:

> In his book of *Memorialia* Massurius writes, "A *paelex* among the ancients was called that woman who nevertheless lived with a man although there was no wife." Today we call this woman by her real name, girlfriend, or by the slightly more fashionable name concubine. In his book on the Jus Papirianum Granius Flaccus writes, "The woman now commonly called a *paelex* is one who sleeps with a man who has a wife. Certain [authorities call a *paelex*] one who is in the house instead of a wife and without benefit of a wedding. Her the Greeks call *pallake*."[219]

> This very old law demonstrates ... that a woman was called a *paelex* and considered shameful who usually kept company with a man in whose hand and control [*in manu mancipioque*] there was another woman for the sake of marriage. Moreover *paelex* is as if *pallax* [i.e., as if *pallakis*]. Like many others, this word comes from Greek.[220]

> Today not only women but also men who sleep with others are called *paelices*. The ancients properly call a *paelex* one who was married to a man who had another wife. To this class of women is also applied the punishment which Numa Pompilius ordained by this law ....[221]

There were two legal views on what was a *paelex*, neither of which embraces the Plautine sense of hired prostitute. According to Masurius Sabinus the *paelex* was the concubine of an unmarried man. Granius Flaccus knew this opinion as well as that held by Gellius, who believed a *paelex* was the mistress of a married man. The epitome of Festus blunders in calling a *paelex* the second wife of a bigamist. Thus, we know four kinds of *paelex:* hired prostitute, common-law wife, mistress of a married man, and a woman involved in bigamy. Recall Numa's law, "Let not a *paelex* touch Juno's altar. If she touches it, let her sacrifice a female lamb for Juno after she has let down her hair." From this law Gellius and his source inferred that the man had a legal wife *in manu mancipioque!* Granius Flaccus commenting on the Jus Papirianum, which apparently contained this royal law,[222] favors the one opinion but acknowledges the other. I conclude that these were mere opinions formed by inference from "Numa's" law, which says nothing whatsoever about the marital status of her partner. The very fact that agreement did not prevail among students of the law at a time when *paelex* "prostitute" or "mistress" was current[223] indicates ignorance on the part of the learned. But Juno's altar is being protected, not married women. Further, the learned inferences were drawn when Juno was indeed considered a goddess of marriage. No ancient supporter of this view has adduced any reason that leads us to believe that Juno did protect marriages. On the contrary, the extant ancient testimony points to Tellus and Ceres as the deities involved in weddings, marriages, and procreation.[224]

Finally, Juno Sororia's function must be treated, since a situation similar to that of a *paelex* has been brought into connection with the cult of this Juno. On 1 October, according to the calendars, sacrifice was offered to the *tigillum sororium*. This beam figures in an aetiological tale of Horatius, who purified himself by walking under the beam that hung above the altars of Juno Sororia and Janus Curiatius (perhaps also called the Janus Junonius).[225]   In a series of articles H. J. Rose developed the thesis that this expiation was a rite of passage appertaining to initiation into the thirty Roman curias. Rose argues that *sororius* and the verb *sororiare* refer to the growth of pubescent youngsters and have no relation to *soror* "sister." He further connected the ceremony with the religious activities of the Matralia, which, unlike Matronalia on 1 March, is marked on the calendars at 11 June. The Matralia was celebrated at the temple of Mater Matuta and was closed to all female slaves. On this occasion the Roman mothers traditionally prayed for the children of their siblings. Rose believes that the prayer was actually said for *pueri sororii*, the mother's own children who were attaining sexual maturity. Thus Juno Sororia, whose altar stood under the *tigillum sororium*, presided over the puberty of children of both sexes.[226]

The majority of Junonian epithets that were, and still are, adduced in support of the contention that Juno was a goddess of marriage have no known cult associations whatsoever; some can even be interpreted as not pertaining to marriage. Furthermore, the non-cultish epithets can be traced back no further than Varro, whose view of Juno as moon, earth, air, etc., hardly emerged from an examination of her cult. Not a single Juno who enjoyed a state cult bears an epithet that compels us to believe her career began with women preoccupied with a desire for husbands and fertility. If Juno is sometimes addressed *mater*, Jove, Mars, and many other gods are addressed *pater*. Perhaps the oldest of these epithets is *Opigena*, which has all the appearances of being derived from cult.

Opigena. By ancients and moderns the epithet *opigena* has been construed as evidence that Juno brought help to women in childbirth, or as a mythological compound meaning "daughter of *Ops*," i.e., the Roman Rhea.[227] Linguistically, *opigena* has no connection with bringing help in childbed; rather, it appears to mean "producing material prosperity." Furthermore, Ops was worshipped at the Regia, where Juno too was worshipped. According to the pontifical archives, *ops* was a form of address (*indigitamentum*) accorded Bona Dea, one of whose attributes was the royal scepter of Juno.[228] In this connection we must remark the recitation of *versus Iunonii* with *versus Ianuli* and *Minervii* in the Salian *axamenta*.[229] Presumably such hymns were integrated into the worship of Mars, who oversaw the beginning of vegetable growth and warfare in his month. Second, Juno appears with other strange company in an old harvest sacrifice: "Before you harvest, in the following manner you must sacrifice a *praecidanea* pig. To Ceres sacrifice a *praecidanea* sow before the following crops are stored: spelt [*far*], wheat, barley, beans, and turnip seeds. With incense and wine first address yourself to Janus, Jupiter, and Juno." [230] Cato then quotes the prayer formulas for Janus and Jupiter to accompany the rites for Ceres, but omits further mention of Juno. The omission does not compel us to expunge Juno's name, nor is her presence in a harvest ceremony any stranger than that of Janus and Jupiter. [231] The Salians also prayed to both Janus and Juno. Second, Juno, Janus and Jupiter were addressed only before the storing (*condere*) of certain produce, among which are the spelt and barley, grains which were otherwise set before the thirty curial Junos with the first fruits. [232] The storage of these primitive crops at harvest recalls the festivals of Opiconsivia (25 August) and Opalia (19 December), both of which must be related to the two Consualia on 21 August and 15 December, four days before the rites for Ops. [233] If the Latin word for sacrificial dinner *epulum* is related to *ops*, [234] it is clear that Juno Opigena is not "Juno who brings help in childbirth" [235] but "Juno who produces the goods of this earth."

Cinxia. This epithet the ancients assigned to Juno as the goddess who undid the bride's girdle. [236] An analogous adjective is *anxius*, from *ango*, which means either "distressed" or "distressing." Thus *cinxia* means either "girded" or "girding," not "loosening the girdle" of anyone. Since compounds and derivatives of *cingere* ordinarily apply to men at arms, Juno's epithet *cinxia* might have referred either to her own girding as a war goddess or to the belt or strap of the soldiers she protected in her role of Populona. [237]

Iterduca and Domiduca. The Romans explained these Junos as "she who leads the bride into marriage" and "she who leads the bride to her new home." But just as both *iter* and *-duca* are familiar military terms, "he who leads the way or the march," the *domiduca* "home-bringer" may be related to a deity who leads soldiers home from war (cf. *domi militiaeque, duelli domique*, etc.). [238]

Pomana and Ossipagina. These Junonian epithets are met only in Arnobius 3.31. Juno Pomana, goddess of fruits, is not surprising when we recall *opigena*, the Junonian section of the Salian hymns, and the address to Juno at the harvest festival. Although Arnobius does not explain Ossipagina, he mentions a goddess Ossipago who hardens and strengthens infants' bones. She is recorded among a number of deities who have no relation with Juno (Arn. 4.7-8). The compounds *ossipagina* and *ossipago* seem to mean "bone-setter." [239] Insofar as the mere names are concerned, they imply broken bones and nothing about toddlers; Juno Ossipagina can also be related to anyone with a broken bone, even to a warrior.

Pronuba. We first learn of Juno Pronuba, Juno Matron of Honor, from Varro. The epithet is never found in cult, nor can it be connected with a goddess of any Roman wedding ceremony. Like that of other epithets, its application to Juno is no older than Varro's *Antiquities of Divine Matters*, and certainly cannot be shown to have been used in cult. Vergil (*Aeneid* 4.166-68), introduces Juno into the circumstances of Dido and Aeneas' union:

> prima et Tellus et pronuba Iuno
> dant signum; fulsere ignes et conscius aether
> conubiis, summoque ulularunt vertice Nymphae.

This is a peculiar wedding ceremony, Roman and yet not truly a wedding. Juno, protectress of Carthage, is involved in the heavenly portents (see note 205). Juno here is Caelestis (see below, sect. 15) as opposed to Tellus: Heaven and Earth. Thus the Servian commentaries: "Pronuba Iuno." quae nubentibus praeest. Iunonem autem dedisse signa per tempestatem constat et pluvias quae de aëre fiant. Varro pronubam dicit quae ante nupsit et quae uni tantum nupta est; ideoque auspices deliguntur ad nuptias. In any case, a *pronuba* was a person involved in the wedding (cf. Festus p. 282 L), and chosen for a kind of good omen. Juno plays the bridal attendant in the epic because she was by Vergil's day a marriage goddess; she is not invoked in the Roman ceremony. [240] Finally, Juno and Tellus, Heaven and Earth, participate in the ceremony; they are not the object of it.

What kind of deity was Juno before she was considered almost exclusively a goddess of women, childbirth, and marriage? Was she originally a patron of the state and a war-goddess? A no must be the answer to the latter question, for a war-goddess does not become a marriage goddess any more easily than the latter becomes the former. Juno was related early to childbearing and pubescence. The Roman male's *iuventus* spanned the period from puberty to the forty-fifth year, when the citizen ceased to be a *iunior* eligible for annual military service and entered the ranks of the *seniores*. [241] The sense of *iuno* that fits all circumstances is the deity or spirit of youthfulness. After all, both women and men dwell on the retention of their youth. At war, Juno protected the man eligible to bear arms, the *iuvenis*, a word often used for soldier; thence she assumed the function of the tutelary deity of sovereign peoples. For the woman capable of bearing children, Juno from the time of puberty oversaw childbirth and marriage. Her female worshippers had to be married women. Few unwed women, I guess, would want to entreat such a deity. The woman who swore by her *iuno* was putting her fertility in jeopardy, because it protected her youth. Nor did widows participate in her cult. The Secular Games included only *matres familias nuptae*. After the burning of Rome, the matrons who observed the vigil and offered the suppers were *feminae quibus mariti sunt*. [242]

Although no ancient authority refers the menopause to Juno's cult, it is implicit in the notices on Mena and Fluvionia. Even if we were told that women ceased to participate in Juno's cult after the menopause, we need not assume that Juno began as a goddess of women alone. Everyone is young once.

Juno was associated with Jupiter and Minerva in the protection of Rome; with Janus, Minerva, and probably Mars in the Salian ceremonies of March; with Jupiter, Janus, and Ceres in the rites before the storing of certain agricultural produce; and with Janus Curiatius under the *tigillum sororium*. In her most primitive cult, Juno received a dinner that included first fruits and a meal prepared from such grains as *far*, which the Romans grew in the historical period mostly for religious purposes. Juno's meal seems a fair return to the goddess as well as a means to preserve the *iuno*, the youth, of the Roman curias and *populus*, or of any state.

The political circumstances of Juno's widespread Roman cult ought not to be forgotten. She belonged to the Capitoline triad who were the chief deities of Rome.

In every curia, which shared in the oldest state assembly, she was worshipped. She protected the *populus*. When Fidenae, Veii, and Carthage were destroyed and their estates became the property of the Roman people, their Junos were invited to Rome and worshipped. After a bitter war with the remaining members of the Latin League, Rome dissolved the league and turned her attention to the loyal Lanuvium, which she had not humbled. With calculated piety, the Romans' chief magistrates annually paid homage to the chief goddess of Lanuvium, Juno Sispes Mater Regina. Adopting the Tusculan rite and creating a priesthood to supervise Tusculan religion, the Romans united Tusculan Juno with the Juno of a Roman grove between 381 and 375 B.C., in order to consummate the marriage of Rome and Tusculum. Octavian's treatment of Perusine Juno exemplifies his equivocal treatment of Perugia; this Juno's fortunes fell to a low state from which only a Perusine emperor raised them to survive total oblivion.

After the temple to Lucina, the Romans erected four more temples to Juno during the Republic. In 349, a general vowed a temple to Moneta in a war with the Gauls; he dedicated it in 344. [243] In 197, a general vowed a temple to Sospita in a war with the Gauls; he dedicated it in 194. [244] In 189, a general vowed a temple to Regina in a war with the Ligurians; he dedicated in 179. [245] After his triumph, Caecilius Metellus Macedonicus dedicated in 146 B.C. two temples, one to Juno Regina, which held Stator's statue, and the other to Jupiter Stator, which held Regina's statue. [246] It is fairly urged that none of these Junos earned temples because of a gift of female fertility. [247] The Romans hoped to win the support of a native deity from their enemy. Now, we turn to some of the Italian deities who are syncretized with Juno at least by name.

11. JUNO AND HERA LAKINIA

An old goddess with whom the Romans later identified Juno was the deity worshipped in a temple on the promontory of Lakinion, whom the Greeks called Hera Lakinia. [248] Early Roman contact with the cult can be inferred from the fact that the promontory was the southeastern limit of the Roman fleet stipulated in a treaty invoked at the outbreak of the Tarentine War in 282; the treaty may not have been struck before 311, when the Romans created their first military fleet. [249] The Romans and their near neighbors, however, could have learnt of this great shrine from anyone who plied the Italian seas and landed at Latium long before the end of the fourth century. The temple of Lacinian Hera enjoyed wide fame in antiquity, and students of western Greek religion assume that the place and the deity were religiously cultivated before the Greeks came to the west. The site of the cult lies a distance of some seven miles from the nearest town, Croton, whose citizens supervised it, and seems to be the vestige of a religious center attended by the inhabitants of the surrounding territory before its conversion to the worship of Hera. [250] The Crotoniates made Lakinion the rallying point of the league over which they exercised hegemony, and which the goddess presumably protected. Regular pilgrimages (*panegyreis*) of the Italiotes were attracted thither, and there is even a hint that both Italiotes and Italians venerated the goddess together. [251] Certain cult attributes of this Hera resemble those of the northern Juno. Her temple was sited on the height of the promontory [252] in a grove. [253] The obscure poet Lycophron gives to Hera of Lakinion and to Hera of Argos the epithet *Hoplosmia*, which evidently means "heavily armed." [254] Milo, the famous Crotoniate athlete, is said to have been sculptured as her priest standing in an attitude of prayer upon a shield. [255] Nor are these indications alone in confirming her military capacity. Her temple received the spoils of war. [256] Hera Lakinia was nonetheless a goddess specially revered by women, [257] although the reverence may have been secondary and related to cults of Hera in old Greece. It is unlikely that the Crotoniates consciously made a goddess of female fertility into a warrior and league patron. Pyrrhus and Hannibal paid their respects to Hera Lakinia, [258] and they were not seeking female fertility any more than her male priest. Furthermore, Aeneas was said to have stopped over at Lakinion on his way to his destined home and to have left a bronze cup inscribed with his name. [259] Finally, woven into the legend of Heracles in Italy are the wife of the eponymous Croton, Laurete by name, and king Latinus and his daughter Laurine, all of whom are mythologically connected with the founding of Croton or Hera's temple at Lakinion. [260] Hera's great sanctuary in the Greeks' New World apparently had old ties with the northern people of Latium, strong enough to hang a Roman mythology therefrom.

12. JUNO AT PATAVIUM

Far north on the Adriatic coast, in Venetic Patavium, stood a temple to Juno in which the Patavinians dedicated the prows and spoils of ships taken in war. Livy, who no doubt saw these offerings in his hometown, says the temple was old, and attributes the dedications to the result of a battle with the Spartan Cleonymus at the end of the fourth century. Furthermore, he tells us, his fellow townsmen continued to hold an annual ritual naumachy in the middle of the town to commemorate their ancestors' victory. [261] Although Livy does not explicitly name Juno or her Venetic counterpart as the patroness of warfare and protectress of the town, we may assume that the goddess of Patavium was the community's protectress, received spoils in this capacity, and accordingly was worshipped by means of ritual battle.

13. JUNO QUIRITIS OF FALERII

Because the Faliscans consistently allied themselves with neighboring Veii against their cousin Romans, whose language was remarkably similar to their own, the chief goddess of their town Falerii deserves special attention. We have already remarked the existence of Juno Quiritis at Falerii, and related her cognomen to that of the thirty Roman Junos of the curias. [262] Her archaic cult was preserved intact down to the beginning of the Christian era, although her city was dismantled and her people transported.

In 241, the two consuls directed their war-weary legions in a combined assault upon Falerii, which fell under a six-day siege. The Faliscans surrendered to the discretion of the Roman people by *deditio*, witnessed the destruction of their town, moved to a new and less defensible site, and forfeited half their territory. They did not suffer the same fate as Fidenae and Veii, their old allies, for the times had changed; the old civil community of Falerii was permitted to survive in another place. It is thus unlikely that any proper evocation of gods was performed by the Romans. In any event, the old temple of Juno Quiritis emerged unscathed from the rebellion.[263]

In his *Roman Antiquities*, Dionysius asserts the belief that Juno of Falerii was a colonial descendant of Hera of Argos. The temples and cults of the two closely resembled each other: the goddess's precinct was supervised by holy women, the first phase of sacred ceremonies was entrusted to a virgin called the basket-bearer (*kanephoros*), and sacred choruses of virgins sang their ancestral hymns to the goddess. [264] The Romans arranged comparable choruses of twenty-seven virgins for Juno Regina, who had been brought from Veii. [265] The Faliscan holy women are unparalleled at Rome, unless Dionysius merely refers to *matronae*. The basket-bearer would be perplexing if Dionysius himself had not given further details of the Latin institution he intended. When he describes the religion of the curias he says that the Roman curial religious system rests upon borrowing from the Greeks. The Greeks employed *kanephoroi* and *arrhephoroi* in the ceremonies which the Romans entrusted to unmarried maidens called *tutulatae* because they wore a special head-dress (the *tutulus*). The boy and girl attendants as a group were called *camilli*, after a Pelasgian and Etruscan custom;[266] for Dionysius, these Pelasgians are identical with the Pelasgians who had lived at Argos and brought Hera's cult to Falerii. [267] The young Roman acolytes of whom Dionysius is writing were *camillae* and *camilli.* [268] Although Dionysius may have equated their roles, and then applied the term basket-bearer, a title unknown to Italic cult, his description of the banquets that were set for Juno Quiritis in all thirty curias [269] includes baskets with the earthenware on the curial tables. [270] Therefore, the curial *camillae tutulatae* probably carried the baskets for the tables. If this interpretation of Dionysius' choice of words is correct, then the Faliscans also offered Juno dinners. [271] The cult of Juno Quiritis seems to have lasted sometime after Dionysius. One Faliscan inscription informs us of a male priest of Juno [272] and redresses the one-sided account of the Greek.

The *Book of Colonies* records a Faliscan Junonia established by tresviri. [273] Whether this was a normal three-man colonial commission or the three men for restoring the Republic is not known. The forfeiture of one half of the Faliscan territory [274] made land available for colonization after 241. However, names such as Carthago Junonia, Scolacium Minervium, Tarentum Neptunia, and Narbo Martius were not given to colonies until over a century later, although a colony named Saturnia was sent to the Etruscan Ager Caletranus in 183. The choice of name betrays Rome's constant respect for Juno and for the sentiments of the local inhabitants.[275]

Indeed, the Roman temple of Juno Quiritis in the Campus Martius has sometimes been thought to house the evoked Juno of Falerii.[276] Although the evocation of Juno is clearly out of the question, the temple may have been vowed by one of the consuls who took Falerii in 241. Since Livy's account of this and subsequent years is lost, we have no details from the period, but nothing prevents the assumption that the temple housed a Juno of a Roman curia who came to occupy a religious pre-eminence.

On the Caelian Hill was a small shrine (*delubrum* or *Minervium*) of Minerva Capta whose epithet Ovid explains four ways. One of his explanations rests upon the assertion that this Minerva was captured at Falerii and brought to Rome.[277] If Ovid is correct, the participle *capta* forestalls any discussion of an evocation of Minerva, since the Faliscans restored or maintained Minerva's cult in New Falerii[278] as if she had never been taken away.

Although the Roman people wished revenge on Falerii in 241,[279] the citizen body and its *sacra* were left intact. The decision doubtless was made because the Romans had nothing to fear from this quarter except a bad example of secession from their network of alliances. No other allied state was likely to follow the Faliscans' example.

14. JUNO AT CAERE AND PYRGI

In the Etruscan town of Caere stood a large temple in which have been found cooking wares, cups, and plates that date back to the sixth century. The early pottery, made under Greek influence, has sparse or illegible Etruscan writing, but many cups of the third century bear in Greek letters the full or abbreviated name of Hera. The temple and its ritual wares for kitchen and table must have belonged to the Etruscan Uni, identified with Hera (Uni is the named mother of Hercle on Etruscan mirrors) and borrowed (like Greek Apollo and Heracles) by the Etruscans from their Italic neighbors.[280] The remains of cooking pots and tableware point to a shared custom of giving both Juno and Uni sacral suppers. Fragments of fictile halos and a part of an antefix found in the Caeretane temple indicate the iconography of Juno Sispes, known from elsewhere in Etruria.[281]

There were also found pieces of two painted tiles, arranged as a mural, which display the lower portions of two warriors with shields and the fragment of a female face (Uni?).[282] The representation of armed warriors on the wall of Uni's temple demonstrates devotion to a deity that protects the warrior.

The recent archaeological finds at Pyrgi, Caere's port, have yielded even greater surprises. In the precinct of a temple, now so close to the sea that water and frogs fill it, were found in 1964 three gold rolls. Before discussing their pertinence to our study, we must examine the ancient testimony on one of the shrines at Pyrgi. In 384/3, Dionysius of Syracuse sacked a temple at Pyrgi dedicated to Leukothea, carried off 1000 talents, and realized 500 talents from the booty. [283] The Romans equated Leukothea with Mater Matuta (connected at Rome with Portunus, god of the port), whose Roman temple Camillus rebuilt and rededicated along with the temple of Juno Regina from Veii. [284]

The wealthy Leukothea, whose temple and its environs yielded so much to the tyrant of Syracuse, was certainly known by another name at Pyrgi. In the vicinity of her temple three gold plaques were dedicated by the Etruscan Thefarie Velianas. [285] Needless to say, the Phoenician epigraph, if not perfectly understood, is better understood than the similar Etruscan Inscription A. The following translation of the Phoenician inscription is that of Fitzmyer: [286]

> To the Lady Astarte [is dedicated] this shrine, which Thebariye' Velanaš, the king over Kaysriye', constructed and which he donated in the month of the Sacrifices to the Sun as a gift in the temple. *And I built it* because Astarte requested [it] from *me* [in] the third year of *my* reign in the month of KRR, on the day of the burial of the deity. And may the years of the statue of the deity in her temple be years like *the stars of El* [or: *these stars*].

To the Pyrgan goddesses Leukothea and Eileithyia, whom the authors mention, we must now add Semitic Astarte and the Latin Uni, with whom Astarte was identified at Pyrgi. This unusual plenty of goddesses occasions confusion in the quickened discussion of Pyrgan cults. Elsewhere the present writer demonstrates, first, that the Pyrgan temple to which the "shrine" was given as a "gift" belonged to the sea-goddess Venilia, and second, that the sea-goddess Venilia was equated with Leukothea by the Greeks on account of the "burial of the deity" who was the temple's goddess. The burial of the deity was commemorated in the Phoenician tablet by the Caeretane king as if it had taken place before the foundation of the shrine or "holy place" for Uni-Astarte. Furthermore, an epiphany or oracle of Juno can be directly related to Matuta, who represented Leukothea to the Romans. [287] Finally, Strabo 5.2.8 clearly stated that the temple of Eileithyia which Dionysius had sacked existed in his time. Many recent authors have tried to introduce Eileithyia's temple into a discussion of the temples and the tablets that Colonna has uncovered, but the newly found temples were overwhelmed long before Strabo knew of the contemporary existence of Eileithyia's shrine. Consequently, the temple of Eileithyia cannot have been the temple that contained the new inscriptions and the latterly installed Astarte. [288] In any event, the combined deity Uni-Astarte is not the major deity to which the temple was dedicated; the temple of the tablets belonged to Venilia. We may proceed to discuss the connection of Juno and Astarte without concern for Eileithyia.

Etruscan Inscription A is said by its first editor to yield roughly the same information as the Semitic text, although Thefarie Velianas' Etruscan title seems to be absent. In Etruscan Inscription A (12-13) the phrase *Atranes zilacal* is met: the former word is a masculine personal name [289] in the genitive case, the latter a feminine noun, also in the genitive case, that is to be related to the Etruscan word *zilath*, usually rendered by "praetor." [290] Such a formula is paralleled three times in Umbrian. At Iguvium: *uhtretie T.T. Kastruçiie* and *uhtretie K.T. Kluviier.* The word *uhtretie* is an abstract name of an office, in the locative case; *Kastruçiie* and *Kluviier* are the personal names of the officers, in the genitive case. [291] From the vicinity of modern Foligno: *oht. C.V. Vistinie Ner. T. Babr., maronatei Vois. Ner. Propartie T. V. Voisiener.* The abbreviated *oht.* should be resolved *ohtretie*, as at Iguvium, and *maronatei* is also in the locative case; both names of offices are followed here by the personal names of the officials in the genitive case. [292] Hence I render the Pyrgan *Atranes zilacal* (as if L. *in Atranii praetura*) "when Atranes was zilath." In a word, this is the eponymous date of the dedication, inconsequential to, and omitted from, the Phoenician inscription, just as Uni was omitted. Although eponymous, the *zilath* Atranes need not have been the chief (republican) magistrate at Pyrgi or Caere. Yet it is equally possible that the "king" of Caere, Thefarie Velianas, may have served as an officer similar to Rome's demoted *rex sacrorum*. This might explain the two means of dating: by the eponymous *zilath* and the regnal year. We have already discussed the political and sacral king's cult for Juno Regina.

Most Etruscan texts show the copyist's care in preserving interpuncts between words. The two new Pyrgan texts are no exceptions. Hence the single word in Etruscan A, line 3, *unialastres*, would seem to indicate the syncretism of two goddesses *uni* and Ishtar. Furthermore, both deities originated with other peoples. Etruscan Uni shows the loss of Latin *y-*. The Piacenza liver exhibits *uni* for *Iuno* and *ani* for *Ianus.* For this reason a search for Italic cult borrowed along with a goddess can be justified (see note 8). The cult of Uni-Astarte revealed by both the new Etruscan inscriptions betrays further proof of Etruscan borrowing from the Italic cult of Juno. At the end of the two Etruscan dedications stands the word *pulumchva*, which Pallottino proposes was a ceremony to be performed annually for Uni. [293] The suffix *-chva* is recognized in other Etruscan texts. [294] The word to which the suffix is attached, *pulum*, has a non-Etruscan ring to say the least; [295] it does, in fact, resemble the Latin *epulum*, and refers to the Junonian sacral suppers already noted for Caere, Rome, and Lanuvium. One might have expected an Etruscan rendition *eflum*, *efulum*, or the like. First of all, the syllable *e-* may have been treated as prothetic, since such an *e-* is discernible in Etruscan and was certainly attached to some ritual Latin words. [296] On the Cippus Perusinus, which records the funerary disposition of one family in relation to another, [297] the word *fulumchva* is attested (*CIE* 4538 B 5-6). Funerary and sepulchral dinners are extremely well attested in ancient Italy, especially on gravestones, and found mention in the inscribed testamentary dispositions of the dead. [298] Hence *fulumchva*, an annual supper at the grave of the dead, is quite appropriate to the context of the dead Etruscan's instructions.

Although *epula* for gods other than Jupiter are uncommon at Rome, we nowhere have preserved the precise Latin term for the dinners of the Junos of the curias and the *populus.* [299] Nevertheless, a supper for Uni-Astarte fits perfectly with the cult of Juno. The apparent retention of the Latin case-ending in *pulum* and *fulum* suggests that the word was a borrowing from Latin into Etruscan, and not vice versa. There are probably fifteen occurrences of *vinum* in that form on the Zagreb mummy-cloth alone. Words borrowed from Greek into Etruscan exhibit a similar reduction of -ων,-ουν to -*un* or -*um*, [300] which may have been influenced by the retention of Italic accusative endings. In the case of *vinum* and *pulum*, archaic Latin -*om* was rendered by -*um*. The Phoenician text of Pyrgi does not mention any banquet to the goddess; yet the Phoenician stars can be related to Etrusco-Italic cult practice, as the stars designating the proper inauguration of the temple. [301] They might be embroidered upon a *toga picta* worn by a cult statue. Such gorgeous attire Apuleius gives to the Queen of Heaven manifest: "per intextam extremitatem et in ipsa eius planitie stellae dispersae coruscabant earumque media semenstris luna flammeos spirabat ignes." [302] The banquets founded in both the Etruscan inscriptions from Pyrgi were not to be seen by the reader of the Phoenician text *in situ.* Hence, mention of the dinners would have been inappropriate in that context. The stars, howsoever they were represented, were presumably visible to the reader.

Once we grant the similarities in the Etruscan cults of Juno that show cultural exchange, we can find other parallels in the two cultures. The very old tile found at Capua, [303] the Etruscan town of Velthur (L. Volturnum), preserves in uncertain context the offering of a cup (*caper*) by a certain priest (*pricelu*) to Uni (*unial*). [304] On the Zagreb mummy-cloth (XII 10) we meet the phrase *unialti ursmnal athre*, which Trombetti compares with the phrase on the Capuan tile. [305] Olzscha, however, is correct in assuming that *athre* is a verb of offering and that *unialti* is a double genitive meaning "in the temple of Uni," which requires no mention of the building itself. [306] For our purposes the *ursmnal*, modifying *unialti*, is important: it may be only a gentilicial adjective, or it may be the eponymous adjective of an Etruscan curia or similar political unit. [307]

15. JUNO AND ASTARTE

If Juno's original relation to womankind remains vague in our meager sources, Astarte had been venerated for her fecundity long before she ever came to Etruria. Despite the probability that the Etruscan and Phoenician inscriptions of Pyrgi record a dedication in a political context, the Phoenician Ishtar cannot be divorced from fertility cult. Yet the Astarte at Pyrgi may represent a political protector of the statesman; she is found in the Semitic Near East in the same role. [308] Among the western Phoenicians, however, Ishtar did not enjoy great cult, if we are to trust the evidence of silence in the Carthaginian sphere of influence. In her stead was Tin(n)it Pene Ba'al, who apparently originates among the Libyans of northwestern Africa. In Hellenistic syncretism Tin(n)it is identified with Hera and, less frequently, with Demeter. Ishtar, on the other hand, enjoyed an identification with Aphrodite, if her name was not borrowed as Astarte. [309] Thus, according to the *interpretatio Romana*, Tin(n)it would have been the Italic Juno, and Ishtar Venus. [310] Manifestly such strictly formulated equations as have been accepted by students of Carthaginian religion will not bear close scrutiny beside the unequivocal composition of Uni-Astarte. In turn, the Pyrgan union raises anew questions of the identity of the Carthaginian goddess, called Juno Caelestis in Roman Africa, who is often merely named as Caelestis in order to avoid the ineffable name. Despite the mere appearance of a late distinction in Carthage between Tin(n)it, who is often named, and Ishtar, who is conspicuously absent, the former may likewise once have been no more than the effable name of the ineffable Ishtar, spoken in Libyan. [311] In Roman times, moreover, the cult of Aphrodite-Venus encroached upon the cult of African Juno, which may point to a vestigial unity of rite antedating the supposed divorce of Tin(n)it from Ishtar and going back to a time when Ishtar and Etruscan Uni might have been viewed as one and the same. [312]

One of the oldest historical references to the gods of Carthage raises further doubt as to the validity of identifying Juno Caelestis with Tin(n)it rather than with Astarte. In 215 B.C., Philip V of Macedon concluded a treaty with Hannibal on Italian soil, to which Hannibal and the Carthaginian elders with him swore. [313] Although it has been suggested that the oath preserved in Polybius was taken on both sides, the oath of the Carthaginians alone is recorded. Hence the gods in Greek guise must be considered principally Punic: Zeus, Hera, Apollo, the *daimon* of Carthage, Herakles, Iolaus, Ares, Triton, Poseidon, the gods who fight for us (the Carthaginians), Sun, Moon, Earth, Rivers, Lakes, Waters, all gods of Carthage, all gods of Macedon, all gods of Greece, and finally, whichever gods of the army protect the oath. Clearly Hannibal was not inviting a charge of Punic perfidy by this oath, for it is hard to imagine he has omitted a single deity, and consequently hard to identify any Punic gods with the Greek names. [314] But the name of Hera and the more or less explicit *daimon* of Carthage leave open the door to an informed guess.

The Romans have left us the clue to the identification of the *daimon* of Carthage. To the Romans the *daimon* of a place or a political unit was the *genius*, the community's procreative force. Charles-Picard and others suggest that the *genius* of Roman Africa is the goddess Tin(n)it, because the iconography of the *genius* is a goddess with lion's head, which they also ascribe to Tin(n)it. [315] Be that as it may, Ishtar of Babylon was called "the lioness of the gods." [316] The *genius* of Africa can be equally identified with Astarte or Tin(n)it, if they are not the same deity. Presumably the *genius* of Roman Africa was the same deity who had served as *daimon* of Carthage before its destruction in 146. We are thus led to a discussion of the religious end of the independence of Carthage.

In 146 B.C., Scipio Aemilianus destroyed the city, and in the fashion of every good Roman commander he summoned its chief deity from the city. Before him in Roman history stood the Junos from Italic and Etruscan towns enshrined in Roman temples. Fortunately we possess the prayer recited for the evocation of the *daimon* of Carthage: [317]

There is a ritual hymn [*carmen*] of this sort by which the gods are evoked whenever a city is besieged: "If god, if goddess be in whose care the Carthaginian army and state are,[318] you especially, that one who have assumed the protection of this city [*urbs*] and army [*populus*], you I pray and entice and seek pardon from you that you may abandon the Carthaginian army [*populus*] and their state [*civitas*], that you may quit their sacred places and precincts and city, that you may depart from them and [thereby] cast their army [*populus*] and state into the depths of fear, dread, and oblivion, that you may surrender and come to me and mine at Rome, and that our sacred places, precincts, and holy city may be more to your liking and that you may be put over me, the Roman people, and my soldiers so that we may know and understand. If you will have done as I ask you, I vow that I shall make precincts and games for you." One must offer victims with the same words and examine the authority of the entrails so that they promise future events. Once the deities [*numina*] have been evoked, the cities and armies [*exercitus*] are cursed [*devoveri*], but only dictators and imperial officers can curse with these words.

Although Macrobius does not tell us the name of the god or goddess who eventually came out of Carthage to Rome, he does mention the cursing (*devotio*) of seven towns, Carthage, Corinth, Fregellae, Gabii, Veii, Fidenae, and the textually corrupt *Stonii* or *Tonii.* We have already discussed the likelihood that Rome's Juno Caprotina came from Fidenae by evocation. The curse of Gabii probably rests on no better evidence than that Gabii's Juno consented to the Gabinians' adherence to "isopolity" with Rome. [319] Veientine Juno of the king has already been discussed.

When C. Gracchus gave the name Junonia [320] to the colony unsuccessfully planted in 122 B.C. on the territory of defunct Carthage, he was inviting the favor of a Roman goddess of state and a Punic goddess who had recently been taken to Rome. The Romans gave the same name to a colony situated in the territory of Old Falerii, where Juno Curitis' temple still stood. [321] Juno's protection of the Carthaginians is met again and again in Vergil's *Aeneid.* [322] No matter what Punic deity she represented to the Romans, Juno had been summoned from Carthage to Rome in 146. For centuries the location of Carthaginian Juno's cult at Rome remained unknown; then, in the late nineteenth century, a dedication to the *Virgo Caelestis praestantissimum numen loci montis Tarpei* and to her priestess was found on the flank of the Capitoline citadel. [323] As its editor noted in 1896, this inscription belonged to Caelestis worshipped in the area where today stands the church of S. Maria in Aracoeli, whose name still bears witness to the cult of Juno Caelestis established after Punic War III. [324] Juno Caelestis joined Juno Moneta and Venus Erycina on the Capitol and Arx. The latter goddess, installed during the second Punic War, had close ties with the Carthaginians (see below).

Basanoff (pp. 63-66) argues that the altar of this Caelestis belonged to Hera Hoplosmia, which Hannibal dedicated and Scipio Africanus the Elder brought from Lakinion after Punic War II; and that the Juno from Carthage, taken at the end of Punic War III, was sent home with the colonists to Junonia in 122/1 B.C. Not only are both these statements without foundation in ancient testimony, they are also inherently improbable conjectures. First, Hera Lakinia is not called Ourania or

Caelestis; second, Gracchus would have been a mad man to send the goddess home in the face of the violent political opposition, even if sacral law permitted such an act; and third, Basanoff's evidence for Punic War II (Serv. on *Aen.* 12.841: sed constat bello Punico secundo exoratam Iunonem) is without value for four reasons: 1) *exorare* is uniquely recorded here in this kind of context, and is not a religious technical term for *excantare* or *evocare* despite Basanoff's arguments (see his index, p. 219), but a religious term (see Beutler *TLL* s.v.) that means "to placate, soften," etc.; 2) any Roman general might have obtained the gracious support of Carthaginian Juno by prayer, which is all that *exorare* does mean (cf. Ennius in Serv. on *Aen.* 1.281), and even in the ritual of evocation, recited for days on several occasions, successful enticement is neither implicit nor guaranteed (cf. Dion. Hal. *AR* 3.69); 3) Servius' notice nowise involves Scipio Africanus, is misleading because *constat* does not include Livy, and, at any rate, may be simply a duplication of the event of Punic War III; 4) in 174/3 B.C., a Roman censor quarrying the temple of Hera Lakinia for a shrine he was building in Rome was compelled to restore what he had taken, because of the Romans' great veneration of the Greek temple (Livy 42.3). Basanoff's arguments do not merit credence, especially in light of the comment by Servius on *Aen.* 12.841: constat bello Punico secundo exoratam Iunonem, tertio vero bello a Scipione sacris quibusdam etiam Romam esse translatam. Juno was placated during Punic War II; such is the ancient inference from Roman success. The same Juno was brought to Rome by another Scipio in Punic War III: the evocation which Macrobius attests. Furthermore, Servius and Macrobius derive their information from the same source and complement each other. Macrobius lifted from his source the antiquarian lore in *Sat.* 3.8.8-9.16 on *Aen.* 12.836, which Servius ("Danielis" from corrupt marginalia) partly excerpted from the same source to comment on *Aen.* 12.836, the entry just before his comment on 12.841. Whereas Macrobius fails to name Juno as the evoked goddess, Servius gives almost only that detail and omits discussion of the ritual hymns, one of which is translated above. As for the continued worship of Juno in Africa Proconsularis and the name Junonia, it stands to reason that local cults might be officially revived by Roman colonists in conjunction with the natives, in order to preserve the *pax deum* of a place. To restore the cult utensils and statues, acquired by evocation, was tantamount to a Roman surrender, particularly after the cursing of a site. (Cicero, Verr. 2.1.19.50, wryly calls one of Verres' early depredations *expugnatio fani antiquissimi et nobilissimi Iunonis Samiae;* he would not have used *expugnatio* so pointedly if Juno had not been involved.)

The question of what actual Carthaginian deity, who was the tutelary *daimon* or *genius* of Carthage, came to Rome as Juno Caelestis remains uncertain. If Tin(n)it is the Hera of the Hannibalic treaty with Philip, and if the *daimon* of Carthage is distinct from that Hera-Tin(n)it, then Astarte may be the tutelary god. [325] The new evidence from Pyrgi points to an old syncretism in an Etruscan city numbered among Rome's first allies outside Latium, while the older eastern evidence supplies a parallel, if only coincidental, practice. The Indo-European Hittites, like their distant and later relatives the Latins, followed a procedure of evoking the gods of their conquered enemies. From a single text we learn that from many towns the Hittites invited Ishtar alone to come and live with them in the land of Hatti. [326]

16. JUNO IN VERGIL AND OVID

Although the rules of quasi-historico-religious poetry do not demand strict adherence to the facts of history or the data of cult, Vergil in his *Aeneid* and Ovid in his *Fasti* reflect some aspects of the *iunones* discussed in this chapter. Both poets ascribe to Juno of Carthage weapons and war-chariot, accoutrements of the Italic Juno. [327] Vergil centers Punic Juno's cult in a grove (*Aen.* 1.441-49). Ovid has Juno herself tell us of her scepter. [328] Into the pre-Roman and archaic Roman past, Vergil and Ovid project the Junonian function of making peace and friendship among Trojans and Italians, Latins and Sabines. [329] Ovid's Juno alludes to her hundred Roman altars, which no doubt included the curial shrines and the altars of the evoked Junos (*F.* 6.55). Besides the months named after her in Latin communities, the town walls of Tibur and Praeneste belong to her care (*F.* 6.56-63). The prodigious sow and her twelve sucklings are offered to Juno by Aeneas at the site of Alba; [330] this seems to have been the foundation of the cult of a Juno Albana. [331] His victims are the same as the monthly hosts of the king's queen for Juno in the king's house, yet in this instance the sacrificant is the leader of his people.

Finally, and most remarkably, Vergil describes the allies of Aeneas marshalled for war. From *Populonia mater* comes a force of 600 men. [332] And upon the other Etruscan allies—

> sequitur pulcherrimus Astyr,
> Astyr equo fidens et versicoloribus armis.
> ter centum adiciunt (mens omnibus una sequendi)
> qui Caerete domo, qui sunt Minionis in arvis,
> et Pyrgi veteres intempestaeque Graviscae.[333]

Astyr, the captain of the forces from Caere, her port Pyrgi, and neighboring Graviscae, is none other than Phoenician *astres* of Pyrgi, dimly remembered but not forgotten.[334]

A deity at the head of an armed force does not astonish the reader of Vergil's *Aeneid*. The poet's choice of legendary names and characters follows this tendency. Some of his heroes have divine mothers. Ocnus of Mantua named Vergil's hometown after his mother Manto, whose name, according to the commentator, was derived from Mantus, an Etruscan underworld god. [335] The mighty Turnus' mother was named Venilia, an obscure, goddess, and his grandfather was the deity Pilumnus. [336] Vulcan sired the chieftain Caeculus.[337] Capys may bear the name of the Etruscan falcon after which Capua was named. [338] Vergil allows himself greater latitude with women: Camilla, whose name is the title of young sacrificial attendants, plays a prominent role in the epic, [339] and its final book is filled with the deeds of Juturna, cast as Turnus' sister, who was indeed a water goddess. Though he was a minor figure, Astyr's name suits the context very well. Aeneas, too, is known to have enjoyed cult in certain places.[340]

17. JUNO AND VENUS

The orthography of the prince's name varies. In the manuscripts of Vergil it is spelt *Astyr*, which may be only a conscious attempt at an alien archaism, as *Thybris* for *Tiber*. Servius Danielis on *Aeneid* 10.181 (cf. on 9.771) offers a spelling which is adduced to support a connection with the Iberian Asturians: quidam "Astur" pro "Astures" accipiunt, apud quos equi et equites optimi perhibentur. Lastly, Charisius (281 K, 370 B) gives *Astor*. All variants exhibit a short vowel whose precise nature could not be determined in ancient times. Although farfetched, the introduction of the Spanish Astures calls to mind the island and river Astura, whose mouth lies seven miles southeast of Antium in Latium.[341]

Although Astura has no manifest connection with Vergil's Etruscan captain, the Astura river had a haven at its mouth which still received ships after Antium's harbor had ceased to admit shipping. An island and harbor at a river's mouth would have been a natural site for a marine station. The Antiates, neighbors of Astura, practiced piracy in conjunction with the Etruscans before and after they took in Roman colonists. [342] Hence, the Latin deformation of the Etruscan *astres*, itself a deformation on foreign tongues, could be *Astura* and could be related to Etruscan influence on the Latian coast. Direct Phoenician contribution of the goddess to the cults of the Tyrrhenian coast now merits examination.

In the treaty between Rome and Carthage, struck in the late sixth century, the Latian peoples specifically protected from Carthaginian injury are the Ardeates, Antiates, Laurentes, Circeians and Tarracinians. [343] The regulation of trade among Rome, Carthage, and their allies presupposes cultural contacts. But our evidence does not end with this secure inference. Astura Island is very likely to have been the site of the Phoenician trading post. The island could have been named after Astarte, just as the Phoenicians apparently gave the original name to the island Junonia, which was one of the Isles of the Blest, i.e., the Canaries (Pliny *NH* 6.202-205, Mart. Cap. 6.702). Hanno, the Carthaginian general, dedicated in the precinct of Juno at Carthage the hides of "female gorillas" acquired on his famous voyage (Pliny *NH* 6.199-200).[344]

Strabo (5.3.5-6) supplies us with the oldest coherent discussion of this Latin area. Besides his comment on Astura, which he calls *Stora*, [345] he notes that the Laurentes of Lavinium possessed a great temple of Aphrodite, to which all Latins came and where the Ardeates supervised the cult, and that the Ardeates themselves had their own Aphrodision near Ardea, whither the Latins came on pilgrimage. Pomponius Mela mentions the Aphrodisium of Ardea, but quite remarkably he also uses the Greek name. [346] So, too, Pliny retains the Greek name and treats the place as a town that no longer existed. [347] The Roman application of a non-Latin name to the sacred place rests upon the epithet of the goddess *Venus Frutis* who was worshipped at Laurentine Lavinium. Cassius Hemina tells us the cult statue of this Venus was brought to the Ager Laurens from Sicily by Aeneas. [348] Frutis should be no other than the Venus of Mount Eryx in western Sicily, worshipped by the Elymians, Carthaginians, and Siciliotes, among others. [349] The Laurentine or Ardeate shrine of Venus Frutis had a special and obviously rarely used Latin name *Frutinal* (Festus 80 L), which suggests an explanation for the use of a Greek word for the Ardeate shrine.

Scaliger was the first to propose that *Frutis* is a deformed Etruscan rendition of *Aphrodite*; the suggestion was rejected by some a half century ago, [350] but today is accepted. [351] Schilling goes on to suggest that the Rutuli or Etruscans brought Frutis from Sicily and called her by a Greek name. [352] When Cassius Hemina tells us the cult statue of Frutis was Sicilian, we can be sure we are dealing with a non-Latin deity who had not been transformed by the Julii into an ancestress. Our information takes us even further into the Latin past.

Amid the panic of the war with the Carthaginians in 217, the Roman Decemviri Sacris Faciundis sacrificed at great cost in the forum of Ardea. [353] After the defeat at Lake Trasimene in the same year, Fabius Maximus, freshly appointed dictator, had the same decemvirs consult the Sibylline Books because of the dead consul's religious negligence. Among other suggestions, the Books advised building a temple to Venus of Eryx and vowing a sacred season of spring (*ver sacrum*). [354] Hence, the Ardeate connection with Venus Erycina appears older than Hemina's report or the goddess' importation to Rome. The assumed connection receives support from the vow of a sacred spring, [355] because the Ardeates at one time resorted to a sacred spring that had earned them a nickname. [356] Finally, in the vicinity of Astura was the promontory of Venus in the territory of Circeii. [357]

The goddess of Lavinium and Ardea had a non-Latin name that was related by the Romans directly to Aphrodite of Sicilian Eryx. The form *Frutis* betrays an archaic identification at the time of strong Etruscan influence in Latium. The island Astura and the haven of the Astura River evince a name similar to Astur, captain of the Pyrgans, Caeritanes, and Graviscans. The specific citation of the Laurentes, Ardeates, Antiates, and Circeians in the Roman treaty with Carthage confirms the existence of Carthaginian interests along the coast, where a cult under foreign influence can be demonstrated. The Antiates, in whose territory Astura Island lay, were associated in maritime ventures with Etruscans. The toponym seems to bear reference to a shrine to Astarte even older than any identification with Roman Venus. [358]

Finally, we note how similar are the circumstances of Astarte's introduction to Pyrgi, ca. 500, and Venus' introduction to Rome in 217. Both shrines were apparently built at oracular suggestion. The awesome presence of Hannibal in Italy, the sacrifices at Ardea in the first place, and the importation of Venus Erycina in the second place are no mere coincidence. Therefore, any oracular powers of the

Astarte at Pyrgi need not be traced immediately to Cyprus.[359] Both Naevius and Ennius attribute Anchises' power of prophecy to a gift of Venus.[360] Naevius himself served in Sicily during Punic War I, and could have known the Erycinian cult at first hand, particularly if he participated in the lengthy siege of Lily-baeum.[361] At any rate, Roman contacts with Cyprus and knowledge of Aphro-dite's oracle there are unlikely for the late third century. Venus' oracular gift would presumably have been known from the temple at Eryx. Furthermore, East Phoeni-cian contacts with the Western Mediterranean were perhaps already interrupted by the time the king of Caere installed Astarte at Pyrgi.[362] We agree that the shrine of Erycina is a more likely immediate source of the Phoenician inscription from Pyrgi,[363] since Erycina was thought to have affinities with Cyprus and to have bestowed the power of prophecy. The language of the Semitic inscription can be understood as the product of ritual conservatism at Mt. Eryx.

On the other hand, we prefer to seek in Caere the oracle that first prompted Thefarie Velianas to construct the shrine for Uni-Astres. A Caeretane oracle is attested, and its later activity fits well with the nature of the Roman religious crisis early during the Hannibalic War. Among the prodigies of 218 B.C., Livy (21.62.5) reports *Caere sortes extenuatas.* In response a *lectisternium* was ordained at Caere (Livy 21.62.8). Remarkably enough, in the same year at Juno's. Lanuvian temple two prodigies occurred, which prompted gifts both at Lanuvium and at Rome to Aventine Juno. Furthermore, the state suffered the expense of a supplication for Fortune *in Algido* (cf. Ogilvie on Livy 3.2.6), and at Rome a *lectisternium* for Iuventas and victims for Genius.[364] A connection between the Caeretane *sortes* and Fortune is to be found at Praeneste, where Fortune's great shrine housed a dispensary of oracular lots. Cicero makes clear that cult statues of Jupiter and Juno sat in Praenestine Fortune's lap.[365] In the second century A.D. a statue of Trivia was set up in the Junonarium, somehow related to this Praenestine shrine.[366] The Praenestine Junonarium, evidently an internal shrine, invites comparison with the Pyrgan shrine of Uni-Astres. The request made of Thefarie Velianas by Uni-Astres could well have come from such Caeretane oracular lots as Livy mentions. Such lots were perhaps issued from the Caeretane temple of Uni-Hera (see above sect. 14). For the prominence given the failure of the oracular lots at Caere should be closely tied to the events of 217 B.C., when the decemvirs sacrificed at Ardea, apparently to Frutis, and subsequently promoted the introduction of Venus Erycina into Roman cult.[367] Also in the second year of the Hannibalic War, the Caeretanes were alarmed by the blood running in their natural baths and in the next year by the same waters running cold from their hot sources.[368] Hannibal's threat to Italy upset the normal course of religion everywhere. In 217 there occurred at Falerii prodigies also worth recording (Livy 22.1.11): Faleriis caelum findi velut magno hiatu visum quaque patuerit ingens lumen effulsisse; sortes sua sponte attenuatas unamque excidisse ita scriptam: "Mavors telum suum concutit." We ought not be deceived by the name of Mavors into believing that the Faliscan oracle was his. When the Romans destroyed Falerii in 241 B.C., and transported its people from the former hill site to a new home on the plain, the one temple left standing beyond doubt was that of Juno. [369] The Faliscan *sortes attenuatae* in 217, barely twenty-four years after the refoundation of Falerii, ought to be attributed to the old cult of Juno; lots from a new shrine would hardly have so excited the Faliscans as to attract the attention of the Roman priest who recorded the prodigy. The Faliscan *sortes attenuatae* of 217 resemble the Caeretane *sortes extenuatae* of 218. Besides oracular lots, oracular dreams prompted worship. Caesar Octavian brought Juno from Perugia to Rome, and left her former town open to reoccupation, at the behest of a dream (see above).

The rash of special attention to religious demands at Caere, Falerii, and Ardea, coupled with similar attention to Juno of Rome and Lanuvium and with the importation of Venus Erycina, bespeaks the Italian terror of Hannibal. Yet it is worth emphasizing that Juno and Venus, both syncretized with Phoenician Astarte, stand out. The peculiar behavior of the *sortes* at Caere and Falerii, where they very likely came from the temple of Juno or some such source as the Praenestine Junonarium, leads to the supposition that the original impetus to Thefarie Velianas' gift for Uni-Astres came from a Caeretane *sors*, and that it was reinforced by Erycine cooperation out of some political or mercantile consideration. If the evidently Junonian *sors* at Falerii could read, "Mars is brandishing his spear," then a Caeretane *sors* might once have read, "Uni is requesting a shrine." Such a request would have been effectively addressed to a "king" who, though agreeable to the expenditure, found it expedient to meet the request with a joint shrine for which he sought alien support.

The sole surviving Semitic inscription from Eryx (*CIS* I 135) begins with precisely the same dedication as that of Pyrgi: "To the lady Astarte," etc. It is dated by sufetes. [370] One foundation legend of Carthage relates that Elissa picked up a priest of Jupiter, his family, and eighty prostitutes from Cyprus before reaching Carthage. [371] The practice of temple prostitution also obtained on Mt. Eryx. [372] The prophetic Cyprian Aphrodite [373] may have reached W. Sicily via Carthage. The similarities between Cypriote Phoenician and the Phoenician of the Pyrgan inscription [374] can thus be traced to the cult on Mt. Eryx, which was akin to that of the Phoenicians on Cyprus. [375]

A Phoenician reverence for the same goddess may be pinpointed elsewhere on the western coast of Italy south of Astura. At Circeii is the promontory bearing Venus' name. [376] At Minturnae near the coastal shrine of Marica stood a *sacellum* of Pontia Aphrodite. [377] These are insignificant places insofar as our evidence goes, but their very insignificance attests the vanished Phoenician trader. When Hanno returned home around 500 B.C. and deposited the gorillas' hides in the precinct of Carthaginian Juno, where they stayed till the conquest of the city, [378] he acknowledged the miraculous support the goddess had lent his seafaring.

The shrine of Pyrgan Uni-Astres, the haven of Astura/Stura, the Circeian promontory of Venus, and the precinct of Pontia Aphrodite at Minturnae represent to us the activities of the Carthaginian traders on the central Tyrrhenian coast. The powerful goddess of Ardea and Lavinium, called Aphrodite or Frutis, documents the presence of some old and powerful deity worshipped along this coastal strip.

Tradition refers her to Mt. Eryx. The situation or name of all these goddesses ties her to the sea.

18. CONCLUSION

Yet our concern remains the identity of Astarte and Juno at Pyrgi. The question why Thefarie Velianas chose to honor Uni-Astres goes partly unanswered. If we are correct in arguing that the shrine of this goddess was situated in Venilia's temple, [379] in the temple of a sea-goddess, the emphasis is on Caeretane trade relations with Phoenicians. To Juno of Carthage the great explorer Hanno offers the spoils of his expedition to the outer seas, where the island Junonia lay. Since Astarte had no regular home at Pyrgi, the temple of Venilia appeared appropriate to the ruler of Caere. Why, then, is Astarte one with Juno? In truth, neither Astres nor Uni originated with the Etruscans. If our interpretation of the word *pulumchva* is near the truth, the cultus of Pyrgan-Caeretan Uni coincides with the Italic cultus of Junonian suppers. Italic Juno meant political and military strength for towns and townsmen, and she became a similar deity for the Etruscans of Capua, Rome, Veii, Perugia, and Cortona. At Caere, too, the "king" must have recognized this divine power. Whatever else she was for the peoples of central Italy, for Thefarie Velianas and for the king of Veii she meant more than marriage, fertility, and child-bearing; [380] Juno bestowed protection and aggrandizement on whomever she favored. Hence she had to be taken from any town whose conquest was intended to be final, for with her went the community's *iuventus* in all its senses. It did not matter at all whether a Juno had actually exercised pre-eminence in the conquered community. For the Romans—they were her abductors—it was the practice to deprive the fallen of her support. If Rome's enemies had no major fortress town, or presented a concerted front of many communities, the Roman general could simply vow a temple to Juno. It is probable that no occasion for an evocation was offered in the campaigns against the Gauls and Ligurians when the commander vowed a temple to Juno.

Only a mighty god could have represented Astarte to the Etruscans. Evidently Etruscan Turan, who in one instance represented to them the Aphrodite of sexual love, did not convey the full capacity of the Phoenician goddess, who was mistress of cities and patroness of exploration. With due regard for her capacity, Thefarie Velianas installed her in the temple of Venilia. The installation was a state act prompted by Uni and Astarte. The Junonian supper annually secured the deity's continuing favor. We may assume that the favor lasted long, and proved efficacious, because Vergil recalls that Astyr, an Etruscan captain of armies, rode to the aid of the Trojans, just come from Carthage and Mt. Eryx.

The Romans sought Juno's support not only when they wished to annihilate their enemies, but in their imperial diplomacy. Juno Lucina enjoyed a temple upon Tusculum's adherence. In Lanuvium her consuls annually paid Rome's homage. At

Falerii, she was allowed to live on as if her people had not rebelled during the final hours of the First Punic War. In sending colonists to settle land formerly under her protection, the Romans named the Faliscan and Carthaginian colonies Junonia after her. Especially those who went to colonize abroad for the first time on land laid under curse needed more than Gaius Gracchus' protection. And the strange natives of the place needed to be reassured that the intruders had not come to antagonize the local divinities. Octavian ceased to worry over Perugia after her Juno quit the town. Wherever she was worshipped, and whatever the phenomena of her cult the Romans observed, Juno could increase the power and majesty of the Roman people, at home and at war, and could almost grant them everlasting victory. This the Roman wives had begged of Juno on the Capitol at the Secular Games. They asked the same from other gods and goddesses. Only Jupiter had heeded such prayers as long as Juno.

CHAPTER TWO

ADHERENCE TO THE AVENTINE CANON
AND THE *LEX TIBURTINA*

In 1952 G. Mancini republished his collected inscriptions of Tibur, modern Tivoli, as volume 4, fascicule 1 of *Inscriptiones Italiae*.[1] Mancini included in the collection some texts which had never been published before and offered a list of these new finds at the end of the volume. Among his documents not previously edited was a fragmentary marble tablet (no. 73) from Marcellina, which lies about 8 kilometers by road northeast of Tivoli.[2] Mancini did not say how recently the tablet had been found. A rather poor photograph accompanied his text. The site of the find was not within the ancient town, and the tablet's original circumstances cannot be ascertained. However, its situation suggests a shrine on country property. Presumably much of this district, too, was given over to resort villas.[3]

Mancini recognized the precise character of the broken tablet's text, and with a few references to some other epigraphic texts and to some authors he offered excellent restorations. The tablet is broken on the righthand side, but in such a way that the bottom, uninscribed portion survives intact, so that the frame and the last line indicate the extent of loss. Two lines (7 and 11) are fully restored within the degree of certainty for which any epigraphist dare hope (see figure 8). The text contains some known formulas from prayers and a reference to the so-called sacred law (*lex*) derived from Diana's temple on Rome's Aventine Hill. Mancini's restorations were not argued, and with rare exceptions students of Roman law or religion have not taken this document into account.[4] Further, the extraordinarily important restoration of the next to last line depends upon an authority whom Mancini fails to cite in his omnibus list of references. In addition, Mancini seems unaware that the text on which he based this restoration had been condemned by students of the text and of Roman religion. Even after its publication in 1952, no notice was taken of the documentary confirmation of the literary text, so that no less an expert than Kurt Latte demanded again the excision of the offensive deity's name.[5] The text in question is a prayer for use at a sacrifice as preserved for us by Cato the Elder in the *De agricultura*. This work has been recently edited anew for the Bibliotheca Teubneriana. In this edition Mazzarino retained the manuscript reading in our passage (134) but did not invoke the authority of the Tiburtine tablet.[6] If for no other reason, this document needs to be made better known as an example of the hazards of dogmatic assertion. In due course, the pertinent section of the tablet that supports the text of Cato will be treated.

Besides a study and partial revision of the Tiburtine text, this chapter also treats the situations in which we encounter the epigraphic evidence of these sacred regulations emanating from the Roman shrine of Aventine Diana.

The following text of the document, which for convenience sake may be called the Lex Tiburtina, is an expanded and modified version of Mancini's. Because the entire sentence, whose last words survive at the present top of the stone, can be restored, my text is two lines longer, and thus bears line numbers different from Mancini's text:

1. [– – – si quis tergere ornare re]-
2. [ficere volet quod benefici causa fiat, ius]
3. fasq[ue esto. ceterae leges huic arae eaedem]
4. sunto q[uae arae Dianae in Aventino monte]
5. dictae sunt. *vacat* [Ceres – – –,]
6. tibei signum Bona[e Deae hac lege do dico]
7. dedicoque uti sies vole[ns propitia populo]
8. Romano Quiritibus, *vv* m[ihi, domo municipi]–
9. oque meo, coniugi, liberis, [familiae meae]
10. conlegaeque meo. *vvvvv* si om[motum exta]
11. ad aram redit, Ianum Iovemq[ue et Iuno]–
12. nem in aram vino praefatus es[to. *vvvv*]

1-2 *suppl.* Palmer 3 eaedem *Palmer, cetera* Mancini 4 *suppl.* Mancini 5 Ceres] *Palmer,* Iuppiter optime maxime] *Mancini* 6 *suppl.* Mancini 7 vole[ns propitius populo] *Mancini,* propitia *Palmer* 8 m[ihi, domo municipi]oque *Palmer,* [item domui praedi]oque *Mancini* 9 familiae meae] *Palmer,* gentique meae] *Mancini* 10 om[motum exta] *Palmer,* om[*legit Mancini* 11 *suppl.* Mancini 12 *suppl.* Mancini.

Before discussion of all restorations, something should be said about this *lex* and similar *leges*, especially those whose texts parallel this Tiburtine document and permit its restoration. The Aventine temple of Diana had within its precinct a bronze column inscribed with regulations governing meetings and festivals for all Latin cities belonging to a newly founded alliance under Roman leadership, and also inscribed with the names of the Latin cities that had participated in formulating the regulations (see below, n. 13). A presumed outgrowth of the regulations of a Latin festival is to be detected in the inscribed references to the appropriate Aventine rule for donation, consecration, and dedication of temples, sculptures, utensils, and like instruments destined for a divinity. A further extension of the rules embraced the matter of inviolable refuge or asylum, which had serious consequences in archaic Latium (see below).

The regulations on cult and instruments are termed *leges*, and in context must be construed as a body of holy law. The body of rules is twice mentioned outright. The older mention is known from the dedication of an altar to the Numen of Augustus Caesar by the people of Narbo in Gaul between 11 and 13 A.D. In the present study this document will be called the Lex Narbonensis, although it also goes by other and longer titles.[7] The second mention of the Aventine rules is found on the dedication of an altar to Jupiter at Illyrian Salona(e) in 137 A.D. This dedication is hereafter called the Lex Salonitana.[8] At the Italian town of Ariminum the local aedile dedicated a temple to Salus Augusta and apparently applied the rules of Aventine Diana to the temple.[9] Hence there are at least three surviving pieces that should be adduced in any discussion of the Tiburtine tablet. Moreover, a statue base from African Mactaris was dedicated to Diana Augusta in such terms as to invite comparison with the Aventine rules. It is called hereafter the Lex Mactaritana.[10]

Besides these four documents, parallels are to be found in the inscription recording the text of the dedication and the rule of the temple of Jupiter Liber which was set up in 58 B.C. at the Sabine village of Furfo. Hereafter it is called the Lex Furfensis.[11] It is our oldest fully preserved regulation of this kind.[12] The Lex Tiburtina remains the only citation of the Aventine regulation to be found in central Italy; the other citations are met in towns of colonial status.

The rules of Aventine Diana were not the only canon law acknowledged by the Romans. In his *Roman Antiquities*, Dionysius lends the impression of the high antiquity and Latin universality of a series of enactments by Latin towns adhering to a new league headquartered at the Aventine shrine by the Roman king Servius Tullius. The shrine itself enjoyed a right of asylum of which all Latins could avail themselves. Consequently, Dionysius' discussion, which is the sole literary allusion to the shrine's pre-eminence, constitutes a basis for any discussion of the Aventine canon. However, the antiquarian does not mention, indeed no author mentions, the canon to which the four inscriptions refer.[13] The existence of other regulations than the Aventine canon suggests a special function for the "Latin" canon.

A gift for Hercules at Praeneste was offered under the rules of the altar of Salus, which perhaps was that of the famous Quirinal temple at Rome. The Praenestine text reads: L. Gemenio(s) L.f. Pelt. / Hercole dono / dat lub(en)s mer(i)to / pro sed sue(is)q(ue), e(is)de(m) leigibus / ara(e) Salutus. The Latin of this dedication is by no means normal or certain. Some editors prefer to construe *ede* for *idem*, i.e. Gemenio(s), and to supply *dedit* or a like verb governing *ara(m)*. However, this cippus was found with two other dedications to Hercules, who should not be so closely associated with Salus. With Jordan I have taken *edem* as *eisdem* just as *sue* = *suis*, and *ara(e)* as a genitive with *leigibus*. If the latter interpretation is not accepted, *ara* can be understood as an ablative dependent on *e(is)de(m)*. On this interpretation Gemenios gave a gift to Hercules in accordance with the same canon as at the altar of Salus (or of the altar of Salus).[14] References to the rule or canon under which an offering was made ought to be explicit. The interpretation of the Praenestine offering, which is now rejected, says that the same person gave or dedicated an altar of Salus merely according to the rules. The reader of the inscription ought to know which were the *leges*. Thus the Julian clan at Bovillae dedicated an altar to Vediovis Pater under the Alban rule or liturgy: Vediovei patrei genteiles Iuliei. Vedi[ov]ei aara leege Albana dicata.[15] As in the other cases, so here the document also specifies the *lex*. The Praenestine piece must be understood to contain a like specification.

The dedications at Latin Praeneste and Latin Bovillae are surely older than the Latin Tiburtine dedication, but they contain no quotation from their peculiar canon.

The inscribed rules of Narbo and Salona, as well as the dedication of Ariminum, inform us of the existence of the sacral canon of Diana's Aventine altar, which may also have been observed at African Mactar. A fourth rule is known from a mutilated document found at Brixia, where an official of the colony set up the tablet in accordance with a now nameless sacral rule.[16] The *lex* or *leges* applied to religious foundations sometimes appear to have been noted because they did not originally belong to the place or to the god receiving the offering. At Ariminum, Narbo, Salona, Tibur, and perhaps at Mactar, the applicable canon came from Rome's Aventine shrine of Diana. At Praeneste the rule of the altar of Salus, which I maintain stood at Rome, was observed in the dedication to Hercules. At Bovillae the Julii observed the Alban canon.

The surviving lower fragment of the Tiburtine rule may be divided into three sections, which are distinguished by blank spaces at lines 5 and 10. The brief blank space at line 8 seems not to mark a new section. Enough survives to supplement a part of the lost beginning of the tablet. I have restored only the one sentence whose end is still inscribed on the stone. The first five lines contain the rules of the local shrine, rules which were shared with Aventine Diana. The second section, lines 5-10, records the dedicatory formula of a statue of Bona Dea to a deity. The third and last section, lines 10-12, gives instruction on the preliminary ceremony, which is normally called the *praefatio*. The last line is followed by space for five more lines of text; the space was never carved, and was perhaps never intended to be.

The restorations and surviving text are explained in the following commentary.

LINES 1-3

Parallels

Lex Narbonensis, lines 13-14 of side: si quis tergere, ornare, reficere volet, quod beneficii causa fiat, ius fasque esto.
Lex Furfensis, lines 6-7: utei tangere, sarcire, tegere, devehere, defigere, m<u>n-dare, ferro oeti, promovere, referre <liceat ius> fasque esto. (mandare *lap.*, mundare *Orelli*, emendare *alii*; liceat *add. omnes*, ius *Palmer.*)
Lex Mactaritana, lines 5-6 of front: . . . neve ab alio [quo nisi ab eis o]mnibus, quibus ornandum tergendumve erit, contingatu[r . . . line 1 of left side: – – – redi]ntegretur – – –

The formula that ends with *fasq[ue* has been wholly restored from the Lex Narbonensis, wherein this stipulation on cleaning, equipping, or remaking stands after the dedication of the altar and before a clause on sacrifice. The closest similarity besides the Lex Narbonensis stands in the Lex Mactaritana, which itself was partly restored from the text of the Lex Narbonensis. The Lex Furfensis has a long opening sentence, the emended end of which I quote here. I have added *ius* in order to make the conjunction *-que* conjoin. Editors have already remarked the omission of *liceat* governing the infinitives. I have not however taken the Lex Furfensis as a model for the restoration of the Lex Tiburtina because the Lex Furfensis cannot be brought into a close relation with the Aventine canon.

In the Tiburtine situation it will become clear that this clause is cited from the rule of an already existing Tiburtine shrine to which a donation is being made. Hence the dedicant is acting upon the right to equip (*ornare*). Despite its mutilation, the Lex Mactaritana records a situation like that on the Tiburtine tablet. This rule belongs to the dedication of a statue of Diana Augusta (see below) and cites the regulation on modification of shrines (see above). The Mactaritane temple, in which the statue was placed, was under the control of the chief priest of Apollo (*sacerdotum Apollinis primus*).[17]

LINES 3-5

Parallels

Lex Salonitana, line 8: ceterae leges huic arae eaedem sunto quae arae Dianae sunt [i]n Aventino monte dictae.

Lex Narbonensis, lines 21-23 of side: ceterae leges huic arae titulisq(ue) eaedem sunto quae sunt arae Dianae in Aventino.

The restorations of line 3 and 4 are Mancini's except for the word *eaedem*, which I add. With praiseworthy insight, Mancini recognized that the words *sunt q*[---] *dictae sunt* belonged to a known formula to be found in dedicatory regulations. Since the soundness of the dedicatory formula of lines 6-10 is beyond our doubting, the regulatory precedent of the dedication must have been cited. Mancini however does not tell us on what he bases his supplements. The formula is nearly the same as that on the Lex Salonitana. There is no space on the Tiburtine tablet for the *titulisq(ue)* of the Lex Narbonensis. Both of the above parallels contain *eaedem*. Mancini does not say whether he considered and rejected this word because of space. While the restoration may appear too long (it contains thirty-two letters), the total of letters in line 3 would also be thirty-six. Line 7, whose restoration is certain, comprises a total of thirty-six letters. Therefore *eaedem*, which must stand for the sense of the sentence, has been restored here.

At this point belongs a discussion of the last line of the dedication from Ariminum.[18] After the text recording the local aedile's dedication of the temple of Salus, which he had promised (*ex voto*), are the letters *H.A.S.A.H.L.Q.D.R.IN.A.* The very abbreviation demonstrates the author's belief in its easy comprehension. Thus it has been expanded: h(aec) a(edes) S(alutis) A(ugustae) h(abet) l(eges) q(uas) D(iana) R(omae) in A(ventino). This abbreviated statement might have been Mancini's precedent for omitting *eaedem*, but he does not refer to this dedication.

Within the framework of discussion on dedicatory canons the question arises why the Ariminian temple of Salus Augusta was not dedicated according to the canon of Salus.[19] The answer first to mind is that the Aventine canon seems to have gained universal application, for it was valid in Gaul, Illyricum, and perhaps Africa. However, there is another and better answer, which may contribute to our appreciation of the Aventine canon's universality. Since its foundation the colony of Ariminum had enjoyed special ties with Diana of the Aventine. Ariminum was sent out as a Latin colony in 268. The town itself was divided into seven *vici* or neighborhoods. We know the names of these *vici*: Dianensis, Velabrus, Cermalus, and Aventinus.[20] While the Vicus Aventinus by itself does not indicate a special tie with Diana of the metropolis, the name of the Vicus Dianensis surely points in that direction. An extraordinary survival of this almost unique relation between Rome and a colony is recorded by *CIL* VI 133: Dianae Sanctai Ariminenses. The provenience and precise nature of this Roman inscription are not preserved. The present writer has collected hundreds of documents for a work on Roman metropolitan and colonial *vici*. What we have in the case of this Roman dedication is either a gift from the people of Ariminum or a gift from some Romans resident in a Roman neighborhood called Ariminum.[21] It seems more likely that the townsmen of Ariminum made an offering to a favorite deity in the metropolis.

We know very little about the organization of cult in the new Latin or Roman colonies. However, the tradition makes king Servius Tullius' foundation of the cult of Diana on the Aventine an attempt to secure Rome's hegemony of the Latin League.[22] Hence, the Latin colonists might have appropriately venerated the goddess. Moreover, the canon of Diana's Aventine temple will have served as the model for sacral law in Latin colonies in terms consonant with Dionysius' report of the Aventine inscription. An unusually rich documentation on the case of Ariminum, which has reached us by accident, allows us to speculate on the origin of the canon's universality.

According to Mancini's restoration, the Lex Tiburtina applied to a local altar. This assumption is suggested by reference to the altar in lines 11 and 12. It should be made clear, however, that the dedication of the altar is not what is being recorded by the actual tablet. The first five lines contain quotation from the *lex* of the local altar that was previously dedicated in accordance with the Aventine canon (*leges*) and is, at the time of inscription, still subject to the canon. The dedications of the Lex Narbonensis, Lex Salonitana, and even the Lex Furfensis make mention of the *leges* in the formulary of dedication. They are absent from the formulary of dedication in the next section of the Tiburtine tablet. The sentence on the canon restored in lines 3 and 4 precedes the words of dedication. In the Lex Narbonensis and Lex Salonitana, the statement on the Aventine canon also immediately precedes the words of dedication.

LINES 5-10

Parallels

Lex Narbonensis, lines 24-34 of the sides: hisce legibus hisque regionibus sic, uti dixi, hanc tibi aram pro imp(eratore) Caesare Aug(usto) p(atre) p(atriae), pontifice maximo, tribunicia potestate **XXXV**, coniuge, liberis genteque eius, senatu populoque R(omano), colonis incolisque col(oniae) Iul(iae) Patern(ae) Narb(onis) Mart(ii), qui se Numini eius in perpetuum colendo obligaverunt, doque dedicoque uti sies volens propitium.

Lex Salonitana, lines 9-10: hisce legibus hisce regionib(us) sic, uti dixi, hanc tibi aram, Iuppiter optime maxime, do dico dedicoque uti sis volens propitius mihi collegisqu[e], meis decurionibus, colonis, incolis coloniae Martiae [I]uliae Salonae, coniugibus liberisque nostri[s].

For the moment other parallels for the clause *uti sies volens* etc. are not adduced. In both laws the quoted parallels follow immediately upon the phrases restored in Lex Tiburtina, 3-5.

Mancini wrote "partem habemus legis arae Bonae Deae dicatae simillimae legi antiquissimae quae scripta Romae in aede Dianae in Aventino fuerat," after he restored the invocation *Iuppiter optime maxime* in line 5. On these points he has gone astray. Nowhere in the surviving text is the god of the altar named; Bona Dea's image is being given to some other deity (it is not *signum tuum, Bona Dea*), to whom presumably the altar belonged. This tablet records the dedication of the image and not the altar. The regulations governing the altar are quoted, but the actual tablet commemorates the dedication of the image.

The statue of Bona Dea constitutes a gift to the altar and its deity. The Lex Narbonensis, lines 16-19 of the side, provides for a gift in a manner more explicit than what is restored in line 1-3 of the Lex Tiburtina: "si quis huic arae donum dare augereque volet, liceto; eademque lex ei dono esto, quae arae est."

Mancini's mistaken restoration of the invocation of Jupiter Optimus Maximus comes straight from the dedication of the Lex Salonitana, which the Lex Furfensis perhaps reinforced. In the former case, however, Jupiter received an altar and in the latter Jupiter received a temple. In contrast, Jupiter is not invoked in the Lex Narbonensis, where the altar is that of the Numen Augusti. Thus we must ask who would have received a statue of the Bona Dea at Tibur. The answer is partially implicit in the ceremony of the last section of the Lex Tiburtina. Insofar as information exists, the subsequent ceremony can concern only Ceres. Further, other strong connections between Ceres and Bona Dea are known to us.

Reserving for the moment any discussion of the unique ceremony, I turn to Bona Dea and Ceres. Bona Dea is known from several inscriptions and one author to have been occasionally venerated in the country.[23] Thus we encounter the four mayors of Laverna overseeing Bona Dea's wall, gate, porch, and precinct, which were voted by a decree of the *pagus*.[24] A pontifical slave named Felix honored his namesake Bona Dea Agrestis Felicu(la) on the Via Ostiensis.[25] At Aquileia is found not only Bona Dea Pagana, but more important, Bona Dea Cereria.[26] Bona Dea and Ceres were not associated only at Aquileia. Classical Roman authors confused and identified Ops, Ceres, and Bona Dea.[27] Ceres was joined to Ops in Roman cult 'on 10 August.[28] In a document of the year 85 A.D., a freedwoman commemorated her placing gods in the shrine of the Antiate Ceres.[29] The Tiburtine donation of the statue of Bona Dea to Ceres is supported and confirmed by external evidence even without the ceremony described in the last section of the Lex Tiburtina.

Besides the right of donation implicit in the verb *ornare* restored from other regulations to line 1, clauses on donation are inscribed in the Lex Furfensis, Lex Narbonensis, and the Lex Brixiana. The last preserves the phrase: "si quot donum pecuniave aut stipes huic signo dono datae erunt." The Tiburtine tablet is the record of the gift of an image of Bona Dea (*signum*) to the altar (*ara* of lines 11 and 12 and restored in line 3). A similar or the same situation is recorded by the Lex Mactaritana: "simula[crum Dianae Augustae hac lege do dedico] uti extra e[am legem n]umquam me sentio dedicare." The statue and the base that carries the inscription seem to have stood in a shrine of Apollo.[30] The Tiburtine tablet records the dedication of an image of Bona Dea to Ceres.

The reason for the offering was expressed by a time-honored formula *uti vole/ns propitia*, etc. The prayer phrase is first attested by Cato in his instructions on the ceremony, which resembles that in the last section of the Lex Tiburtina. So, says Cato, one prays: uti sies volens propitius mihi liberisque meis domo familiaeque meae.[31] Variants are the prayer to whatever god lurks in a grove, "uti sies volens propitius mihi domo familiaeque meae liberisque meis," and to Mars, "uti sies volens propitius mihi domo familiaeque nostrae."[32]

Equally old as formulas are the prayers spoken at the Ludi Saeculares at which similar imprecations are found in the inscribed proceedings of the years 17 B.C. and 204 A.D.:

> uti sitis] volentes pr[opitiae p(opulo) R(omano)], Quiritibus, XVvirum collegi[o, mihi, domo, familiae].

> fitote v[olente]s propitiae p(opulo) R(omano), Quiritibus, XVvirum collegio, mihi, domo, familiae.

> uti sies volens propitia populo Romano], Quiritibus, XVvir(is) s(acris) f(aciundis), no[bis, domibus], familiis.[33]

> fito volens propi[t]ius p(opulo) R(omano), Q(uiritibus), XVvir(um) collegio, mihi, domui, fa[miliae].[34]

For an obvious reason I have made *propitia* agree with *Ceres*, whereas Mancini restored *propitius* to agree with *Iuppiter*. This line is securely restored by the formula and in conformity with the length of line inscribed to the right margin as estimated from the surviving lower portion of the carved frame.

Mancini made two wrong supplements: *praedi]o* in line 8 and *gentique meae* in line 9. It is inconceivable that *mihi* was omitted. The officiant mentions himself in the Lex Salonitana, in Cato's three ceremonies, and in the proceedings of Ludi Saeculares after the Populus Romanus, Quirites, and the College of Fifteen Men. Mancini's [*item*] seemed necessary to overcome the punctuation implicit in the blank space of an indeterminate length after *populo*] *Romano Quiritibus.* Moreover, I am now informed that there survives a trace of an *M* at the break of line 8.[35]

The act of the Tiburtine officiant is a civic ceremony, for his *conlega* is included in line 10. Therefore, after *mihi, domo* I restore *municipi]o.* Tibur was a municipality. There is no record of a *vicus, pagus,* or other governmental unit in this district, or any district of the Ager Tiburtinus. The last word of line 8 must be either the priesthood or the civic unit responsible. Since the officiant had only one colleague, I have assumed that he is a magistrate.[36] The imprecation on behalf of the municipality runs parallel to that in the Lex Salonitana for the "decurions, colonists and residents of the colony of Martia Julia Salona," which precedes the imprecation for the wives and children.

Thereafter the dedicant mentions his wife and children. In the Lex Salonitana the wives and children come at the end after the officiant, his colleagues, the local senators, colonists, and residents, and appear to be the wives and children of all these classes. In Cato's prayers wives were omitted, the children follow the officiant in one instance, and the household follows in the second instance and is omitted from the third. Wives and children are not to be found in the comparable prayers of the proceedings of the Secular Games.

In line 9 Mancini made the highly improbable restoration *gentique meae.* Apparently he based himself on the Lex Narbonensis *pro imp(eratore) . . . coniuge, liberis genteque eius.* The *gens* in this case is the imperial house, not the clan of the dedicant. Such a statement fits the offering to the Numen Augusti; it is not appropriate to a local magistrate, and is misapplied to the Lex Tiburtina. The *familia,* "household," is named after the *domus* by Cato and by the Fifteen Men in all their prayers. The *familia,* which comprised the slaves, is now restored to the Tiburtine tablet.

In the last place stands the dedicant's one male colleague—who appears to be an afterthought, since I assume that *meum,* not *nostrum,* modifies *municipium.* In the Lex Salonitana the *collegis* directly follows *mihi,* and in the proceedings of the Secular Games the College of Fifteen Men, who were the virtual colleagues, stands between *Quiritibus* and *mihi.* The abnormal statement of the Lex Narbonensis omits the emperor's colleagues but cites the senate and Roman People after his clan. Although each recipient of the Tiburtine goddess's blessing is found in other formulas, there is still no evidence of a universally fixed formula in this request for blessing.

A useful, but not exact, analogue is recorded in the very old censorial formula addressed by one censor to his herald for summoning the Roman men: "quod bonum fortunatum felix salutareque siet populo Romano Quiritium reique publicae populi Romani Quiritium mihique collegaeque meo, fidei magistratuique nostro."[37]

Although it served a different function from a prayer *volens propitius*, this formula's *rei publicae populi Romani Quritium* supports the restoration [*municipio*] to the Lex Tiburtina, which is otherwise unparalleled.

The order of these parties receiving the blessing of the gods is tabulated below with the evidence of Cato *Agr.* 134 as *I*, Cato *Agr.* 139 and 141 as *II*, the Lex Salonitana as *III*, the Ludi Saeculares as *IV*, the Lex Tiburtina as *V*, and the censorial formula as *VI*:

	I	*II*	*III*	*IV*	*V*	*VI*
mihi (nobis)	1	1	1	3	[2]	3
liberis	2		7		6	
domo	3	2		4	[3]	
familiae	4	3		5	[7]	
coniugi (-ibus)				6	5	
populo Rom. Quiritibus (Quiritium)						
rei publicae p. R. Q.				1	1	1
[municipio]					[4]	2
decurionibus coloniae			3			
colonis coloniae			4			
incolis coloniae			5			
collegae (-is)			2		8	4
collegio				2		
fidei magistratuique nostro						5

LINES 10-12

Parallels

Cato *De agricultura* 134: prius quam messim facies, porcam praecidaneam hoc modo fieri oportet: Cereri porca praecidanea porco femina, prius quam hasce fruges condantur, far, triticum, hordeum, fabam, semen rapicium. thure, vino Iano Iovi Iunoni praefato, prius quam porcum feminam immolabis. Iano struem ommoveto sic: "Iane pater, te hac strue ommovenda bonas preces precor, uti sies volens propitius mihi liberisque meis domo familiaeque meae." fertum Iovi <om>moueto et mactato sic "Iupiter, te hoc fercto obmovendo bonas preces precor, uti sis volens propitius mihi liberisque meis domo familiaeque meae mactus hoc fercto." postea Iano vinum dato sic: "Iane pater, uti te strue ommouenda bonas preces bene precatus sum, eiusdem rei ergo macte vino inferio esto." postea Iovi sic: "Iupiter, macte isto fercto esto, macte vino inferio esto." postea porcam praecidaneam immolato. ubi exta prosecta erunt, Iano struem ommoveto mactatoque item, uti prius obmoveris; Iovi ferctum obmoveto mactatoque item, uti prius feceris. item Iano vinum dato et Iovi vinum dato, item uti prius datum ob struem obmovendam et fertum libandum. postea Cereri exta et vinum dato.

Cato *De agricultura* 141.2: Ianum Iovemque vino praefamino, sic dicito, "Mars pater, te precor etc."

Cato *De agricultura* 141.4: item cultro facito struem et fertum uti adsiet: inde obmoveto.

Festus p. 222 Lindsay: obmoveto, pro admoveto dicebatur apud antiquos, ut alia, quae supra relata sunt.

The first parallel is a ceremony quoted in its entirety. The second and third are merely excerpts from a different ceremony. The last is a gloss on the legal imperative.

Without any reference to Cato, Mancini brilliantly restored line 11 after leaving unrestored line 10 where he read *si om*[– – –. I have restored the assimilated supine of the archaic verb *obmovere* and made it dependent upon *redit.* The supine's object *exta* exactly completes the line.

The last section instructs the reader to perform the preliminary ceremony, *praefari*, at the altar. Similar instructions on sacrifice are found in the regulations from Furfo, Narbo, Salona, and Brixia. However we receive no precise help from our paralleled regulations on this point. Only the Catonian material lends direct support. The four regulatory texts do commence with a condition. The Lex Furfensis runs *si quei ad huc templum rem deivinam fecerit Iovi Libero aut Iovis Genio, pelleis coria fanei sunto.* Narbo's regulation reads *sive quis hostia sacrum faxit, qui magmentum nec protollat, id circo tamen probe factum esto*; and that of Salona has the latter formula with the addition of *hic* after *quis.* The Lex Brixiana is too mutilated to tell us anything except that its formula differs from all others.

The conditional clause of the Lex Tiburtina fits well, but has no precise parallel. The comparable clauses in the two other texts are placed before the clause on the Aventine canon, which preceded in lines 3-5 of the Lex Tiburtina. In terms of the order of similar injunctions, the regulations can be summarized as follows. Lex Narbonensis: rule on cleansing and so forth, condition of sacrifice, rule on giving a gift, application of Aventine canon, dedication of altar with imprecation for blessing. Lex Salonitana: condition of sacrifice, application of Aventine canon, and dedication of altar with imprecation for blessing. Lex Tiburtina: rule on cleansing and so forth, application of Aventine canon, dedication of statue with imprecation for blessing, and condition of sacrifice. The condition of sacrifice is the same at Narbo and Salona, while at Tibur the condition is derived from a special regulation in Ceres' cult.

The Tiburtine text differs from all other regulations save, perhaps, the Lex Mactaritana in that it records the gifts to an already founded altar; it is not the dedicatory tablet of the major foundation. The *praefatio* of wine for Janus, Jupiter, and Juno is attested only for a ceremony in behalf of Ceres. On other grounds, good reasons were adduced earlier to restore Ceres as the recipient of the image of Bona Dea. Ceres seems the only likely deity to whose altar the celebrant returns in line 11. The last section of the Lex Tiburtina calls for the officiant to address his preliminary prayers to Janus, Jupiter, and Juno while he offers wine, if he returns to the altar. Insofar as our present evidence permits us to speculate, the officiant returned to the altar to sacrifice to Ceres. Ceres received the vitals of the *porca praecidanea.* Hence, basing myself on the last sentence of Cato *Agricultura* 134, I restore *si om[motum exta] ad aram redit.*

The above-quoted passage from Cato makes clear that Ceres received a female pig before the harvest. Bona Dea also received the female pig. [38] The author of the Tiburtine text has merely added a single and peculiar condition after the recorded dedicatory formulary. It resembles the peculiar last clause of the Lex Furfensis: "If you will have sacrificed to Jupiter Liber or Jupiter's genius at this shrine, the skins and leather will become the property of the shrine." The shrine's income was derived from the sale of such remnants of the victims. The peculiar condition of the Lex Tiburtina envisages a sacrifice for Ceres, whose altar is receiving the image of Bona Dea. If the celebrant returns to make the offering of the vitals, he must remember the preliminary ceremony, peculiar to Ceres, which he did not perform for Bona Dea.

No doubt can adhere to Mancini's supplement of line 11, which he took from Cato's instructions on the harvest rites for Ceres.

In 1598 Johannis Meursius published at Leiden an edition of Cato's *Farming.* Among many suggested emendations was the deletion of *Iunoni* from section 134. Although most modern editors have retained *Iunoni*, they did so at the risk of incurring the wrath of students of religion. Meursius saw that no prayer to Juno is quoted or cited by Cato, and that Juno is omitted from the *praefatio* in section 141. His analogy is useless, because the latter ceremony is a *suovetaurilia* for Mars, and the former is a harvest ceremony for Ceres. *Iunoni* is not happily deleted by conjecture of a corrected dittography. The religious argument that Juno has nothing to do with Ceres must be otherwise proven. At least, Le Bonniec tried to understand a relation between Juno and Ceres. [39]

K. Latte betrayed his prejudice by asserting that *Iunoni* must be expunged as a gloss, and by commenting, "Die schlecht erhaltene späte Inschrift Inscr. Ital. IV, 1, 73 (3./4. Jh. n. Chr.), scheint direkt von Cato abhängig zu sein. In jedem Fall handelt es sich um archäistische Spielerei." [40] If Cato were the source of this inscription, we should find mention of a dedication of an image of Bona Dea in Cato. If the author of the tablet followed Cato, we should expect him to imitate the phraseology of the *uti sies volens propitius* prayers in Cato, and to follow Cato in the *si . . . ad aram redit.* Indeed, if the Lex Tiburtina had been derived from Cato, Mancini could have restored it to its entirety beyond doubt. Latte does not argue or prove his case. To cap this monument of dogmatism, Latte did not demonstrate how *Iunoni* was a gloss and why it belongs to the third or fourth century. Even if we allow that Latte hedges ("scheint"), we cannot overlook the fact that Cato's text reads, and read, *Iunoni*. No single authentic ancient text displays a precise coincidence of word or context with the Lex Tiburtina. Thus we have no warrant to posit a forgery or epigraphic joke. And even if a parallel text were forthcoming, it would hardly damage the validity or authenticity of the Tiburtine tablet.

Mancini's restoration of the last line *praefatus es[to* yields unusual Latin. Consequently I offer some syntactical parallels of the verbal substantive and imperative and the participle and imperative:

1. si nox furtum faxsit, si im occisit, iure caesus esto.
2. eius piacli moltaique dicator[ei] exactio est[od].
3. si quis arvorsu(m) hac faxit, [civ]ium quis volet pro ioudicatod n(ummum) <L> manum iniect[i]o estod.
4. damnas (= damnatus) esto (plus infinitive).
5. aera militaria ei omnia merita sunto.[41]

The first and fifth of these examples may be taken as perfect passive participles, which would be analogous to *sive quis hostia sacrum faxit, qui magmentum nec protollat, id circo tamen probe factum esto.* [42] Howsoever the last sentence of the Lex Tiburtina is construed, its sense is clear enough. If the officiant returns to the altar to offer Ceres the vitals, there must be a preliminary ceremony for the three other deities.

The Catonian ceremony prescribed the offering of a sacrificial animal's vitals (*exta*) to Ceres. Such vitals were sometimes the *augmentum* and sometimes the *magmentum*. The relevant part of the Lex Narbonensis and Lex Salonitana is rendered, "If anyone who does not bring forth the vitals will have sacrificed a victim, nevertheless let the sacrifice be considered rightly done anyhow." Presumably the god expected the vitals, but if they were not forthcoming the sacrifice was not invalidated.

Unlike *magmentum*, the simple *exta* are mentioned as being offered in various ways. [43] The Latin verbs used are *dare, reddere, porricere*, as well as the archaic *obmovere*, which we have already adduced here. Festus reports that *obmoveto* was superseded by *admoveto*. I find this later usage attested only in one case, in which three men are compelled to resign their flaminate because they applied the vitals with too little care. [44]

The *exta* of a victim which were to be offered to the god could be presented raw, boiled, or roasted on spits. Raw vitals needed no lengthy preparation and are not relevant to the Lex Tiburtina. In the case at hand the officiant goes away while the vitals are being prepared and returns to offer them upon the altar. The text is highly compressed so that we must review the elaborate ritual whereby vitals were given to a deity.

Ancient definitions of the *dies intercisus*, which was marked *EN* on the calendars, record the fact that the victims were slaughtered in the morning and their vitals were offered in the evening. [45] Regardless of the worth of the explanation, the definition suffices to indicate a considerable passage of time between the beginning of the ceremony and its completion. An important difference in preparing the vitals lay in their cooking. Ancient authorities distinguish between those boiled in a pot (*aula* or *olla*) and those broiled on spits. [46] This distinction directly bears on the cult of Ceres, as we now know from the so-called *lex sacra* of Lavinium which is to be dated to the third century B.C.:

Cerere(m) auliquoquibus
Vespernam poro.[47]

According to this bronze plaque, Ceres was to be worshipped with vitals cooked in the pot. *Vesperna* is taken to mean either the evening meal or the deity of the evening meal. It is worth remarking that the *exta* were offered in the evening of a *dies intercisus.* [48] The interval of the boiling must have been considerable.

At the beginning of the official year 176 B.C., the two consuls, Cn. Cornelius and Q. Petilius, offered the customary bovine victim to Jupiter. Petilius' victim yielded no "head" on the liver, and he was ordered by the senate to sacrifice until he obtained a worthy victim. Meanwhile Cornelius participated in further senate proceedings until he was summoned by his runner, left the senate, and returned to inform the Fathers that the liver of his victim had been flushed away. He did not believe the report of his sacrificial assistant and bade him drain the pot in which the vitals were cooking. Then he saw the rest of the vitals intact, but not the liver, which had unaccountably disappeared. Petilius' second report of a failure to find a whole liver in three subsequent victims heightened the alarm of the senate, which ordered more sacrifices.[49]

The lapse of time implicit in this tale makes clear why the Tiburtine officiant "returned" to the altar to offer the vitals, if he offered the vitals at all. A precise parallel to the restored *si om[motum exta] ad aram redit* does not survive. Ovid's aetiology of the origin of Remus' Luperci Fabii yields the *redire*, in what appears to be a reflection of religious ceremony represented as the return from a plunder party:

> ut rediit, veribus stridentia detrahit exta,
>   atque ait, "haec certe non nisi victor edet."
> dicta facit, Fabiique simul. [50]

However, the best examples of a similar liturgy are to be found in the proceedings of the Arval Brothers.[51]

1. . . . ture et vino in igne in foculo fecit immolavitq(ue) vino, mola cultroque Iovi O(ptimo) M(aximo) b(ovem) m(arem), Iunoni Reginae b(ovem) f(eminam), Minervae b(ovem) f(eminam), Saluti publicae p(opuli) R(omani) Q(uiritium) b(ovem) f(eminam); exta aulicocta reddidit.

2. item IIII kal(endas) Iunia[s] in luco deae Diae Alfenius Av[i]tianus promagister ad aram immol(avit) porcil(ias) piacul(ares) I[I] luci coinq(uendi) et operis faciund(i), ibi vacc(am) honor(ariam) imm(olavit) et inde in tetrastylo revers(us) subsellis consed(it), deinde reversus ad aram ext[as] reddidit porcil[i]ares. item in circo in foculo arg(enteo) cespiti ornato extam vacc(inam) redd(idit) et in tetrastylo reversus est et in codice cavit et praetextam deposuit et in pap[i]lione suo reversus.

3. fruges libantes cum calatoribus et public(is) ad aram retulerunt (*sc.* fratres).[52]

It should be emphasized that none of these rites concerns Ceres, although the *exta aulicocta* of the first example must be identical with the archaic Lavinian cult of Ceres. In the first example the *exta* are being "given back." In the second example the officiant leaves the altar after the immolation, sits down in the tetrastyle shrine, goes back to the altar and gives back the vitals of the pigs of atonement. In the third case the Brothers carry the fruits back to the altar. Although none of these proceedings fully details the officiants' every action, they sufficiently demonstrate their comings and goings. The Iguvine tablets also preserve several instances in which the religious officiants returned to their former function.[53]

The idiom of restoring the vitals (*exta reddere*) upon the altar is found beyond the proceedings of the Arval Brothers, and was recognized as a religious technical term.[54] The other technical term, *exta porricere*, literally "throw the vitals forward," seems as common as *reddere*.[55] Perhaps the word *poro* on the bronze tablet for the cult of Lavinian Ceres is no mere coincidence; it appears to be the adverb *por(r)o* related to the preverb in *porricere*. The verb *porricere* "throw forward" resembles the phrase *protollere magmentum* of the Lex Narbonensis and Salonitana. Whatever the linguistic argument for *poro* as adverb, another interpretation is available. *Poro* should parallel *auliquoquibus*, the instrument of sacrifice, ablative case. If the analogy holds good, *poro* is the ablative of *porrum* "leek." Only one known offering of an onion is recorded. Valerius Antias, Ovid, and Plutarch tell a delightful tale of how the onion, hair, and certain fish came to be given Jupiter Elicius to expiate a thunderbolt. Elicius' shrine was situated on the Aventine Hill.[56] Further, the onion was notoriously applied in ancient medicine of the learned and common kinds.

The last section of the Lex Tiburtina provides for the eventuality of returning to the altar (of Ceres) for the purpose of giving her the vitals of a victim. The officiant must perform the preliminary ceremony (on behalf of Ceres) by which he addresses Janus, Jupiter, and Juno with a libation of wine upon the altar. The offering of the vitals did not constitute a necessary part of the liturgy. In the terms of the Lex Narbonensis and Salonitana, it was a *magmentum.* Accordingly provision is made for the special preliminary rite which was necessary in the case of the Cereal cult, at least insofar as the surviving evidence indicates.

CONCLUSION

The twelve lines of Tiburtine text have been restored with attention to the language preserved in similar documents and literary texts and to the length of the lost portion of the lines, which has been estimated on the basis of two lines, 7 and 11, containing formulas of reasonable certainty. The summary in Table 1 of the number of letterspaces indicates the extent of each line and of each restoration. As it is restored, I translate: "[If anyone wishes to cleanse, equip (and) repair because it would be done as an improvement, it is meet] and just. Let there be [the same canon for this altar as] is laid down [for Diana's altar on the Aventine Hill.] [Ceres,] to you I [give, utter] and dedicate a statue of Bona [Dea in accordance with this rule] so that you may wish well (and) be [well disposed] to the Roman [people], to the Quirites, to [me, to (my) house, to] my [municipality], to (my) wife, to my children, [to (my) household] and to my colleague. If he returns to the altar for

Table 1.　　Letterspaces in Each Line and Each Restoration

Line	Preserved	Estimate (7)	Estimate (11)	Restored	Vacat	Line Total
1	0			21		21+
2	0			35		35
3	4	(32	27)	32		36
4	6	(29	25)	28		34
5	10	?	?	5	(4+)	15+
6	15	(±9	17)	18		33
7	20	(16	15)	16		36
8	17	(14	13)	15	2	34
9	21	(12	12)	12		33
10	18	(±9	+9)	9	±5	32
11	22	(10	8)	8		30
12	24	(6	6)	2	±4	30

[offering the vitals], he must address a preliminary prayer with wine to Janus, Jupiter and Juno."

The adoption and publication of the Aventine canon at Tibur raises questions about the precedents and extension of sacral canons of religious conduct.

The Diana whose Latin shrine was reared on the Aventine by Servius Tullius was considered to be the same as Ephesian Artemis, and a deity borrowed from Ionia by way of the Phocaeans of Massilia.[57] However, the similarity in cult statues which was remarked in antiquity cannot be decisive in authenticating the ancient belief, because there exists no certain date for the installation of the statue in the Roman temple.

Another similarity between the Ephesian and Roman cults has been remarked in recent times. Between 39 and 35 B.C., Mark Antony wrote to the Asiatic community of Plarasa-Aphrodisias in the name of all the triumvirs and confirmed former benefactions, which he covered by inclusion of a senatorial decree and a now-lost letter of the dead Julius Caesar.[58] Caesar apparently assured the Asiatic community that its temple of Aphrodite would retain its privileges as a legal refuge (*asylos*) and enjoy the same rights and veneration as the temple of Ephesus. The right of asylum which Ephesian Artemis later gave as a model can be dated earlier than Alexander,[59] and has every likelihood of being much older. Under the emperor Tiberius the claims of the Ephesians and Aphrodisians were scrutinized, along with those of other "Greek" shrines. Besides the goddesses just mentioned, credentials of inviolable refuge were adduced for Diana Leucophryne by the Magnesians, who derived their arrangement from L. Cornelius Scipio Asiagenus and Cornelius Sulla; for Jupiter and Trivia by the Stratonicenses, who, like the Aphrodisians, had documentation from Caesar and his son; for Diana Persica by the

Hierocaesarienses, who traced their privileges to Cyrus; and for Venus Paphia and Amathusia, along with Jupiter of Salamis, by the Cypriotes who outstripped the embassies bringing merely human proof.[60]

Daube argues that the application of rights and privileges enjoyed by Ephesian Artemis upon the Aphrodite of Plarasa-Aphrodisias indicates the existence of an old law at Ephesus which was applicable in other places at other times, as was the Aventine canon, and which was a model distinct from the Aventine canon. Daube did not investigate, or know of, the connection between Aventine Diana and Ephesian Artemis which the ancients asserted. Further, he is wrong in denying the right of asylum prevailing at the Aventine shrine. Indeed, he seeks out the pertinent clause of the senate decree to illustrate an argument on the Latin use of the Latin legal (future) imperative, which is preserved in the Greek translation.[61] Of course, Daube's interpretation of priorities remains insusceptible of proof. Such details of two disparate cults may have been roughly coincidental, and in fact suggested the ancient speculation on the Ephesian origins of Diana Aventina. The opposite argument could be made on behalf of the priority of the Aventine canon, which was Caesar's precedent. Viereck, Mommsen, and Dittenberger agree that the most relevant Greek phrase seems to be a rendition of the Latin *eodem iure eademque religione quo iure quaque religione*. Indeed, this Greek seems to be a translation from the Latin:

ὅ τε] τέμενος θεᾶς Ἀφροδίτης ἐν πόλει Πλαρασέων καὶ Ἀφροδεισιέω[ν
καθιέρωται, τοῦτο ἄσυλον ἔ]στω ταυτῷ {τῷ} δικαίῳ ταυτῇ τε δεισιδαιμονίᾳ
ᾧ δικαίῳ καὶ ᾗ δεισ[ιδαιμονίᾳ Ἀρτέμιδος Ἐφε]σίας ἐστὶν ἐν Ἐφέσῳ.
κύκλῳ τε ἐκείνου τοῦ ἱεροῦ εἴτε τέμενος εἴτ[ε ἄλσος ἐστίν, οὗτος ὁ] τόπος
ἄσυλος ἔστω.[62]

Caesar, to whom the Aphrodisians owed their privileges, knew Ephesus, where, so he said, he twice spared Artemis' monies. The cities and peoples and tribes of Asia honored him in Ephesus in 48, when he was on the way between Pharsalus and Egypt: "To Gaius Julius Caesar son of Gaius, chief pontiff, imperator, consul for the second time, descendant of Ares and Aphrodite, god manifest and universal savior of mankind." Despite his insouciance Caesar took pains to record in his account of the civil war the local prodigies at the moment of his victory at Pharsalus.[63] No doubt the miracles enhanced his stature everywhere. Moreover, in making his own record Caesar may have been playing out his role of chief pontiff. The few surviving dedications to Caesar give emphasis to his priesthood.[64]

The Aventine canon could never have escaped a chief pontiff's knowledge. Moreover, Caesar might have seen the usefulness of its broader application by designating the putative ancestral shrine of Ephesian Artemis as a legal paradigm for Asia. The procedures under Tiberius, which were partly recounted above, illustrate the problem.

In 22 A.D. the flamen Dialis demanded a province—which contrary to holy law would have taken him from Italy—and argued that in the past chief pontiffs had forbidden the flamen to quit Italy solely because of personal spite. The debate that ensued resulted in the submission of the dispute to the chief pontiff, Tiberius, who postponed decision and took up other matters. In Tacitus' account the lengthiest business was that of the *asyla* in eastern cities. Tiberius put the business in the senate's hands in order to convey to them the mere form of their ancient power, while he strengthened his own power.[65] Despite Tacitus' emphasis on the princeps' function, the matter at hand seems to have been pontifical. After the senate exhausted itself listening to the several embassies, it consigned the matter to the consuls, who were charged with resolving some of the claims and reporting to the senate. The final decisions were embodied in a senatorial decree. More than fifty years before, the senate had officially acted upon the triumvirs' request concerning Plarasa-Aphrodisias. That request concerned more than just the privileges of Aphrodite's shrine.

A brief review of the pontiffs' competence in settling claims and deciding cases that involved the character of property and the propriety of dedications will serve two purposes. First, it will show the desirability of such a fundamental canon as that of Diana's Aventine altar. Second, it will show by what authority Caesar or any other chief pontiff, sometimes in concert with the senate, might have established a precedent in sacral law by rendering a judgment. From the review there emerges the probability that Julius Caesar successfully imposed a Roman mode of religious law in the east. Moreover, a finer appreciation of the catholic canon of Aventine Diana can be gained by following its extension both to the Greek east in a different form and to a place like Tibur, which ought to have preserved its own ancestral law.

Land and other property were distinguished under the law into three kinds, insofar as the gods were concerned: *religiosus*, *sacer*, and *sanctus*. The chief pontiff and the college of pontiffs regularly oversaw cases involving these distinctions, and issued decrees. It is ordinarily believed that the chief pontiff himself had the right to issue edicts. Be that as it may, the pontiffs enjoy pride of place in the development of Roman jurisprudence irrespective of holy law.[66] Mainly from sepulchral inscriptions, we gather details on the differences in land (*locus*).[67] Only one verbatim decree of the pontifical college survives to us. It concerns a reburial in a sepulchral shrine (*sacellum*).[68] The pontiffs' permission is often noted.[69] In one instance action was taken *ex auctoritate et iudicio pontificum*.[70] Another unique funerary document, which is not grammatically correct, preserves the interesting notice that "whosoever has made a fire by the altar should know that he will argue his case before the pontiffs."[71]

From a few historical passages emerges a clearer picture of the pontiffs' decisions. In 208 B.C. the pontiffs forbade the dedication of a one-chamber temple to the two deities Honor and Virtus, partly because of any subsequent problem arising from expiating prodigies. In 200 B.C., the chief pontiff delayed the consul's public offerings because of the source of the monies to be expended. The magistrate referred the matter to the entire pontifical college, which settled it. Similarly, in 194 the same chief pontiff asserted that the sacred season of spring (*ver*) had been improperly accomplished. First he brought the matter to the pontifical college on whose authority he reported to the senate. In consequence of the pontifical decision (*arbitratus*), the senate decreed that the rite would be repeated.[72]

Cicero cited two precedents in the case involving the restitution of his property after he returned from his exile. The older can be dated to 154, when the censor consulted the pontiffs on the matter of dedicating a statue. For the college the chief pontiff responded that only a person put in charge by the people could dedicate it. The later case is dated to 123, when the urban praetor followed the senate's suggestion and referred a faulty dedication by a Vestal virgin to the pontifical college. Again, the chief pontiff responded for the college.[73] In Cicero's own case the pontiffs decreed that he should repossess his property *sine religione* because it had not been dedicated in accordance with legislation of either assembly. However, Cicero let the matter undergo further discussion in the senate.[74] Of course in this case the chief pontiff could not have participated in the deliberations because he was warring in Gaul.

The events of 22 A.D. may be reconstructed in light of the Republican precedents which Tiberius seems to have promoted. In reporting other religious matters put to Tiberius (as chief pontiff), Tacitus introduces the question of the Greek *asyla*. Tiberius consigned the matter to the senate even though it concerned defaulting debtors, slaves, fugitive criminals, and revolutionaries who availed themselves of divine protections. The senate even went so far as to evaluate the local cults (*ipsorum numinum religiones*) while testing the rights (*iura*) asserted by the several eastern communities. The embassies adduced considerable religious history (see above). Besides the term *religio*, Tacitus supplies us with the phrases *perfugium inviolabile* and *sanctitas*, so that we can appreciate the Roman holy law at issue. When the senate admitted the embassies to an audience, the Ephesians came first. The order of the subsequent audiences seems to have been based on the chronological priority of the Roman grants beginning with Lucius Cornelius Scipio (cos. 190 B.C.). From Tacitus' silence we infer that the Ephesians adduced no Roman grant of privilege. To my mind, the only reasonable explanation of this anomaly lies in the fact that Julius Caesar had treated the precinct of Ephesian Artemis as the very model of Diana Aventina's temple, and that, further, the same Caesar led the Ephesians to suppose that the Aventine canon was derived from Ephesus. Consequently, Tiberius' senate first heard the Ephesians, but did not hear from them a normal statement of a specific proconsular edict or letter.

Although Tiberius' role in these proceedings is hidden from us, Tacitus illumines his actions in the account immediately following that on the eastern *asyla*. In opposition to a senator's proposal that the fetials preside at certain games, Tiberius based his arguments on the distinctions between priesthoods and on the adherence to precedents.[75] Tacitus seems to have dealt at great lenght with Tiberius' conduct of his high pontificate at this point in his account of the year 22. In the reign of Claudius a comparable case was handled. The emperor released the Ilienses of Asia from all tribute on the grounds that they were ancestors of the Romans, and that king Seleucus had enjoyed friendship and alliance with the Romans when he acknowledged the privilege of Ilium. The Greek document Claudius followed suggests how important were arrangements dating back at least to the second century B.C.[76]

Alert to republican practice and keen on observing every propriety, Tiberius involved the senate in adjudicating the claims of several eastern cities to maintain religious refuges, some of which had been confirmed or conferred by Roman commanders. Aphrodisias-Plarasa took its grant from Caesar. By the senatorial decree under the triumvirs, this community could maintain an asylum enjoying the same rights and sanctity as Artemis' Ephesian shrine. Whatever the historical merits of an Ephesian origin for the cult of Aventine Diana, which is not uttered before the time of Julius Caesar, Caesar extended to the Ephesian shrine a primacy in rules of asylum, and from thence extended the rule to another refuge, that of his ancestress Aphrodite. Caesar could not extend pontifical rules to foreign soil.[77] Instead, so I have argued, he created a like canon by basing himself on the rules of Aventine Diana and asserting her dependence on, and derivation from, Ephesian Artemis.

At this point we must turn to Ampolo's recent research. Starting from the coinage of the Caesarian, L. Hostilius Saserna, he argues that the goddess represented is Artemis of Massilia and not Aventine Diana. The coin would commemorate Caesar's Gaulish undertakings and his siege of Massilia. Further, Ampolo would relate the connection of Aventine Diana with Ephesian Artemis to the Ephesian geographer Artemidorus of ca. 100 B.C. Artemidorus, whose works did not survive antiquity, is cited for a geographical item in the same paragraph where Strabo (4.1.8) equates the Massiliote Artemis to the Ephesian goddess. Strabo often drew on Artemidorus, especially in matters of Gaulish interest (4.1.11; 4.4.6). Further, Artemidorus is quoted on Alexander's restoration of the temple of Ephesian Artemis (14.1.22). Strabo knew of his embassy to Rome, where he successfully appealed for the recovery of revenues from certain lakes to the treasury of Ephesian Artemis; for his diplomacy the Ephesians honored him with a golden statue placed in the goddess' temple (14.1.26). Although Strabo is one of several sources responsible for our knowledge that Aventine Diana's statue resembled that of Ephesian Artemis (see n. 57: neither Livy nor Dionysius knew Artemidorus), none of the informants on this point cites Artemidorus. Quite possibly Artemidorus, or an even earlier authority, made the identification from the archaic appearance of the statue. Ampolo wants to confirm the Ionic character of the Aventine idol, mediated through Massilia and dated to 550-500 B.C., while it is also argued that the (purported) image of Aricine Diana betrays Campanian influences. None of the items in the argument on the artistic date or identification of the cult statues appears to me susceptible of proof. I especially miss Artemis' mammosity.[78] At all events, Caesar first acknowledged the extensibility of the Ephesian privileges, which seems to be patterned upon the extension of the Aventine canon.

The Aventine canon was acknowledged and partly published in Narbo and Salona. It was applied to a temple at Ariminum. All these communities were sometime colonies. I previously have suggested that the Aventine canon became catholic because it was adopted at first in Latin colonies that might have been organized with Diana's special protection. [79] After the foundation of the Latin colonies of Italy it was exported to the provinces of Gaul and Dalmatia, and may have been translated to Asia by "discovery" of its eastern predecessor. In terms of Roman imperialism, its appearances abroad are easily explicable. Its appearance in Latin Tibur is not so easy to explain and to understand, since Tibur was independent until *ca.* 90 B.C., and thereafter maintained municipal status. Moreover, it was a Latin community rich in the heritage of its own religion.

Until the era of the Allies' War, Tibur preserved its independence [80] from Rome, although its proximity to the imperial seat could have created certain extraconstitutional ties. We can speak of Tibur's relation to a federal cult of Diana such as is met on the Aventine Hill.

Tibur was one of eight Latin communities that participated in the cult of Diana of the Aricine *nemus* at an uncertain, but very early, date. [81] The Tiburtines preserved their observance of the cult of Diana Nemorensis, whom they also called Opifera, at Tibur. [82] Perhaps she is identical with the local Lady Artemis. [83] According to Martial, Diana of Tibur enjoyed her own woods. [84] The Tiburtines began to worship the federal Diana of Aricia at a very early period, and extended their worship even to their own town, where they brought her Aricine cult name, Nemorensis.

The prominence of Diana's worship at Ariminum and at Rome by that Latin colony's citizens was discussed above in relation to the dedication of an Ariminian temple of Salus according to the Aventine canon. Moreover, the early borrowing of the canon by colonies has been attributed to their Latin character. [85] Ariminian loyalty to a Roman Diana should thus not astonish us. However, among many dedications to Diana in the Aricine grove is found an old bronze tablet recording a dedication by Ariminum's consul on behalf of the people of Ariminum. [86] When the Latin colonies were planted under the protection of Rome, and with application of holy law from outside the colony, they could have preserved and developed their ties not only with Aventine Diana but also with Aricine Diana. Although it is inherently probable that Diana of the Aricine grove had her peculiar regulations, the existence of an Aricine canon transferable to Latin colonies of the Latin peoples cannot be demonstrated.

Tiburtines were prepared to accept cult regulations from the Aventine shrine of Diana, who presumed derivation from Aricia, because they had long ago participated in the Aricine cult and had kept it in Tibur itself. Even though Tibur was not a colony and never received a colonial settlement, Tibur could have acknowledged and adopted the Aventine canon on the grounds of long-standing, and formerly independent, worship of the Aricine Diana.

The fragment of the Tiburtine dedication in which some reference to the Aventine canon was made instructs us in the modes of Roman imperialism. The Romans applied the regulation of a putatively federal shrine of the Aventine Diana upon the religion of Latin colonies. It is possible, but not susceptible of proof, that the Latin colonies originally took their regulations from the Latin shrine of Aricine Diana, the putative forebear of Aventine Diana. The Romans believed that their

Aventine shrine was modelled on the Ionian organization of the Ephesian Artemis, who had come indirectly to Rome by way of the Massiliotes (and, perhaps, the Latin Aricia). When the modes and intent of Roman colonization had been altered,[87] a once-free town like Tibur could accept the Aventine canon in Italy, while in Asia chief pontiff Gaius Caesar could grant to Aphrodite of Plarasa-Aphrodisias the privileges and inviolability enjoyed by Artemis of Ephesus, thereby introducing religious usage from Rome whither the same goddess was thought to have migrated more than 500 years before.

Dionysius of Halicarnassus not only imparts the information on Ephesian Artemis' identity with Aventine Diana, but also advises his readers of the regulatory decrees made by the federated cities that adhered to the Latin shrine of Aventine Diana established by Servius Tullius.[88] We should like very much to know whether Tibur's name stood on the Aventine pillar, as it did on the Aricine document Cato recorded. On the morrow of the fourth-century Latin War, the Romans may have asserted a subtle dominion over such cities as Tibur and Praeneste, which were destined to remain independent, by commanding their submission to the Aventine canon. In certain instances the Romans made religious settlements with the Latin parties to this war. The Aricines became Romans in 338, while the people of Tibur and Praeneste are said to have lost some territory. Moreover, they could not preserve special relations in matters of marriage and contract with the rest of the Latins, and they were forbidden to foregather as Latins.[89]

This was the era that witnessed the Roman adoption of the Tarentine Games for the grandeur of the Roman people.[90] In the transactions of these games appears the oldest mention of the formula *uti sies volens propitius populo Romano Quiritibus*.[91] It is not beyond the realm of possibility that Roman priestly law was extended to Latin colonies and to the few truly Latin republics of Latium in the wake of the Latin War, even though the colonies and Latian republics preserved political independence.[92]

Another avenue of imperial religious expansion lay open through the old Roman colony of Antium. At the same time that Tiberius Augustus weighed the request of the Dial flamen for an overseas command (see above), the Roman knights vowed a gift to Fortuna Equestris in return for Livia's recovery of good health. Although its payment presented a problem because no shrine of such a Fortuna was situated in Rome, "it was discovered that Fortuna Equestris had a temple at Antium and that in the towns of Italy all rites, precincts and statues of the gods were subject to Roman law and sovereignty. Accordingly the gift was set up in Antium." From Tacitus' report the precedent of this comprehensive assertion was then established. Theretofore not even the colony of Romans was clearly capable of receiving a Roman ex-voto without authority from a Roman priest. His subsequent discussion of the Dial flamen's position strongly implies that Tiberius as chief pontiff uttered the innovative decision.[93] Long before this opportunity had presented itself to Tiberius, Julius Caesar had hastened the process in the same official capacity when he based himself solely on the Aventine canon to assert the peculiar rule of sanctuary adhering to the antecedent shrine of Ephesian Artemis.

CHAPTER THREE

THE GODS OF THE GROVE ALBUNEA

The recently found epigraphic dedications from the territory of Lavinium, modern Pratica di Mare, have advanced our knowledge of the Latins' archaic debt to Greek religion and myth. The oldest epigraphic find, which belongs to the fifth century, is a dedication to Zeus' sons *Castorei Podlouqueique qurois*. This Lavinian offering records the cult of Castor and Pollux, only slightly modified from the Greek in name and epithet. Moreover, their cult, which spread inland as far as Tusculum at least as early as the sixth and fifth centuries, now appears to have been borrowed directly from Greeks in Southern Italy, not through any Etruscan intermediary.[1]

The two sons of Zeus serve to demonstrate how deeply and how early Greek cult had permeated Latium, and could have influenced the development of local religious habits without roughly imposing itself on a reluctant and supposedly primitive population. This chapter does not concern the Greek cults at Lavinium proper; rather, the gods of an extensive cult shrine lying some five miles inland from Lavinium, and within her ancient territory, demand our close attention. By two separate discoveries we have learned of Parca Maurtia, Neuna, Neuna Fata, and the Lares.[2] Professor Guarducci illumined the cult setting of these four altars, or bases, by drawing our attention to passages in two poets who describe an oracle of Faunus operating in a grove while his petitioners slept in order to receive the prophetic vision. The Parcae and Fata are known to us mostly from Latin literature, especially from the poets. Faunus, usually overlaid with attributes of the Greek Pan and satyrs, seems from the main tradition to have been without local cults, for he appeared here and there in the countryside and seldom tarried long. The description of his incubation shrine has invited the modern learned comment that it represents the fashion of the Greek world. Despite Guarducci's two lucid publications, little research has been conducted to improve our appreciation of the entire site and of the nature of its deities.

The sacred grove and the deities will be discussed here as the cult center it once was. In the course of the discussion occasion will arise to point out the relation of the Parcae or Fata(e) to the Secular Games held at Rome. Since the oldest mention of a Parca is to be found in Livius Andronicus, Rome's oldest poet, we can here extend our knowledge of the beginning of Latin literature and its close relation to native religion. The dedication to the Lares requires a review of the nature of the *Lares*. The epithet *Indigetes*, which was applied both to Aeneas and to Jupiter in worship near this cult center, and finally the deity Vediovis, whom the Roman Julii venerated at Bovillae, close to this woodland shrine, will also be reviewed. Examination of the cult of, and the relation to, Vediovis will lead us at last to the Tiber Island in Rome, where were worshipped not only the great alien incubation god

Aesculapius, but also Vediovis, Jupiter Jurarius, and Faunus. On the Island is met the wedding of the two Latin earth deities, Vediovis and Faunus, with imported Gaulish demons called *Dusii*.

1. TOR TIGNOSA

All four dedications were found at a place called Tor Tignosa, which lies near Stazione di Pomezia on the road leading from Albano Laziale (Albanum) to Pratica di Mare (Lavinium). The first three cippi face the modern road, which Guarducci remarks may be an ancient way. They were found on a small hill one kilometer from Zolforata. In both her studies Guarducci rightly emphasizes the importance of the names Zolforata, Ponte Zolforata, Sorgenti di **Acque** Zolforea, and Casale Zolforatella[3] to two ancient descriptions of a grove cult of Faunus (see Figure 9). The older description comes from Vergil's *Aeneid* 7.81-106:

> At rex sollicitus monstris oracula Fauni,
> fatidici genitoris, adit lucosque sub alta
> consulit Albunea, nemorum quae maxima sacro
> fonte sonat saevamque exhalat opaca mephitim.
> hinc Italae gentes omnisque Oenotria tellus
> in dubiis responsa petunt; huc dona sacerdos
> cum tulit et caesarum ovium sub nocte silenti
> pellibus incubuit stratis somnosque petivit,
> multa modis simulacra videt volitantia miris
> et varias audit voces fruiturque deorum
> conloquio atque imis Acheronta adfatur Avernis.
> hic et tum pater ipse petens responsa Latinus
> centum lanigeras mactabat rite bidentis,
> atque harum effultus tergo stratisque iacebat
> velleribus: subita ex alto vox reddita luco est:
> "ne pete conubiis natam sociare Latinis,
> o mea progenies, thalamis neu crede paratis;
> externi venient generi, qui sanguine nostrum
> nomen in astra ferant, quorumque a stirpe nepotes
> omnia sub pedibus, qua sol utrumque recurrens
> aspicit Oceanum, vertique regique videbunt."
> haec responsa patris Fauni monitusque silenti
> nocte datos non ipse suo premit ore Latinus,
> sed circum late volitans iam Fama per urbes
> Ausonias tulerat, cum Laomedontia pubes
> gramineo ripae religavit ab aggere classem.

"Worried by the apparitions, the king went to the oracle of his prophetic father Faunus and took counsel from the clearing of the grove of lofty Albunea which, because it is the greatest of woods, echoes with its holy spring and emits the stench of dense sulphuric vapors. From this place the peoples of Italy and the whole of Oenotria seek ambiguous responses. When the priest has brought gifts to the place and under the silence of nighttime has lain upon the spread hides of slaughtered sheep and sought sleep, he sees many images flying about in wondrous wise and hears indistinct voices and enjoys the conversation of the gods and addresses Acheron from the depths of Avernus. Seeking in this place at that time the responses, Latinus himself duly sacrificed a hundred sheep, and spreading their fleece he lay for a while upon this cushion. Suddenly from the depth of the grove came the echoing voice: 'Thou shalt not seek to bind your daughter in matrimony with Latian alliance, my son. Nor shalt thou trust the betrothal already made. Foreign bridegrooms shall come to raise to the stars our fame by their line. Descendants from this race shall witness all things moved and ruled under their feet from the rising to the setting of the sun.' Latinus did not himself utter from his lips how his father Faunus had given these responses and warnings in the silence of the night. But Rumor had flown far and wide carrying the account to all the cities of Italy when the sons of Troy tied up their fleet on the river bank."

Latinus, king of Lavinium, was the son of Faunus, son of Picus. Faunus is here represented as the prophetic god of a grove overwhelmed with sulphuric vapors. Vergil names the place Albunea and makes no mention of a long journey from Lavinium to the cult center. Many scholars have insisted that Albunea must refer to the equally obscure Sibyl Albunea of Tibur, and that Latinus had gone to Tibur for his oracle. However, the discoveries at Tor Tignosa fully vindicate Bertha Tilly[4] and equally support Guarducci's argument that the rather extensive area dotted with names derived from the sulphur springs is where Latinus met his prophetic father. Of the Sibyl Albunea we shall say more below. Vergil's *alta Albunea* is the tall woods (*sub alta Albunea nemorum quae maxima*) with its grove clearing (*lucus*) which Faunus haunted. As we see later, this region of Latium contained another place sacred to the god which was kept by sailors.

A proper cult of Faunus is implicit in *sacerdos . . . videt . . . audit . . . fruitur . . . adfatur*, by which Vergil describes the normal procedure of receiving a vision. In the dead of night the priest brings his offerings to the grove and lies down to sleep on the skins of slaughtered sheep; whereupon he experiences visions and voices, and even converses with the god of the Netherworld. Thus Latinus slaughtered a hundred ewes and in his sleep heard from the grove Faunus' injunction against his daughter's marriage to Turnus, king of Rutulian Ardea, and advice to await the arrival of a foreign son-in-law. Faunus not only favored Aeneas, but showed himself the partisan of the Latins and Trojans in the war with the Rutulians; he apparently also had a special prominence in determining matters of marriage. These three points will be taken up in due course.

The second ancient testimony on the Faunian oracle comes from Ovid's *Fasti* 4.649-72:

Silva vetus nullaque diu violata securi
    stabat, Maenalio sacra relicta deo:
ille dabat tacitis animo responsa quieto
    noctibus; hic geminas rex Numa mactat oves.
Prima cadit Fauno, leni cadit altera Somno;
    sternitur in duro vellus utrumque solo.
Bis caput intonsum fontana spargitur unda,
    bis sua faginea tempora fronde tegit.
Usus abest Veneris, nec fas animalia mensis

ponere, nec digitis anulus ullus inest;
veste rudi tectus supra nova vellera corpus
    ponit, adorato per sua verba deo.
Interea placidam redimita papavere frontem
    Nox venit, et secum somnia nigra trahit;
Faunus adest, oviumque premens pede vellera duro
    edidit a dextro talia verba toro:
"Morte boum tibi, rex, Tellus placanda duarum:
    det sacris animas una iuvenca duas."
Excutitur terrore quies: Numa visa revolvit,
    et secum ambages caecaque iussa refert.
Expedit errantem nemori gratissima coniunx
    et dixit "Gravidae posceris exta bovis."
Exta bovis gravidae dantur, fecundior annus
    provenit, et fructum terra pecusque ferunt.

"There was an old grove which had never been cut by an axe because it was left holy for the god of Arcadia. In the quiet of the night he used to give responses to the mind in repose. Here King Numa slaughters two sheep: the first died for Faunus, the second for Sleep. The fleecy hides are spread upon the hard ground. Twice spring water is sprinkled upon his uncut head, twice he binds his temples with beechen branches. He abstains from sexual contact. And it is forbidden to put meat on his table or to wear a ring on his fingers. Clothed in simple fashion, he puts the fresh fleece over his body and addresses the gods in his own words. In the meantime comes Night with her becalming brow wreathed in poppy and brings in her wake the blackness of dreams. Faunus appears, and grinding the fleece under his hard hoof he speaks from the blessed bed, 'King, thou must appease Earth by the death of two cows: let one heifer give up two lives at the rites.' Repose was scattered by the fright. Numa thought over the visions and reported the ambiguities of the obscure orders. His spouse, who much pleases the grove, interpreted these words for her puzzled husband: 'You are asked for the inwards of a pregnant cow.' The inwards of a pregnant cow are given. A more bountiful year comes, and the earth and its flocks bring forth fruit."

Although Ovid is here influenced by Vergil, he has given us further details. His purpose was the explanation of the Roman festival of the *Fordicidia* on 15 April, when the Romans both on the Arx and in the thirty curias sacrificed pregnant cows to Tellus. Numa has sought a cure for the pestilence and sterility of Rome's herds and fields. He has recourse to Faunus in a grove that was no longer standing in Ovid's account. That the woods had suffered no harm from an axe recalled to the reader's mind the scrupulous care shown to such existing holy groves and their trees, dead or damaged by the elements, as we can still meet in the accounts of Rome's Arval Brethren (*ILS* 5042-48).

Numa slaughters two ewes. Then come details wanting in the *Aeneid*. The petitioner does not cut his hair, which he sprinkles with the water of a spring and twice-over binds with a branch of beech. He avoids sexual contact, the consumption of meat, and any ring on his finger. As Latinus before him, Numa lies down on the sheepskins and in sleep learns that Earth will be appeased by one cow yielding two lives. Whereas Latinus had received a rather clear statement from Faunus, the Roman king has to take away ambiguities, normal at any rate among oracles, to his counsellor Egeria. To this Faunus' expertise in matters of marriage, we must add his solution to the besetting problem of pestilence and infertility. The oracle's relation to Tellus, "Earth," will become clear later. Incubation oracles maintained a close relation to the powers of earth.

Ovid's report of Numa's abstinence from sexual intercourse and from meat, and the interdiction of any ring, recalls some of the many prohibitions imposed upon the priest of Jupiter and his wife, the flamen and flaminica Dialis. In treating the union of Dido and Aeneas, the fuller Servian commentary adduces an archaic wedding ceremony that is called *confarreatio.* It was still kept by the priest of Jupiter, for, to put the matter correctly, any candidate who aspired to this priest-hood would have been married under the terms of this rite. Besides the essential speltcake (*libum farreum*) it was also necessary that the priestly bride and groom sit on two stools spread with the skin of the sheep victim.[5] This hide was not used in incubation. However, the wedding ceremony latterly observed only by a patrician priest seems to have suggested to Ovid some of the details of ritual abstinences. Moreover, Latinus' consultation of his oracular sire was all the more appropriate if Vergil kept in mind the obsolete wedding ceremony while he wrote of the marital destiny of Latinus' daughter.

The hides of sacrificial animals also recur in this preventive remedy: "When an eagle-stone is fastened to a pregnant woman or animal with a strip of a victim's hide, it will stop the parturition and must not be withdrawn except at the time of labor; somehow the vulva slips out. But if the stone is not taken away at the time of labor, she will not bring forth at all."[6] When one sacrificed to Jupiter Liber or his *genius* at Furfo, the hides of the victim became the property of the shrine.[7] The revenue to the shrine from the commerce in the hides was based upon the public desire for the commodity in private religion, such as in marriage or in effecting cures. The *genius* of a deity betokened its procreative force.

The nature of Faunus' cult center is unequivocally clear. By incubation, the priest or king obtains knowledge through the vision and voice of the god who actually appears to the sleeping petitioner. The details of cult practice can be paralleled in reports of oracles both in southern Italy and Greece. Deubner can cite the Faunian incubation in almost every aspect of known incubation shrines and their practices.[8]

Many examples of Faunus speaking from the woods, but not operating at a particular incubation shrine, are found in Latin letters. In *Roman Antiquities* 5.16, Dionysius reports that a hero Horatius or Faunus (*sic*) called from his sacred pre-cinct (*temenos*) to the Roman army under P. Valerius Poplicola and cheered them to a nocturnal victory over the Veientines. Livy, however, gives a different version of these events of 509 B.C.; his report names the deity Silvanus and places the event at the *Silva Arsia.*[9] Livy also makes explicit the god's words: uno plus Tuscorum cecidisse in acie; vincere bello Romanum. Faunus/Silvanus could also advise on warfare. In this case the oracle came gratuitously. Later we shall have occasion to mention the Roman clan of Valerii in other connections with prophets.

The regular cult of Faunus did not enjoy any widespread fame in antiquity. Indeed, the only account can be found in Horace's *Ode* 3.18, to which his older scholiasts have added only the obvious. Yet Horace cannot be dismissed, for he very probably reports an actual festival which the scholiasts call the Faunalia. On the nones of December, 5 December, the country district (*pagus*) observes a feast of Faunus in the meadows through which the god passes. A kid was sacrificed and wine poured on an old-fashioned altar. For the occasion the woods scatter the ground with falling twigs and leaves in honor of Faunus. The ploughman himself dances the ceremonial three-step dance. Whatever else this festival was, the intent of the *pagani* was the fertility of their district. Thus, we seem to be dealing with an earth god who brought increase. This aspect agrees with the incubation at his shrine of Albunea and with the advice given to Numa on a cult for Earth.

Other than the Horatian poem to Faunus, we know of only one possible Faunian festival held yearly. Some Romans believed that the Lupercalia on 15 February belonged to Faunus, but his involvement in the festival is by no means clear or certain. The one peculiarity of the cult which might be Faunian was the goatskin which the Romans called Juno's cloak. [10] The Lupercalian Faunus bears all the marks of the Lycaean Pan, and the festival is represented as the foundation of Arcadian Evander. [11] Yet Livy offers a slightly different version. He says that the god was Pan but bore the Roman name of Inuus. [12] The identification with Inuus has important connections with the shrine at Albunea, to which we return below.

The Fauni first appear in Latin literature when Ennius proclaims the new era of poetry in a proem to the seventh book of his *Annals*. The connection made by Ennius, whose lines Varro and Cicero preserve, brings the Fauni together with prophets (*vates*) and the old poetry in Saturnian measures. [13] Varro explicitly identifies Fauni as gods of the Latins and expresses his belief in a Faunus and Fauna whose names are derived from *for, fari*, a root to which he also assigns Fatuus and Fatua. [14] Faunus cannot be reckoned as a linguistic derivative of *for, fari*. But the notion inherent in the activity will be treated below with regard to Fatuus and Neuna Fata. Macrobius, partly drawing on Varro's *Antiquities of Divine Matters*, Book 15, gives Bona Dea the titles Fauna, Ops, and Fatua on the basis of the *indigitamenta* in the pontifical books. He derives Fatua from *for, fari*, and Fauna from *favere*. These data seem to belong with Varro's discussion of the Dii Novensiles and *Aeneas pater indigens*. [15] The historian Justin tells us the story of how the Lupercalia was founded for Pan, called Faunus, and attributes a wife Fatua to Faunus. Thus he describes Fatua: "quae adsidue divino spiritu inpleta veluti per furorem futura praemonebat. unde adhuc, qui inspirari solent, fatuari dicuntur." [16] Madness constitutes a commonplace in descriptions of oracular religion even though it might be short-lived. The verb *fatuari* is unique and requires our further attention.

The name Faunus cannot come from the verb of speaking *for, fari*. If we consider Faunus the earth god who could nurture crops and beasts, we are allowed to understand Faunus < *favonus*. There is, however, another acceptable derivation given below. As Ernout and Meillet rightly point out, *fătuus, -a, -um* cannot be derived from *fātus*, perfect participle of *for*, and the quantity of the *a* in *Fatuus/a* is unknown. [17] Semantically, the notion of *fatuus* "speaking, prophet" becoming "garrulous" and then "fool" has a splendid analogy in our "silly" in contrast with German "selig," both derived from soul/seele. All difficulties disappear if we assume that *fătuus* comes from *făteor*, a derivative of *for*, *fatus*, but with short vowel. Thus *for* directly yielded *făta*, the deity called Neuna Fata at Tor Tignosa, and through *făteor* "to admit (the truth)" also yielded *fătuus*. The adjective *fatuus* is composed as *praecipuus*, *adsiduus*, *continuus*, and, most important, Inuus. Before examining the nature of Inuus, I stress Justin's choice of language *divino spiritu inpleta* and *inspirari*.

When a human being served the gods as vehicle for a prophecy, Latin expressed the activity by *divinare* a denominative verb "to be *divinus*." The concept resembles what the Greeks expressed by *entheos* and *enthousiasmos*. The verb *fatuari* means "to be the spokesman." No wonder, then, that Pliny describes the medicinal herb *natrix*, "whose roots smell of a goat when they are pulled up. In Picenum they use it to drive away from women what are called by wonderful belief the *fatui*. I myself would believe that there are kinds of mad souls of this sort which may be helped by such a medicine."[18] Popular lore attributed the name *Fatui* to certain spirits possessing mad minds. Pliny's information belongs to a much more elemental level of thought than Varro's etymological research. The root Pliny treats reminds us of the properties attributed to the mandrake in later ages.

The ancient comment on Vergil's oracle of Faunus had supported the location near Lavinium long before the recent epigraphic discoveries imposed silence on the supporters of the Tiburtine shrine:

> Certain authors consider Pan, Inuus and Faunus the same god because some in Italy keep his feast annually, others monthly. Moreover, Faunus was reckoned the king of the Aborigines, who taught a gentler life to his fellows living the life of beasts, and the first to consecrate places, buildings and groves to certain divinities. Accordingly, shrines (*fana*) take their name. He is also believed to have been accepted into the number of the gods. Consequently he has an oracle in Albunea, a Lavinian forest. There is another belief that Fauns appear in groups because they are often sighted in the Italian countryside away from the cities.[19]

Although this commentator may have known his Horace and his Vergil, he also knew some students who posited monthly rites for Faunus, also known as Inuus.

If Livy alone had called the god of the Lupercalia Inuus,[20] we might have dismissed him. But the identification with Faunus is very old indeed. Vergil mentions the archaic Latian community Castrum Inui.[21] The very name authenticates its antiquity. Much before Vergil, Lycophron makes Aeneas found his thirty stations among the Latins and Daunii, so that Stephanus, citing Lycophron, states that there was a Latian town Daunion.[22] Daunion must be Castrum Inui, for the Daunii of Apulia revered and maintained the oracles of Podaleirios and Kalkhas, whose ceremonies much resemble Faunus' cult of Albunea.[23] Moreover, a possible linguistic connection between Faunus and Daunus has been advanced.[24] Be that as it may, Vergil persists in calling the Rutulians or Ardeates Daunii and speaks of Turnus and Juturna's *Daunus parens*.[25] Hence, we must seek Castrum Inui, otherwise Daunion, near Ardea. When Ovid describes the journey of Aesculapius' snake to Rome, he remarks how after Antium it kept its head on the rudder *donec Castrumque sacrasque Lavini sedes Tiberinaque ad ostia venit.* [26] And Silius Italicus makes Castrum the ally of Ardea:

> Faunigenae socio bella invasere Sicano
> sacra manus Rutuli, servant qui Daunia regna
> Laurentique domo gaudent et fonte Numici;
> quos Castrum Phrygibusque gravis quondam Ardea misit,
> quos, celso devexa iugo Iunonia sedes,
> Lanuvium . . . . [27]

The *Fons Numici* is the stream in Laurentine territory where there was a shrine of Aeneas. It may have been situated near the cult center of Albunea (see below). More pertinent now is Faunus' advice to King Latinus that he not marry his daughter to Turnus. Turnus enjoyed the support of the town Castrum Inui, but Latinus had the god himself on his side. Immediately before Turnus' death Vergil remarks the Faunian involvement in the war (*Aeneid* 12.766-80):

> Forte sacer Fauno foliis oleaster amaris
> hic steterat, nautis olim venerabile lignum,
> servati ex undis ubi figere dona solebant
> Laurenti divo et votas suspendere vestis;
> sed stirpem Teucri nullo discrimine sacrum
> sustulerant, puro ut possent concurrere campo.
> hic hasta Aeneae stabat, huc impetus illam
> detulerat fixam et lenta radice tenebat.
> incubuit voluitque manu convellere ferrum
> Dardanides, teloque sequi quem prendere cursu
> non poterat. tum vero amens formidine Turnus
> "Faune, precor, miserere" inquit "tuque optima ferrum
> Terra tene, colui vestros si semper honores,
> quos contra Aeneadae bello fecere profanos."
> dixit, opemque dei non cassa in vota vocavit.

"By chance there had stood on this spot a wild olive with bitter leaves sacred to Faunus. At one time the wood was honored by sailors who had attached thank-offerings to it when they were spared from loss at sea and had hung upon the tree the clothes vowed to the Laurentine god. But the Trojans had thoughtlessly uprooted the holy tree so that they could cross a cleared battlefield. Here stood Aeneas' spear, hither the throw had planted it and held it with pliant root. The Trojan put his weight (*incubuit*) on his weapon and wished to wrench it with his hand and to pursue with the flight of the spear the man whom he could not catch in running. Then, frightened out of wits, Turnus said, 'Faunus, I pray thee, pity me. Earth, best of all, hold the weapon, if I have ever observed your worship which the men of Aeneas, to the contrary, desecrated.' He spoke and summoned the god's help upon his successful vows."

The poet describes a place near the shore where the sailors might have made offerings to the Laurentine Faunus. However, this Faunus, as well as Earth, was dutifully worshipped by Turnus and, on that account, should have been the Inuus of coastal Castrum Inui if Inuus could be called a *divus Laurens.*

The singular *castrum* specifies a fortified or defensible coastal headland. Else-

where in Latium it is met in the Laurentine place name Castrum Troiae, so important in the development of the Trojan mythology in Latium. [28] There are two
places on the Latin coast where Castrum Inui may have been situated: either Torre
Caldara o Solferata, about six kilometers north of Anzio or along the Fosso dell'
Incastro, which runs from Ardea to the sea (see Figure 9). The former place may
recall the sulphuric activity, the latter may preserve the very name Castrum. In any
event, Castrum Inui lay not far from Lavinium and Albunea, somewhere between Lavinium and Antium.

Servius, who confuses Castrum Inui with Castrum Novum in Etruria, also identifies the god with Pan, Ephialtes, Faunus, Fatuus, and Fatuclus. He translates Ephialtes into the Latin Incubo and etymologizes Inuus *ab ineundo passim cum omnibus animalibus* "from his indiscriminate mating with any animal." [29]

Faunus is he who "goes in" and he who "sleeps in." Augustine also knows
something of this interpretation: Silvani and Panes are commonly called Incubi
because they wantonly seek out and lie with women. They closely resemble the
Gaulish demons, the Dusii. [30] In the same tradition stands Isidore: "Pilosi, qui
Graece Panitae, Latine Incubi appellantur, sive Inui ab ineundo passim animalibus
unde et Incubi dicuntur ab incumbendo, hoc est stuprando. saepe enim inprobi
existunt etiam mulieribus, et earum peragunt concubitum: quos daemones Galli
Dusios vocant, quia absidue hanc peragunt inmunditiam. quem autem vulgo
Incubonem vocant, hunc Romani Faunum ficarium dicunt." [31]

Isidore's account shares equally in the words of Servius and Augustine. But the
latter does not mention Incubo or Inuus or Faunus *ficarius*, and the former does
not mention Incubi or Dusii or *ficarius*. Isidore has derived his report from the
ultimate source of Servius and Augustine. Isidore gives the Varronian list of Sibyls
(see below) in *Etym* 8.8, and quotes Varro's etymology of *vates* in *Etym* 8.7.3.
Varro was the ultimate source of all three authors. On the Dusii of the Gauls we
shall say more later. [32]

The formation of *inuus* from *ineo, inire* has been cited in connection with
fatuus. The notion of the lascivious Pan or satyr has imposed the construction of a
sexual entry upon *inuus* as well as upon *incubus* and *incubo*. Nevertheless, we may
equally well understand these words as descriptive of the advent and epiphany of
Faunus with reference to the practice of his petitioners. Incubo and Incubus are the
nightmares, or its demon-like *ephialtes*. The Latin speakers have applied to the
oracular agent the very act of their incubation. [33] Implicit in the application is a
notion incongruent with Greek custom. To the Latin mind the oracular Faunus also
slept in. When Faunus entered, he was *inuus*. This epithet refers not only to his
epiphany for oracle but to his propensity to flit hither and yon:

> Faune, Nympharum fugientium amator,
> per meos finis et aprica rura
> lenis incedas abeasque parvis
>   aequus alumnis. [34]

The feeling for a Faunus Inuus or Incubus expresses something of the Greek *entheos* and *enthousiasmos.* It recalls Justin's *divino spiritu impleta* and *inspirari* when he speaks of Faunus, Fatua, and the act *fatuari.* So, too, the concept of *divinare* conveys the sense of oracle-seeker and dealer representing the inner god. In discussing Neuna Fata, Indigetes, and the cult of the Tiber Island we return to the inward operation of the deity and to incubation.

Before closing the section on the shrine of Tor Tignosa, I take up its relation to Albunea and the Sibyls. The list of Sibyls given by Isidore comes without citation from Varro. Lactantius preserves the list, which he drew from the *Antiquities of Divine Matters* dedicated to Caesar as chief pontiff. [35] Only the three Italian Sibyls here interest us. Varro identified the fourth Sibyl, the Cimmerian whom Naevius mentioned in his *Punic War* and Calpurnius Piso in his *Annals;* the seventh, Cumaean Sibyl named Amalthea, Herophile, or Demophile; and the tenth, Albunea of Tibur. It was Demophile who tried first to sell the Roman king Tarquinius Priscus nine prophetic books and finally sold him only three at the far greater price. Albunea had a shrine by the banks of the Anio River where her statue, holding books, had been found in the rapids. Dionysius tells us that the Sibylline Books were burned in the fire on the Capitoline and had to be recollected later. Evidently the canonical ten Sibyls whose identity Lactantius preserves supplied the basis for the new collection. Since Dionysius cites Varro's *Antiquities of Divine Matters*, the fruits of the research for the texts were evidently embodied in Varro's research on Roman religion. [36]

Cumaean Amalthea recalls the name of the nurse or she-goat who reared the infant Zeus on the island of Crete. To this Zeus we return later. The very name Demophile, the dealer in Sibylline Books, counters Tarquin's royal arrogance. The Cumaean Sibyl enjoyed great renown as the source of Rome's *libri fatales* and the prophetess to the wandering Aeneas. However, Naevius and Calpurnius Piso seem to have made the Cimmerian Sibyl author of Aeneas' prophecy, and perhaps also the bookseller. The many accounts of the land of the Cimmerians bring to mind the cult center of Faunus at Albunea. From Homer to Paul the Deacon we are given a picture of people dwelling in everlasting twilight, without sun and warmth, and guarding an entrance to the Netherworld. Circe sends Odysseus to Hades' realm and to the Cimmerian land by way of Ocean. There Odysseus spoke with the dead, and thence returned to Circe. [37] To a Roman, Circe's homeland was Circeii, on a promontory south of Antium. In his *Epitome* of Festus Paul locates the Cimmerians in a valley between Baiae and Cumae. [38] The Sibyl of the Cimmerians was not the Cumaean Sibyl, at least for Varro.

A specific Campanian locality of a Faunian cult can be identified in the *Silvani lavacrum*, which also went by the name of Mammaea, Alexander Severus' mother. This spa was situated at the resort town of Baiae. Although Silvanus is frequently a humble personal name in late antiquity, the name may refer to the god who was often confused or identified with Faunus. Faunus and Inuus are met in coastal Latium. Silvanus is met elsewhere under similar circumstances. [39]

A different sort of Sibyl was Tiburtine Albunea. Her cult was by a river in a Latian district famous for its sulphur springs. The name *Albunea* is very likely to be

derived from the word root in *Alba Longa* and *Alpes*, which refers to the mountains. The Numicus River, beside which sat the shrine of Aeneas, flows through the
district where the dedications to Parca Maurtia, Neuna Fata, and the Lares were
found. Vergil called the place Albunea and mentions its holy spring and sulphuric
vapors. Albunea denotes the origin of the waters, as even Horace suggests by his
domus Albuneae resonantis at Tibur, which echoes Vergil's *Albunea, nemorum
quae maxima sacro fonte sonat* in Lavinian country. [40] The name of the Laurentine
grove and the Tiburtine Sibyl is very old. Vergil and Ovid attribute the Grove
Albunea to Faunus. His cult was to be found in many places, and especially, we can
only suppose, at Castrum Inui. However, neither poet mentions any other deity at
Albunea than Faunus, although Vergil may imply the presence of an Albunea.
Others there were at Albunea, and two of them belong to the oracular kind.

No matter how similar are the poetical descriptions of Albunea and its cult to
Greek accounts of certain incubation shrines, we are dealing with a cult center truly
Latin in origin. Nor ought we to wonder at the appearances of similarities with
Greek rites. It was located in the territory of a town where the almost unadulterat-
ed Dioscuri received an offering in the fifth century.

2. THE THREE GIFTS

Three cippi, found at Tor Tignosa, faced the road and were lined up in a group,
which read from left to right:

1. Parca(e) Maurtia(e) dono(m).
2. Neuna(e) dono(m).
3. Neuna(e) Fata(e).

All three cippi as well as that for the Lares are now exhibited in Michelangelo's
Great Cloister in the Museo Nazionale delle Terme at Rome. Their size, which is
roughly the same, confirms that they were set up as a series. Guarducci reckons
their date to the end of the fourth or beginning of the third century, and likens
them to the early Latin dedication from Pisaurum. [41] Degrassi dates them to the
first decades of the third, and certainly no earlier than the middle of the fourth,
century, the era of Rome's wars with the Samnites and of Rome's first Greek
conquests and allies (Naples).

Degrassi points out that the shape of the cippi, truncated pyramids, is common
for archaic dedications. Furthermore, such dedications either contain the god's
name alone or add the simple *dono(m)*, whether or not the dedicant records his
own name. The record of a "gift" does not tell us whether we have a base or an
altar, or neither. The tops are roughly 58 by 58 centimeters. The dedication to the
Lares, which does not belong to this series, is contemporary and has the same
shape, but its top is 17 by 19 centimeters. The smallness of this cippus seems to
suggest that the stone by itself was the *donum*.

The first editor of the three texts laid the foundation for all future study when she adduced this passage from Aulus Gellius:

> antiquos autem Romanos Varro dicit non recepisse huiuscemodi quasi monstruosas ra-
> ritates, sed nono mense aut decimo neque praeter hos aliis partionem mulieris secundum
> naturam fieri existimasse, idcircoque eos nomina Fatis tribus fecisse a pariendo et a nono
> atque decimo mense. "nam 'Parca,' " inquit, "immutata una littera a partu nominata,
> item 'Nona' et 'Decima' a partus tempestivi tempore." Caesellius autem Vindex in lec-
> tionibus suis antiquis "tria," inquit, "nomina Parcarum sunt: 'Nona,' 'Decuma,' 'Mor-
> ta' " et versum hunc Livii, antiquissimi poetae, ponit ex 'Οδυσσείᾳ :

> quando dies adveniet, quem profata Morta est [43]

> sed homo minime malus Caesellius "Mortam" quasi nomen, cum accipere quasi Moeram
> deberet. [44]

> "Varro says that the ancient Romans did not accept oddities of this sort as monstrous,
> but reckoned the delivery of a woman in her ninth or tenth month happened according
> to nature, and on that score they created names for the three Fates from the act of
> delivering, and from the ninth and tenth month. For 'Parca,' he says, 'was named from
> *partus* by altering a letter; likewise "Nona" and "Decima" from the seasonal term of the
> delivery.' Moreover Caesellius Vindex says in his work on ancient readings, 'There are
> three names of the Parcae, "Nona," "Decuma," "Morta," ' and he establishes the evi-
> dence of this verse from the *Odyssey* of Livius, our oldest poet:

> When the day comes, whom has Morta foretold?

> But Caesellius, who is not at all bad, took 'Morta' as a name when he ought to take it as
> a form of 'Moera.' "

In the same chapter Gellius cites Varro's *Antiquities of Divine Matters*, book 4, on the periods of human gestation, so that the above-quoted statement before intro-duction of Caesellius' name is attributed to the same book. [45] Elsewhere Varro writes after deriving *fatuus* from *for, fari*: "ab hoc tempora quod tum pueris consti-tuant Parcae fando, dictum fatum et res fatales. ab hac eadem voce qui facile fantur facundi dicti, et qui futura praedivinando soleant fari fatidici; dicti idem vaticinari, quod vesana mente faciunt: sed de hoc post erit usurpandum, cum de poetis dice-mus." [46]

For Varro, as for most Romans, the Parcae are goddesses of childbirth (*partus*) who establish the lifespan of children by issuing a *fatum*. Combined with what Varro is reported by Gellius to have written, the word Parcae was bestowed on the three Fata. Varro knows the names of Nona and Decima. But he did not know or, if he knew, did not apply the third name, Morta.

Other Fata are mentioned by Tertullian, who was very probably reading the same book of Varro: "ita omnes idolatria obstetrice nascuntur, dum ipsi adhuc uteri infulis apud idola confectis redimita genimina sua daemoniorum candidata profitentur, dum in partu Lucinae et Dianae eiulatur, dum per totam hebdomadem Iunoni mensa proponitur. dum ultima die Fata Scribunda advocantur, dum prima etiam constitutio infantes super terram Statinae deae sacrum est." [47] Although this passage does not make clear the relation between the Fata who are Parcae and the Fata who are Scribunda, from further information which is discussed with Neuna Fata, it appears that the Scribunda might be a group of Fata.

Varro's Nona is the Neuna of Albunea. However, it is generally agreed that Decima is a Varronian invention which does not belong to Latin cult. [48]

Caesellius Vindex, Gellius' second authority, does not stand too high in Gellius' esteem; Gellius begrudgingly calls him *minime malus*. Elsewhere he castigates Caesellius (*homo hercle pleraque haut indiligens*) for his misinterpretation of Ennius in his *Ancient Readings*, cites Terentius Scaurus on Caesellius' lack of linguistic good sense, and finally, allowing that Caesellius might be intelligent, *hautquaquam ineruditus*, faults him for his strictures on the poetry of A. Furius Antias. [49] Gellius does not inspire us with confidence in Caesellius. Nevertheless, he seems to have preserved accurately the line of Livius. What he says about Morta the Parca is astonishingly precise, although we could not have praised his research without the dedication to Parca Maurtia.

3. PARCA MAURTIA

The three Parcae are frequently met in Latin literature, are often undistinguished from the three Fata, and normally represent minor divinities who watch over the lifespan of man. Parcae and Fata are patterned after the Greeks' three Moirai, whose names Clotho, Lachesis, and Atropos are everywhere found in Latin literature. Among the Greeks these sisters often join forces with the goddess of childbed, Eileithyia, who was equated with Latin Juno Lucina. Thus, Varro naturally coupled Juno Lucina and the Fata (see above). Indeed, few very old signs of a proper Latian cult of the Parcae or Fata existed before the discoveries at Tor Tignosa. Almost no ancient statement from learned authors can be trusted with regard to Latin religion, because the configuration of the three deities, however named, took its inspiration from Greek literature. The consequences differ markedly from the consequences obtaining at Tor Tignosa and Lavinium. The archaic dedication to the Dioscuri demonstrates definite borrowing by one religion from another, whereas the frequent intrusion of the Parcae and Fata into Latin belles-lettres reflects the influence of a parent literature upon its child. In the simplest terms, the notion and activity of the three goddesses represent Greek concepts. Today, however, we can see how important are the purely Latin names Parca and Fata. Further, we can trace their introduction into Latin literature to Rome's first poet, a poet operating in a Greek tradition and translating a still surviving Greek epic.

Although Parca and Fata belong together in Latin cult, the three dedications at once raise the question of the generic name of the deities. Later Romans treat the Parcae and Fata as one and the same. Now it is clear that the latter were also Fatae, and at least nine in number (see below). Although only one Parca is found at Tor Tignosa, she is distinguished by an adjectival epithet so that we are justified in assuming the existence of other Parcae. Since the sense of Neuna Fata cannot be slighted as a modern Varronian interpretation, we are further prompted to seek the origin of these Parcae or Fata. It is all well and good to answer that the three are patterned after three Greek Moirai; we ask how the identification of Parcae or Fata with the Moirai was made in the first place. A simpler solution can be had from assuming that among the nine Fatae were counted the three Parcae, one of whom was Parca Maurtia. To this solution we return later.

The ancients held that *parca* was an adjective from *pario*, "to give birth." There exist a few dissenters from this interpretation. Servius and Isidore remark that *manes* is a euphemism like Eumenides, Parcae, *bellum* and *lucus*. [50] If *parca* concerned childbirth, *parca* is not a euphemism unless Servius and Isidore believed that they were concerned with death. Rather, they had in mind *parca* < *parcere*. The ancient derivation from *pario* was made on the basis of Roman knowledge of the Moirai. The natural linguistic interpretation of *parca* points to *parcere*. In any case, the word cannot come from *pario*. [51]

The verbal substantive *parca* takes its meaning from *parcere*, which has two senses in Roman religion. [52] The older "to curb, hold in check, restrain" is met in Plautus, as well as in the ceremonial caution *parcito linguam* "keep quiet." [53] Later, the verb becomes "to spare, save" and can be found among the Latin poets in the alliterative and assonant opening of prayers *parce, precor*. [54] Finally, *parco* can have the pejorative sense of "to be niggardly." Assuming for the moment that a *parca* had some control over life, we can apply any of the meanings of *parco*—or, for that matter, all its meanings—to the deity's activity. The plurality of *parcae* suggests that the worshipper could address himself to a particular function. The epithet Maurtia underscores this probability, even though we have no knowledge of other epithets applied to a Parca.

Maurtia is without doubt an adjective from a name of Mars, *Mavors*. Thus, early in the second century a military tribune dedicated some of his booty *Maurte*. [55] A later pronunciation of Maurtia would have been *mortia,* not *martia*, which is derived from *Mart-*. Guarducci and Weinstock see the linguistic connection and discuss the similarity to the Roman deity Numisius Martius, the power called *heries Martea*, and the Iguvine Cerfus Martius. [56] The last is a combination of the notion inherent in the Latin cognate *ceres* "growth" and of the life force found in certain cults of the Roman Mars.

The oldest surviving Latin prayer contains repeated invocations of Mars by the Arval Brethren, whose title bespeaks their care for Roman tilthland. Without its threefold repetition I render the famous Arval hymn: "Help us, Lares. . . . Marmar, let not blight and destruction rush in any more. . . . Be full, fertile Mars. Leap the boundary, stand right there. . . . By turns will he summon all the spirits of the seeds. . . . Help us, Marmor. . . . Rejoice!" [57]

The combination of Mars with the Lares has interesting implications for any interpretation of Parca Maurtia and the Lares together at Albunea. The prayer, which is usually dated to the fifth century, was uttered to gain the help of the Lares and Mars (more properly three: Marmar, Mars, and Marmor, lest the deity somehow fail to respond) in keeping off the natural ravages from the fields and in making fertile the land.

Cato the Elder provides us with two ceremonies concerning Mars. The first is a ritual for the good health of the cattle. It is performed in broad daylight in the woods, just as the Arval hymn was recited in the grove of Dea Dia. The offering for the cattle was made to Mars Silvanus. [58] The second Catonian ceremony is the lustration of farmers' land with the procession of pig, sheep, and bullock (*suovitaurilia*). Mars was addressed at great length with a prayer reminiscent of the Arval hymn, here reproduced in part:

> Mars pater, te precor quaesoque, uti sies volens propitius mihi domo familiaeque nostrae; quoius rei ergo, agrum terram fundumque meum suovitaurilia, circumagi iussi; uti tu morbos visos invisosque, viduertatem vastitudinemque, calamitates intemperiasque prohibessis defendas averruncesque; utique tu fruges, frumenta, vineta virgultaque grandire beneque evenire siris; pastores pecuaque salva servassis duisque bonam salutem valetudinemque mihi domo familiaeque nostrae. [59]

> "Father Mars, I pray and beseech thee to be willing and generous to me, to our house and household; on that account, I have ordered the sacrificial pig, sheep and steer be led around my field, my land and my estate; that thou keep off, hold off, and push off seen and unseen illnesses, bereavement and desolation, disasters and storms; and that thou allow the fruits, the crops, the vines and the reeds to grow and turn out well; that thou keep safe the shepherds and the flocks and that thou give welfare and health to me and to our house and household."

The *lues* and *rues* are now detailed. The protection of man, beast, land, and crops is sought. Here we have a means of assaying the sense of Parça Maurtia. Mars must help the men, ward off ills, increase the production of vegetation, and keep safe herdsmen and herds. In cult Mars is not niggardly, but he curbs unwanted evils and spares the life of man, beasts, and flocks.

This function of Mars comports with Numa's petition from the oracle of Faunus at Albunea. Numa seeks the god's help in driving off pestilence. Faunus counsels the slaughter of pregnant cows for Tellus, "Earth," to gain remission and productivity. Cato's *lustratio* of the land achieved the same purpose. So, too, Mars Silvanus must be approached for the sake of the cattle's health. In this case Mars belongs to the woods, as do the *Lar agrestis Silvanus* and Faunus, who is elsewhere confused with Silvanus. [60]

Horace's feast of Faunus on the nones of December resembles the ceremonies to Mars. The setting in meadows and woods is kept by the country district (*pagus*). The god passes through the territory as Mars is invited by the Arval Brethren to leap the boundary and to remain on the land. The magic of the three-step dance is inherent in the threefold repetitions in the Arval hymn, is explicit in the dances of Mars' Salians at Rome, and is conducted by the farmers of the *pagus* in veneration of Faunus.

Wherever Faunus is styled by the authors a king of the Aborigines, he is given for a father Picus, the woodpecker. The bird is prominent in Roman augury and regularly associated with Mars as the *picus Martius*. Two examples will suffice. Miss

Guarducci draws our attention to a report in Dionysius.[61] In his *Antiquities* Varro listed the communities of the Aborigines located in Sabine country. At Tiora Matiene (should we understand Martiana?) was an oracle of Mars, which resembled the oracle of Zeus at Dodona. Mars prophesied through the mouth of a woodpecker sitting on a wooden column. At Iguvium one unit of the community owned an *ager tlatius* of *picuvius Martius* and another an *ager* bearing its own name and also that of *picuvius Martius*. The former field may indicate an *ager latius* (cf. Latium). A part of the cereal produce of both fields was turned over to a priestly brotherhood. [62]

Mars' woodpecker issued oracles or, more commonly, by its appearance and flight advised those taking the auspices. It might also have watched over certain fields. There is no certainty that Parca Maurtia was oracular or protective of the land and its dwellers; however, the grove Albunea was set aside for oracles, and the later Parcae were in a sense prophetic. Certainly Neuna Fata is by name prophetic. Faunus' advice to Numa concerned the life of Rome and a sacrifice to Tellus "Earth." As guardians of childbirth, the Parcae interested themselves in similar activities but also restricted themselves to human kind. Parca Maurtia suggests a much broader sphere of operation. Her name Maurtia reflects some kind of cult for Mars in the Grove Albunea. This grove belonged to Faunus, whom legend made the son of Picus "Woodpecker."

4. MORTA, LIVIUS ANDRONICUS, AND THE SECULAR GAMES

What appeared to be an obvious connection between Parca Maurtia and Andronicus' Morta has met with scholarly opposition. Miss Guarducci recognized the connection and suggested good reasons for the poet's choice of Morta over Maurtia or Mortia. In this section I propose to review the career of the first Latin poet, insofar as it can shed light on our subject, to evaluate his craft of translation, and to discuss the place of the Moerae in the Secular or Tarentine Games, a festival he could have witnessed and, perhaps, written for. This survey will produce new information and interpretations toward the understanding of Latin cults and letters, as well as promote Guarducci's identification of Maurtia with Morta.

On the unsure authority of the tragic playwright Accius, Cicero tells us that Andronicus, a native of Tarentum, was brought to Rome as a captive. [63] The name Andronicus certifies the validity of the tradition that makes the playwright a former slave. No contemporary or slightly younger poet bears a Greek cognomen that was the residue of slavery. At the year 187 B.C., St. Jerome reports his manumission by Livius Salinator, whose children he had taught. Jerome's notice can be traced to Suetonius' research into the lives of the poets; in his brief history of education, Suetonius makes Livius Andronicus and Ennius school teachers who composed Latin pieces for their pupils' study. [64] In fact, Andronicus sold his first play to Roman magistrates in 240 or earlier (see below). Since no available evidence bears witness to a slave's selling plays to the magistrates, Andronicus should have been a freedman in 240. Jerome's year, 187 B.C., very probably marks the date of the playwright's death (see below). Accius not only reports his capture in 209 B.C. but also his birth in Tarentum. We are not obliged to accept Accius' notice of the birthplace if we can find a reason for the mistaken date, 209 B.C., and for confusion of the city Tarentum of southern Italy with the Tarentum of Rome's Campus Martius. The source of chronological confusion is apparent in the person of the Roman prefect of Tarentum from 214 to 209 (see below). In 249, and again in 236, the Secular Games, then called the Tarentine Games, were observed at the Tarentum in the Campus Martius; their name and place could have been confused with a birthplace of Andronicus.

Andronicus bears the gentilicial name of the plebeian clan of Livii, whose members were recently prominent in Roman politics during the generation of Andronicus' productivity. Jerome, following Suetonius, puts the playwright in the *familia* of a Livius Salinator. The Livii had become ennobled by the consulship of M. Livius Denter in 302 B.C. Two years later the same Denter was among the plebeians who first attained the pontificate, Rome's paramount priestly college. In his pontifical capacity, Denter coached Decius Mus through the prayer formula of a *devotio* before the pontiff was made a propraetor, and the commander surrendered his life in 295 B.C. [65] Livius' part in the *devotio*, as well as the *devotio* itself, may be apocryphal, but it remains a piece of the tradition of the Livii.

Surviving records next yield the name of M. Livius Salinator, son of Marcus and grandson of Marcus. He was a *decemvir sacris faciundis* with Manius Aemilius Lepidus in 236. The conjunction of the two careers is worth remarking, since Denter had been consul in 302 with M. Aemilius Paullus. The two decemvirs of 236 are recorded in their capacity of presidents at the Secular Games (see below). Although this M. Livius Salinator, the oldest to bear the cognomen, is usually distinguished from the consul of 219 and 207 with the same names and lineage, the decemvir and consul are very probably one and the same M. Livius Salinator. Their identity does not depend on the fact that the consul was, factually speaking, the first bearer of the surname Salinator; rather, the supposed chronological gap between 236 and 219 is specious. The decemvir of 236, Aemilius, died in 211 B.C. Thus, no timespan impedes the identification of the decemvir Livius with the consul Livius. Moreover, C. Livius M.f. M.n. Salinator, who was pontiff from 211 to 170, must be the consul's son. The son became pontiff early in his career, for he did not hold the curule aedileship until 204, the year of his father's last magistracy, the censorship, during which Marcus Livius imposed the new salt tax which earned for him and his family the cognomen Salinator.

Marcus Livius, later to be surnamed Salinator, first reached the consulship in 219. He was not only the clan's second consul, but was the colleague of L. Aemilius M.f. M.n. Paullus, a direct descendant of M. Livius Denter's colleague in 302. In 218 both consulars went on an embassy to Carthage, where the famous Roman ultimatum for the surrender of Hannibal met rejection. Upon his return Livius chose to go into exile after his conviction by an assembly. The events surrounding his trial, conviction, and withdrawal are by no means made clear in our meager sources. The cause is usually attributed to Livius' military conduct in 219, but he had just triumphed over the Illyrians. Another cause may be sought in the Roman government's policy toward Carthage. There survives an important item which bears on the situation. Pacuvius Calavius, a powerful Capuan politician, was married to the daughter of Appius Claudius and had given his own daughter in marriage to M. Livius, perhaps a son of Marcus Livius (Livy 23.2.6; cf. 23.4.7-8). In 215 Pacuvius Calavius led Capua's defection from its alliance with Rome, and promoted a Capuan treaty with Hannibal. It is not impossible to imagine Livius' withdrawal of 218 in terms of a disaffection from Rome's belligerence, or in light of his known connections with a Capuan noble whose loyalty to Rome in this particular war was slight and might prove negligible.

Only in the year following Capua's capture in 211 did Livius return from his self-imposed exile. It was the eighth year since his conviction. His first public act was the defense of his kinsman, M. Livius Macatus, accused of some misconduct before the senate. This Macatus is probably the Roman commander at Tarentum from 214 to 209. M. Livius (Macatus) had been put in charge of the Tarentine garrison by M. Valerius Laevinus, one of the two consuls who persuaded Salinator to come back to Rome in 210. [66] The name of the commander at Tarentum and the last year of his command contributed to Accius' belief that the Tarentine poet Andronicus was brought to Rome in 209. Except for some literary milestones, which are remarked below, no other incident in the careers of the Livii can be adduced in tracing Andronicus' life.

Andronicus' literary productivity is said to have commenced with the staging of a play in 240. At that time the decemvir, whom I identify with the consul of 219 and 207, is the only known Livius Salinator active in public life. Other Livii who appear later in the century are the Roman son-in-law of Pacuvius Calavius, M. Livius; the M. Livius Macatus defended by Salinator in 210, who is very probably the same as the Roman prefect of Tarentum; and, finally, C. Livius Salinator, who was pontiff from 211. The only Livius who could have been Andronicus' master is the decemvir of 236. He not only bears the name Salinator but also, I argue, first gained the name in 204 B.C. Andronicus and Salinator must have been contemporaries. Therefore we must assume that M. Livius Salinator had no children old enough for Andronicus' instruction before 240, and that his manumission preceded the education of the young Livii.

It is customary to date the poet's birth to *ca.* 272, when the Tarentine War ended; this seems improbable. Andronicus must have come to Rome with a knowledge of his ancestral literature, and followed a Latin literary career lasting from 240 B.C. into the first decade of the second century. He could not have received a well-grounded training in Greek literature much in advance of the fall of Tarentum. I reckon that in that case he must have died around the age of 90 immediately after his last play in 191 B.C. (see below). Such reckoning allows for a stripling of 9 years to reach Rome in 272. A nine-year-old boy, I submit, could have retained his mother-tongue but could not have brought a profound knowledge of Greek literature with him. Those who choose to uphold the traditional birthdate and origin of Andronicus must demonstrate the source of his knowledge of Greek literature. It cannot be reasonably supposed that he was educated in Greek letters at Rome, even though Greek may have been taught there some time earlier in the third century. It seems best to reject Accius' birthplace of Andronicus when we reject, as we must, the date of his capture in 209; then we may assume that he came from Tarentum after the Tarentine War, or that he never came from Tarentum.

Accius himself apparently had to reconcile certain given facts in his predecessor's career. For one thing, he had to find a Livius operating in Greek territory. Consequently, he turned his attention to M. Livius, the commander at Tarentum from 214 to 209, and the only Livius whom we also know to have been assigned to Greek-speaking lands. However, the fallacy inheres in the mistaken ancient assumption that a Livius had to capture Andronicus. Andronicus could have been bought on any market and come from anywhere. It remains to recall that the Romans were taking Greek captives in Sicily from 264 to 241, during the first Punic War. Syracuse, briefly Rome's enemy, was renowned for its theater. Agrigentum, too, was not without its glorious tradition of learning before the Romans sacked it. [67]

Andronicus presented his first play in 240 B.C., the year before Ennius' birth. M. Varro is responsible for publishing these data in his *Antiquities* and his *Poets*. [68] In fact, stage plays (*ludi scaenici*) had been given at Rome for over a century. [69] Accordingly, Andronicus' play is considered the first translation from Greek into Latin. Andronicus may even have written other plays in an established Roman tradition before he brought forth a direct translation from the Greek. The next date in his life is marked by his composition of a hymn for the purificatory ceremony in the Aventine temple of Juno Regina. [70] The year was 207, when the consuls C. Claudius Nero and M. Livius Salinator were awarded a triumph for their splendid victory at Sena on the Metaurus River. Not only was Marcus Salinator consul in the year of this purification, but C. Livius Salinator was a member of the pontifical college that decreed the singing of the hymn by twenty-seven maidens in procession. [71] Seven years later the same ceremony was held, but P. Licinius Tegula wrote the hymn. [72] One of the consuls supervised the entire proceedings, but we cannot be sure that either consul had participated in 207. P. Licinius Tegula may have been a protegé of another pontiff, P. Licinius Crassus Dives, Gaius Salinator's colleague.

The last date in Andronicus' career is 191 B.C. Accius, who thought Andronicus came to Rome from Tarentum in 209, placed his first play in 197 B.C., when the games were given for the dedication of Juventas' temple, which Marcus Salinator had vowed at the battle of Sena. Cicero vouched for these games and the year on the basis of Atticus' and his own research into old archives (*antiqui commentarii*), although he did not agree that this was Andronicus' first play. [73] While we can fully agree with Cicero on the beginning of Andronicus' career, we cannot agree on the year of the games for Juventas. In a securely embedded religious notice for the year 191 B.C., Livy reports that C. Licinius Lucullus was named *duumvir* to dedicate the temple to Juventas which Salinator had vowed in 207, and as censor had contracted for in 204, and to give the games for the dedication. [74] This Licinius was one of the initial *tresviri epulones.* [75] M. Salinator's death between 203 and 191 is to be inferred. His son, the pontiff, was praetor in 191, absent from Rome with the Aegean fleet. However, the father or his heirs doubtless saw to the performance of Andronicus' piece.

We suggested above that Jerome's notice of Andronicus' manumission and *floruit* in 187 represented the poet's death year (see above). The play given in 191, which Accius believed to be his first and dated to 197, was apparently his last play. Accius himself was born in 170 B.C., but his data on Andronicus' life cannot be trusted.

Now Andronicus' art of translation invites our examination. The fragments of his dramas do not enlighten us on the subject of Morta. Morta was found in his translation of the *Odyssey* (fr. 11 M):

> quando dies adveniet, quem profata Morta est.

How does Andronicus handle the Greek names of gods and mythical figures? First of all, the poem opens with an invocation of Camena where Homer had called on a Muse. Camena was one of a number of water-sprites whose shrine lay just outside Rome's Porta Capena. We meet in ancient and some modern authors the assertion that he chose Camena because its original form *Casmena* had suffered rhotacism and *Carmena* suggested *carmen* "song." That explanation of his choice of words is nonsense. Indeed Andronicus did write *Casmena*, the pronunciation of his day. But *Casmena* never became *Carmena* (or Carmenta) except in incompetent linguists' minds. Andronicus doubtless chose Casmena because of the holy spring of the Camenae, which called to the poet's mind the spring of Hippocrene. Andronicus expected some Roman familiarity with the Greek tradition of holy waters and prophecy, as we witness in this line from one of his tragedies (fr. 37. R.[4] from Festus, p. 408 L):

> quo Castalia per struices saxeas lapsu accidit.

Most of the other Livian versions depend on commonly accepted equations: Saturnus for Kronos, Mercurius for Hermes. Or he employs crude patronymics in similar fashion: *filia Atlantis, filius Latonas.* In the latter instance, Andronicus had available the common Italian form of Leto, and in the former he simply reduced the Greek name to a Latin declension as he does with the variant Ulixes and with Calypso, Circa, and Cyclops. So, too, he retains Pylos and Patroclos.

Andronicus' pattern in rendering the Muse into Camena is met in two other cases. One is Morta and the other is the patronymic of the Muse, *diva Monetas filia docuit,* "goddess daughter of Memory," for such is his notion of Mnemosyne. Although the Roman pantheon abounded in divinities originating in substantial notions such as Fides, Spes, and Fortuna, the Romans had no knowledge of a divine *Memoria.* Latin literature stood at its beginnings, so that no literary tradition existed when Andronicus first wrote. Andronicus brilliantly took the epithet of a goddess and converted it to an entirely new use. Moneta belonged to Juno and to Juno alone. [76] Andronicus believed that it meant "Remembrancer," which would have translated *Mousa*. However, he gave the name to the mother of the Muses, whom the Greeks called Mnemosyne. We cannot ascertain how much Andronicus himself contributed to the Latin understanding of *Moneta*, for it will be clear in a moment how willing he was to seek his own fresh renditions of some Greek mythical persons in Latin religion. What remains important is Andronicus' use of only the epithet of a major Roman deity to express the name of a lowly figure in Greek poetry. In like fashion the poet had begun his version with a call to Camena. The physical situation of the shrine of the Camenae, a wooded valley with fresh waters running from their source, was inducement enough for Andronicus' translation. Its effect was profound, both in the era of classical poetry and in the reaction of Quintus Ennius and of his patron, Fulvius Nobilior. [77] After Cicero quotes at *Brutus* 18.71 the now familiar Ennian lines on the old poetry of the Fauni and *vates*, he turns our attention to Livius Andronicus and to his Latin *Odyssey, tamquam opus aliquod Daedali*. The shift of devotion from Camena to Muses represents the disavowal of the native tradition whose practitioners were Andronicus and Naevius.[78] The Fauni and *vates* recall us to the character of Morta.

With customary acumen, Miss Guarducci recognized the Andronican Morta, which Caesellius Vindex preserved for Gellius. In Andronicus Morta represents the Parca Maurtia of Tor Tignosa. Vindex calls Morta a Parca. Andronicus found this Homeric line four times (with a variant introduction):

μοῖρ' ὀλοὴ καθέλῃσι τανηλεγέος θανάτοιο. [79]

Caesellius Vindex identified Morta and Moira in "quando dies adveniet, quem profata Morta est." Gone from the Latin is a notion of destruction and grief. In their place have been put the prophetic quality of a deified Moira *profata* and the very suggestion of death in the form of the new name *Morta*. Guarducci herselt saw that *mors* had contributed to Andronicus' choice of the form: [80] what ought to have been *Maurtia* or *Mortia* has been rendered Morta. However, Andronicus paid no heed to a principle of identity when he invoked Camena and called her the daughter of Moneta. What Andronicus intended by *profata Morta est* was the feeling of destined death, a death destined by prophecy. His choice of verbs recalled to his reader's mind the cult association of Neuna Fata with Parca Maurtia. Yet Morta does not spare, for she is death-dealing, in contrast with Homer's bland "portion." The kind of deity after which the translator successfully strove had linguistic analogues in Anna Perenna, Flora, and Lara. Therefore opposition to the poet's identification Morta = (Parca) Maurtia[81] simply denies the poet his method and his imagination, by appealing to linguistic rules—as if he had cared a fig for the rules when he had the power to rob Juno of an epithet to render Mnemosyne, and to seek his inspiration at the Roman springs of the Camenae.

Guarducci also realized how the three Greek Moerae had influenced the development of three Parcae or three Fata. In passing, she remarked the nine victims of two kinds which the Moerae received at the Roman Secular Games, [82] although she did not pursue the important problem of the Moerae and the Secular or Tarentine Games. Before looking at the Moerae in this ceremony, we must ask what Livius Andronicus knew of Roman Moerae.

Some years ago Lily Ross Taylor pointed out that the worship of the Moerae was not instituted at Augustus' Secular Games in 17 B.C. but goes back at least to the time of Fabius Pictor. [83] In 496 L. Postumius vowed a temple to Ceres, Liber, and Libera during a famine which had prompted the dictator to consult the Sibylline Books. The Books told him to initiate this cult. Both the cult and the temple were inspired by Greek artists and Greek religion. The temple itself was constructed from the spoils of the Latin War, and was dedicated in 493. [84] The help of the gods was commemorated by circus games (*ludi Cereales*) on 19 April. Dionysius of Halicarnassus gives us a lengthy description of the procession or *pompa* (note the Greek name) that preceded the games even before the Punic Wars, as Fabius Pictor informed him.[85] The list of the gods whose statues, garbed in traditional Greek costume, were carried in the *pompa* is most illuminating. Here is Dionysius' list, which he notes was only partial: Zeus, Hera, Athena, Poseidon, Kronos, Rhea, Themis, Leto, Moirai, Mnemosyne, Persephone, Eileithyia, Nymphai, Mousai, Horai, Charites, Dionysos, Herakles, Asklepios, Dioskouroi, Helene, and Pan. Doubtless many of these gods had pure Latin equivalents. However, we have already witnessed the early arrival of the Dioscuri at Lavinium. That dedication must be roughly coeval with the institution of this *pompa*, which Postumius is said to have vowed. According to Fabius Pictor, the Romans had known statues of the Moerae, Mnemosyne, and the Muses since the fifth century. At least we can certainly trust the annalists' warrant of their arrival before the Punic Wars. The Sibylline Books had prompted the importation. Theoretically, Livius Andronicus' readers would have recognized the Muses and Mnemosyne and the Moerae! It is not at all unlikely that ordinary Romans preferred to call them Camenae, Moneta, and Parcae.

The importation of many Greek deities was urged by the Sibylline Books. An early cult of the three Fates is supposed on the basis of the Tria Fata, whose statues stood near the Curia Hostilia and lent their name to that sector in late antiquity and the Middle Ages. [86] The oldest reference to this trinity tells us something else: "equidem et Sibyllae iuxta rostra esse non miror, tres sint licet: una quam Sextus Pacuvius Taurus aed. pl. restituit; duae quas M. Messalla. primas putarem has et Atti Navi, positas aetate Tarquinii Prisci." [87] Indeed the three statues are not identified as Fata for almost 200 years after Pliny. The encyclopedist considered them among the oldest statues in Rome, even though he knew them only in a restored state. His attribution to Tarquinius Priscus rests upon that king's purchase of the Sibylline Books from the Sibyl herself. Perhaps they were no older than the statues of Alcibiades and Pythagoras which the Romans installed in the Comitium at the instance of Apollo Pythius during a Samnite War. [88] In any event, the three Sibyls were relatively ancient. In the discussion of the Ten Sibyls whom the Romans canonized we saw that there were just three Sibyls in Italy: Cumaean, Cimmerian, and Tiburtine. [89] The last bore the name of Albunea, also the name of the cult place where Parca Maurtia and Neuna Fata were honored. It seems very likely that the three Sibyls honored with statues were the three Italian Sibyls.

The Romans who restored the statues also attract interest. Sex. Pacuvius Taurus bears a fine Campanian name recalling the Capuan magnate who, in 215, had Claudian and Livian connections, and the Brindusine who practiced poetry and painting at Rome in the second century B.C. As plebeian tribune in 27 B.C., Sextus Pacuvius proposed the plebiscite naming the month of Sextilis after Augustus Caesar.[90] M. Messalla, who restored two of the Sibyls, belonged to the Valerian clan which claimed the institution of the Secular Games. He may be one of the *quindecemviri sacris faciundis* in charge of the celebration in 17 B.C. In 210 one of the two men responsible for bringing M. Livius Salinator back to Rome was the consul M. Valerius Laevinus. In 214, the same Valerius had put M. Livius Macatus in charge of the Roman garrison at Tarentum. It was his protegé, kinsman of the disaffected Livius, who wanted a defense in 210. In 280, Laevinus' ancestor had been one of Rome's less successful consular adversaries against the Tarentines and Epirotes.

Legend has it that the Roman Secular or the Tarentine Games were founded by the first consul, Valerius Poplicola, to commemorate an ancestor's discovery of the cult of Dis and Proserpina at an altar, twenty feet underground, at a place in the Campus Martius called Tarentum. According to the legend, Valerius followed the prophecy of his household Lares at a time of great plague and journeyed down the Tiber in search of relief for his physically afflicted children. He came to a halt at Tarentum because of the vaporous exhalations from hotsprings. In due course he uncovered the altar of the two deities, who saved his children.[91] The name Tarentum evinces a common Latin toponymous formation (compare Aventinus, Ferentum, Laurentum, etc.). As the Romans' horizon expanded, they adapted the formation to non-Latin place names (compare Beneventum, formerly Malventum, Grumentum, Agrigentum). Hence, the Greek city Taras was called Tarentum. It is hard to believe that the Romans named a piece of the Campus Martius after a Greek town, to which they also later gave a Latin name![92]

Tarentum resembles the site of Faunus' oracle at Albunea. There existed in both places vaporous exhalations. Dis and Proserpina belong to the ranks of Netherworld deities. Ovid made Numa Pompilius seek at Albunea a divine solution to the problem of pestilence. The cult of Dis and Proserpina was founded toward the same solution, and the games were held every century to ensure the avoidance of pestilence. In a moment we shall see parallels between the two shrines of Tarentum and Albunea.

The appropriate dates in the cycle of the Secular Games were a disputed matter even in antiquity. When Claudius gave his games in 49 A.D., he evoked laughter from the Romans for having the herald proclaim the usual formula that no one living had witnessed them before or would witness them thereafter, and brought Suetonius' wry censure for his claim that Augustus had miscalculated his date of the games, whereas the same Claudius had taken the occasion in his *Histories* to praise Augus-

tus for his right reckoning and observance of the proper interval. [93] Augustus'
games were held in 17 B.C., but such games were already planned before Vergil's
death. [94]

Augustus is said to have reckoned a *saeculum* of 110 years rather than the even
century. However exactly he reckoned it, the Princeps did not come close, because
the preceding games took place in 146 B.C. Although the ancient debate on the
exact length of the *saeculum* may have been quickened by Augustan calculations,
it did not take its beginnings from the Augustan discussion. Rather, the vacillation
between 110 and 100 years is to be sought in the third century, B.C.

The chief source for the chronology of the games is to be found in the seven-
teenth chapter of Censorinus' book on the birthday. We are also well served by the
partial survival of the inscribed proceedings of Augustus' games in 17 B.C. and
Septimius Severus' in 204 A.D. (see below).

Censorinus records the following observances of the Secular Games:

Number	Year		Cycle		Authority
	a.u.c.	/ B.C.			
	245	/509			(P. Valerius Poplicola cos.)
I	298	/456			(M. Valerius Maximus cos.)
II	406	/348	110	(108)	(M. Valerius Corvus cos.)
III	505	/249	100	(99)	Valerias Antias, Livy
III (bis)	518	/236	110	(112)	Fasti Capitolini
IV	605	/149	100		Antias, Varro, Livy
IV	608	/146	100	(103)	Calpurnius Piso, Cn. Gellius, Cassius Hemina
IV	628	/126	110		*comm. XVvirorum*
V	737	/17	110	(109)	

Miss Taylor rightly emphasizes the value of the prayers in the Secular ceremony for
Rome's sovereignty over the Latins, which date the first actual performance of the
games to 348 B.C. when the Romans witnessed Latin attempts to withdraw from
their alliance. [95] The next games fell in 249, almost a century after the first. The
time was the first Punic War, which has not left a discernible trace in the Secular
prayers. After the mention of the "third" games and before mention of the
"fourth," a lacuna occurs in Censorinus, followed by the names of the consuls of
236 B.C. In addition to the evidence of this consular year in Censorinus, the Fasti
Capitolini at 236 B.C. have the additional notice of M'. Aemilius M'.f. and M. Livius
M.f. M.n. Salinator as the two *decemviri sacris faciundis* who presided (*magistri*) at
the "third" Secular Games. I have discussed this pair of decemvirs at length above.
Miss Taylor and others are quite right in calling these names additions to the Fasti
Capitolini, but equally wrong in insisting upon the invention of these games to fit a
110-year "Valerian" cycle. [96] Only three of the above-listed games are "Valerian."
Those of 509 belong to no cycle. Those of 456 are reckoned after the games of
348, but are 108 years earlier because of consul Valerius. Those of 236 follow the
games of 348 after 112 years. Indeed, the first putative observance of a 110-year

cycle falls in 126, is reckoned on the year 236, and is recorded by the *commentarii quindecemvirorum.*

The games of 126 are universally condemned as Augustan forgeries. The forgery was based on the actual games of 236. If no games had been given in 236, and if Augustan research had "invented" the games of 236, there would have been no cycle of 110 years. I thus repeat that the games of 236 were well and properly recorded in the archives, and were transferred to the Fasti Capitolini as the base for the purported cycle of 110 years; this cycle was purportedly affirmed by the games of 126 B.C., which were, in fact, a hoax. The games should have been given in the Forties, an intention reflected in Vergil's fourth eclogue (see below). The games of 126 were the base for the reckoning of Augustus' games of 17 B.C., which were proclaimed for the cycle of 110 years. [97]

Augustus' calculation rested upon the priestly archives, and he chose to lend more authenticity by adding to the Capitoline Fasti the names of the two decemvirs to the year 236 B.C. However, the celebration of 236 is not only supported by the mutilated section of Censorinus but also finds confirmation in a passage that troubled Miss Taylor. Augustine, in discussing the Romans at the time of the first Punic War, writes:

> tunc magno metu perturbata Romana civitas ad remedia vana et ridenda currebat. instaurati sunt ex auctoritate librorum Sibyllino m ludi saeculares, quorum inter centum annos fuerat instituta felicioribusque memoria neglegente perierat. renovarunt etiam pontifices ludos sacros inferis et ipsos abolitos annis retrorsum melioribus. nimirum enim, quando renovati sunt, tanta copia morientium ditatos inferos etiam delectabat, cum profecto miseri homines ipsa rabida bella et cruentas animositates funereasque hinc atque inde victorias magnos agerent ludos daemonum et opimas epulas inferorum. [98]

> "The Roman state was greatly upset by fear at that time and rushed into useless and ridiculous remedies. In accordance with the authority of the Sibylline Books the Secular Games were repeated. Their observance had been founded for a hundred years and had died out when memory failed in happier times. Again the pontiffs renewed the games devoted to the gods of the Netherworld even though these very games had been previously abolished in better years. For it is no wonder that, when the games were renewed, the enriched gods of the Netherworld took delight in the vast crowd of dying men, when indeed unhappy men performed mad wars and gory hostilities and victories deathdealing to both sides, as well as games for the spirits and sumptuous banquets for the Netherworld's deities."

Miss Taylor felt that Augustine was saying that first the decemvirs gave the Secular Games and then the pontiffs had them produced anew. Also, she felt that Varro was responsible for this report. Nevertheless, it escaped even the quick eye of Miss Taylor that we already have other indications of a renewal of the games. Varro is indeed the source. Augustine cites him a few lines before. In the *Antiquities,* Varro had researched the names of the ten Sibyls and the origin of the Sibylline Books. He dedicated his work to Julius Caesar. [99] Augustine used both Varro's *Antiquities* and *De scaenicis originibus.* [100] Varro had insisted on the hundred-year cycle, for he dated games to the year 149, whereas the historians living at that time,

Piso, Cn. Gellius, and Cassius Hemina, witnessed them in 146 B.C. Augustine mentions only the hundred-year cycle. He took this from Varro. Varro knew no 110-year cycle, because he was dead when Augustus prepared to give the Secular Games of 17 B.C. Varro could have found in Caesar an interested reader of his chapters on the Sibyls, because the games ought to have been given in 49 or 46 (the fourth eclogue of Vergil anticipates an early project for Secular Games which were deferred to 17 B.C.; see below, sect. 15). Varro, on the other hand, discovered the fact that the games of 249 B.C. had been found wanting in some way. On that account the pontiffs, to whom such serious matters were normally submitted for judgment, ordered another production of the games. This fell in 236 B.C. Varro must have realized that the games of 236 B.C. merely compensated for the games of 249 and did not alter or rephase the cycle. For Augustus they were a godsend: his games would fall almost 220 years thereafter. His loyal quindecemvirs searched the records and came up with spurious games in 126 and the authentic names of the decemvirs of 236, which were properly recorded on the Fasti Capitolini as an afterthought, not as an invention.

If anyone wants a reason for a second observance of the Secular Games in 236, he does not have far to seek. In 249 B.C., the consul P. Claudius Pulcher commanded the Roman fleet that sank at Drepanum, and his colleague L. Junius Pullus lost his fleet off Camarina. Obviously the games of 249 B.C. had no visible effect on Rome's well-being. The pontiffs waited; and after the war they ordered the Decemvirs to renew the games.

The Secular Games included three days and three nights of continuous stage-plays. At Augustus' celebration they comprised *ludi Graeci* and *ludi Latini.* In 236 B.C., there was only one playwright, so far as we know, fit to write for such *ludi scaenici.* Consequently, I propose, M. Livius was appointed one of the presidents of the second observance so that his protegé and client, Livius Andronicus, might compose the play(s), just as the same Andronicus composed the hymn in 207 when the same Marcus served in the consulship and his son Gaius served as pontiff.[101] If this reconstruction of the circumstances surrounding the games of 236 is near the truth, we now possess the origin of Accius' contemptible errors in the chronology and life of Livius Andronicus. Accius insisted that Andronicus had come from Tarentum as a captive in 209 B.C. He erred in part because of the name of the Roman commander of the Tarentine garrison, M. Livius. In addition, we may suppose that he had knowledge of Andronicus' composing *ludi Graeci* for the *Ludi Tarentini.* Such a tradition could easily have led him to the inference he was willing to draw from the activities of the garrison commander.

Before examining the cult of the Ludi Tarentini, let us return for a moment to the statues of the three Sibyls that stood in the Comitium. M. (Valerius) Messalla restored two of them because his family claimed the Secular Games as a Valerian foundation. The benefactor is very likely to be identified with one of the *quindecemviri*, Potitus Messalla or Messalla Messallinus, who participated in Augustus' celebration.[102] The third Sibyl was restored by Sextus Pacuvius Taurus in his capacity as plebeian aedile. Possibly the tragic playwright M. Pacuvius had written for the Secular Games of 146, and this aedile—by right or by fancy—claimed him for an ancestor.

Livius Andronicus could have learned of Parca Maurtia from the performance of the Tarentine Games. Miss Taylor adduces the evidence of Fabius Pictor to show that the Moerae were not new to the Games in 17 B.C., and belong to the earlier ones. [103] The Sibylline Books called for the following sacrifice recorded in the priestly *acta*: [104]

> nocte insequenti in Campo ad Tib[erim deis Moeris imp(erator) Caear Augustus immo-
> lavit agnas feminas IX] prodigivas Achivo ritu eodemq[ue ritu capras feminas IX, preca-
> tusque est hoc modo]:
> "Moerae, uti vobis in illeis libri[s scriptum est, quarumque rerum ergo quodque melius
> siet p(opulo) R(omano) Quiritibus, vobis VIIII] agnis feminis et IX capris femi[nis sa-
> crum fiat: vos quaeso precorque uti imperium maiestatemque p(opuli) R(omani)] Quiri-
> tium duelli domique au[xistis utique semper Latinus obtemperassit, incolumitatem sem-
> piter]nam victoriam valetudine[m populo Romano Quiritibus tribuatis, faveatisque
> p(opulo) R(omano) Quiritium legionibusque p(opuli) R(omani)] Quiritium remque
> p(ublicam) populi R[omani Quiritium salvam servetis, uti sitis] volentes pr[opitiae po-
> pulo Romano] Quiritibus, XVvirum collegi[o, mihi, domo, familiae, et huius] sacrifici
> acceptrices sitis VIIII agnarum feminarum et VIIII capraru[m feminarum propri]arum
> inmolandarum; harum rerum ergo macte hac agna femina inmolanda estote, fitote v[o-
> lente]s propitiae p(opulo) R(omano) Quiritibus, XVvirum collegio, mihi, domo, familiae.

This same ceremony and prayer were kept in 204 A.D. by Septimius Severus, [105] and presumably by Domitian, whose coins show the rites. [106]

There are many indications that this prayer is basically quite old. Miss Taylor has demonstrated the pertinence of the clause on the preservation of the Romans' control over the Latins, which belongs to the era of 348-340 B.C. The necessity to repeat the games given in 249 B.C. can be viewed in light of two military disasters when the decemvirs' prayers for the Roman people's grandeur, safety, victory, and strength were followed by the loss of two flotillas. The prayer gives verbal echoes of Cato's ceremonial prayer to Mars, even to the alliteration of *v*'s. The prayer is not repeated here, but the parallels are striking (see above, sect. 3).

In passing, Miss Guarducci remarked the nine ewe and she-goat victims. The Sibylline Books prove to be conservative, indeed. For the nine victims must have been for the nine goddesses, among whom were Parca Maurtia and Neuna Fata. The Greek name of the goddesses is preserved in the *acta*, but Horace will have none of it (see below). The (nine) Moerae bear the Greek name, but they are Latin god-desses. Their total number is now attested at Albunea. As Miss Taylor has shown, the prayer is principally directed at them to preserve the Latin alliance intact. The only Latin state that did not quit the Roman side during the great Latin War (340-338 B.C.) was Lavinium. [107] The gods of Lavinium heard the prayers of the Ludi Tarentini. The Romans' Campanian allies in the same war recorded their loyalty on a plaque in the Roman temple of Castor. Such an offering was appro-priate to cavalrymen. [108] Castor was Greek, and was very likely also connected with

Lavinium (see above). At the Tarentine Games of 348, the Greek influence had not been fully felt, and the number of Moerae or Parcae remained nine in honor of the nine goddesses of Tor Tignosa.

The era between the Latin War and the first Punic War is the period to which the three dedications of Tor Tignosa are assigned. In that time the cult still throve, at least away from Rome. In due course, the number of Parcae and Fata(e) was changed to that of the Moirai, and the Nona or "ninth" of the group suffered a different interpretation of her name. The dedications of Tor Tignosa confirm Miss Taylor's keen arguments in favor of a founding date on the eve of the Latin War.

Besides rites for the Moerae and other deities of the Secular Games, Terra Mater also received a pregnant sow.[109] It is no wonder that Ovid has Numa seek the oracle of Faunus at Albunea, and that the god counsels the sacrifice of the pregnant cows, which was in fact the *Fordicidia* for Tellus "Earth." If Ovid did not attend Augustus' games, he had the poem of Horace to remind him.

Here are Horace's lines on the two rites:

>   vosque veraces cecinisse, Parcae,
>   quod semel dictum est stabilisque rerum
>   terminus servet, bona iam peractis
>   iungite fata.
>
>   fertilis frugum pecorisque Tellus
>   spicea donet Cererem corona;
>   nutriant fetus et aquae salubres
>   et Iovis aurae.[110]

Carmen composuit Q. Horatius Flaccus, runs a line of the priestly *acta.* And so he did, in a tradition reminiscent of Livius Andronicus' composition for Juno Regina in 207 B.C.[111] Horace doubtless imitates Catullus (64.306: *veridicos Parcae coeperunt edere cantus*), but Horace's Parcae merely tell the truth and keep the boundary markers of the empire standing safe. Horace chooses to use only the Latin name of the deities, with an allusive *fata*, whereas he names Ilithyia and Lucina and Genitalis for those whom the *acta* call Ilithyiae.[112] The longstanding association of the Ilithyiae and Moerae at the Secular Games and in the old procession for the Ludi Cereales (see above) reinforced the Romans' opinion on the nature of the Parcae, who resemble the Moerae in number and in overseeing childbirth.

Horace's involvement in a grandiose patriotic holiday, in his mind celebrated every 110 years, has a tradition behind it. The Romans so esteemed Andronicus' hymn of 207, which was sung "to make the state to thrive," that Minerva's Aventine temple was given in his charge. In it, "writers" and "players" met and presented offerings. This guild was created to honor Andronicus.[113] In a word, since the year 207 the state had formally acknowledged the religious eminence of those writers whose artistry contributed to the welfare of the state. The state had not thriven in 249 B.C.

Let us summarize the discussion of Parca Maurtia. The goddess was a *parca* whose function was derived from Mavors or Mars. She spared man, beast, and the growing vegetation of the field and forest. Conversely, her powers might abate so that she might be said to deny life through the blight. Parca Maurtia appears only once in surviving Latin literature. Andronicus translated Homer's impersonal *moira* into the deity Morta. The poet rendered one idea with a new word that both conveyed the notion of death and called to the reader's mind the function of Parca Maurtia. He probably learned of Parca Maurtia in connection with a special production of the Tarentine Games of 236 B.C., where the nine Moerae or Parcae were worshipped not just for the sake of the Roman people's general welfare but equally for their empire's greatness, with particular regard for the preservation of their Latin hegemony. The goddesses invoked at the Tarentine rites numbered nine, which was the total of the Fatae in archaic times. The Italian Sibyls promoted the games through the oracular books of fate. The three Sibyls evidently shared a common iconography with the three Fata, for the former's statues were later identified as the latter. In Latium the only Sibyl whose statue is otherwise known is the Tiburtine Albunea, with a book in hand, found in the Anio River. Besides being the name of this Sibyl, Albunea was also the name of the Lavinian cult center where Parca Maurtia and Neuna Fata were worshipped.

Of equal importance remains the fact of Aeneas Indiges' veneration in the same area, for there is no Roman treatment of his legendary exploits in Italy that omits mention of Sibylline prophecy. Naevius, who first rendered the story of Aeneas into Latin poetry, noticed at least the Cimmerian Sibyl. [114] Despite the evidence of our authorities on the situation of the Italian Cimmerians, who dwelt in murky darkness and caves, it now seems possible to suppose that the earliest Latin understanding of Aeneas' visit to an oracle might have set the scene in the vicinity of the "grotto" of Albunea by Lavinium, where the Trojan's landfall first became part of Latian legend. [115]

In reply to Odysseus' request for direction to the land of the Cimmerians where he might consult Teiresias, Circe says (*Od.* 10.508-12):

ἀλλ' ὁπότ' ἂν δὴ νηὶ δι' Ὠκεανοῖο περήσῃς,
ἔνθ' ἀκτή τε λάχεια καὶ ἄλσεα Περσεφονείης,
μακραί τ' αἴγειροι καὶ ἰτέαι ὠλεσίκαρποι,
νῆα μὲν αὐτοῦ κέλσαι ἐπ' Ὠκεανῷ βαθυδίνῃ,
αὐτὸς δ' εἰς Ἀΐδεω ἰέναι δόμον εὐρώεντα.

Hades' δόμος εὐρώεις is perhaps reflected in a line of Livius Andronicus: "celsosque ocris arvaque putria et mare magnum." [116]

The troublesome *arva putria* may be echoed by Vergil's description of Albunea, *saevamque exhalat opaca mephitim* (*Aen.* 7.84). Homer's Ocean has become Andronicus' *mare magnum*. His lofty hills (*celsos ocris*) have no place in Homer, but they fit a description of Alban Hills that provide the distant backdrop to the *mise-en-scène* at Albunea. Andronicus surely knew the one deity of the place, Parca Maurtia, and could have followed a Latian tradition of Cimmerians and prophecy at Albunea. Such shifts in localization are habitual in poets. The association of Circe and her putative home at Circeii with the voyage to the land where lay the entrance to the Netherworld may countenance a transfer to Albunea, which Vergil endows with the ordinary mythological description of a Netherworld (*Aen.* 7.91: *imis Acheronta adfatur Avernis*; cf. *Od.* 10.513-15).

Although we cannot be certain of a Cimmerian Sibyl at Albunea, we are fully entitled to emphasize the relation of the Moerae and their nine victims at the Secular Games for Dis and Proserpina to the goddesses Parca Maurtia and Neuna Fata at Albunea. The goddesses belonged to a Latian cult of the Netherworld and of prophecy, and enjoyed veneration at Rome on two periodic occasions, the annual *pompa* for the games for Ceres, goddess of growth, and the centennial celebration by which the Romans sought from the Nethergods a prolongation of their Latin hegemony. Both ceremonies antedate the first Punic War and the introduction of the Trojan legend into a Roman literature generated after the first Punic War.

The Tarentine Games of 236 B.C., which compensated for the games in 249, were produced by one of two decemvirs who is associated by name and tradition with the first man to translate Greek drama to a Latin stage. In the foregoing discussion the career of Livius Andronicus has been reconstructed. The playwright alone could have competently brought Greek plays in the Greek language onto the Roman stage in 236. The ceremonies were held at the Tarentum, a place in the Campus Martius bearing a Latin name. The name of this sacred precinct or of the Ludi Tarentini very probably induced the early Roman literary historians to believe that Andronicus called Tarentum his birthplace. Again in 207 B.C., the same M. Livius promoted Andronicus' literary pursuits by another decemviral commission for a hymn in honor of Juno Regina. It called for the performance of twenty-seven maidens just as Horace, 190 years later, composed his Secular hymn for twenty-seven boys and twenty-seven girls. In 204 the same M. Livius planned the temple to Juventas, which he had vowed in 207 B.C. When it was finally dedicated in 191, Andronicus' last known literary commission was given on the stage. Four years later, Andronicus was dead after a long career coeval with that of M. Livius Salinator, who deserves title to being the first Roman literary patron.

In subsequent generations the Romans lost sight of nine Fatae, of the original meaning of the name Nona, and of the origin of the epic Morta. The former yielded folk etymology, and the latter lived on in Andronicus' outdated *Odyssey*, where it eluded explanation by the erudition of a few Latin scholars. The discovery at Tor Tignosa reopens closed doors and considerably adds to our appreciation of the all-too-little-known Andronicus.

5. NEUNA FATA

Although the Fata of classical Latin usage are the plural personifications of the neuter *fatum*, "the spoken word," at Tor Tignosa the deity Fata is singular and feminine. She is the indubitable ancestress of the three Fata. Miss Guarducci recognized her name to be an agent noun from *fari*. [117] Earlier in this essay it has been demonstrated how *fata* is related to the deities Fatuus and Fatua, associates of Faunus, through *fateri* < *fari*. [118] Although *Fata* "the speaker" need not have been originally feminine (cf. *agricola*), both Fata and Parca are female at Tor Tignosa, as their adjectival epithets show.

The Fatae were a class of goddesses who numbered at least nine. The second cippus in the row of three bears the simple dedication *Neuna(i) dono(m)* "offering to the Ninth Goddess," the third and last, the mere dative *Neuna(i) Fata(i)*. I have already suggested that Parca Maurtia was one of the Nine, and also one of the three Parcae who belonged to the Nine. [119] A group of Nine is assured by other evidence to be discussed in a moment. As a class of goddesses, the Nine were primarily prophetic; their presence at Albunea thus comports with all that we know about the nature of its religiosity. Whereas Parca Maurtia can be closely related to the cult of Mars, the Fatae have no particular connection with other deities. Our ignorance is determined by the almost complete lack of an epithet like *Maurtia* applied to them. Indeed, *Neuna* by its very position suggests the original rank and not necessarily a divine function or sphere of activity.

As deities, Fatae speak the divine word, which appears to have been the *fatum*. Thus they closely resemble Sibyls, who indeed were not themselves divine but merely spokesmen of the divine word. Throughout Roman history the books for which the Roman college of Two, Ten, and Fifteen Men cared were called either the *libri Sibyllini* or *fatales*. It is not impossible that the latter name first referred to the Fatae rather than to the *fatum*. As we observed above, the statues of the Three Sibyls, which Pliny the Elder believed went back to the royal era, were later called the *Tria Fata*, so we can assume that the iconography of the prophetesses ultimately resembled the iconography of the prophetic godesses. The fact remains that the Fatae, at first nine in number, came to be identified with the Parcae. In my opinion the latter numbered three, one of whom was Parca Maurtia. Thereafter the three Parcae/Fata came to be identified with the three Greek *Moirai*, and to share a principal control over life and death. Further, I suggest that even at the time when the Tarentine Games were instituted, in the middle of the fourth century, the deities received nine victims of two kinds because they were nine. Their immediate origin seems to have been neither at Rome nor in Magna Graecia; they came from Lavinium, more exactly Tor Tignosa. To go the final step, I also suggest that the Sibylline Books or "Books of Destiny" were first acquired from the putative Sibyl of the region Albunea. This suggestion does not preclude Hellenic influence on the books or the Sibyl or the cult of Albunea. To the contrary, the relatively ancient cult of Castor and Pollux at Lavinium, who were only slightly latinized in name and epithet, points to early religious contacts between Latins and Greeks of southern Italy. Thereafter, the first telling of the Trojan inroads into Latium set Aeneas' consultation of the Sibyl at the Grove Albunea. Under these circumstances, Albunea of Tor Tignosa may have been reckoned the Cimmerian Sibyl, whom the epic poet Naevius and the annalist Calpurnius Piso mentioned. However, in the canonical account Aeneas is made to consult the Cumaean Sibyl, the most famous of all the

Sibyls in Italy. The Roman Sibylline Books, at least, seem to have been attributed to the Cumaean Sibyl *ca.* 433 B.C., but were probably as old as or older than the Capitoline temple of Jupiter, Juno, and Minerva. [120] Such an attribution did not necessarily overwhelm the prevalent belief in a Lavinian provenience, for the Tarentine Games evidently preserved the Latin number of Parcae/Fatae from their inception at the instance of the Books. Besides the diplomatic concession to a loyal Lavinium as member of the Latin League, the inclusion of the Nine in a ceremony primarily for Dis and Proserpina demonstrates the Nine's involvement in life and death.

Weinstock stresses that the Parcae and Fatae supervised matters of birth, [121] and lays stress on the Fata Scribunda whom Varro had summoned on the last day of the "week" following a child's birth. The Fata Scribunda must comprise a division of the Nine Fatae. Their name suggests the Writing Fatae, and thereby such Fatae as wrote on leaves or on *sortes*, which were usually wooden chips. Beyond the single notice we know nothing more of these Fata. [122]

Before an examination of the Nine Gods, an identification of another Fata of the Grove Albunea may be hazarded. Throughout the last half of the *Aeneid* one inhabitant of Lavinium stands opposed to the Trojans, to her daughter's marriage to Aeneas, and thus to her husband Latinus' adherence to the oracle of Faunus at Albunea. Queen Amata hoped for the victory of the Daunian Turnus of Ardea. In Vergil's epic gods sometime appear as human participants. There are, for example, Juturna, Venilia (Amata's sister), Astur, and some deified ancestors such as Picus and Faunus. [123] Amata could belong to this class of epic heroines. The name *amata* is older than Vergil; the Romans' chief pontiff appointed a Vestal Virgin by speaking the formula *ita te, Amata, capio.* [124] The explanation of the name was found in the person of the first Vestal Virgin, who was so called. [125] Like Fata and Stata (Mater), *amata* appears to be the agent noun "lover." The function of loving is frequently attested by Plautus in formulaic phrases that refer to variable divine subjects "loving" mortals. [126] The title (not the personal name) of the Vestals properly refers to the priestesses' love for their Vesta. The Roman title or personal name could not have influenced Vergil in selecting a name for King Latinus' wife; rather, the name should have come from Lavinian cult. The form of the name is that of Fata's. Although it remains only conjecture, the Lover may have stood beside and among the Sparers and the Speakers. [127] After Plautus' time even the formula of loving gods passes into desuetude. It is no wonder, then, that a Fata Amata also lost her place in a group that became thoroughly hellenized and reduced in size.

The Nine Goddesses of Albunea have a parallel in the Nine Gods of Ardea and the Di Novensedes, who are met in several places. At the outset of this section I stress the fact that the Nine Fatae must be distinguished from the nine gods, even though they all apparently share a common function. The Fatae are female and came from the Grove Albunea to the Romans' Tarentine Games (at least, our present evidence admits only this history). The male Nine Gods and the Novensedes have no actual connection with the cult center at Tor Tignosa.

With one mistaken exception,[128] Neuna is agreed to mean "ninth." From Ardea, Lavinium's southern neighbor, comes a dish in which is written *neuen: deiuo*, that is, *Novem Deorum*.[129] With it is a cup under whose foot is inscribed *Titoio(m)*, which Vetter renders *Titi proprium*, "this belongs to Titus."[130] Vetter attributes the Novem Dei and Neuna to the *novendial* of funerals and the cult of the dead.[131] On the other hand, Weinstock brings Neuna into close relation with Nundina Dea, who presided over the ninth or purificatory day (*dies lustricus*) after a child's birth, when he received his formal name.[132] In both cases the name is thought to reflect the number nine observed in a *nundinae* or *novendial*, but Vetter assigns it to funeral observances and Weinstock to ceremonies fixed after birth. In truth, there is no indication in the case either of Neuna Fata or of the Novem Dei that allows us to bring them into direct relation with these cults of birth or death.

The other group of deities here adduced are the Dii Novensedes. Unfortunately, these obscure and by no means frequent gods shared with the Di Indigetes the foundation of G. Wissowa's thesis of two kinds of Roman gods, the native gods (*indigetes*) and the new-comer gods (*novensedes*).[133] Their importance was magnified out of all proportion to their occurrence in Roman or Latin religion.

At the Roman colony of Pisaurum, one of fourteen archaic cippi reads *Deiv(eis) No[v]esede(bus) P(oplios) Poplio(s) Pop(li) f(ilios)*.[134] The other cippi contain dedications to Apollo, Fides, Juno, Juno Lucina, Mater Matuta, Salus, Diva Marica, Diana, Feronia, Juno Regina, and Liber, and all belong to the same shrine at roughly the same time. Not one of the other gods belongs to a cult of the dead. Although the Junos and Diana might be construed as deities of childbirth, the rest of the gods have no pertinence to a cult of birth. The Pisauran cult setting of the Dii Novensedes does not lend support to any interpretation of their origin, nature, and cult. However, the one inscribed cippus does demonstrate the existence of a cult.

In the literature the Novensedes first appear as Novensides, who according to Varro, notorious in his pursuit of Sabine antecedents of Romans and their institutions,[135] are among a troop of Roman gods of Sabine origin. Varro has nothing to tell us about their function.

Next in chronological order comes a long section of Arnobius containing a number of Roman opinions:

> Novensiles Piso deos esse credit novem in Sabinis apud Trebiam constitutos. hos Granius Musas putat; consensum adcommodans Aelio, novenarium numerum tradit Varro, quod in movendis rebus potentissimus semper habeatur et maximus; novitatum Cornificius praesides, quod curantibus his omnia novitate integrentur et constent. deos novem Manilius, quibus solis Iuppiter potestatem iaciendi sui permiserit fulminis. Cincius numina peregrina novitate ex ipsa appellata pronuntiat: nam solere Romanos religiones urbium superatarum partim privatim per familias spargere, partim publice consecrare, ac ne aliqui deorum multitudine aut ignorantia praeteriretur, brevitatis et conpendii causa uno pariter nomine cunctos Novensiles invocari. sunt praeterea nonnulli qui ex hominibus divos factos hac praedicant appellatione signari, ut est Hercules, Romulus, Aesculapius, Liber, Aeneas.[136]

"Piso believes that the Novensiles are nine gods established among the Sabines at Trebia. Granius thinks they are the Muses; Varro agrees with Aelius and passes on the novenary number because in moving matter it is considered the greatest and strongest; Cornificius, the guardians of novelties because all things are united and adhere in novelty through their oversight. Manilius, the nine gods to whom alone Jupiter gave the power to hurl his bolts. Cincius declares that they are foreign deities called after their very newness. For the Romans are accustomed to assign the cults of conquered cities to private families or to consecrate them publicly. And lest some of the gods be neglected because of their great number or ignorance, Cincius says, all the gods are invoked by one title for the sake of brevity and neatness. Further, there are some men who teach that such gods made of men are designated by this title, as Hercules, Romulus, Aesculapius, Liber, and Aeneas."

This summary is of primary importance for any understanding of the gods. Arnobius' name *Novensiles* presupposed **novenses < novus* and conforms with the view of Cornificius and Cincius, the antiquarian, that the root of the word points to the deities' foreignness. Varro, who presumably followed Calpurnius Piso, the annalist, in assigning them a Sabine origin, attributes their name to the number "nine," as had Piso and Aelius Stilo (Varro's teacher) and his contemporary Granius Flaccus, and as Manilius did after him. The function of the Novensedes is also variously reported. Varro, Granius, and Aelius considered them the Muses and presumably female, although Piso had made them masculine as do all other authorities. Varro especially related them to the power of the novenary number. Cornificius and Cincius, relying on an etymology from *novus*, place them in charge of newness or identify them with new, i.e. foreign, gods. Although the Varronian discussion may have included reference to the *nundinae* and *novendial*, none of these authorities, according to Arnobius' report, gave them control over birth and death. Manilius connects them with Jupiter the sender of lightning. Finally, some anonymous authorities held that the Novensedes were deified heroes. This view seems to depend on *novus* "newly made gods," and a confusion with the Indigetes (see below). Evidently only one author, Cornificius, attempted an etymology of the second element in Novensedes by using the phrase *praesides novitatum*. In a moment we shall return to this analysis.

After this miscellany of opinion we meet Livy's report of the prayer which chief pontiff M. Livius Denter used in assisting at Decius Mus' *devotio*:

Iane, Iuppiter, Mars pater, Quirine, Bellona, Lares, Divi Novensiles, Di Indigetes, Divi quorum est potestas nostrorum hostiumque, Dique Manes, vos precor veneror, veniam peto feroque, uti populo Romano Quiritium vim victoriam prosperetis hostesque populi Romani Quiritium terrore formidine morteque adficiatis. sicut verbis nuncupari, ita pro re publica <populi Romani> Quiritium, exercitu legionibus, auxiliis populi Romani Quiritium, legiones auxiliaque mecum Deis Manibus Tellurique devoveo. [137]

"Janus, Jupiter, Father Mars, Quirinus, Bellona, Lares, Divi Novensiles, Di Indigetes and gods whose power extends to our men and the enemy, Di Manes, I pray you, I entice you, I seek and I bring pardon, that you may generously bestow upon the army of the Roman people vigor and victory and that you may attack the enemy of the army of the Roman people with fright, fear and death. As I declare by words, so do I consign the

legions and auxiliaries with me to Earth and to the Di Manes on behalf of the common-
wealth of the army of the Roman people, of the army, of the legions and of the
auxiliaries of the army of the Roman people."

We shall have further opportunity below to discuss the *devotio*. For the time being
we add that the formula for the *devotio* of Carthage in 146 B.C. required an
invocation of Dis pater, of Veiovis, and of the Manes, and further required an oath
by Tellus the Earth, which, when the oath was spoken, was touched with the two
hands, and an oath by Jupiter. [138] In the Livian prayer the Divi Novensiles are
definitely connected with souls of the dead or Di Manes, the goddess of "Earth"
Tellus, the goddess of war Bellona, and "the Gods to whom belongs control over
our men and the enemy." In the Carthaginian *devotio*, Dis, Veiovis, the Manes, and
Tellus surely belong to the cult of Earth and the Netherworld, realm of the dead.
However we shall reserve further discussion of these gods, the Lares and Indigetes
to the sections on the Lares of Tor Tignosa and the Di Indigetes.

Harking back to the cult of the Grove Albunea where we encounter Neuna Fata,
we recall the presence of Mars *pater* and Tellus in the prayer and draw attention to
the offering to Parca Maurtia and Numa's consultation of Faunus on behalf of
Tellus, who must be made to ward off the bane from the land by means of unborn
calves sacrificed at the Fordicidia. In a sense, both life and death derive from the
cult at Albunea. However, the Divi Novensiles in the one prayer are not necessarily
related to Neuna Fata, for they are not prophetic.

Finally we come to the sixteen inscrutable divisions of the sky, attributable to the
Etruscans. Martianus Capella (1.46) assigns to the second region Jupiter, Quirinus
Mars, the Lar Militaris, Juno, Fons, the Lymphae, and the Dii Novensiles. Jupiter,
Quirinus Mars, and the soldiers' Lar reflect the presence of Jupiter, Mars pater,
Quirinus, and the Lares in the *devotio*. Fons and the Lymphae or Nymphae have
connections with the cult of the Grove Albunea. Both Vergil and Ovid mention the
waters; Lympha is addressed at Tiburtine Aquae Albulae; and the Nymphs are to be
discussed below on the River Numic(i)us. [139] In the aggregate, the deities of this
region of the sky do not constitute deities of life and death.

To summarize our ancient knowledge of the Dii Novensedes, they are nine male
deities who on one occasion received an offering at Pisaurum. Calpurnius Piso and
Terentius Varro held them to be Sabine. Nothing in their cult, evinced by one
dedication, one mention in a lengthy prayer, and one reference to a division of the
sky, indicates their certain function. When Granius Flaccus argued for their identification with the Muses, he probably based himself only on their number and did
not have in mind the Muses' inspiration and Neuna Fata's prophecy.

The name *novensedes* was analyzed by Cornificius, who is very likely Q. Cornificius Longus, author of the *De etymis deorum*,[140] to mean *praesides novitatum*.
Vetter holds that the title combines "nine" and "sitter," "Neunsitzer." The Nine
Sitters sat by a corpse for the nine days of the *novendial*. [141] There seems no room
to doubt the composition of *novem* + *sedes*, for the Nine are attested at Ardea and
the Ninth Fata at Tor Tignosa. Even in Wissowa's interpretation, the name contains
the root *sedere*, "Neuinsassen." [142] However there is another variation to be con-

sidered which comprises *novem* + *en* + *sed-*, namely, the "Nine who sit in." I offer this interpretation without designating where they sit or why they are thought to sit anywhere.

Before turning to the Lares and Aeneas Indiges, I recapitulate the discussion of Neuna Fata. The Ninth Speaker is one of Nine Speakers who, I argue, comprised three Parcae. One subgroup also seem to have been the Fata(e) Scribunda(e). According to conjecture, the epic queen of Lavinium named Amata could have been a Fata. The Fatae were also confused with the Sibyls. Moreover, the *libri fatales* may have been first acquired from a Lavinian source. The prominence of the number nine in Latin and Italic cult is met also in the Novem Dei of Ardea and the Dii Novensedes, whose function is quite obscure even if their name allows nearly certain etymology. Wissowa put unwarranted stress upon a contrast between Dii Novensedes and Dii Indigetes, who he believed were imported and native gods respectively. Wissowa, of course, knew that the ancients attributed to Aeneas Indiges a shrine by the River Numic(i)us, which may have run by the site of the Grove Albunea. Wissowa and many others would never have dreamt that Neuna Fata had been honored near the shrine of Aeneas Indiges. Nor could Wissowa have divined a close link between the nine and the twice-nine victims the Moerae received at the Tarentine Games and the Nine Fatae implicit in the dedication of Tor Tignosa.

There may indeed be a real link between Novensedes and Indigetes. This link may be sought at the cult center of Tor Tignosa.

6. THE LARES OF TOR TIGNOSA

Between 1958 and 1970, it was believed that a fourth monument recorded a dedication to the single Lar Aeneas. In the latter year Kolbe published his new reading of the text,

Lare Vẹsuia Q. f.

The proper reading has rendered inappropriate much that Guarducci and Weinstock wrote. Kolbe, struck by the single Lar, reviewed some of the evidence of the Lares' cult without resolving the problem of the identity of the one Lar. As it happens, he was led astray by the former reading, which required the understanding of a single Lar Aeneas. Since, however, Lares always come in groups of at least two unless the one Lar is specified by an epithet (e.g., *familiaris*, *agrestis*, *victor*), all religious testimonies require us to assume that the dedication at Tor Tignosa was made to the plural Lares, and to read

Lare(bus) Vesu(v)ia Q(uinti) f(ilia).

Kolbe's reading now gives us the name of one worshipper at Tor Tignosa, Vesuvia daughter of Quintus Vesuvius. Two men of that name and two Sexti Vesuvii are known from an old inscription on a carved shield with a head of Minerva that was found somewhere in Rome. [143]

In this section the several kinds of Lares will be examined, with some attention to Weinstock's discussion of their nature as dead ancestors. The place of the Lares beside the other gods of Tor Tignosa will also be emphasized. Since our newly recovered dedicant was a woman, women's devotion to the Lares will come under review.

The Lares are encountered throughout the history of Roman and Latin religion. They rank very low in any Roman divine hierarchy, but are widespread and often endowed with many identifying cognomens. This is not the case at Tor Tignosa. The nature of that deity is to be demonstrated.

Weinstock argued that the now-non-existent Lar Aeneas meant the Hero Aeneas, that the dedication was made to a dead ancestor, and, further, that the Lares were, one and all, dead ancestors. [144] Much could be added to his evidence of *Lar*, rendered by the Greek *hero*, and *indiges*, by the Greek *genarchēs*, by citing the congruence of the flower cult for Lares and for the dead at graveside, by citing the mutual influence of the iconography of the Lares' compital altars and sepulchral altars, which Altmann studied years ago, [145] and by citing an apparent linguistic relation of *lar* with *larva* "ghost." In the course of a decade, while preparing a study of *vici* and *compita*, the present writer has amassed hundreds of references to diverse Lares and their cults. The evidence, if it tells us anything, says that Lares were not dead ancestors. Whatever *indiges* means, it is not another word for Lar, as Weinstock argued.

Underworld deities usually receive nocturnal sacrifices at some time of year. There is no indication that the Lares received a regular night sacrifice. The Lares' animal victim is a white pig. Delian representations, the oldest surviving, belong to the public cult of the *Competaliastai* on the island. [146] Although there exist variant types, Lares, public and private, are shown in tunics dancing or toasting, a rhyton of wine in hand. There is nothing in their types to indicate the dead, or Roman ancestors. Their want of *gravitas* is phenomenal. The festival of the Lares took place in crossroads after the winter solstice; it was a movable festival ordinarily falling, in Rome and Roman territory, in late December or early January. It was usually observed by slaves and freedmen who held games (*ludi Compitalicii*). The Compitalia was also held in the countryside. The site of the festival could be at country crossroads, urban intersections, or the convergence of rural property lines; all were *compita*. [147]

Next we turn to the Lares' spheres of activity, besides crossroads and intersections. The oldest surviving Latin prayer, the hymn of the Arval Brothers, has the Lares associated with Mars and the spirits of the seeds in an agricultural context. Mars is asked to leap the boundary, a notion related to the intersection of boundaries (*compitum* and *limen*). [148] The Lares also had a rôle to fill in making the bride's marriage happy. [149] The Romans officially paid honor to their dead on fixed days in February. The dead ancestor has nothing to do with marriages. Indeed, the Lares were associated in imperial cult with the Genius, a procreative force; they thus received a youth's *bulla* when he came to manhood. [150]

The Lares' epithets have great pertinence here. The most famous is *Augusti* which was applied before the Principate, at least as early as 59 B.C., in a dedication by twenty country slaves of the territory of Mantua. [151] When Augustus shared his name with the Lares, [152] he surely had better sense than to endow dead ancestors with a sense of increase and prosperity. The Lares Augusti of the *vici* and *compita* supplant the Lares Compitales or the Lares Vicinales. [153] Leaving aside the Lares of domestic cult, which bear either one of the epithets *familiares, domestici,* or a family name (e.g. Volusiani), I mention the thirty Lares Grunduli or Grundiles or Grundules, called after "grunting" pigs; [154] the Lares Permarini, who had a Roman temple; the Lares Praestites, who occupied an old Roman temple and whose name evidently means "protector (of the City);" the simple Lares Publici; Lares Salutares; the group of three altars to the Lares Semitales, L. [C]uriales, and L. Viales; Lares Querquetalani. [155] Martianus Capella (1.45 ff.) records among his deities of the sixteen celestial regions these Lares: I Salus ac Lares; II Lar Militaris; IV Lar Caelestis and Lar Militaris; and X Lar Omnium Cunctalis. Something like a Lar Militaris is represented on a relief in the Vatican Museum. Although it is now immured, it seems to have been the side-panel of an altar. Thereon a Lar, wearing a mantle over his tunic, sits on a horse wearing a panther-skin saddle. [156] I have elsewhere dealt with the Lares Hostilii and the Comitium, who were also Lares of the Roman people. [157]

A single Lar is *Silvanus Lar agrestis.* [158] The Lares and Silvanus otherwise appear together. [159] Furthermore, one of the compital shrines of Delos depicts a Pan with pipes standing between two garlanded trees. The round altar of the Lares Vicinales of Ostia in the Piazzetta dei Lari has two similar goat-legged figures variously called Silvani, Pans, Fauns, and Satyrs. [160] Suffice it to recall for the moment that the dedication to the Lares at Tor Tignosa was found in the place of Faunus' oracle, and that Faunus is notoriously confused with Silvanus and the local deity, Inuus. Capella's *Lar Omnium Cunctalis* "All Lar of All Things" may be considered a rendition of Pan (= *omne*), who was the Romans' Faunus or Silvanus (see below). If he is Pan, he supplies an analogue to *Silvanus Lar agrestis.*

Another solitary Lar, again with epithet of course, is met in the territory of Clusium, where a woman raised a dedication to Lar Victor. [161] The epithet is common to Jupiter, but here recalls the plural Lares Militares.

The Arval Brothers' agricultural Lares, the Lares of intersections (*compitales*), of increase (*augusti*), of neighborhoods (*vicinales*), of grunting swine (*grunduli* etc.), of maritime victory (*permarini*), of protection (*praestites*), of the people (*publici*), of health (*salutares*), of paths (*semitales*) and of roads (*viales*), of oak groves (*querquetulani*), and the Lares of a curia, soldiers, and heaven have very little to do with the dead ancestor. Indeed, only one pair of Lares might support the operation of identity with dead ancestors. They are the Winged Lares (*alites*), which gave their name to a Roman neighborhood. [162] Not all winged creatures represent the ancient dead (e.g., Cupid). The Roman Lares may have haunted intersections just as the Romans buried their dead by the roadside. The words for a haunt and haunted, *larva* and *larvatus* can be derived from Lar, but spooks and ghosts and haunts are not always dead ancestors. The Lares resemble the Greeks' *hermai* and Hermes in this context.

In a discussion of the usually plural *Di Indigetes* we return to another Underworld context of the Lares. For the moment I content myself with Lares in general. We do not know for certain whether the Lares originated on the household hearth (*focus*) or out of doors in the fields in conjunction with Mars at a boundary line. This question encapsulates an old scholarly debate, which perhaps has no solution. However, the oldest attested sphere of activity was at the boundary. The *lar familiaris* belonged to the *familia*, which was not a family, but slave holdings. [163] This peculiar adoration occurs quite early at the crossroads within Rome itself. For in a pontifical religious notice for the year 428 B.C., Livy (4.30.7-11) records that the people were resorting in time of drought, scurf, and illness among men and beasts to foreign and abnormal rites *in vicis sacellisque*, so that the (plebeian) aediles were charged with preserving Roman gods from foreign modes of worship. The only gods worshipped in all the urban neighborhoods were the Lares. Evidently slaves, freedmen, and sojourning foreigners (compare Vicus Tuscus) were already changing the nature of the native cult of Lares. Indeed, the oldest representations of the Lares are Greek, and there is literary evidence even older than the visual representations. [164] When the Lares were worshipped at a *compitum*, each Lar presided over his own bailiwick. A person approaching a crossroads or boundary intersection recognized his own Lar as well as the Lar of another person or another people. Lares were always both domestic and alien. By definition of the deity's operation, for every domestic Lar there had to be an alien Lar. The strangeness of the Lares inheres in their cult, which was practiced by the Romans from the time of its oldest historical notice. Centuries later, every slave and freedman in Italy especially kept the Lares, whose public cult was commonly open to them and publicly supervised by them. In a very real sense, the Lares belonged to aliens in the city and in the country. Most Lares are in the plural, because the oldest Lares of which we are informed oversaw a *compitum* where more than one road or boundary line converged or crossed. The description of a *compitum* as a shrine makes clear that its form corresponded to the number of Lares for each line or road. [165]

Like any god for everyman, the Lar brought what everyman wanted. The Lares were worshipped wherever neighbors or the household most naturally gathered for holiday. The accident of ancient economics consigned them to a cult chiefly in the hands of the lowest form of human kind; they became the gods of the non-Romans in Rome.

The daughter of Quintus Vesuvius honored the Lares at Tor Tignosa. Just as boys would present their childhood lockets to the Lares on coming of age, Roman girls offered the Lares their breastbands, dolls, headdresses, and soft balls. When she married, a Roman bride brought three coins to her husband's house: the first for her husband, the second, which she kept in her shoe, for the hearth's Lares Familiares, and the third, which she kept in her purse, for the neighborhood compital shrine. [166] None of these occasions alone accounts for Vesuvia's giving the cippus.

More light on the problem comes from the town of Luna, where a freedman and two slaves gave Lares to the *iuno* of their mistress for her health (*pro salute*). [167] The donation of these Lares evidently recompensed the *iuno* for the health the mistress enjoyed after illness. The *iuno* of Roman women was closely related in the popular mind to the *genius* of Roman men. In Roman houses, and at the cross-roads, the Lares were associated in cult with one of several kinds of *genius*. [168] The man's "procreative force" and the woman's "youthfulness" wanted to enjoy health. One dedication to the Lares Salutares is known in Rome, where there were three distinct Vici Salutares, locations of the Lares' neighborhood or compital cult. [169]

Silvanus was once styled the "wild Lar." This god, whom we have already seen likened to Faunus and associated with the Lares, sponsored "health clubs," *collegia salutaria*, a euphemism for funeral societies. Earlier Cato counselled his farmers to sacrifice for the health of their cattle to Mars Silvanus in the woods. By implication, Cicero situated certain shrines of the Lares in holy groves. [170] This brings us back to the grove of Albunea where Faunus kept himself.

Faunus, who was believed to be worshipped in the rites of the Lupercalia, presumably operated in their general purificatory functions, including the expulsion of barrenness (see below). King Latinus approached Faunus on the matter of his daughter's marriage. The Lares, too, were regarded by brides. King Numa approached Faunus on the matter of pestilence, in a poetic passage composed with reference to the habits of the flamen Dialis and with allusion to his marriage rites. According to legend, a voice from the Lares Familiares prophesied to Valesius the restoration of his children's health if he would undertake the trip that resulted in the founding of the Secular Games. In 428 B.C., the Romans were introducing strange rites into the ceremonies of their neighborhoods against drought and sickness of men and beasts; in other words, ill health was fought through rites at the numerous altars of the Lares. Finally, again, Mars Silvanus kept the cattle healthy when he was worshipped in the woods.

Vesuvia's dedication was located near the dedication to Parca Maurtia. In the discussion of the sense of the epithet Maurtia, the Arval hymn was cited to illustrate how the Lares and Mars were implored to keep off blight and destruction. Indeed, in other proceedings the Arval Brethren sacrificed two wethers to the Lares and two sheep to the Mother of the Lares, when they treated the trees in the holy grove of the Arval goddess Dea Dia. [171]

The Lares are found in the prayer of *devotio* along with Mars, just as the Lar Militaris is found with Quirinus Mars in one of the heavenly regions recorded by Martianus Capella. However, the plural Lares are conjoined with Health, *Salus*, in another region by the same authority. [172] There were two aspects of this conjunction of Mars and the Lares; one of war and destruction, another of health.

Faunus and Fata had prophetic or oracular powers. This power is attributed to the Lares Familiares of Valesius, the founder of the Secular Games. Moreover, the same power inheres in the legend of Servius Tullius' paternity, in which the Lar of the hearth took the form of a penis of fire. [173] These are very slim evidences of prophetic Lares because they have no foundation in cult, unless we choose to take Vesuvia's dedication in close regard to the character of the other gods of Albunea.

There is otherwise ample indication that the Lares of Vesuvia's dedication are to be related to the matter of her marriage or her health. At Luna, Lares were returned to a woman's *iuno* for her health. In other instances the Lares were invoked against drought, illness, blight, and destruction. Some of the Roman neighborhoods where the Lares were worshipped bore the name of health. At the time of their marriage, Roman maidens customarily honored both the Lares of their new home and the Lares of their new neighborhood. Accordingly, Vesuvia's dedication beside those to Parca Maurtia and Neuna Fata need cause no surprise when it is linked to the story of Latinus' search for divine guidance on the subject of his daughter's marriage.

The ancients, of course, had no certain knowledge of the beginnings of the cult of the Lares in Lavinium or elsewhere. Normally, they attributed the beginnings of the Latin cult of the Penates to their importation from Troy by Aeneas.[174] In a poem commemorating Valerius Messallinus' elevation to the quindecimvirate, Tibullus develops a Sibylline prophecy for Aeneas. The prophecy originates with an unidentified Sibyl, although the poet mentions four Sibyls, including her of Tibur—that is, Albunea. Before the actual prophecy Tibullus writes that Aeneas had carried the Lares from Troy, and in the prophecy he makes the Sibyl say that the Lares will have a home in a foreign land where Aeneas will be the *deus indiges* of the Numicus River.[175]

In his epic, Silius Italicus displays some of his erudition on ancient Latium by narrating the pleas of a Saguntine ambassador who cites the Ardeate origin of Iberian Saguntum:

> per vos culta diu Rutulae primordia gentis
> Laurentemque Larem et genetricis pignus Troiae,
> conservate pios, qui permutare coacti
> Acrisioneis Tirynthia culmina maris . . . .
> . . . vetus incola Daunus,
> testor vos, fontes et stagna arcana Numici
> cum felix nimium dimitteret Ardea pubem,
> sacra domumque ferens et avi penetrali Turni,
> ultra Pyrenen Laurentia nomina duxi.[176]

> "By the long-worshipped originators of the Rutulian race, by the Lavinian Lar, and by the talisman of mother Troy (I beg) keep from harm the dutiful sons who were compelled to migrate from Ardea's walls to the Herculean heights of Saguntum . . . . A former native of Ardea, I call upon you to witness, springs and ponds of hidden Numicus, when prosperous Ardea dispatched her surplus young men, I bore the holy utensils and talisman of the house of Turnus and brought the name of Lavinium beyond the Pyrenees."

So spoke the ambassador from Saguntum, who represented to the Romans his city's putative descent from Latin migrants who had kept the cults of both Lavinium and Ardea. The Laurentine Lar is consciously linked with the Trojan tutelary deities that came first to Lavinium and then to Rome. Here the Lar is distinct from the Penates (*pignus*). Appealing to the piety owed the Aeneas of the River Numicus (see below), the ambassador reminds his audience that he fulfilled for Saguntum the role that Aeneas had played for Troy, by carrying the holy objects to the new land.

We know today how important such claims of kinship (*cognatio*) between Latian cities and overseas peoples were considered during the era of the Punic Wars. [177]

Tibullus and Silius permit the suggestion that the Lares whom Vesuvia honored at Tor Tignosa may have been viewed as deities imported from Troy by Aeneas, who in both instances is recalled as god of the Numicus.

From consideration of the character of the cults at Tor Tignosa, great importance is attached to Vergil's representation toward the end of the fifth book of the *Aeneid* (lines 719-45). The dead Anchises is sent to his son Aeneas by Jupiter, with the god's counsel to seek Latium after visiting the Cumaean Sibyl, who will escort him to the abodes of Dis after sacrificing black sheep. Upon Anchises' ghostly retirement, Aeneas stirs up the fire upon the two altars at his father's burial mound near Segesta in Sicily and offers sacrifice of spelt and incense, "Pergameumque Larem et canae penetralia Vestae." This hexameter was the model for the just-quoted line of Silius, "Laurentemque Larem et genetricis pignus Troiae."

Thus the Trojan origin of the Lares is confirmed as a tradition for Lavinium and Rome. Further, their veneration after the appearance of the dead Anchises would seem to link the Lares to divine intervention of a partially prophetic nature. In the next section are discussed another facet of Anchises' prophetic powers, another appearance of a god like the Lar, and in addition the source of the sacrificial waters of Vesta associated in Aeneas' rites for the Trojan Lar.

Whatever the Romans believed to be the origin of the Lares, the Lares of Tor Tignosa are to be construed in terms of their promotion of health and welfare, which could have affected Vesuvia's youthfulness. Further, the fact of Vesuvia's marriage may have prompted the dedication. To a lesser degree of certainty, the evidence allows us to surmise that the Lares of Tor Tignosa had some divine connection with the incubatory nature of the shrine. The cult of the Lares was appropriate to the grove of Albunea, for they are known to have been worshipped in woods and to have had a worshipful care of woods. In any case, we can no longer seek a cult of Lar Aeneas at Tor Tignosa.

7. AENEAS INDIGES

Despite the Greek language, Dionysius of Halicarnassus has left us the best description of the Latin cult of Aeneas. Not far from Lavinium, a battle took place between the Latins and Trojans on one side and the Rutulians and Etruscans on the other. Afterwards Aeneas was nowhere to be seen. Next to the river where they had fought, the Trojans and Latins honored Aeneas.

καὶ αὐτῷ κατασκευάζουσιν οἱ Λατῖνοι ἡρῷον ἐπιγραφῇ τοιᾷδε κοσμούμενον·
"πατρὸς θεοῦ χθονίου, ὃς ποταμοῦ Νομικίου ῥεῦμα διέπει."
εἰσὶ δ᾿ οἵ λέγουσιν ἐπ᾿ Ἀγχίσῃ κατασκευασθῆναι αὐτὸ ὑπ᾿ Αἰνείου, ἐνιαυτῷ
πρότερον τοῦ πολέμου τούτου τελευτήσαντι. ἔστι δὲ χωμάτιον οὐ μέγα καὶ
περὶ αὐτὸ δένδρα στοιχηδὸν πεφυκότα θέας ἄξια. [178]

"And the Latins built him a *heroon* adorned with this inscription:
(This is the shrine) of the Father and God of the Earth, who has charge of the River Numicius' stream.
Some assert that Aeneas had built it for Anchises, who passed away the year before this war. It is a modest mound of earth around which have been planted rows of trees which are worth seeing."

Dionysius considered the form of the monument to be local; that is, he attributes its building to the Latins, not to the Trojans. The "mound" is the Latin *tumulus*, which may be literally a mound or a stone construction similar to the imperial mausolea. At any rate, it is not a shrine for Lares, which were either round towers (*compita*) or marble tetrastyle shrines (*aediculae*). Dionysius calls the Lares' shrine a *kalias*, not a *khōmation*. [179] Of course, the inscription is much more telling. First of all, the name of the deity was missing, and thus the shrine might be attributed even to Anchises. Secondly, the god was a divinity of the river's stream, his realm the Earth. The appellation *khthonios* comports with Numa's visit to the Grove Albunea during pestilence to learn of a ceremony on behalf of Tellus. A tentative Latin translation of the title in the inscription is *deus pater* (or *parens*) *inferus*. [180]

Besides Dionysius, Pliny is said to give a proximate location of the shrine of Aeneas: in principio Ostia . . . oppidum Laurentum, l<u>cus Solis Indigetis, amnis Numicius, Ardea . . . . [181] The shrine must have been situated between Lavinium and Ardea. Many authorities agree on a site at the Numic(i)us River, over which Aeneas was thought to keep watch. [182] Castagnoli's report of his team's excavations in the territory of Lavinium establishes the site of the shrine of the Sun at Troia which is at the mouth of Fosso di Pratica (see Figure 9). Further, Castagnoli argues that the Fosso di Pratica is the ancient Numicus. More recently P. Sommella has published his excavation of a sepulchral shrine by the Fosso di Pratica that he identifies as the *heroon* for Lar Aeneas. [183] Caution in dealing with a "deity" whose name was attached to "his" shrine only through ambiguities should be ever exercised, especially when the "deity" may have never been. Dionysius distinguishes between the shrine of the Sun, with its two altars located by dry pools near the seashore, and the site of the Numician divine father. [184]

There is not the slightest evidence that Sol (Indiges) and Aeneas (Indiges) are identical. The very existence of this Sol Indiges or *genarchēs* is doubtful. [185] The location of the shrine of Aeneas Indiges is not certainly known beyond its proximity to the river whose diety in fact occupied the shrine. Whether the Numicus is identified with the modern Fosso di Pratica or the Rio Torto, the upper reaches should have been the site for the cult of its deity. In both cases, the river's headwaters lie near Tor Tignosa (see Figure 9). [186]

Although the god of the Numician shrine was not Aeneas, Aeneas was indeed cultivated at Tor Tignosa on at least one occasion. Before turning to the nature of the Di Indigetes, whose religion is more important than any putative cult of Aeneas or of Sol Indiges, we examine some details of Aeneas' legend in Latium.

On his way to the Promised Land, Aeneas and his Trojan followers are said to have made landfalls where subsequent religious indications of their presence certified the route of the voyage. All evidence for the cult of Aphrodite, Aphrodite Aineia, and Aineias the hero was collected by Dionysius of Halicarnassus: Pallene, a temple of Aphrodite and a city called Aineia; on Cythera, a temple of Aphrodite; on Zakynthos, a temple of Aphrodite, housing two antique wooden statues of Aphrodite and Aineias, where racers ran the course of Aphrodite and Aineias and ended at the temple; at Leucas, Actium, and Ambracia, temples of Aphrodite Aineia; also Ambraciote was the *heroon* of Aineias, with its wooden figure of Aineias supervised by the "handmaids" (*amphipoloi*); at Anchises' Harbor (i.e., Onchesmos), a temple of Aphrodite; Aphrodite's Gulf (i.e. Portus Veneris), Aeneas' first Italian landfall; at the shrine of Hera Lakinia, a cup given by Aeneas; atop Mt. Elymus, an altar of Aphrodite Aineia; in Aegesta (Segesta), a temple of Aineias. [187] At last, Aeneas comes to Latium, where he pitches camp at Troia, four stades from the sea. He sacrifices to the Sun who bestowed fresh water upon his band. The altars of the Sun already stood on the site; Dionysius considered them of Trojan architecture.[188] Upon the fulfillment of one prophecy, Aeneas spies the pregnant white sow destined to fulfill another. He follows her for twenty-four stades until she stops on a hilltop. Then, Dionysius reports two versions of a new prophecy. From the woods an invisible god is heard to tell the Trojan to build his city. Or, discouraged by the site's very desolation, Aeneas falls into a sleep in which enters the dream vision of a god like one of his ancestral gods (*theos patrios*). His vision admonishes him to build on the site. Accordingly, Aeneas founded Lavinium, which he named after his local wife. [189] The two accounts reflect the two kinds of known Faunian prophecy. The ordinary mode of Faunian statement relied on disembodied sylvan voices; the unique Faunus of the Grove of Albunea spoke by entering the dream of persons resting upon the hides of slaughtered victims. Surely, the two tales told of Aeneas' foundation incorporated the religious phenomena of Faunus. Further, the *theos patrios* who appeared in Aeneas' dream could have been one of the Penates or the Lares.

In Vergil's telling of the tale, Aeneas (emotionally resembling his wooden statues at Zakynthos and Ambracia) lays himself down to sleep on the bank of the Tiber. While asleep, Aeneas experiences a vision of *deus Tiberinus*, who counsels him on building the city. Upon awakening, Aeneas prays to the *nymphae Laurentes.* Only then does he see the sow, whom he sacrifices on the shore. [190] Vergil's variation from the standard "Laurentine" version can hardly be explained by his ignorance of the Faunian oracle of which he is a chief source.

The god of the Tiber River comes to Aeneas in a dream. Upon awakening, Aeneas sacrifices to the nymphs of Laurentine country. In contrast, the same admonition is made to Aeneas elsewhere and by one of two methods consonant with the oracle of Faunus. Whereas Faunus was not a rivergod, the deity of the Numicus River was subsequently identified with Aeneas or his human and prophetic father Anchises. The Numicus River also harbored nymphs, or at least the one nymph who was purported to be Anna the sister of Dido, or Anna Perenna.[191] The Numician nymphs perhaps otherwise received Aeneas' offering to the Laurentine nymphs mentioned by Vergil. Nymphs were also worshipped at the Aquae Albulae, which belonged to Tibur and perhaps to Albunea, the Tiburtine Sibyl whose name is also that of Faunus' grove.[192] Although no explicit statement confirms it, the shrine of the river Numicus may have been an oracular center attached to the grove of Albunea. In a version that has left only circumstantial traces, Aeneas will have been counselled by the *Pater Numicius* and have sacrificed to the local nymphs. Because of his destined identification with that god, Vergil's Aeneas must experience the dream apparition of another river.

Nowhere does Dionysius revert to the subject of Aphrodite's cult in his discussion of Aeneas in Italy. Nevertheless, the history of Aphrodite can supply a link with Dionysius' earlier account and the development of a cult of Aeneas. From Strabo we know that in the territory of Lavinium and of Ardea were precincts of Aphrodite. Even at that in Lavinian country which all the Latins shared, the Ardeates occupied the priesthood.[193] Latin authors call it by a Greek name, Aphrodisium.[194] Aeneas had brought from Sicily the statue of its deity Venus Frutis.[195] Indeed, these two centers of Aphrodite's cult can be reckoned as ancient signs of the cult of Aphrodite Aineia. Zakynthos boasted a temple of the goddess where the statues of Aphrodite and Aineias stood, and toward which the race of Aphrodite and Aineias was directed. Saguntum, the Spanish town whose beleaguerment marked the start of the second Punic War, was thought to have been named after Zakynthos. Yet Ardea was also considered the metropolis;[196] the Ardeate shrine of Aphrodite must have been presumed to have been dedicated to the Aphrodite of Zakynthos, where Aineias was also worshipped. Aeneas brought the Sicilian Venus Frutis to the Lavinian shrine. Perhaps she was also presumed to have been the Aphrodite Aineia who had an altar on Mt. Elymus. Further, the foot-race of Zakynthos may have paralleled similar meets at the Lavinian Aphrodisium, where all the Latins resorted under Ardeate supervision. In any event, as late as the first century of this era, the shrine(s) still bore a foreign goddess' name, and thus attested the continuing belief in some kind of alien worship.

Another archaeological article shared by Saguntum and Zakynthos, as well as Ardea, must have been the similar cult statue of the goddess. On Zakynthos she and Aineias were carved in wood, and were thought very old on that account. The eastern coastal communities of Spain held comparable statues of Ephesian Artemis, which Massiliotes installed in temples they founded at all their coastal stations. (Indeed, this practice was thought to have inspired the beginnings of Aventine Diana at Rome.)[197] The Hellenic wooden cult statues of eastern Iberia surely contributed to formulation of kinships overreaching Gaul and Italy. The Romans used one such statue to explain the origins of Frutis, with whom Aineias will have been associated.

The cult of Aeneas appears to have emerged from the shrines called Aphrodisia, which had a history as Trojan or Greek foundations. Their Aphrodite can be related to Aphrodite Aineia in the belief in the origin of one cult statue, and in the transmission of *sacra* from Troy to Zakynthos to Ardea to Saguntum. The putative identity of Aphrodite Aineia was reinforced by a Lavinian place called Troia.

When the Latins were exposed to the legend of Aeneas, they conceived divergent stories on the foundation of Lavinium that contained references to the Faunian prophecies. One legend made Aeneas see the dream vision of a *theos patrios*, much as a voice of divine advice spoke from the hearth where Valesius was praying to the Lares Familiares for the health of his children. Ultimately that voice prompted the foundation of the Secular Games, which were dedicated to Nethergods. [198]

The site of the shrine to the Numician deity may be sought in the vicinity of the cult of Faunus and the Lares. Aeneas' appearance in Lavinian cults, first and solely documented by the purported Numician shrine must be traced to the cult of the Aphrodite who dominated two neighboring Aphrodisia. Whatever the goddess' beginnings, her actual cult either suggested that of Aphrodite Aineia or had been adapted to it. Aineas was her cult partner, who was on one occasion revered at or near Albunea, an incubation shrine.

Aeneas Indiges, or Pater Indiges who was reputed to be Aeneas, was one of several traditional names of the god of the Numicus. Although Dionysius knew of an attempt to recognize Anchises as the deity of the Numicus,[199] no positive identification was available from the shrine's inscription, which honored an anonymous god. The fourth traditional identification was that of Jupiter Indiges, who was equated to the dead Aeneas. [200] However, Jupiter substantiates Latin divinity, whereas Aeneas substantiates Trojan divinity only in the company of Aphrodite (Aineia).

Jupiter also represents one of the few native divinities of incubatory oracles, which must carry importance in any discussion of the gods of Tor Tignosa. If Jupiter was the god of the Numicus, the authority of the river god's shrine did not record the identity. Before examining Jupiter Indiges and the Di Indigetes, we can summarize the section on Aeneas Indiges and the god of the Numicus. Our single reliable authority for the actual shrine at the Numicus refuses to vouch for a certain identity of the god. Indeed, he transmits an anonymous *pater theos khthonios* "who watches over the Numicus River's flow." The *pater* is manifest in Pater Indiges and Iuppiter Indiges. Indiges, on all heads, ought to be the Latin for *khthonios.* Since the ancients had no sure idea of the meaning of the Latin word, Dionysius' Greek rendition is no more useful than any of the etymologies retailed in antiquity (see below). Aeneas had once belonged to the Aphrodisia of the vicinity of Lavinium and Ardea. Whoever the deity of the Numicus River, he was a Nethergod. His shrine was a burial mound. The sepulchral aspect invited Latins to put a name to the putative dead, even though no dead man was commemorated on the shrine's tablet. The natural consequence of the urge to name was the dubious application of Aeneas or his sometimes prophetic father, who, so we are told, forecast the son's becoming *immortalis* and *indiges.* [201]

Two very similar "heroes" who also participated in the Trojan War had *heroa* in Italy, where incubation rites took place. On top of Mt. Drion (Garganus), north of Sipontum, Kalkhas' *heroon* admitted petitioners of oracles who offered a black ram. They slept on its hide to receive the prophecy. At the foot of the hill near the sea, and close to a stream of water that cured animals, was situated Podaleirios. Podaleirios boasted Asklepios' paternity, a fact which brings him into a family of incubation demigods. In Podaleirios' *heroon* the petitioner slept on the skins of slain sheep. [202] These oracles resemble Faunus' rites. The curative powers of the stream recall Numa's intention in seeking Faunus' advice. The name *heroon*, without further comment, and the semi-divine nature of the pair, conform to the bare facts of the shrine sometimes attributed to Aeneas. Moreover, the two *heroa* of the Greeks were situated in the country of the Daunii. The people of Ardea were occasionally called Daunii, because their king Turnus had Daunus for father. [203]

Although all three *heroa* were occupied by demigods or deified men in the historical period, the occupants of the *heroa* were imported from the east. It follows that the shrines existed before the importation of the demigods. Little likelihood subsists in the possibility of direct influence or relation between Mt. Drion and the Numicus River. Rather, the nature of such Italic holy places called for structures resembling the *heroon*; the *tumuli* invited the installation or attribution of Greek and Trojan heroes. Since the rites of incubation appear to be Indo-European inheritances of Greeks, Italians, and Gauls, [204] they too attracted identification with Greek ceremonies appropriate to heroes and demigods. Vacillation between Aeneas and Anchises in identifying the Numician god reinforces this notion of the historical development, for Anchises demonstrated prophetic powers on several epic occasions. [205]

The Roman Vestal Virgins were compelled by sacral law to draw water from springs: for their holy uses, it could not pass through pipes. [206] The waters were used for ordinary cleansing or for preparation of sacrificial foodstuffs. However, a water libation to the goddess Vesta had to be drawn from the spring of the Numicus. [207] Beyond this brief notice, no indication of peculiar powers of the Numicus River survives. The curative virtue comparable to that of Podaleirios' stream may have inhered at one time in the Numicus. In any case, the waters were blessed by the presence of their own earthgod. Juturna's nearby spring possessed healing qualities. [208]

Aeneas was thought by some to have been worshipped as a *deus indiges* at the Numicus River. Without the evidence of the Lar Aeneas and the certitude we could derive from an explicit inscription on his purported tomb, we can only assume that a proper cult of Aeneas was known at, or inferred from, the Aphrodisia of Aphrodite Aineia near Lavinium and near Ardea. Both Aphrodisia were supervised by Ardeates who claimed kinship with Zakynthos, where Aphrodite and Aineias had a cult center. Aeneas may have been linked to the Numician shrine because it was situated by the incubation center of Faunus, in which was found Vesuvia's dedication to the Lares. In one version of the legend, Aeneas brought the Lares to Latium and founded Lavinium on the counsel of a voice from the woods, or a dream vision of a deity like his ancestral god. The former admonition resembles the operation of Fauns, and the figure of the dream may have been a Lar. In any case, the two divine activities tend to evoke Faunus and the incubation rites.

8. SOME PRIESTS OF LAVINIUM

Two fragments of a choliambic poem preserve a few precious bits of Lavinian lore: [209]

– – – Numice Lavinas	– – – sacer]dote
– – – v]irecta Pilumni	– – – inae
pon]tifex sacris votum	
– – – c]lara sanguis Aenea	– – – p]risci
– – – m]aximus petitorum	– – – I]ulo
– – – p]rosperetis eventus	
– – –a iura Laurentum.	

The *virecta Pilumni* are found as the *lucus parentis Pilumnus* in the Aeneid, [210] where Pilumnus is the divine maternal grandfather of Aeneas' enemy Turnus. [211] The pontiff was a local priest (see below). Here he seems to invoke the gods who are to bestow success. The verb *prosperetis* recalls the formulae of prayer *uti sitis prosperi*, etc. [212] The "line of Aeneas" also finds mention in Iullus, the Trojan's fabled son and eponymous founder of the Iulii. From this inscription can be inferred that the Lavinian pontiff prayed to the Numicus on behalf of the descendants of Aeneas and Iulus, who were the actual imperial house. Moreover, Lavinian law and custom prevailed (*iura Laurentum*). The noun *petitor* recalls the use of *responsa petere* and *somnia petere* in Vergil's description of Faunus at Albunea, and *veniam petere* by Decius at the *devotio*. [213]

A much later inscription honors a

> [Priscilia]no Maximo c(larissimo)
> v(iro), vati primario, quaestori candidato,
> praetori urbano, pontifici maiori, pontifici
> dei Solis, electo ad legation(em)
> provinciae Asiae, patrono et curatori
> L(aurentium) L(avinatium), sacerdotales
> et populus. [214]

The priests and people of Lavinium chose to glorify a senator of Rome who held priestly office among them. Surely the *vates primarius*, the only official *vates* known to me, was the man in charge of divination at the grove of Albunea, where, like Latinus and Numa, he could learn Faunus' wishes. [215] The first pontificate was perhaps that held by the author of the choliambs. The second pontificate of the Sun-god oversaw the cult and shrine on the coast where Aeneas had prayed when he first landed. Maximus' election to an embassy sent to Asia seems as important as his Roman magistracies and Lavinian priesthoods. Since Asia was the homeland of Aeneas and his Penates, Maximus and his fellow envoys may have gone there on religious business out of ancestral interests. Dionysius reports that the wandering Trojans reaffirmed their kinship with those peoples where shrines of Aphrodite (Aineia) were located. International custom called for treaties of *syngeneia*, such as that apparently mentioned in the fragmentary letter of a Roman magistrate to the people of Ilium, or that preserved on the senate decree of Lanuvium. [216] The third and last epigraphic document demonstrates the existence of Lavinian diplomatic instruments.

A famous inscription, wherein Claudius' inverted digamma was written for *v*, provides several important items in the history of the Lavinian priesthoods that bear on the gods of Albunea:

> Sp(urius) Turranius L(uci) f(ilius) Sp(uri)
> n(epos) L(uci) pron(epos), Fab(ia)
> (tribu), Proculus Gellianus, praef(ectus)
> fabrum II, praif(ectus) curatorum
> alvei Tiberis, praif(ectus) pro pr(aetore)
> i(ure) d(icundo) in urbe Lavinio,
> pater patratus populi Laurentis
> foederis ex libris Sibullinis percutiendi
> cum p(opulo) R(omano), sacrorum
> principiorum p(opuli) R(omani)
> Quri(tium) nominisque Latini, quai
> apud Laurentis coluntur, flam(en) Dialis,
> flam(en) Martial(is), salius praisul, augur,
> pont(ifex), praif(ectus) coh(ortis)
> Gaitul(orum), tr(ibunus) mil(itum)
> leg(ionis) X. locus d(atus) d(ecreto)
> d(ecurionum). [217]

A *pater patratus* served in a college of Fetials, the priests in charge of treaties and other diplomatic acts. This priesthood might have made treaties of *cognatio* or *syngeneia*. Turranius' function was the constant renewal of a treaty with Rome. The renewal substantiated the Lavinian autonomy. [218] The renewal was worked in accordance with Sibylline Books. Surely these books were Lavinian. Their existence reinforces the tie between Rome and Lavinium around 350 B.C., when the Secular Games were instituted, at the instigation of the Roman Sibylline Books, for the majesty of the Latin name. The Sibylline Books of Lavinium perhaps reflect the existence of a defunct local Sibyl that bore the name Albunea, as was argued above, and were kept by the *vates primarius*. Although the title of Turranius' office in charge of the holy foundations of the Roman people and Latin name seems lost, it must have been another Lavinian priesthood. Its supervision would have extended to the Penates as well as any Latin deities. The Latin deities would have included the goddess of the Aphrodisium, where all the Latins worshipped, and all deities worshipped according to the holy canon of Alba, the town founded by Iullus and destined to be the metropolis of many Latin communities. Among the latter deities we know only the name of Vediovis, whom the Julii revered (see below).

In these three documents are seen several aspects of Lavinian cult, which can be clarified in terms of the religion of the grove of Albunea. The *vates primarius* is a likely officer to oversee incubation and oracles at Albunea and to maintain the local Sibylline Books. The pontificate noted in all three inscriptions could have watched over the cult of Aeneas inferred from the fragmentary choliambs, which allude to Laurentine law. The Lavinians could have maintained a treaty of kinship with ancestral peoples in Asia, for they had a Fetial simply for renewing their treaty with Rome. At Lavinium, another priesthood preserved the ancestral rites and cults of the Roman people and the Latin name.

Neighboring Lanuvium maintained a treaty of kinship with Sicilian Centuripe. Ardea maintained kinship ties with Iberian Saguntum, a town that sometimes claimed descent from Zakynthos. Besides the putative etymological link, there existed a similarity between the cult of Aphrodite Aineia and Aineias on Zakynthos and the Latian Aphrodisia in the Laurentine and Ardeate territory. All the Latins acknowledged the religious superiority of Lavinium because there the foundations of Latin cult were laid and kept, and because in the territory was a federal shrine of Aphrodite (Aineia), who had come from Sicily. It follows that the Aphrodite in the similar Ardeate precinct came from Zakynthos. Since the Lavinians traced their ancestry to Troy, whose very name was preserved on their shore, they seem to have honored an elected ambassador to Asia, because he represented them or the Romans at the Asiatic metropolis. Such apparently were the traditions, not the facts.

For a fuller appreciation of the deities of Albunea, we must now turn to some Roman gods and their peculiar cults, to the Di Indigetes, to Vediovis of Bovillae and Rome, and to Faunus, whose Latin cult we have only partly touched and whose Gaulish counterpart came to Rome from the north.

9. DI INDIGETES

The vague plurality of the Di Indigetes can be examined from three viewpoints. First, there survive one actual dedication on stone and a prayer embedded in an author, to which can be added a similar prayer. These pieces convey to us some idea of how the Latins understood the Indigetes. Second, some authors, mostly poets, composed invocations including the gods *indigetes*. Last, learned opinion on the significance of the word *indiges* attempted explanation of deities whose character was already blurred in antiquity. After examining the evidence, I shall propose alternative etymologies of the word, linguistically unimpeachable and religiously consonant with the newly uncovered evidence from Tor Tignosa. Since the word *indiges* must have had a linguistic life of its own as an adjective, it is susceptible of analysis. Such is not the case with all divine names. For instance, if *lar* ever meant anyone but *lar*, we shall probably never know who it was.

In the discussion of Neuna Fata has been included Livy's prayer of self-sacrifice (*devotio*), which purports to go back to the fourth century. The deities the self-sacrifer invoked were Janus, Jupiter, Mars pater, Quirinus, Bellona, Lares, Divi Novensiles, Di Indigetes, Divi of the enemy, and Di Manes. The *devotio* was made to these last gods, who were the dead, and to the Earth, Tellus. In the prayer are met the idioms *veniam petere*, which recalls *petitorum* in the Lavinian choliambs, and *vim victoriam prosperetis*, which recalls *prosperetis eventus* in the same inscribed holy poem. From the invocation we see that the Di Indigetes are not identical with the Lares or the Di Manes. The latter are surely the dead ancestors of the self-sacrificer and his army. All other deities appear to be public gods. Moreover, the Di Indigetes are associated with Jupiter, who was the father *indiges* of the Numicus in one interpretation, and with the Lares. [219] Since the deities invoked are adapted to a context of warfare (Mars, Quirinus, Bellona, and perhaps Janus) and of death (Di Manes and Tellus), the formulary prayer for the *devotio* of a city offers an analogue.

Macrobius incorporated into his dialogue a lengthy disquisition on the summons of alien gods and the cursing of a city. In the latter case he quotes from Sammonicus Serenus who in his turn cites the two prayers extracted from the Furius who wrote in the latter half of the second century B.C. [220] The following text is the prayer spoken by Scipio Aemilianus at Carthage in 146:

> "Dis pater, Veiovis, Manes, sive vos quo alio nomine fas est nominare, ut omnes illam urbem Carthaginem exercitumque quem ego me sentio dicere fuga formidine terrore compleatis quique adversum legiones exercitumque nostrum arma telaque ferent, uti vos eum exercitum, eos hostes eosque homines, urbes agrosque eorum et qui in his locis regionibusque agris urbibusque habitant abducatis. lumine supero privetis exercitumque hostium urbes agrosque eorum quos me sentio dicere, uti vos ıeas urbes agrosque capita aetatesque eorum devotas consecratasque habeatis ollis legibus quibus quandoque sunt maxime hostes devoti. eosque ego vicarios pro me fide magistratuque meo pro populo Romano exercitibus legionibusque nostris do· devoveo, ut me meamque fidem imperiumque legiones exercitumque nostrum qui in his rebus gerundis sunt bene salvos siritis esse. si haec ita faxitis ut ego sciam sentiam intellegamque, tunc quisquis votum hoc faxit ubiubi faxit, recte factum esto ovibus atris tribus. Tellus mater teque Iuppiter obtestor." cum "Tellurem" dicit (*sc.* imperator), manibus terram tangit. cum "Iovem" dicit, manus ad caelum tollit. cum votum recipere dicit, manibus pectus tangit.

> "Father Dis, Veiovis, Manes, or you under whatever name it is meet and just to name you, may all of you fill with flight, fear and dread that city of Carthage and army which I feel I am designating and those men who bear arms and missiles against our legions and army; and may you lead away that army, those foemen, those men, their cities, their fields and those who live in these places, quarters, fields and cities; may you rob of the light above the army of the foemen, their cities and fields of the men whom I feel I am designating; may you consider cursed and condemned those cities, fields, animals [221] and lives in accordance with those rules by which everytime foemen are especially cursed and consigned. Upon my faith and upon my magistracy on behalf of the Roman infantry, [222] our army and legions, I give, curse and consign them as substitutes that you gods allow me and my faith and our command, legions and army of men who are participating in this endeavor to be safe and sound. If you should do this in such a way as I know, as I feel and as I understand, then whoever should have made this vow wherever he should have made it, let it be done with three black sheep. I call on thee to bear witness, Earth, and on thee, Jupiter." When he says "Earth," he touches earth with his hands; when he says "Jupiter." he raises his hands to heaven; when he says that he assumes the vow, he touches his chest with his hands.

Since the commander consigns the enemy to the Netherworld of earth, he invokes Dis, Veiovis, and the Manes, who also are the recipients of the three black sheep. The Manes are also met in the individual *devotio* of self-sacrifice, which ends with consignment to the Di Manes and Earth. In cursing Carthage and the Carthaginians, the general makes Jupiter and Tellus, Heaven and Earth, witness the act. Of course, consignment to the latter means death. Heaven must deny the "light from above" (*lumen superum*).

From what is thought to have been the sometime territory of the village where Gaius Marius was born comes the single dedication to the Di Indigetes. It is dated to 4 B.C.:

> C(aio) Calvisio L(ucio) Passieno co(n)s(ulibus), M(arcus) Menius M(arci) f(ilius) Rufus [s]a[c](erdos) VI, L(ucius) Vibidius L(uci) f(ilius) sac(erdos) II Iovi Atrat(o) et Dis Indigetibu[s] cum aedicl[a] et base [statuae] d(e)i et porticu d(e) s(uo) l(ibentes).

The attention of students of Roman religion is fastened on the Jupiter who received worship with the Indigetes. In the *Corpus*, Mommsen printed *Aer[i]s et*, although he doubted his own interpretation of the copy from which he worked because the letters given as E and T were practically vertical strokes susceptible of being seen as I, E, L, or T. His conjectured epithet is never used of Jupiter, is not appropriate to an association with the Di Indigetes, and above all is abnormal for being the genitive of a noun that is Greek in origin. Not satisfied with Mommsen's reading A. Giannetti recently visited the almost inaccessible mountain-top, over 1700 meters high, where the inscription was carved on living rock evidently cut to resemble a throne. He has made a new reading of AIRAI ET, which Degrassi would emend to AEREA ET because Giannetti allowed that the second and fifth letter could also be either E or T. Degrassi, however, could not understand his *aerae*, an unknown vocable, and so imported the opinions of others which are neither appropriate nor clarifying. [223] Rather, the second alternative, ATRAT ET, must be followed.

Since the Di Indigetes belong to the realm of curses and the Netherworld, Jupiter Atrat. should somehow be brought into relation with such a cult. The abbreviation *atrat.* will thus be considered as a derivative of the adjective for "black," *ater*, used to describe sacrificial victims and certain unlucky days in the liturgical calendar. Further, from Festus' *Epitome* we learn of a kind of black deity: furvum bovem, id est nigrum, immolabant A[e]terno. Not only are black victims required in certain instances of Roman sacrifice, but also the use of black or white vessels is specified for a certain religious occasion at Iguvium. [224]

Although we can be confident that the god Aternus has a name derived from the same root as Jupiter's cognomen Atrat., we must seek an explanation of the abbreviation *atrat.* for *atratus* or Atratinus. The latter word serves as surname to the earliest Sempronii and was revived by a Sempronius at the very end of the republic. The name suggests a toponym, but no other evidence on the origin of the Sempronii survives. [225] There is a remote possibility that Jupiter took his epithet from the Sempronian clan or from its toponymous cognomen describing the clan's origin.

The well-attested word *atratus* comes from a hypothetical verb *atrare* "to blacken," and means "clothed in black." It resembles *albatus, candidatus,* and *purpuratus*. The adjective *caeruleatus* is once used to describe a naked man made up to impersonate a sea-god. Accordingly, Jupiter could have been garbed in black or covered with black: either his statue had a black garment draped upon it, or the sculptured garment was painted black, if *atratus* were to mean "clothed in black." Another explanation calls for the fleshly parts of the god's image to have been painted black as the impersonator of the sea-god was smeared dark blue. The penis of the statues of the god Priapus was painted red. Evidently the entire statue or the face of Jupiter Capitolinus was painted with red lead paint (*minium*) every fifth year. Otherwise, the statue was garbed as a triumphant general. Although no evidence of a black-painted statue survives, *atramentum*, a word for black paint also derived from **atrare*, is known to have been applied to paintings. [226] Since all statues, whether of stone or clay, were painted in antiquity, a black pigment must have been used wherever appropriate to a sculptured representation. No doubt a black Jupiter was as unusual as a Bearded Fortuna and Hercules, Hercules with a Locket, or Fortuna Covered with Birdlime. [227]

Marcus and Quintus Cicero knew of a River Atratus that had once run with blood. [228] Their personal knowledge would suggest that the river flowed in the vicinity of Arpinum, their hometown, in whose territory the shrine of Black Jupiter and the Di Indigetes was perhaps situated. Their hilltop shrine is sufficiently distant both from Casamari and Arpino to allow speculation that it was situated in the territory of Sora, a town notorious for its religiosity. [229] Indeed, one of the few fragments of Valerius of Sora touches upon the nature of Jupiter. [230] Arpinum and Sora had once been occupied by Volscians. L. Sempronius Atratinus was buried on a site between Formiae and Caieta, also originally Volscian country. [231] This reviver of the house of the Atratini perhaps reckoned his ancestral homeland to have lain in the settlements of Volscians. From the viewpoint of religious phenomena, Jupiter Atratus and the Di Indigetes can be related to Dis or Apollo Soranus, who was worshipped in a peculiar fashion atop Mt. Soracte. [232] Whatever the location of the River Atratus, its name attests a meaning of the verbal adjective that connotes neither clothing nor painting. Unless *Atratus* is analyzed as having the ethnic suffix -*at*- in the wrong declension (cf. *Arpinates*), the river bore the name Blackened, suitable for a stream susceptible of a prodigious flow of blood. The black (*ater*) precinct of Lucerian Deives still flows with black waters (see below, sect. 10).

Black or Blackened Jupiter took his epithet from one of three situations: 1) his entire statue or its bodily parts were painted black; or 2) his statue was draped with an actual black garment; or 3) only the carved garment of his statue was painted black, to represent his black garb. The epithet recalls both the aspect of his representation and the name of the god Aternus, who received dark victims. Like victims were also accorded Jupiter Summanus and Vediovis, a different manifestation of Jupiter. Later we shall meet these deities. That Black Jupiter was a god of the Netherworld seems assured by his association with the Di Indigetes, who are known in a cult setting only by this inscription. Moreover, this kind of cult on a desolate hilltop finds its analogue in the cult on Mt. Soracte. The proper reading and interpretation of Jupiter's epithet reinforces whatever else we know about the Indigetes from Latin authors.

On the inscription we find that the priests of the several gods were elected annually, and that one was in office for a sixth term and the other for a second. Menius and Vibidius offered a statue implicit in the word *basis* or explicit as restored by Degrassi. It was very probably a statue of the Black Jupiter, who, with the Di Indigetes, was installed in the shrine (*aedicla*), which had a colonnade porch. Except for the annual office of the double priesthood, no peculiarity of cult emerges from the text. What is somewhat peculiar is the shrine's foundation cut from the rock on which the commemorative inscription was carved.

Now the poets enter the discussion. Most of these passages pretend to be prayers. First, Vergil's *Georgics* 1.498-501:

> di patrii Indigetes et Romule Vestaque mater,
> quae Tuscum Tiberim et Romana Palatia servas,
> hunc saltem everso iuvenem succurrere saeclo
> ne prohibete. satis iam pridem sanguine nostro
> Laomedonteae luimus periuria Troiae.

The adjective *patrius*, which is met in Dionysius' Greek translation of the Numician dedication, refers to the Trojan ancestry in the last quoted line. In his last work Vergil was to hail Aeneas Indiges. Others called the Numician deity Pater Indiges or Jupiter Indiges. The adjective *patrius* yields two interpretations. It may bear the force of the honorific salutation of the gods *pater*, or signify "ancestral" and, thus, "native" or "tutelary." Dionysius of Halicarnassus employs the comparable Greek *patrios* to render the dedicatory inscription on the *heroon* to the Numicus river and, in a different sense, to describe the *theos patrios* who appeared in Aeneas' dream after the pig chase.

Ovid, who also believed that Aeneas became the divine Indiges (*M.* 14.581-608), closes his *Metamorphoses* (15.861-70) with echoes of Vergil's *Georgics* and with new material:

> di, precor, Aeneae comites, quibus ensis et ignis
> cesserunt, dique Indigetes, genitorque Quirine
> Urbis, et invicti genitor Gradive Quirini,
> Vestaque Caesareos inter sacrata Penates,
> et cum Caesarea tu, Phoebe domestice, Vesta,
> quique tenes altus Tarpeias Iuppiter arces,
> quosque alios vati fas appellare piumque est:
> tarda sit illa dies et nostro serior aevo,
> qua caput Augustum, quem temperat, orbe relicto
> accedat caelo faveatque precantibus absens!

Aeneas' divine companions can be no other than the Penates and other ancestral gods installed in Lavinium. Quirinus must be the Romulus of the *Georgics* and the god of the Livian prayer of self-sacrifice, just as *Gradivus genitor* is the *Mars pater* of the same prayer. Vesta occurs also in the *Georgics*. Jupiter occurs in the Livian prayer of self-sacrifice, as well as in the dedication of Casamari.

The obscure Lucan yields the next mention of the Indigetes (*Bellum Civile* 1.556-60):

> Indigetes flevisse deos, urbisque laborem

> testatos sudore Lares, delapsaque templis
> dona suis, dirasque diem foedasse volucres
> accipimus, silvisque feras sub nocte relictis
> audaces media posuisse cubilia Roma.

The poet writes of the awful portents witnessed at the outbreak of the Caesarian civil war, with which we can compare Tibullus 2.5.77. Lucan seems to say that statues of the Indigetes were reported weeping, and those of the Lares sweating. Such prodigies were far from uncommon. Lucan and the inscriptions of Casamari alone allude to the existence of figures of the Indigetes. Here the Indigetes are coupled with the Lares, an association also met in the Livian prayer.

Silius Italicus' *Punica* contains the greatest attention to the Indigetes. The nymph Anna is said to have a shrine near that of Aeneas, *Indigetis castis contermina lucis.*[233] On the next occasion Silius lists the gods who favor the Romans at war with Carthage (*Pun.* 9.290-95):

> hinc Mavors, hinc Gradivum comitatus Apollo
> et domitor tumidi pugnat maris; hinc Venus amens,
> hinc Vesta et, captae stimulatus caede Sagunti,
> Amphitryoniades, pariter veneranda Cybele
> Indigetesque dei Faunusque satorque Quirinus
> alternusque animae mutato Castore Pollux.

Apollo belongs to the mythology and counts not at all. Mars has been invoked twice before along with Quirinus. Vesta is found in Vergil and Ovid. Hercules' presence is explained by Silius. Castor and Pollux are Lavinian and are the Greek or Trojan counterparts of the Penates. Cybele, too, came from Troy. Venus represents the mother of Aeneas, the goddess of the Aphrodisia in the territories of Lavinium and Ardea. And, finally, Faunus appears with the Indigetes. Faunus is also Lavinian. At *Punica* 5.626, Silius had written of the *litora Fauni Appenninicolae*, and he resumes at 8. 356-59:

> Faunigenae socio bella invasere Sicano
> sacra manus Rutuli, servant qui Daunia regna
> Laurentique domo gaudent et fonte Numici,
> quos Castrum Phrygibusque gravis quondam Ardea misit.

The "sons of Faunus" comprise the peoples of Lavinium and of Ardea, which controls Castrum—that is, the Castrum of Inuus, an epithet of Faunus. The last use of the gods is met in an oath of Scipio (Africanus), who first calls on Capitoline Jupiter and Juno and then (*Pun.* 10.436-39):

> Indigetesque Dei, sponte en per numina vestra
> perque caput, nullo levius mihi numine, patris
> magnanimi iuro: numquam Lavinia regna
> linquam nec linqui patiar, dum vita manebit.

There can be little doubt that Silius connected the Di Indigetes with Lavinium and its gods, beside whom he numbered the Faunus who was a founder of the Lavinian and Rutulian (Ardeate) peoples.

In late antiquity the Dii Indigetes remain archetypal protectors of the State. Symmachus speaks of asking peace from the ancestral gods who are the Indigetes. [234] Claudian joins them to Venus, Mars, Vesta, Cybele, and Juno. [235]

Without a Roman context and within the Latin poetic tradition, an anonymous translator, quoted in Macrobius' *Commentary on the Dream of Scipio*, rendered Hesiod into

> Indigetes divi fato summo Iovis hi sunt:
> quondam homines, modo cum superis humana tuentes,
> largi ac munifici, ius regum nunc quoque nacti.

> τοὶ μὲν δαίμονες εἰσι Διὸς μεγάλου διὰ βουλὰς
> ἐσθλοί, ἐπιχθόνιοι, φύλακες θνητῶν ἀνθρώπων
> πλουτοδόται· καὶ τοῦτο γέρας βασιλήιον ἔσχον. [236]

Both Macrobius' discussion and the Hesiodic sentiment attest the sense of *daimones* and *indigetes* as deified men, for which the Latin had reserved *divus* at least in cases of imperial apotheoses. However, learned opinion among the Roman erudite made *indiges* a word for deified man.

Since Varro believed that Aeneas assumed the title *indiges* upon his death and deification, the word *indiges* could signify a deified man in learned circles, without having a foundation in religious realities. Varro's erudite influence very probably bears the ultimate responsibility for Arnobius' definition of Indigetes, *qui in flumen repunt et in alveis Numici cum ranis et pisculis degunt.* [237] Moreover, the previous examination of Arnobius' collection of learned opinion on the Di Novensiles revealed that somehow he and others confused them with the Indigetes in calling the Novensiles deified men, among whom are listed Hercules, Aesculapius, Romulus, Liber, and Aeneas. [238]

Learned opinion derived from antiquity has been the source of considerable misconceptions on the Indigetes and on Roman religion in general. The great expounder of the field, Georg Wissowa, divided the Roman gods into the native gods who were the Indigetes and the foreign, imported gods, who were the Novensedes. His pervasive influence has left lasting impressions on any serious student who resorts to his handbook, even though since Wissowa's time much ink has been spilt over the etymon of *indiges*, which cannot equal *indigena*.

In the epitome of Festus' lexicon the entry on Indigetes seems to suggest an etymology from *dico*, because they are gods "whose names may not be published." [239] In other words, the Indigetes must be anonymous because their true names are ineffable. The Bern scholiast contains the fullest linguistic treatment of the word. [240] Like the Lares and Di Consentes, the Di Indigetes have no individual names, or their individual names are not known. This suggestion approximates the lexicographer's. According to Nigidius, they are named because they lack nothing, *nullius rei indigent.* The same suggestion is offered by Servius (on *Aen.* 12.794), who cites Lucretius as his authority. All comments include the etymology *in diis agentes,* "living with the gods," when deified men is urged as the meaning. [241] Ordinarily the commentators distinguish the *di patrii* from the *Di Indigetes* when they are found side by side in the *Georgics.* However, Servius (on *Aen.* 12.794) reports a body of opinion wherein they are identical, and the latter take their name from the verb *indigetare,* "to invoke." The Bern scholiast alone reports an identity with the Greek *emmykhos* "night-dweller," "sleeper-in," etc., which is also a Greek epithet of Hades. None of the learned etymologies suggested in antiquity deserves acceptance. Only the last item conveys the cult of the gods, for they were invoked in moments of grim, deathdealing activity.

By the poets the Indigetes are reckoned among the gods of the state, who should protect the Roman people in moments of crisis; or, in Lucan's epic, the portentous behavior of their statues foretold the doom. Silius Italicus sets them with Faunus, a deity not otherwise appropriate in a catalogue of deities assisting Romans at war. Faunus' incubation shrine at Albunea lay in the vicinity of the shrine of the god of the Numicus, called variously Aeneas, *pater,* and Jupiter Indiges. Unattributed opinion makes the Indigetes *ennukh(i)oi.* The Indiges of the Numicus River was thought to be Aeneas. In the formula of the self-sacrifice, the Lares and Indigetes are invoked. On the eve of the Caesarian civil war, by their images, the Indigetes and the Lares yield similar portents, which Lucan reports together. In a section leading into the development of Etruscan religious lore, Censorinus refers to the uncivilized Italy where nymphs and *Fauni indigenae* occupy the woods. [242]

If Faunus was an *indiges* as well as a partner of the Indigetes, the nature of the Indigetes is immediately ascertained. In a previous section Inuus, another name of Faunus, was subjected to linguistic analysis and yielded the etymon *in + eo,* "entering." Since the Indigetes are associated with Faunus, it is just as likely that their name once clearly indicated a similar notion. Accordingly, we are dealing with a compound of *ind-* (= *in-*) and either *ag-* or *agy-,* "doing in" or "saying in," as we suggested *novensedes* might be analyzed as the "nine sitting in."

Faunus and his oracular ilk, including Aesculapius, also reckoned a deified man or *indiges,* entered into dreams, were active in dreams and places, and spoke into the heads of consultants. Also *incubus* suggests the communion on the side of the human petitioner. The verbal noun *indiges, -etis* is analogous to *praestes, sispes,* etc.

Against a compound with the root of *aio* is *adagium,* where the *a* is not reduced. However, *prodigium* perhaps comes from *agy-.* The Roman warning deity of Aius Locutius or Loquens supports the analysis. (see below). A *deus indiges* would be a "god who speaks within" if this analysis of the compound is accepted. On the other hand, a compound of the root of *ago* is without fault. A *deus indiges* would be a "god who does within," if this analysis of the compound is accepted.

Both compounds can be linguistically supported by Iguvine *ahtu:*

Iuvie unu erietu sakre pelsanu fetu, arviu ustentu, puni fetu, taçez pesnimu ařepe arves. pune purtiius, unu suřu pesutru fetu Tikamne Iuvie; kapiře peřu preve fetu. ape purtiius suřu, erus tetu. enu kumaltu, kumate pesnimu. Ahtu Iuvip uve peraknem peřaem fetu; arviu ustentu puni fetu. Ahtu Marti abrunu perakne fetu; arviu ustetu; fasiu preseçete ařveitu; peřae fetu; puni fetu; tra ekvine fetu. Açetus perakne fetu.

"Offer to Jovius one ram from the temple property, to be buried. Present grain offerings,

sacrifice with mead and pray silently with (offerings of) fat and grain. When you have
made the presentation, present one pig-*persondro* to Dicamnus Jovius. Make a mound in
a separate place for the bowl. When you have presented the pig-*persondro* distribute the
erus. Then grind (the grain) and pray with the ground (grain). To Ahtus Jupiter sacrifice
a young boar brought from away. Present grain-offerings and sacrifice with mead. To
Ahtus Mars sacrifice a young boar brought from away. Present grain-offerings, add
spelt-cakes to the parts cut off, sacrifice the victim upon the ground, and sacrifice with
mead. Sacrifice across the (Via) Equina, Sacrifice a victim brought from away, to the
Ancites."[243]

These four sacrifices took place when the Atiedian Brothers, grouped for viewing
the auspices, took the auspices. Although both Poultney and Ernout agree the *ahtu*
can represent the root *ag-* or *agy-* or neither, the presence of the word with Mars and
Jupiter, both oracular gods, in conjunction with the auspices, and the presence of
Dicamnus Jovius, "the speaker of Jupiter," appears to ensure an oracular notion
inherent in *ahtu.* [244] Poultney admits uncertainty in the name *Açetus*, which is
rendered by Ancites, gods of Vestinian Furfo known from *CIL* IX 3515. Perhaps
they, too, are **aientes*, but their name is surely not the Iguvine generic term for
Ahtus Jupiter and Ahtus Mars, since they received distinct sacrifice. Relating the
Açetus to another root, Ernout likens them to the Di Indigetes. [245] The collocation
of *Tikamne*, the two *Ahtu*, and *Açetu* with Jupiter and Mars seems indisputable
evidence of oracular terms, however *Ahtu* and *Açetu* are analyzed.

On balance, the word *indiges* seems better treated as a compound of *ind-* and
agy-, "speaking within." This derivation fully explains the nature of the deity of
Tor Tignosa. Faunus' incubation cult, of which we shall say more below, presupposed a god who spoke to petitioners, to Latinus and to Numa as well as to
Aeneas in a quandary over the site of his city. The god of the river Numicus had the
title *indiges.* Although that river does not stand in the record as oracular, Vergil
makes Tiberinus appear in Aeneas' dream on the founding of his city, whereas
Dionysius tells us of a disembodied voice or a dream vision of a *patrios theos* in the
same circumstances. Likewise, a voice of the Lar Familiaris addressed Valesius on
how to find a cure for his ailing children, and thus impelled him toward foundation
of the Secular Games at the Tarentum in the Campus Martius.

The Greek words *entheos* and *enthousiasmos* convey the notion that the god
and the man have somehow become one. Even if its precise semantic structure
eludes us, the first linguistic element of the Greek words is cognate with Latin *indo*
(*endo*). Among the Romans were found not a few unusual and faceless divine
corporations. The *penates* "belonged to the larder" (*penu*), the *consentes* "kept
company" (*con* + *sum*), the *manes* were "good," and finally the *novensedes* constituted the "nine who sit in." Further search for identity of this kind of god seems
hopeless. If the *novensedes* were at some time identical with the Nine Fates or
Speakers, the Speakers spoke while occupying the place of incubation. The *indigetes*, on the other hand, were inner voices or workers that filled dreams or passed
bodiless through nature's dark and covered places. As a divine group, the Indigetes
could have embraced Jupiter, Faunus, and certain river (or spring) gods.

The Indigetes originated as oracles haunting woods and dreams. If they were dead ancestors, they were dead ancestors who offered praeternatural counsel. Such divinity belongs to the ground, the earth, the Netherworld. Accordingly Dionysius used *khthonios* of the Numician god. They were invoked at the self-sacrifice in battle; they were worshipped with Black Jupiter. While the Lares sweated on the eve of civil war, the Indigetes wept.

Presumably, they had statues somewhere in Rome. In any event, the Roman consuls and pontiffs performed annual sacrifice to the *indiges* of the Numicus. [246]

At Rome four divinities are related to oracular incubation: Jupiter, Aesculapius, Faunus, and Vediovis. The Julian clan held the last god in special esteem. Since the Julii also considered Aeneas their ancestor through his son Ascanius-Iullus, who founded Alba Longa, their family shrine at Bovillae merits examination before we pass on to Rome. [247]

10. VEDIOVIS OF THE JULIAN CLAN AT BOVILLAE
AND DEIVES OF THE MAGIAN CLAN NEAR LUCERIA

The god Vediovis or Veiovis is young Jupiter or an anti-Jupiter or non-Jupiter. [248] At the cursing of Carthage, Aemilianus invoked Dis, Vediovis, and the Manes. In such company Vediovis did not attract many offerings. From first to last Vediovis was what Jupiter was not, but he was sometimes mistaken for Jupiter. At the Bovillae was found an altar with this inscription: *Vediovei patrei genteiles Iuliei. Vedi[ov]ei aara leege Albana dicata.*[249]

Bovillae, lying 10 kilometers distant from Zolforata, which can be taken for the center of the incubation cult, received the rites of fallen Alba which Iullus had founded (see Figure 9). The Lavinians maintained a priesthood that oversaw the *sacra principia* of the Roman people and the Latin name, which is to say the so-called Alban peoples. The Julian clan kept a family shrine at Bovillae. Although he never mentions Vediovis, Tacitus speaks of the place.

In 17 A.D., Tiberius dedicated a structure for ceremonial goods (*sacrarium*) on behalf of the Julian Clan and statues for Divus Augustus at Bovillae. These dedications are reported with the dedication of a Roman arch commemorating recovery of the standards lost by Varus, and of a temple to Fors Fortuna at the park Caesar bequeathed to the people while Germanicus triumphed over the Cherusci, Chatti, and Angrivarii. [250]

Upon Poppaea's delivery in 63 A.D., Nero decreed thanksgivings, a temple to fertility, a contest like the Actian games, golden statues of Fortunae on the Capitoline couch, and circus games for the Julian clan at Bovillae and for the Claudian and Domitian clans at Antium where Nero had been born and where Poppaea had given birth. [251] The newborn was celebrated at a shrine whose religion could be traced back to Iullus of Lavinium. This religion provided a link between Lavinium and Rome. On both occasions of Julio-Claudian observances at Bovillae, the emperor also honored the goddess Fortuna.

On the model of the Titii Sodales, which were commonly mistaken for priests of King Titus Tatius, Tiberius founded the Sodales Augustales to maintain worship of the Divus Augustus. [252] His statues were apparently installed at Bovillae after institution of the priesthood, in which members of the Julio-Claudian house served.

On the Roman capitol the *ara gentis Iuliae* stood in close proximity to statues of Liber Pater, Jupiter Africus, and Numa Pompilius, and to Germanicus' war-trophies as well as Romulus' hut. [253] It was a considerable pile, for it had a podium. Perhaps it resembled a marbled precinct like that of the Altar of Peace. More important than the hut where their ancestor Romulus had lived was the temple of Vediovis, which stood in the same complex behind the Tabularium (see below). If Tiberius first built the altar of the Gens Julia—a conjecture consonant with his institution of the Sodales Augustales and dedication of his adoptive father's images at Bovillae—he cannot have ignored the fact of his family's devotion to Vediovis, whose temple had stood in the vicinity for two centuries. Moreover, the house of Titus Tatius, whose sodales were Tiberius' model, once stood where temples of Juno Moneta and Vediovis rose. [254]

Nero felt that joy and thanks at the birth of his daughter could be fitly acknowledged by circus games. The occasion required races of some sort. Although Vediovis' survival at the clan's precinct at Bovillae cannot be certified, the games are significant to the appreciation of the cults of some old Jupiters that can be related to incubation or incubation gods. Vediovis himself is not directly connected to the kind of oracle met at Albunea. Rather, Vediovis supplies the link between Rome and Lavinium through Alban cult, and underscores the character of Julian cult. At Rome, Vediovis was quite clearly brought together with incubation gods. However, Roman Vediovis was especially cultivated by a single patrician, Furius Purpurio, under quite peculiar circumstances.

More than superficially comparable is the newly discovered cult of Deives. L. Gasperini recently published an inscription found in the Fogiano (Gargano), presumably in the territory of the ancient Latin colony of Luceria, and dated by him to *ca.* 200 B.C.: Gentiles Magiei Sancto Deiveti facere.[255] The nominative Magiei (rather than -*es*) suggests a later date than the end of the third century. However, the uncontracted form of Dis, now firmly established, seems to support a second-century date.

The *gentiles* represent the Magian clan, as the same noun on the Bovillan dedication to Vediovis represents the Julian clan. The Magii constituted a romanized family of Oscan origins. [256] Together the Magii and Terentii corporately set up a *diuvila* at Capua. [257]

The epithet *sanctus*, which precedes Deives, was especially applied to the god Silvanus. [258] It conforms to other supposed aspects of Deives' cult, which Gasperini rightly brings into the account of the new find. Luceria evidently took its name from sacred groves (*luci*). A chance epigraphic survival affirms the connection. [259] The grove, implicit in the name of Luceria and derivable from the application of the word *sanctus* to Deives, finds confirmation in the explicit descriptions of a notoriously dangerous shrine of Dis known to have been situated in the general vicinity of the findsite of Deives' dedication. [260]

At the navel of Italy in the land of the Hirpinians stood the black grove in the mountain valley of Ampsancti. There sulphuric waters ran so thick that animal victims for Dis or Mephitis were asphyxiated rather than killed by the normal religious attendants. The surrounding terrain was pocked with natural vents from which vapors rose, and at least one cave. Even human beings died upon entering the temple of Mephitis, the sulphurous goddess. The shrine itself was anciently likened to that of the god of Mt. Soracte and to the Plutonia in Asia. [261]

This Hirpinian descent to the Underworld bore the name Ampsancti, recalling *sanctus Deives*, who is cited merely by the name Dis in the ancient accounts. The ethnic Hirpini surely derive their name from the Osco-Sabellian word *hirpus* "wolf," which was the name given to the practitioners of the cult of Dis or Apollo Soranus on Mt. Soracte. [262] The toponymous Soranus reminds us of the town Sora, to whose territory may have belonged the cult shared by Black Jupiter and the Di Indigetes. The Hirpinian grove, the cave, the exhalations of Mephitis, and the direct contact with the Underworld parallel the circumstances of the incubation cult of Faunus. [263] Asiatic Plutonia reinforces the now-certain translation of Dis/Deives from the Greek Plouton. Further, the sulphuric vapors in Ampsancti accord with the unusual and geologically unverifiable description of Roman Tarentum, where Dis and Proserpina were venerated at the Secular Games. [264]

The whole picture of the Hirpinian shrine of Dis and Mephitis resembles the several aspects of the Lavinian cult of Faunus, the general cult of Silvanus, and the wolfmen's cult of the god of Mt. Soracte. The new dedication to Deives renders untenable any attempt to deprive a clan (*gentiles*) of its Underworld deity. [265] Dis and Vediovis are associated by the Romans in cursing. [266] In our subsequent pursuit of the origins of the Roman Vediovis, certain goatish divinities of Gaulish influence will clarify the relationship and character of incubation and the oracular gods Faunus, Vediovis, Jupiter, and Silvanus, as well as the goddesses normally called Fauna and Silvana. Underworld gods not only possessed malevolent powers over human life, but also promoted human health, human fertility, and, through prophecy, human knowledge.

11. SOME JUPITERS OF THE ROMAN CAPITOL

Invocation of the highest god of the Roman state can be expected in all manner of prayers and sacrifices. Because of his great powers and his ubiquity, Jupiter's name does not surprise us when it is so often met. At Tor Tignosa Jupiter left no trace. Near the shrine of Faunus, Jupiter was sometimes recognized as the *indiges* of the Numician flow. The prayer of self-immolation contains a bare invocation of the simple Jupiter. In the other kind of *devotio*, that of a city, Jupiter and Tellus, Heaven and Earth, are called to witness in a prayer to Dis, Vediovis, and the Manes. Our unique epigraphical record of the Di Indigetes conjoins them with a Black Jupiter who is equally unique. Whereas Jupiter ruled the sky, and his name and many sacrifices commemorated a celestial cult of natural phenomena, Jupiter also drew unto himself several divine functions that arose from his capacity to deny what he was supposed to bestow. At the cursing of Carthage, the commander raised his hands to heaven when Jupiter bore witness to a ceremony in which the invoked deities were asked to cut off the light from above in regard to the accursed Carthaginians. The gods Dis, Vediovis, and the Manes presided over a realm without heavenly light and there received the Carthaginians at the cordial request of the Roman commander. Jupiter's suzerainty was founded upon twin bases. He controlled the heavenly light and expelled from that light. His hellish counterpart was played by Vediovis. Real confusion not only in the names but also in the functions occurs in the beliefs and cults of Vediovis and Jupiter. The Romans often could not distinguish the two gods. Their resemblance is not accidental, and suggests to us caution in drawing a hard and clear line between them. Some important differences are manifest. Jupiter enjoyed the oldest of the Roman temples. Vediovis' character did not invite gifts of comparable grandeur.

Vediovis, a reflex of Jupiter, arrived on the Capitol relatively late in Roman history, and was preceded by two Jupiters who far outrank him.

In a long disquisition on the legal terms of the patron and client, Dionysius speaks of Romulus' law in which a violator was *sacer* to Zeus Katakhthonios, just as anyone subject to a death penalty was consigned to the *theoi katakhthonioi*. [267] The word *sacer* is assured by the Law of the Twelve Tables. The Nether Zeus is thought to be Dis. [268] It could equally well be Vediovis who was invoked with Dis and the Manes at Carthage. Be that as it may, Jupiter was the Romans' principal god of oaths. Ancient swearing involved terrible consequences.

Jupiter Feretrius had a Capitoline temple in which Romulus displayed his *spolia opima*, the armor of a slain general, taken by his own hand. After the founder, Cornelius Cossus next deposited the spoils from the Veientine king Lars Tolumnius. The third and last set was put there by Marcus Claudius Marcellus, who despoiled the Insubrian chief Viridomarus. Also in this temple was a flintstone used for striking (*ferire*) treaties. [269] According to a legend retailed by Ennius in his *Annals*, after building the temple to Jupiter Feretrius, Romulus spread out oiled (goat) skins upon which he gave games of boxing and racing. Since the games given by Romulus could not have been recorded, Ennius actually had in mind the games commemorating a rebuilding or refurbishing by Marcellus. The coin minted by P. Cornelius Lentulus Marcellinus around 38 B.C. represents Marcellus holding the *spolia opima* in front of Feretrius' small temple. His coin would seem to commemorate the Marcellan temple (see Figures 11 and 12). [270] Degrassi places the occasion of the Capitoline or Tarpeian Games on 15 October, and does not refute or corroborate previous suggestions that these games for Jupiter Feretrius, apparently called *Ludi Tarpeii*, were the Capitoline Games. [271]

The games are curious. We have met circus games at Bovillae on the occasion of the birth of a princess. Moreover, on Zakynthos, a race of Aphrodite Aineia and Aineias had its goal at the goddess' temple where there were wooden statues of the mother and child. The oiled animal skins forcefully remind us of the incubation at Albunea, where the petitioner lay down to sleep on the raw skins of the victims.

Although Jupiter Feretrius cannot be shown to have served an incubation cult, his greater neighbor Jupiter Optimus Maximus did serve such a cult. If we were inclined to credit embellished legend, we might suppose that Jupiter was thought to appear in dreams so early as 491 B.C. However, the tale that attributes at least two appearances to a Roman, through whom he requested of the senate changes in his games, must be dated to the year 279 B.C.[272]

Plautus' *Curculio* was set in Epidaurus, whence Rome's cult of Aesculapius had been brought perhaps as much as a century before the play's composition. In spite of the Peloponnesian *mise-en-scène*, the playwright makes his players speak of incubation at the temple of Jupiter on the Capitol, where perjured parties wished to "lie in."[273] Plautus' humor perhaps extends to the conduct of P. Cornelius Scipio, who was to conquer Hannibal.[274] From his early years Scipio attended Jupiter Capitolinus before dawn's light, and from him sought counsel. Even in the field Scipio enjoyed divine conversation.[275] Upon his death the Cornelian family had the right of fetching for their funerals his statue, permanently housed in the chapel of Jupiter Optimus Maximus.[276] Apparently Scipio's statue kept after life the watch he had kept in life, a watch of incubation. The very presence of the statue lent to the Cornelian clan such eminence as might draw the envy of the Julian clan when the latter revived its fortunes, political and financial. The statue of Jupiter Africus, which is reported on two military diplomas,[277] was also on the Capitol near the altar of the Julian Clan. Scipios twice conquered Africa. Centuries later, the emperor Nero sought the advice of the Capitoline gods on his departure for Achaea to enthrall the Greeks with his theatrical performances.[278]

Around 278 B.C., a statue of Jupiter Capitolinus was struck by lightning and its head toppled into the Tiber. The god then took the name Summanus, because the statue had stood atop the temple.[279] Yet Varro believed T. Tatius had raised an altar to Summanus.[280] A temple was built to Summanus at the Circus Maximus, which was struck by lightning in 197 B.C.[281] Some ancient authorities derived the name from *sub + man-* meaning nocturnal lightning. This etymology is rejected while the control of lightning is preserved.[282] Given insistence upon the time before dawn when Scipio visited the chapel of Jupiter Capitolinus, the rejected derivation could well be correct: the lightning bolt will have reinforced a folk tale. In any event, *summanus* can indeed refer to the hour of Jupiter's appearance; compare the Greek word *emmykhoi*, equated with the Indigetes.[283]

A quickened interest in the visions of Capitolinus and in Summanus' well-being is witnessed shortly after the importation of Aesculapius, the incubation god *par excellence*. Examination of the cults of Aesculapius, Vediovis, Faunus, and Jupiter Jurarius (another Jupiter of oaths) on Tiber Island is deferred until Vediovis of the Capitol is scrutinized. Discussion of similar Gaulish cults and the victory of Claudius Marcellus will put into focus the nature of the cult of Jupiter Feretrius.

Jupiter himself appeared in dreams so that he might alter his own cult. This same Capitolinus imparted advice to Scipio, who came before dawn to commune with him. After his death the statue of Scipio was housed in his chapel. An offshoot of Capitoline Jupiter's cult was installed at the Circus Maximus (so that this Summanus might be party to the games?). The very name *summanus* can refer to the hour of the night when he was customarily consulted. Jupiter Feretrius was honored with games of such unusual circumstances that his function is guaranteeing treaties and in keeping the extraordinary spoils might be expanded to include incubation cult.

12. VEDIOVIS ON THE CAPITOL AND ARX

According to the body of ancient evidence, three temples to Vediovis stood in Rome, of which two were raised on the Capitol and Arx. Prose and poetic authorities alike confuse Vediovis with Jupiter, from whom he is derived. As a result, the common practice of emendation of texts is unnecessary, especially because the inscribed calendars identify the god in question by the name Vediovis. All three temples were vowed by L. Furius Purpurio, descendant of M. Furius Camillus. The clan claimed superiority in leading Romans against Gauls. The prayer of *devotio*, spoken over Carthage and addressed to Dis, Vediovis, and the Manes, was written down by a Furius who is very probably L. Philus, consul of 136 B.C. and friend of the Scipio who uttered the prayer. [284]   A concise summary of Purpurio's career draws our attention to the Gauls and Ligurians of Northern Italy.

L. Furius Purpurio, military tribune in 210, served with M. Claudius Marcellus, glorious victor over the Gauls in 222. In 200 praetor Purpurio fought Gauls and Ligurians. In 196, consul with M. Claudius Marcellus, son of his former commander, Purpurio fought Gauls and Ligurians. In 189 and 188, Purpurio served on a ten-man commission settling peace terms in Asia at the direction of Manlius Vulso; among the commission's charges was the arrangement with the Gaulish chieftains of Asia. In 183, Purpurio is last known on an embassy to Gauls from across the Alps who had entered the peninsula; he and his two colleagues persuaded withdrawal. [285] Purpurio, expert in fighting against, and treating with, Gauls and Ligurians, is presumed to have learned from the elder Marcellus, whose career against Gauls will be discussed below.

At 35.41.8 (192 B.C.), Livy writes: *aedes duae Iovis eo anno Capitolio dedicatae sunt; voverat L. Furius Purpurio praetor Gallico bello unam, alteram consul. dedicavit Q. Marcius Ralla duumvir.* Vediovis was Purpurio's savior in both Gallic wars, and earned a temple for each. The more famous, and partly surviving, Capitoline temple to Vediovis was situated on the former "asylum" *inter duo lucos* between the Arx and Capitol. Later it was to back on the Tabularium. Its birthday was 7 March. [286]

Aulus Gellius argues the character of Jupiter and Vediovis at length. In the temple between the Arx and Capitol, Vediovis' statue held arrows. Some think him the same as Apollo. A she-goat is offered to the god *ritu humano*, and on that account its figure is set beside the statue of the god. Gellius' verb tenses make clear that he describes a temple and cult of his own day. [287]   The *ritus humanus* is a matter of no little dispute and is discussed below. Ovid describes the same temple but refers to lightning bolts, not arrows. He introduces the she-goat in connection with the story of baby Zeus on Crete. [288] The she-goat has further ramifications on the Tiber Island and is discussed in that connection. For the moment, suffice it to recall the oiled goatskins laid down for the Tarpeian Games of Jupiter Feretrius on the Capitol.

In 1939 this temple was uncovered and the mutilated cult statue of a youthful god was found. [289] To these representations are added three coins of republican date. Around 103, L. Caesius minted a coin with Vediovis and thunderbolt on the obverse, backed by two Lares (see Figures 13 & 14). [290] The conjunction of the Lares with Vediovis recalls the invocation of Lares in the human *devotio* and of Vediovis in the *devotio* of Carthage. Further, the human *devotio* reminds us of the *ritus humanus*, in which the she-goat is sacrificed to Vediovis. On Caesius' coin the two Lares hold spears and a pet dog stands between them. According to Plutarch the Lares wore dogskins. [291] About twenty years later, another coin with Vediovis and Jupiter was minted. On it the young god hurls a bolt. [292] It was coined by three moneyers at roughly the same time as the two other, far more interesting, coins of Vediovis.

Behind Vediovis on a coin of Manius Fonteius were carved a winged infant Jupiter astride a goat, the two caps of the Dioscuri, and beneath the goat a thyrsus with fillets (see Figures 15 & 16). [293] If we accept Sydenham's date of 84 B.C., this coin was apparently minted ten years before the Gaulish command of Marcus Fonteius, whose knowledge of Gaulish custom was reflected in Cicero's speech on his behalf alluding to the Gaul's fondness for human sacrifice. [294] The iconography of this coin is well elucidated by Cook. The thyrsus reflects a common Greek confusion of Zeus and Dionysos. Vediovis' head on the coin's obverse is wreathed in bay, Apollo's greenery. The bay contributed to confusion with Apollo. Cook calls the figure on the goat Jupiter Crescens, and recognizes the winged infant as Cupid's figure. More likely he is the suckling Jupiter the child connected with the oracular cult of Fortuna Primigenia of Praeneste, and also known at Anxur (Tarracina). Jupiter Liber may have begun as a child, for at Furfo in Sabina this god is associated with the Genius Iovis, Jupiter's procreative force.

The she-goat originates in the Cretan cult. [295] Moreover, Ovid purposely introduces the story of the Cretan baby Jupiter and the milk-giving goat into his story of Vediovis on the Capitol. The iconography of this coin is thoroughly Greek. While Fonteius' kinsman, Marcus Fonteius, is best known for his service in Gaul, Furius Purpurio vowed his temples to Vediovis during wars with Gauls and Ligurians.

The last republican coin bearing Vediovis who hurls a thunderbolt was minted by the famous tribune and annalist, Gaius Licinius Macer, who figures Minerva in a quadriga on the reverse. This coin is dated approximately to the period in which Fonteius and the three moneyers issued their coins of Vediovis. [296] Indeed, Macer's office of moneyer must be dated before his plebeian tribuneship in 73 B.C. Otherwise, all three coins dated to the later Eighties can reflect the operations in Gaul, in which Marcus Fonteius finally participated. These began with the year 77 B.C. Moreover, Gaulish belligerence must have preceded Fonteius' campaigns. Veneration of Vediovis in this era suggests a revival of Roman interest in the cult of a Gaulish deity.

Before quitting the Capitol, a last glance at another monument by which military diplomas were permanently posted. On a single diploma: *in Capitolio post Ligures.* [297] Who were these Ligurians? Whatever their shape, their likenesses must have been set up when the Ligurians constituted a free people at war with the Romans. It is not beyond the realm of possibility that these Ligurians were reared when Furius Purpurio's Capitoline temple to Vediovis was erected.

The Arx is the peak next to the Capitol. It is but a stone's throw away, for a slight declivity intervenes. Pliny discoursing on the long life of wooden products:

> non et simulacrum Veiovis in Arce e cupresso durat a condita ⟨urbe⟩ DCLXI anno dicatum? . . . . et in Hispania Sagunti templum Dianae a Zacyntho advectae cum conditoribus annis CC ante excidium Troiae, ut auctor est Bocchus. [298]

> "Is not there also a likeness of Veiovis on the Arx, though made of cypress, which has lasted until today since its dedication in 93 B.C.? . . . . In Spanish Saguntum [cedar beams] were transported to the temple of Diana from Zakynthos with the founders 200 years before the fall of Troy, as Bocchus writes."

This highly compressed statement on the fabulous products of man's carving includes the only mention of Vediovis on the Arx. The subsequent mention of the beams of the temple of Diana at Saguntum is especially interesting because the larger treatment in which we meet these supporting details covers the marvelous statue and beams of Diana of Ephesus. The Saguntine temple appears to have been constructed with material like that of her temple at Ephesus. Zakynthian origin of the temple and cult should be rejected in favor of the real Massiliote inspiration. However, the same antique artisan tradition embraced the wooden statues of Aphrodite Aineia and Aineias at her Zakynthian temple, where the course of the two gods was run. [299]

Vediovis' cypress likeness was installed in a temple on the Arx, which must be the other temple to Vediovis imprecisely mentioned by Livy as *in Capitolio*. The statue was given ninety-nine years after the dedication of the temple. Perhaps it was a centennial offering. The Capitoline temple of Vediovis had been dedicated on 7 March and kept that anniversary. A single calendar (the Fasti Venusini) records a festival for Vediovis on 21 May. [300] This third day for Vediovis (after 1 January on the Island and 7 March on the Capitol) assures the existence of a third temple implicit in the Livian notices.

Not so incidentally, 21 May also held the third of four feasts called *agonia* or *agonalia* in the Roman liturgical calendar. No certain identification of the deities involved in the four *agonalia* survives to us. However the third, annual observance seems to have been kept for Vediovis, the Vediovis of the Arx. The fourth occasion, on 11 December, has the notation *Agon(alia) Ind(igeti)*. This usual resolution of *ind.* is sometimes related to Sol Indiges. The abbreviation could signify *indigetibus* and embrace Vediovis, who was venerated on 21 May, and Faunus, who traditionally received sacrifice on 5 December. [301] Although there are divine candidates available for these festivals on 9 January and 17 March, it is noteworthy that Vediovis of the Island had a feast on 1 January, and Vediovis of the Capitol on 7 March— that is, in the other months in which they observed Agonalia.

The contradiction in Livy's report of the two dedications in 192 now is more apparent than real. Pliny's exactness in naming the Arx as the location of the god's cypress statue supports Livy's statement. The existence of a third feast of Vediovis, on 21 May, confirms it. The Agonalia for the Indigetes or Indiges on 11 December squares with a similar rite for Vediovis on 21 May.

Larger questions on the impetus to Vediovis' installation on the Capitol and Arx, to subsequent offering of the wooden statue, and to minting his image, await the treatment of the gods of Tiber Island and the Gaulish rites and gods. Indeed, very little sense can be made of Roman Vediovis without scrutiny of the circumstances of his installation in temples during warfare with the Gauls and Ligurians. If the Romans chose to dedicate one of his three temples on the May *agonalia* because he somehow resembled the *indiges* or *indigetes* of the December *agonalia*, Vediovis can be counted among the *indigetes*. This hint squares with other circumstances of Vediovis.

13. VEDIOVIS ON THE ISLAND

In 293 a pestilence struck the Romans, who frantically sought relief to the extent of bringing Asklepios in serpentine guise to Rome, where he quit the ship at the Island. There, around 290, a temple was dedicated to him on 1 January. [302] Aesculapius, as the Romans called him, brought from Epidaurus belief in curative incubation. [303] The god's cult was closely linked, in popular opinion if not in fact, with Apollo, who was to lend Vediovis some of his attire.

Aesculapius' importation took place in an era of quickened Greek influence. In 296 the two Ogulnii brothers, already innovators in Roman religion, served as curule aediles. From fine monies exacted of usurers, they improved the Capitol with bronze threshholds, a silver service for the three tables in Jupiter's chapel, and upon the Capitoline temple a statue of the god in a four-horse car. From the same fund, they set at the Ruminal fig-tree a statue-group of the she-wolf giving suck to Romulus and Remus. [304] The Jupiter raised to the temple's height was destined to be Jupiter Summanus (see sect. 11).

At either end of the Comitium the Romans erected statues of Alcibiades and Pythagoras, in response to Delphic Apollo's oracle. The god had ordered statues of the wisest and bravest Greeks in the most trafficked place in Rome. The precise date and occasion of the oracle of Asklepios' father are not given, but since it took place during a Samnite War, it will have occurred shortly after 291, when Livy's narrative quits us. [305]

In 200 Furius Purpurio faced the Gaulish foe. In the heat of battle he vowed a temple to Vediovis if he were to put them to rout. Six years later another man,

C. Servilius, dedicated this temple of Vediovis on the Island, which Purpurio himself had contracted in his consulship of 196 B.C. [306] This brings to three the number of temples vowed to Vediovis by Purpurio, who dedicated none of them. The dedicant in 194 was the C. Servilius who as consul in 203 advanced into Gaul to free his father from Gaulish captivity. [307] The architectural historian Vitruvius (3.2.3.) assigns one temple of Jupiter and Faunus on the Tiber Island to the type of temple called prostyle. Jupiter can be Vediovis, although a Jupiter is known on the Island (see below), and Vitruvius knows the name Vediovis for the Capitoline god. [308] Moreover, in treating Aesculapius Ovid writes:

> Iuppiter in parte est, cepit locus unus utrumque
> iunctaque sunt magno templa nepotis avo. [309]

Ovid means that Aesculapius and Jupiter share either the same precinct or the same Island.

A mosaic dedication in a pavement under S. Giovanni Calibita on the Island reads: C(aius) Volcaci(us) C(ai) f(ilius) har(uspex) de stipe Iovi Iurario [– – m]onimentom. [310] The *stips* belonged to Aesculapius' treasure and was accumulated by public donation. [311] Jupiter of Oaths recalls the curious Tarpeian Games for Jupiter Feretrius, another god of oaths, and Plautus' banter in the *Curculio* on incubation of perjured men in the shrine of Jupiter of the Capitol, which he introduces in conversation on Epidauran Aesculapius. That Jupiter Jurarius and the Jupiter who shared a temple with Faunus and a precinct with Aesculapius are one and the same cannot be proved. We can be sure that Vediovis had a temple on the Island, and that it was dedicated on the same day of the year as that of Aesculapius, a few years short of a century later. [312]

A greater likelihood remains that Vediovis, who was often mistaken for Jupiter, had a single structure with Faunus, since in cult the deities resemble each other, and the gods Vediovis and Faunus were brought to the Island within years of each other and dedicated within days, whereas Jupiter Jurarius is not named by any author and accordingly has little fame.

In sum, the calendars certify the presence of Vediovis on the Island, where his temple kept an anniversary on 1 January, also Aesculapius' anniversary. Livy, Ovid, and Vitruvius speak of Jupiter on the Island; their "Jupiter" is assumed to be Vediovis. Aesculapius brought the Greek mode of incubation to Rome, where he occupied the Island for almost a century without divine company. This foreign god of incubation attracted to the Island other gods of incubation, of whom one was installed through foreign influence.

14. FAUNUS

On the Tiber Island a chapel to Faunus was built. In 196, Gnaeus Domitius Ahenobarbus and Gaius Scribonius Curio, the plebeian aediles, brought charges against many *pecuarii*. From the fine monies imposed on three of them the aediles built the temple. Two years later Domitius as urban praetor dedicated it.[313] This was the same year in which C. Servilius dedicated the Island temple of Vediovis. Faunus' temple was dedicated on 13 February,[314] forty-one days after Vediovis'. The sources of the aediles' funds would indicate some relation to the God on the part of the *pecuarii*, who will have been grazers or sellers of cattle.

The dedication of a temple to Vediovis and to Faunus in the same season suggests that Vitruvius' one prostyle temple of Jupiter and Faunus comprised back-to-back or side-by-side *cellae* of Vediovis and Faunus. Besides the famous and longstanding Capitoline temple of three contiguous chapels, the Romans had a recent precedent of a temple of two chapels, erected at a certain distance in time, in the temple of Honor and Virtus. In 234, Fabius Maximus had built a temple to Honor after his Ligurian command. Twelve years later, M. Claudius Marcellus vowed a temple to Honor and Virtus upon his victory over the Gauls. He renewed the vow at Syracuse. In 208 he rededicated the temple of Honor that Fabius had built 26 years before. However, the pontiffs intervened, and Marcellus was compelled to quit his fraud. In 205 his son dedicated a refurbished *cella* of Honor and a new *cella* of Virtus.[315] The pontiffs' decision rested on the need for a *cella* for each god who was to receive a victim. Vitruvius' *aedes* of Jupiter and Faunus must refer to a single building with two *cellae*, and, since it was prostyle, the chapels might have backed onto each other. However we surmise its aspects, the temple must have had two *cellae*, one for each deity. Moreover, like Honor and Virtus, the two deities should have borne some close relation to each other. This relation is best understood in interpreting Vitruvius' *Iovis* as *Vediovis*.

The year in which Domitius and Scribonius fined the *pecuarii* and started the temple of Faunus was that when L. Furius Purpurio was consul in northern Italy and himself vowed his third temple to Vediovis. Domitius was destined to serve his consulship against the Gaulish Boii in 192/1 B.C.[316] We should like to know whether either Domitius or Scribonius had served with Purpurio in 200, or with any other commander of legions facing the Gauls. No other temple to Faunus ever stood in Rome. Although the aediles were fulfilling an urban function, the religious temper of the era, the religious setting on the Island, and the likely combination of Vediovis and Faunus all tend to an interpretation of Faunus as the god of incubation, who was being linked to the Gauls while he was associated with Vediovis.

The annual feast of Faunus fell on 5 December. The dedication of his temple on 13 February nearly coincides with the Lupercalia, which many ancients believed was a feast of Faunus or Inuus.[317] The goatskin (*pellis caprina*) was used by the Luperci to purify the throng and the Palatine.[318] The goatskin recalls the sacrifices at the incubation center of Albunea and the Tarpeian Games for Jupiter Feretrius. Faunus, of course, was a goat god.

When Ennius rejected the Saturnian meter sung by Fauns and *vates* for the hexameter, he implied that the Fauns served as inspiring songsters.[319] In the Ennian tradition, Fronto calls the *Fauni vaticinantium incitatores*[320] In the first year of the republic, Valerius' army, camped by the *silva Arsia*, heard a great voice which the soldiers thought was Silvanus'. It bespoke the Roman victory. [321] Dionysius uses the Latin name Faunus in telling the same story of the voice of this *phasma* or *daimon*. [322] Faunus is joined to Picus Martius (his ancestor or father) in prophesying for Numa Pompilius in an instance not associated with that same king's incubation at Albunea; the site was the shrine of Jupiter Elicius in the Aventine grove. [323] In the Servian comment on Vergil's *nemora indigenae Fauni*, the student learns that *indigenae* means *autokhthones*, demigods, heroes, mere men, and *scelerati*. Moreover, in quoting the Varronian etymology of Faunus from *fari*, the commentator tells us that Fauni are Fatui if they speak divine matter *per stuporem*. [324] A few lines before, the same commentator gives Varro's view that Faunus was a deified man peculiar to the Romans. [325] In effect, Varro asserted that Faunus was an *indiges*.

Horace tells us of a ceremony for Faunus at the end of winter, which included a sacrifice of lamb or kid in a wood. [326] This festival would have fallen nearer 13 February, when Faunus' temple was dedicated on the Island, than the other Horatian festival of Faunus on 5 December. [327] At the outset of spring, so advises the bucolic poet Calpurnius Siculus:

> tum caespite vivo
> pone focum geniumque loci Faunumque Laresque
> salso farre voca; tepidos tunc hostia cultros
> imbuat: hac etiam, dum vivit, ovilia lustra.[328]

> "Then set up a hearth of living sod and summon Faunus and Lares and the deity of the place with an offering of salted meal. Then let the victim dye the knife with its warm blood: here, too, purify the sheepfold while it still lives."

At Albunea Faunus' incubation oracle contained an offering to the Lares. Nearby there was the shrine of Indiges. The plurality of Indigetes, who were involved with the Lares and other gods at the self-sacrifice, appears to have included Faunus. The same poet wrote an entire eclogue of Faunus' sylvan shrine, where the god himself left a godlike song, carved on a holy tree, in which he prophesied the destiny of Rome. [329]

All the settings of the Faunian prophecies or oracles recall Cicero's ideal legislation: "Let them have groves and seats of the Lares." [330]

In 194 Faunus received his one and only shrine at Rome, which was located on the Island. His assignment to the Island joined him to the Greek incubation god Aesculapius and the Latin Nethergod Vediovis. The immediate impetus was Gaulish. Nevertheless, Faunus belonged with his own kind. His oracular powers were attested at the grove Albunea, by reports of his utterances from woods, by his carved prophecies, and by Ennius' treatment of Fauns and *vates*. Although Fauns became the property of poets, they originated in folkbelief. Faunus was himself an *indiges*. The shrine at Tor Tignosa could have extended even to the *heroon* of the *indiges* of the Numicus River. This *indiges* was occasionally considered Aeneas, an ancestor of the Albano-Roman Julii. The patrician family kept a center for clan religion at Bovillae, where they worshipped Vediovis. In Rome, Faunus has a chapel to himself only in conjunction with Vediovis. Both deities are found only in the ambience of incubation shrines on the Capitol or Island. By Vediovis' temple on the Capitol stood the altar of the Julian clan, and on the Island the deified Julius was honored with a statue (Tac. *Hist.* 1.86). Caesar, too, had defeated Gauls. Finally, both deities received their temples, while the Romans prosecuted an extended war against the Gauls and Ligurians across the Po River.

15. VERGIL'S FOURTH ECLOGUE

The most famous poem in all Latin literature seems to attract minds fevered with Cumaean prophecy and Christian messianism. Vergil's fourth eclogue on the birth of the Child opens with unmistakable reference to planned Secular Games (4-5: ultima Cumaei venit iam carminis aetas; magnus ab integro saeclorum nascitur ordo), after announcing a song of woods worthy of a consul. The subsequent omission of the woods leads the reader to suspect the poet intended *silvae* for *silva* "matter." Upon proclamation of the return of the Golden Age, Vergil calls upon Lucina to assist the child aborning, for Apollo already rules. Both deities received sacrifice at the Secular Games. [331] Gaius Asinius Pollio is addressed as consul of the year 40, when the beauty of the era shall commence and the "great months" shall start. Under his leadership, the Child shall assume divine life, look upon heroes associated with gods (*divi*), and shall rule the calmed world with ancestral virtue. Later this Pollio witnessed the senate decree authorizing Augustus' presentation of the Secular Games in 17 B.C. His son, Gallus, whom some believe to be the Child of this eclogue, was a participating quindecemvir in 17 B.C. [332]

Upon a mythological address to the Child himself, the poet resumes (46-47)

> "talia saecla" suis dixerunt "currite" fusis
> concordes stabili fatorum numine Parcas.

No doubt, these Parcae are the Moerae of the Secular Games. [333] "Approach the highest offices! Soon will come the fullness of time, dear son of the gods, Jupiter's greatest growth. Look upon all creation enjoying the fruits of the coming age. May life and breath stay with me to that moment when I can speak your deeds." Cajoling a smile from the Child, "Begin, little child. No god will invite to table or goddess to bed this child who has not smiled at his mother."

Who was this son of gods, this great growth (*incrementum*) of Jupiter? He ushers in the new age. For all his godliness he shall do deeds worth Vergil's attention. Since the last Secular Games had been given in 146 and the chance for needed games in 46 was lost, the next available year was 36, in a putative cycle of 110 years (probably not discovered). Yet Vergil wrote of the dawn of the new age in terms such as to suggest his acquaintance with the rites of the games he could never have seen.

A Sibylline poem can be no clearer than the Sibylline Books of Destiny. Was Vergil just practicing with an eye toward a commission to write a *carmen saecu-*

lare? Was there a real child? Was he divine or human? Candidates abound.[334] Was he the son of Jupiter? The nourishment of Jupiter?

Vediovis, *parvus Iovis.*[335] Baby Jupiter, child Jupiter, Jupiter not great.[336] The Julian clan worshipped him at Bovillae. When Poppaea Sabina brought forth a newborn babe, Nero held circus games at the clan's cult center at Bovillae after promising a temple to Fertility. The eclogue was composed when Pollio's consulship was destined and not yet entered. Gaius Julius Caesar Octavianus had no wife at the moment. His children belonged to the future. But on 1 January, the New Year's day, the birthday of the temples of Aesculapius and of Vediovis on the Island, in the 712th year of the city, Octavian became the son of god, thanks to senatorial decrees that acknowledged the elder Caesar's divinity and made his birthday a public holiday.[337] And Vergil wrote (15-17):

> ille deum vitam accipiet divisque videbit
> permixtos heroas et ipse videbitur illis,
> pacatumque reget patriis virtutibus orbem.

In the Golden Age to come many goats will bring their full udders to the child, or so Vergil prophesies. It was a safe prophecy. Who would ever blame him? The Mantuan poet witnessed the resurrection of the divine clan of Father Vediovis.

Vediovis was the anti-Jove, invoked with Dis and the Manes when cities were to be cursed. His underworld realm embraced powers of birth, life, and death. Vediovis was fitly hailed in terms of the new *saeculum*, which the Romans welcomed with games for Dis and Proserpina and with sacrifice to the Moerae and Ilithyiae.

The measure of Vergil's Sibylline success can be taken in counting the millions of sacrifices to the Lares Augusti and Genii Caesarum. Vergil lived to speak the deeds of Iullus' father; he never wrote of Vediovis' line. Yet over fifty years after the eclogue the people of Narbo in Gaul voted an altar to the *numen* of Augustus, whom *saeculi felicitas orbi terrarum rectorem edidit.* Besides other feast days, the priests were to observe 1 January with a gift of incense and wine to placate his Divine Will.[338]

At Rome his clan's altar was laid on the Capitol near the temple of Vediovis, perhaps by a dutiful Tiberius instituting the Sodales Augustales. For neighbors the same altar also enjoyed the hut of Romulus (another ancestor!), the statue of king Numa Pompilius, and the trophies of Germanicus.

Finally, in this section which has touched on the ruler cult, we are brought to the Belvedere altar made for some compital shrine of the Lares Augusti. On the still unexplained side Aeneas stands beside a now-mutilated man, bearded and holding an open scroll. At their feet are the white sow and her piglets (see Figure 10). Behind Aeneas is a tree. Mrs. Ryberg says the seated figure with scroll is a *vates.*[339] Simon argues that he is Apollo.[340] Yet he is bearded. Indeed, he is the author of the voice, or the ancestral god, who spoke to Aeneas after he chased the pig to the future site of Lavinium. Is this not Faunus, Latinus' father and Lavinia's grandfather, unrolling a *liber fatalis*?

Vergil's fourth eclogue strikes the first note of many a song for the new age under the new divinity of Caesar, father of his country and of Octavian. The poet alludes to the clan's patron deity Vediovis, Child Jupiter. The poet had little by way of a cult tradition for Vediovis, but adapted the material of the Secular Games which were required by the epoch. The principal male deity of the games had his altar beneath the ground of the Tarentum. He was Dis. Dis, Vediovis, and the Manes were invoked at the cursing of cities. Late antiquity thought Dis and Vediovis identical. [341] By his adaptation, Vergil muted the gloominess of both cults, the cult of Vediovis and of Dis, and elevated them to the heights of personal praise in the frame of Caesar's deification by official act on 1 January 42. The man is dead. Long live the god! The epoch bore the seeds of more war and again more war. The poem was cast in Sibylline phrases, the right tone for the times. Varro had recently published his research on the ten Sibyls among his *Roman Antiquities of Divine Matters.* [342] The entire piece fits the genre of Sibylline prophecy and fulfilled an undoubted purpose, the bewilderment of its audience.

16. CAPRINA GALLA

There survives from the Island a tablet which today commemorates a dedication detached from the object offered. It is dated to the republican era, without further precision:

> L(ucius) Rutilius L(uci) l(ibertus) Artemido(rus),
> A(ulus) Carvilius L(uci) l(ibertus) Diodorus,
> P(ublius) Sulpicius Q(uinti) l(ibertus) Philocom(us),
> mag(istri) conl(egi) Caprina(m) Galla(m)
> ex d(ecreto) d(ecurionum) [f]ac(iundam) coeraver(unt)[343]

The nature of this organization whose three officers make the offerings in the vicinity of Aesculapius' precinct is not immediately manifest. Liebnam had the good sense to suspect Gaulish goatherds who were attached to a cult of Pan. [344] Besnier perversely sees no relation to the Faunus whose shrine was joined to that of Jupiter or Vediovis. [345] The resolution into *caprina(riorum) Gallo(rum)* requires adduction of the word *caprinar(ius)* recorded on a Christian tombstone of 545 A.D.,[346] and the correction of a letter in the second word. To these attempts can be added interpretation of *caprina galla* as an ablative of place where or instrumental ablative in sacrifice, or a genitive/dative Caprina(e) Galla(e) that is rare but not unknown. The ablative of place would be paralleled by these toponyms: a lacu Gallines, Vicus Longus ab statua Planci, V. Longus aquilae, V. capitis Africae, busta Gallica, and the simpler Vicus Tuscus, V. Africus. If this is assumed to be a toponym, the *caprina galla* must be connected with some Island cult, as is also the case of the interpretation *(sacra) facere caprina galla.* This latter ablative presupposes *caprina* for *capra,* the ordinary word for goat (see below). The likelihood of recording a sacrifice of a mere goat is remote indeed. The construction of a genitive makes the organization devotees of the *caprina galla,* which might not have had any significant ties to the Island's cults. The dative after the word *magister* or *collegium* is not unusual, and can often submit to a construction of the indirect object with *faciundum*, since that gerundive sometimes has a subtended noun object. Finally, there exists the easiest interpretation from the viewpoint of what such inscriptions as these record and of what was the commonest Latin rendition. Accordingly, the text printed here says that Rutilius, Carvilius, and Sulpicius, masters of their associations, have overseen the erection of a (statue of) Caprina Galla in accord with a decree of their counsellors. [347]

Who or what was Caprina Galla? The Gaulish herds and flocks were famous, and were cultivated in northern Italy. [348] *Caprina* means "goatish." However, it can be a substantive analogically formed after *gallina* "the Gaulish fowl, hen." Or it can mean goat-goddess. In this case one can adduce *deus Caprio* of the Treveri. [349] Also, Epona, the Gauls' horse-goddess, stands as a perfect parallel in animal divinities. The second element *galla* can mean Gaulish or Woman Gaul: goatish female Gaul or Gaulish goat-goddess. Moreover, these several interpretations amount to about the same kind of deity.

From 200 to 192 B.C., four temples were built in Rome that are to be related directly to the Gaulish or Ligurian wars of northern Italy. Vediovis' cult statue on the Capitol was given a goat statue as a companion, because that animal was offered to him *humano ritu.* On one of the coins of Vediovis the baby Jupiter is transported by a goat. [350] Besides a shrine of Vediovis, the Island also had a shrine of Faunus reared from the fine monies of the *pecuarii.* That the latter was attached to the former shrine has been argued above, on the basis of Vitruvius' text. Moreover, Servius reports that Aesculapius receives goats because the animal is never feverish and is thus appropriate to a god of healing. [351] Aesculapius was the senior deity of the Island, who very probably received a goat victim because it was appropriate to incubation. However, *caprina galla* does not belong to Aesculapius, because Aesculapius has no Gaulish connection, whereas Vediovis certainly, and Faunus probably, received temples under direct Gaulish influence. In subsequent discussion, the Gaulish goat-goddess will be assumed to belong to the cult of Vediovis or Faunus on the Island, and her Gaulish name will be produced from the Latin authors.

If the three masters did not serve an association of the Gaulish Goat Goddess, the nature of the association may be sought elsewhere. The Island has yielded a much later and comparable document on a statue base:

> Semoni Sanco deo Fidio sacrum Sex(tus)
> Pompeius Sp(uri) f(ilius) Col(lina tribu)
> Mussianus quinquennalis decur(iae)
> bidentalis donum dedit. [352]

This same dedicant is noted on another inscription as [*quinque*]*nnalis decuriae* [*sacerdo*]*tium videntalium.* [353] The god Semo Sancus Dius Fidius was a god of oaths, whose divine interests recall the republican dedication to Jupiter Jurarius on the Island. [354] References in the Church Fathers to Semo as Simon the Magician may be taken to prove the deity's presence on the Island as early as the reign of Claudius. [355] Besides Mussianus' records, two other inscriptions from the vicinity of

Semo's temple on the Quirinal Hill document dedication to that god by the *decuria sacerdotum bidentalium.* [356] Apparently the decuria had its headquarters on the Quirinal and was strictly tied to the cult of Semo. The *bidentales* were priests who specialized in sacrificing sheep (*bidentes*), perhaps only at a *bidental*, the place where a lightning bolt was buried. [357]

The decuria of *bidentales* could have been party to a republican *conlegium* whose officers erected the Caprina Galla. Their concern could have arisen from a desire to placate a deity who in some way watched over their *bidentes.* Yet no reason for linking the republican document to the *bidentales* appears compelling at this time.

The *conlegium* most naturally belonged to the Island or its several cults. The neighborhood (*vicus*) on the Island was called *vicus Censori* (or *v. Censorius*, originally). Usually four freedmen *magistri* presided over an urban *vicus.* Although a case for calling the modest government of a *vicus* a *conlegium* can be made for the Republican era, no certain example of *decuria* or *decuriones* subsisting in and for a *vicus* survives. Therefore it would be mere assumption to identify this dedication as the work of the associated residents of the Island neighborhood. [358]

Prosopographical research on the three *magistri* yields very little: in 100 A.D., P. Rutilius P.f. Priscus was *magister vici Censori.* [359] He seems quite distant from L. Rutilius L.l. Artemidorus. P. Sulpicius Q.l. Philocomus was a freedman of a family which was perhaps the Sulpicii Gali or Galbae. The latter cognomen was Gaulish.[360] The praenomen Quintus, however, does not occur among the patrician Sulpicii after the later third century.B.C.

Finally, there remains the probability that the *conlegium* served the cult of Vediovis or of Faunus, since both deities required or received goat victims.

The Gaulish Goat-goddess will have come to Rome with Vediovis or Faunus in the 190's. Toward the end of the republic, three officers of an unidentifiable organization complied with the decision of their organization's council of ex-officers and raised her statue on the Island. Beyond the single document no Roman evidence illumines her character. Now is the occasion to pursue some elusive Gaulish gods who we can demonstrate are the congeners of Vediovis, Faunus, and the Caprina Galla.

17. SOME GAULISH GODS AND THE NETHERWORLD

In this section I propose to deal with several gods known from the classical authors or from epigraphic testimony to be peculiar to the Celtic world. Explanation of the *ritus humanus* proper to Vediovis can come only from the longstanding practice of human sacrifice, which entered Rome under Celtic influence. Moreover, the kind of incubation practiced at Albunea was performed by the Celts. The Celtic identity of the gods whom the Romans interpreted as Vediovis and Faunus in the 190's will also be sought.

Somewhere in central Rome was situated a monument whereat the Gauls involved in the sack of Rome in 390 were said to have been cremated. Although they called it *Busta Gallica*, the Romans had no accurate idea of how the monument received its grim designation. [361] The fragment of a paving contract from the Sullan era holds mention of the site, "from the bottom of the slope at Busta Gallica up to the top of the slope." [362] The Gauls' Pyre was probably located at the foot of the Aventine in the Forum Boarium. [363]

In 225, the Romans buried alive a pair of Gauls and a pair of Greeks. In 220, they buried two more such pairs in the Forum Boarium. The Greek male and female confirm that the Hellenic authority of the Sibylline Books had been invoked. [364] The Gaulish male and female were required by the race of Rome's contemporary enemies, the Insubrian and Boian Gauls of Northern Italy. With the live burial of a male and female, the Romans sought an end to fertility between the pair and the nation which they represented. By direct consignment to the earth, the mode of burial avoided actual bloodletting on the part of the sacrificing people. In spite of these tender feelings, or because of their avoidance of bloodshed, the Romans persisted in such practices. Plutarch brings the initial sacrifice into a proper historical perspective and also tells us that even during his lifetime similar rites are held in November at Rome. [365] In 222, M. Claudius Marcellus won the *spolia opima* from the corpse of the fallen Gaulish chief. In his triumphal glory at Rome he will have restored the temple of Jupiter Feretrius, where the spoils were housed. It was this deity whose games performed on oiled goatskins were noted in Ennius' *Annals*. [366] The unusual games for Jupiter Feretrius found mention in Ennius because they were given to celebrate Marcellus' new building. The Ennian fragment attributes them to Romulus' first structure. No doubt, the last winner of the *spolia opima* believed that was so. This same Marcellus was later Furius Purpurio's commander, and his son was Purpurio's consular colleague. Purpurio reared the three temples to Vediovis.

According to Silius Italicus' over-burdened epic, the souls of the dead seemed to emerge from Busta Gallica while visions haunted men's dreams after the defeat at Cannae. [367] We can only assume that some Romans believed in Gaulish ghosts. For over fifty years nothing is heard of them, besides what we choose to make of Vediovis and Faunus in the 190's. In 143, Ap. Claudius Pulcher snatched victory over the Salassians from previous defeat by obeying the decemvirs, who, again consulting the Sibylline Books, cautioned sacrifice on their borders before any invasion of the territory of the Gauls. [368] In 121, Fabius Maximus confronted the Allobroges at the confluence of the Rhodanus and Isara. On the battle line, he was freed from a quartan fever after 130 Gauls were slain. Upon his return to Rome he laid out a precinct for Fever. [369] Unfortunately, our one notice of the wondrous cure is too brief to satisfy any curiosity. It appears that the mass death of the Gauls was a specific against the quartan. No doubt we could understand the incident if we knew something more about the Gaulish practice of human sacrifice (see below). Caesar reports that the Gauls themselves resorted to human sacrifice when they were seriously ill or endangered in battle (*BG* 6.16.2). Fabius' slaughter of the

Gauls has every appearance of a Gaulish rite against serious illness.

In the year 113, when the Romans suffered a decisive defeat at the hands of the Cimbrians, sacrifice of Gauls and Greeks was resumed. [370] Its efficacy was certainly not proven, but the ban on human sacrifice was not set for another sixteen years (see below). In 101, C. Marius and Q. Lutatius Catulus combined forces to defeat the Gaulish Cimbrians after the former consul's victory over the Teutons. In the same year was recorded the remarkable ceremony: "A goat with burning horns was led through the City and passed through the Naevian Gate where it was abandoned."[371] From these northern victories over the Gauls and Gallo-Germans were taken 160,000 captives who might be enslaved. Fewer survivors were found on the morrow of the victory over the Cimbrians, for they killed themselves and their kinfolk rather than be taken. [372]

In 87 B.C. Marius acquired some slaves, whom he liberated. Calling them *bardyaioi*, Marius unleashed them like beasts to slay all his enemies as well as their own former owners, whose wives and children of both sexes they ill-used. Sick with the carnage, Cinna and Sertorius accomplished their death, to the number of 4000, by having their Gaulish soldiers fire arrows on the *bardyaioi* in their camp. [373] I understand these loathsome creatures of Marius as Gaulish freedmen, whose nickname reflects the Celtic bards and the religious rites of human sacrifice among the Gauls. The bards, who were subsequently recognized as prestigious members of Celtic society by virtue of their songs and poems (see below), appear from the name *bardyaioi* to have been viewed as religiously involved in human sacrifice. Cinna and Sertorius set their Gaulish troops on the bloodthirsty ex-slaves because of the divine business inherent in the entire unsavory episode.

Revenge came in a Gaulish fashion. Marius and Lutatius Catulus had quarrelled over the extent of each other's contribution to the victory at Vercellae in 101 B.C. In 87 B.C., Catulus was among the first to die by his own hand. Catulus had been accused by the tribune M. Marius Gratidianus.[374] When the Sullans resumed the government of Rome, L. Sergius Catilina gratified Sulla, whom Catulus' son had importuned for revenge. Catiline took his brother-in-law Gratidianus to the tomb of Catulus senior on the Janiculum, and there had him taken apart limb by limb. After the demise he took Gratidianus' head and proudly exhibited it to Sulla, who was settled in the temple of Apollo in the Circus Flaminius. [375] This truly barbaric revenge was the Sullan response to the Marian *bardyaioi*. Even Catiline's dangling the severed, gory head in his own hand recalls the Gaulish habit at a battle (see below). Nor ought we to forget that Manlius Torquatus acquired both torque and surname, around 361 B.C., by severing the head of his slain enemy. In 82, however, Romans had come to expect better treatment, at least among themselves. For this study the most important aspect of the atrocities remains the Gaulish inspiration that had its foundation in Gaulish religion.

Pliny the Elder certifies the Roman practice of live burial even under the Flavians, although he also otherwise reports the senatorial decree outlawing human sacrifice in 97 B.C. [377] In a forensic plea Cicero discoursed on the Gauls' habit of human sacrifice. [378] The Druids supervised human sacrifice, which Caesar says was regularly exacted of certain criminals, and occasionally of the innocent. They constructed huge wicker images, enclosed the man inside, and set fire to them. The same Druids asserted their peoples' descent from the god Dis, for their time-reckoning was based upon the night.[379] The Gauls showed a fondness for severed human heads; indeed, Livy would ask us to believe that they made them drinking cups. [380] At any rate, they did nail the recently severed heads of their foe to their houses. [381] Doubtless influenced by his long campaign in Gaul, Caesar determined to combine this Gaulish practice and the Roman rites of the October Horse by nailing the severed heads of mutineers upon the Regia, his priestly headquarters as Roman chief pontiff. [382] Caesar's emphasis upon the Druidical Dis finds pertinence in the existence of a Roman temple to that god only in the eleventh region of the City. That region embraced the Forum Boarium, where the Romans performed their live burials. [383]

The historian Diodorus Siculus and the geographer Strabo wrote ethnographic disquisitions on the continental Gauls which they seem to have extracted mostly from the polymath Posidonius. The description of the Gauls includes the detail that their hairstyle made them resemble Pans and satyrs. Virtually, then, any representation of a Gaúl might have suggested the Roman Silvanus or Faunus. The art of human sacrifice was keenly refined among them. One method called for sending arrows against the victim. As we saw above, Cinna and Sertorius had their Gaulish troops execute Marius' *bardyaioi* precisely in this manner. Another ritual called for stabbing the victim in the back in such a way as to predict the future from his fall, his twitches, his writhings, and spurting of blood. A third kind of human sacrifice recall's Caesar's statement. They made effigies of wood and straw and set them afire. Diodorus says that war prisoners, kept five years, were burned alive on great pyres. Although none of the authors mentions the Gallo-Roman practice of live burial, the unanimity on live burnings indicates to us the first use of the Busta Gallica at Rome. For these permanent (?) pyres commemorated either human sacrifice or cremation of slain human victims. All Gaulish elite was divided into three parts. The first class were the Druids, who supervised much human sacrifice. They were concerned with the care of men's souls; a kind of philosophical priesthood believing in metempsychosis. The second elite group comprised the *vates*, performers of rites. Their title, perhaps an Italo-Celtic word, recalls the *vates primarius* of Lavinium, whom I would assign to the incubation rites of Faunus' shrine at Albunea. After severing the heads of their enemies, Gaulish warriors hung them from their horses. At home they nailed them at the door of their houses. If the slain was important, his head was embalmed and ensconced indoors as a trophy, like modern antlers. Their victories the Gauls hailed with a song over the dead foemen. Perhaps the victory hymn was led and accompanied by the last of the prestigious Gauls, the bards, poets and singers, playing upon a harp.[384] Nothing in our authorities excludes the possibility that the bards were involved in ritual human killing. Further, the very title of Marius' bloodthirsty henchmen betrays one Roman's view of the capacity of the bards.

In discussing divination among the Gauls, Cicero casts doubt on the very existence of the Druids. Centuries later, however, the Gallo-Roman Ausonius demonstrates how the Gauls themselves designated two Druids who were attached to the cult of Belenus while professing rhetoric: *Baiocassi stirpe Druidarum satus* and *stirpe satus Druidum gentis Aremoricae.* [385]

Enchanted by lurid gore, Lucan too attributes human sacrifice to the Gauls. He gives us the names of three deities who enjoyed human victims, Esus, Teutates, and Taranis, but he does not fail to acknowledge Dis. He repeats the threefold division of the Gaulish elite. Lucan's information cannot have come from Caesar or the immediate Greek sources whom we have examined above. Unless he read Posidonius and extracted more than others before him, Lucan may have drawn on Terentius Varro, for Lactantius names the same three gods in a section on human sacrifice that owes much to Varro.[386]

Pliny's comment on human sacrifice at Rome in his own day and on the senate decree of 97 B.C. precedes a brief discussion of human sacrifice in the several provinces of Gaul. He remarks that Tiberius attempted to suppress the responsible Druids and *hoc genus vatum medicorumque.* [387] The *medici* may represent the division of the bards. Ammianus also appears to have a divergent division: *bardi, euhages, drysidae.* [388] Pliny's physicians remind us that Fabius Maximus was relieved of his fever when 130 Gauls were slain.

The efficacy of human sacrifice outweighed the abhorrence. Plutarch's testimony makes the rites annual in November during his own lifetime. [389] According to Pliny, the Gauls of Britain maintained their human sacrifice even after the attempted suppression under Tiberius. However, we would be mistaken if we inferred that Tiberius' attempt met success among the continental Gauls. In 176 A.D., the emperors Marcus Aurelius and Lucius Commodus countenanced canalizing the Gaulish habit of sacrificing the human *trinci* or *trinqui* into the gladiatorial games, whose costs rose with the then general inflation. Among the victims who subsequently suffered were Christians, whose religion put them at odds with the established religion of Rome and the unspeakable practices among the Gauls. [390] In the late fourth century, Jerome edifies his readers with a lengthy treatment of strange eating habits. By eye-witness account he retails the sight of some Gaulish peoples engaging in cannibalism. On Syme's view, he lifted the uncouth practice out of a lost book of Ammianus Marcellinus. Be that as it may, Strabo had written that the Britons and some other Gauls were cannibals. [391]

For at least 300 years the Romans of Italy acknowledged the existence of the Gauls' practice of human sacrifice. On their own admission, the Romans conducted like sacrifices, especially when they faced the Gauls in war. The Roman rites were controlled by the decemvirs, except when Marius, Sulla, and Caesar introduced their own innovations into public life.

The statue of a goat was set beside that of Vediovis on the Capitol because *immolatur ritu humano capra.* [392] Some interpret *humanus* to refer to *humus* and the chthonic character of the god. [393] The cumulative evidence overwhelms that and any like suggestion. The goat was offered according to the ceremony for human sacrifice. At Rome this meant burial of a live goat. If the goat was indeed a surrogate for a human victim, the existence of the ceremony in the cult of Vediovis is not at all surprising. Vediovis received temples at Rome only at the instance of Furius Purpurio fighting the Gauls. The god's name is joined to Dis and the Manes in the *devotio* of Carthage, which was preserved by a subsequent Furius.

Without doubt, Gaulish religious practices infected the Romans as early as 225 B.C., when they buried their first live victims, one pair of which was Gaulish. Claudius Marcellus put his Gaulish spoils in a rebuilt temple of Jupiter Feretrius. This deity's games of boxing and footraces were given on oiled goatskins. He was a lord of oaths, and like Jupiter Jurarius and Semo Sancus Dius Fidius, on the Island. The decemvirs and Marcellus prepared the way for Vediovis, to whom temples were vowed in 200 and 196. Moreover, the statue of Caprina Galla very strongly corroborates the inference from the *ritus humanus* that the Romans also imported Gaulish cult as well as Gaulish gods in the 190's. Therefore we can profitably seek traces of the Gaulish deities whom they introduced after they had introduced human sacrifice.

Thus far, indications of Gaulish origins for Vediovis' new cult in the 190's are soundly based, whereas Faunus' chapel is only inferentially tied to the Gallic wars. The enemies whom the Romans fought in 200 and 196 B.C. lost their identity, or existence, as a result of Roman massacres. When L. Furius Purpurio fought in the north in 200, the Gaulish Insubrians, Boians and Cenomanians, as well as the Ligurian Celinians and Elbans, were arrayed against him. Four years later the same Purpurio as consul faced Boians, Laevians, Libuans, and Ligurians, while Claudius Marcellus, his colleague and son of the victor of 222, fought Boians, Insubrians, and Comensians. In the latter year the aediles vowed the temple to Faunus on the Island, which was shared with Jupiter or, as was argued above, with Vediovis. In 200, Purpurio certainly vowed one of his three temples at Cremona. In 196, Felsina (Bononia) is the only walled community specifically named. [394] Most of the Gaulish campaigns were fought in open country, for the Gauls had few walled settlements and no community of the city-state. Accordingly, their deities could not resemble the kind known to the Romans; they will have been lords of the open country and the dark woods. Ancient information on the Gaulish equivalents of Faunus corroborate our assertion that the Roman aediles had a Gaulish god in mind when they reared a chapel to Faunus in conjunction with Vediovis.

Notices of the Gaulish Dusii are late; they must thus be shown to contain knowledge current in Rome when Faunus was installed in his one and only Roman temple. Although some of the following material has been introduced earlier in this chapter it will be repeated so that the Roman understanding of Faunus can be appreciated.

Augustine introduces the Gaulish deities in a discussion of the nature of angels:

> And since there is a widespread report and many persons certify that they have experienced, or know someone of unimpeachable truth who claims such experience, to wit that Silvani and Pans, whom they commonly call *incubi*, have often wantonly appeared to women and sought and accomplished sexual intercourse with them; further, that a kind of demon, whom Gauls name Dusii, both try and carry out this constant unclean-

ness–many such fine persons assert to the degree that it seems an act of folly to deny it; hence I dare not define whether some spirits embodied by the element of air–for this element is also felt by bodily feeling and touch when the air is fanned–can allow even this kind of lust that they can somehow mix with women who feel them.[395]

Augustine writes as if the Gauls still used the term Dusii. However, the bookishness of his terms can be seen in the use of Latin Silvani and Greek Pans. In any event, he is speaking of wild deities who enter women. Further, his effort to find a natural, or rational, explanation allows us to suppose that these beliefs were still held in his own time. Augustine's European experience took place in Milan, the surviving town of a Gaulish community.

Isidore of Seville is the only other author explicitly to mention the Dusii, in his long chapter on pagan gods:

> Fauns were named from talking (*a fando*) or from the Greek word for sound *phone*, because they seem to tell the future by voice and not by signs . . . . They say that *larvae* are demons made from men who have earned ill deserts. By their nature they are said to frighten children and to chatter in dark corners. According to tales *lamiae* carry off and usually scratch babies and thus earn their name from scratching (*a laniando*). Shaggy creatures are those whom Greeks call *Panitae* and Romans *Incubi*, or *Inui* from entering (*ab ineundo*) animals here and there. Hence Incubi are also called from sleeping in (*ab incumbendo*), that is from violating women. Often they also appear to women and accomplish intercourse with them. These demons the Gauls call Dusii because they accomplish this constant uncleanness. The Romans call Faunus the "Figger," the god whom commonly they call *Incubo*.[396]

Although Isidore's description of the Dusii closely resembles Augustine's, they derive their knowledge from a third source, for Augustine mentions Silvani, Pans, and Incubi, while Isidore treats Panitae, Incubi, Inui, Faunus *ficarius*, and Incubo. Moreover, Isidore's material abounds in etymologies absent from Augustine, and in his treatment of angels Isidore never recurs to the matter adduced on pagan gods. [397]

In his Biblical commentary, Jerome offers more information from the common source but makes no direct reference to the Dusii. "There will dance the shaggy creatures or *incubones*, or satyrs, or a kind of forest man whom some call the *fatui*, "figgers," or understand as kinds of demons." [398] Like Isidore's etymology of Faunus, Jerome's *fatui ficarii* belong to Varro, whom both Isidore and Augustine have drawn on.

Servius, who does not share in the tradition of Christian erudition, comments on Vergil's place *Castrum Inui*: "It is one city of Italy which is called Castrum Novum. Moreover he is speaking of this Castrum of Inuus, that is of Pan, who is worshipped there. Moreover Inuus is the Latin name for the Greek's Pan. Also, Greek Ephialtes, Latin Incubo. He is the same as Faunus, Fatuus, Fatuclus. Moreover he is called Inuus from entering (*ab ineundo*) all animals, here and there, whence he is also called Incubo." [399] Discussions of Faunus, Fauna, Fatuus and Fatua go back to Varro, sometimes by way of uncertain intermediaries. [400]

Augustine, Servius, and Isidore draw on a common source for information concerning Inuus, Incubus (-o), Faunus, Silvanus, and their Greek congeners. The two

Christian authors introduce the Gaulish demons called Dusii in a context similar to that found in Jerome. The material on woodland gods who indiscriminately enter women and are also prophetic can be circumstantially traced to Varro. He could have learned the word from ethnographers on the Gauls, just as Caesar and later Livy resorted to such writings. However, Varro's acquaintance with the Dusii means nothing if it cannot be understood in the context of his religious history. We must thus ascertain the possibility of his knowing a Gaulish word that was recorded as Gaulish at a time when Furius Purpurio and the two aediles were vowing temples to Vediovis and Faunus. Such a possibility exists in the *Annals* of Ennius, who wrote of the period and its war. No doubt he knew of the Faunus and seers *(vates)*,[401] and his epic contained the Gaulish word for slave *ambactus*. [402] Moreover, the fragment that preserves mention of Romulus' games for Jupiter Feretrius can be related to Ennius' presumed inclusion of the Gaulish *spolia opima* won by Claudius Marcellus.[403]

In Plautus' time the superlative *medioximus* was still current, at least to describe the gods occupying the place between the *superi* and *inferi*.[404] When Varro treated the word, it was already obsolete. [405] Martianus Capella chooses to identify angels as *daemones* in Greek and *medioximi* in Latin. [406] This term also comes from Varro, whose *Antiquities of Divine Matters* is quoted by Servius Danielis when he contrasts gods *superi* and *medioximi*. [407] Varro had no interest in angels. The Church Fathers did have that interest, and researched them in Varro's encyclopedia of religion. They were *daemones* in Greek, and a class of Roman deities—Varro loved classes of deities—made up of the *medioximi*, to which belonged Faunus, Silvanus, Inuus, Incubo, and even the Gaulish Dusii. Perhaps Varro found his name of the class in Plautus, and the name of the Gaulish deities in Ennius.

The Gaulish demons called Dusii were equated with Inuus, Silvanus, and Faunus by two Christian authors who otherwise do not discuss such ethnic deities. Their knowledge rests upon the research of Terentius Varro. The god Faunus received a temple on the Island in 196, when Furius Purpurio and Claudius Marcellus were operating against the Gauls in northern Italy. Purpurio certainly vowed three temples to Vediovis while he fought them. It is very likely that Vediovis and Faunus had contiguous chapels on the Island. In any case, Faunus was installed with another god in one building. Also situated on the Island was the figure of Caprina Galla, which ought to be associated with one or both cults. In light of this evidence, Varro appears to have learnt from Ennius that Dusius was the Gaulish name of Faunus.

Before examining the inscribed dedications from Gaulish territory that can cast light on this phenomenon of Gaulish deities and cult at Rome, we turn to a few similar phenomena met in the authors.

Lusitanians, who resemble the Celts in predicting the future by human entrails and the movement of a dying human victim, offer to their god Ares goats, horses, and human prisoners. One of their tribes are the *Bardyetai*. [408] Celtiberians sacrifice during the night of the full moon to an anonymous god. [409] On an island in the ocean at the mouth of the Loire River live Namnite women whom Dionysus seizes and who, in turn, perform secret rites for the god. These female Namnites go to the mainland for sexual intercourse. [410] Near the Timavus River in Italy were holy precincts where wild beasts grew tame. To these were assigned the special brood mares branded with a wolf's head. [411] When Julius Caesar paused at the Rubicon, a tall handsome man appeared seated nearby playing on a reed. Upon hearing his music, the shepherds and soldiers, quitting their posts, rushed to see him. The apparition grabbed a war-trumpet from one of the trumpeteers and leapt into the stream sounding the charge. Caesar followed. [412] Before Caesar's death, the horses which he had dedicated to the Rubicon and left untended ceased eating and wept. [413] These scattered details contribute to questions previously discussed.

The Lusitanians of Spain practice a religion much like that of the Transalpine Gauls. Their war god receives goats, men, and horses. [414] Caesar nailed up the heads of mutineers on the Regia, as a horse's head was exhibited for Mars at the festival of the October Horse. The Lusitanian Bardyetai's name is to be compared with the Marian butchers *bardyaioi*. The nocturnal sacrifice of the Celtiberians recalls Caesar's remarks on the Gauls' descent from Dis, and their reckoning by nights. [415] The Namnite women's devotion to Dionysus and their promiscuity suggest an activity converse to that of Gaulish Dusii. Indeed, Dionysus' constant attendants in Greek mythology are the satyrs, a common equivalent of the Fauns. The prominence of horse coping in northern Italy is borne out by the ubiquity of the Gaulish horse-goddess Epona (see below). Therefore, Caesar's offering of tamed, free-roaming horses to the Rubicon is not surprising. However, the reed-playing apparition does not belong to the horsemen's cult; he is rather a Gaulish Faun or Silvanus, such as that god who once addressed Valerius from the Arsian Wood. If shepherds thronged the apparition, he was perhaps a deity of theirs and also known as a Dusius. Although the accounts bear circumstantial details that are suspect, the reports of Aius Locutius', or Loquens', shrine on the Roman Nova Via attribute its foundation to a nocturnal voice that warned the Romans of the Gauls' approach in 390. Moreover, Cicero specifically conjoins his account of Aius to mention of the Fauns, whose oracular shouts are heard in battle. [416]

Lucian offers unique information on Ogmius, a Gaulish deity whose painted representation he mirthfully describes. Since Lucian lectured somewhere among the Gauls, his description of Ogmius bears signs of authenticity. [417] Although Ogmius is equited with Herakles, he is a wrinkled old man resembling Kharon and Iapetos. His lionskin cloak, club, bow, and quiver mark him as a Herakles. In the painting Lucian views the god dragging many docile men, who are chained in a line by a light chain run through their ears. Ogmius himself has a perforated tongue. In the Lucianic dialogue, a Gaul speaks up and contradicts: Ogmius truly resembles Hermes and professes eloquence. The character of this Gaulish Kharon or Hermes Psychopompos clearly stands out from Lucian's description. The god leads the dead to the Netherworld. His perforated tongue and his mastery of eloquence are combined with the possibility that his name is related to *Ogma*, the discoverer of writing.[418] Ogmius perhaps issued oracles with his perforated tongue, for the northern "Hercules" is cited in two quite disparate accounts of oracles of, or in, the north.

The Massiliotes established Herakles Monoikos (modern Monaco) on the Mediterranean coast; the Greek god was thus known to that part of the world. Quintus Fabius Maximus erected a remarkable trophy' at the confluence of the Rhodanus and Isara rivers, where he won a victory over the Allobroges and Arverni on 8 Augustus 121. Beside the trophy, he reared a temple to Mars and another to Hercules. Perhaps this Hercules masks a Celtic god like Ogmius. The miracle took place at this battle: when 130 enemy soldiers had been slain, his quartan fever quit him on the battleline.[419]

In the territory of Padua lay a fountain cult of and at Aponus. Hercules had uncovered Aponus' hot sulphur springs with a plow. Usually this oracle of Geryon yielded lots. Tiberius, however, tossed golden dice into the waters of Aponus at the instance of one of the lots. Unfortunately, our authority does not say why he consulted the oracle, but only alludes to the lucky cast of the dice portending his rise to the principate. Even at the end of pagan antiquity, the waters of Aponus warded off harmful Fates. Indeed, the sulphuric vapors and the nature of the medicinal waters reeked of the goddesses Tellus and Parcae, since the entire site was endowed with natural fertility.[420] Not only does this oracle of Geryon physically remind us of the Grove of Albunea, but the lot's advice to Tiberius recalls Caesar's often-quoted remark at the Rubicon on the cast of his die. Since Geryon's name betokens cattle, whose skins were employed in Gaulish oracles, the oracles may have begun as an incubation center (see below).

Late antique writers, who, it shall be shown, draw ultimately on Varro, deal with the Gaulish goddess whom we can assign to the sphere of Nethergods and identify with Caprina Galla on the Island at Rome. All surviving mentions of the goddess Fenta are to be found in discussions of the Bona Dea, who is equated sometimes with Fauna. Varro first tells us of the existence of both Faunus and Fauna, who are joined to the *vates* by Ennius.[421] Faunus was merely the putative father of Latinus, according to Dionysius. In one version, Hercules brought a nameless "Hyperborean" girl to Rome, made her pregnant, and then abandoned her to Faunus. Latinus was Herculean issue.[422] At this point must be injected the several explanations of Bona Dea, who was also known as Fauna. Moreover, Fauna, who is variously Faunus' sister or daughter as well as his prophetic wife, also bore the name Fatua, just as on some occasions he was Fatuus. A third name of Faunus' incestuous consort was Fenta.[423] Fauna is a Latin name, Fatua a Latin substantive. Faunus and Fauna were gods of the Latins. Fenta can only be the name of the "Hyperborean" girl whom Hercules imported from the north when he was driving Geryon's cattle. Consequently, the "Hyperborean" Fenta was the female goddess identified with Fauna. According to the traditional story, Faunus wed his own sister or daughter; Fauna, or whatever her name was, must thus have borne a physical resemblance to her husband. She was a goatish goddess. If she was identified with a goddess of the north, and if Fenta, which is a non-Latin word, was her name, Fenta represents to Romans the Gaulish Goat-goddess, or Caprina Galla. Her actual arrival in Rome should be dated to the era in which Faunus and Vediovis were honored by temples vowed by Romans at war with the Gauls of northern Italy.

In the accounts of Fauna, Fatua, and Fenta, Varro's etymologies from *for* and *fanum* are quoted or are implicit. Further, Lactantius and Macrobius cite Varro. Indeed, Lactantius introduces Faunus in regard to human sacrifice for Saturnus, which matter he has just discussed in connection with an oracle quoted in Greek from Varro. Also Lactantius mentions the Gaulish gods Esus and Teutates, the recipients of human sacrifice, whose cult is known also from Lucan. [424] Dionysius quotes the same oracle at greater length. Its inscription was seen by L. Mallius, who was probably Varro's authority. [425] The same Dionysius recognized the human sacrifice for Saturn as a Punic or Gaulish custom which Hercules abolished at Rome. [426] Finally, Macrobius makes Varro his authority for the same Greek oracle and, most probably, for Hercules' modification of Saturn's cult, which Macrobius closely ties to the cult of Dis. [427] In sum, Varro dealt with human sacrifice for Saturn, with Hercules, and with the Bona Dea who was recognized by the names Fauna, Fatua, and Fenta. Varro must have supplied her "Hyperborean" origin as well as her name. Varro's treatment of Fenta incorporated his discussion of Faunus and, further, of the Dusii. The Gaulish gods and goddess will have been made known to Varro both by the cult of the Island, whose records were preserved in (pontifical) archives, and by the poet Ennius, who will have introduced these matters into his epic *Annals*.

Many dedications to Silvanus, Faunus' kindred god, are known from inscriptions. Only one Roman dedication to Silvanus is known from literature. Pliny's faulty text reports the existence of an aged, holy fig tree in front of Saturn's temple, which was extirpated after a sacrifice of the Vestals, when some—now nameless—person overturned the image of Silvanus. [428] This Silvanus may be compared with Faunus and the unclear religious relation of the latter to Saturnian human sacrifice abolished by Hercules. When we examine the actual cults of the Gauls, we shall have occasion to remark the extent of Silvanus' cult.

Pompeius Trogus wrote the first universal history in Latin, and contributed important information on the Gauls, for he was born of a Vocontian family enfranchised by the great general whose name he bore. Justin preserves two valuable pieces of Gaulish lore in his epitome of Trogus. In one book of his universal history, Trogus dealt with the beginnings of Rome, with his own ancestry, and with the Gauls' relations to the Massiliotes, whose territory bordered on the historian's ancestral homeland. Trogus supplies us with a brief allusion to the religious phenomena of Faunus, who "had a wife named Fatua. She foretold the future because she was filled with divine breath as if by means of madness. Accordingly even in my own day those who are inspired are said *fatuari*. Latinus was born of Hercules' seduction of Faunus' daughter. At that time Hercules was driving the cattle of the dead Geryon through Italy."[429] In his condensation, Justin omits the fact that Fatua was both wife and daughter of Faunus. The art of "fatuation" was Gaulish, as we shall see. When a Gaulish chieftain was beleaguering Massilia, a woman appeared in the chieftain's dream and claimed to be a god. Frightened by her threats, the chieftain gave up the siege and received permission to enter the city for worship. When he mounted to the acropolis of Minerva and saw her image, he recognized the goddess of his dreams, upon whom he bestowed a golden necklace, and entered upon a perpetual peace with her people. Subsequently, when Rome was taken by the Gauls, the Massiliotes conscientiously contributed to the ransom of Rome. As it is now epitomized, Trogus retailed his Vocontian ancestry at this point.

De Vries alludes to this dream of Minerva when he discusses how the Irish Druids seek the future through visions and dreams while the petitioner sleeps on bloody cattleskins. Moreover, the high king of Ireland was usually designated by a dream evoked by sleeping on the skin of slaughtered cattle. [430] Lastly, a Gaelic Taghairm, wrapped in cowhide, delivered oracles after a night by water. [431] Such Gaulish oracles were long recognized as similar to the type evinced at Faunus' shrine of Albunea. [432] Lucian speaks of Ogmius' lionskin cloak, which cannot have originated with the Gauls; surely, it replaced the hide of a proper animal victim. [433] Why else was Geryon the oracle at the waters of Aponus? From the Northlands, Hercules brought to Rome Geryon's cattle and the "Hyperborean" girl who is Fenta.

Northern Italy, which was Gaul, and France yield many epigraphic indications of cults, which can be understood in terms of these gods and cults. At Arausio in Narbonensis was found a dedication to the Fatuae Sanctae. [434] The adjective *sanctus* is frequently applied to Silvanus (see below). This was country occupied by Pompeius Trogus' forebears. At nearby Nemausus, an offering was made to the Parcae at their bidding uttered in a dream. [435] At Antipolis, a slave erects a thank-offering to Pan-Silvanus for the health of imperial superintendent M. Julius Ligus. [436] Among the Transalpine Gauls, Silvanus is frequently represented with the instruments of the Gaulish Sucellos. [437] As one might expect, Silvanus himself appeared to command dedications at Apta, Vasio, St. Gilles, and Narbo. [438] Also at Apta survives a simple dedication to Silvanus and the Silvanae who are known from other northern areas. [439] The Silvanae should be likened to the Fatuae and to Fenta. The Gauls across the Alps yield no evidence of Faunian worship, which is possibly found at Cisalpine Aquileia.

Cisalpine Gaul yields many dedications to Silvanus. [440] Moreover, south of the Po River and near the Rubicon, where Caesar's army experienced the apparition of the pipe-playing giant who lured shepherds, several offerings for Silvanus are known. [441]

From Aquileia come two offerings to Fonio, who was implicated in the cult of the Bona Dea. [442] The ancient mythographers believed Bona Dea was also called Fauna; the name Fonio may be derived from that name. [443] The formation of the name is that also met in Caprio of the Treveri, which deity is reckoned a goat god. [444] Among many offerings to the Fatae in Cisalpine Gaul are dedications to the *Fatae Divinae et Barbaricae, Fatae Dervones, Fati Masculi*, and the double Fati and Fatae.[445] Jupiter Summanus, whom we related to incubation at Rome, received his only known offerings in all of Italy from the inhabitants of Milanese territory and Verona.[446] Verona and Aquileia yield evidence of the cult of the Silvanae.[447] Of the considerable dedications to Silvanus, Silvanus Augustus, and Silvanus Sanctus, only one is reported as an offering prompted by a vision.[448] At Rome, some of Silvanus' dedications were made at his command. The most famous document has support in Juvenal and Martial.[449] "By the order of Silvanus let no woman wish to enter the men's pool, even less if she complains about herself. For this statue is consecrated."[450] Another Roman inscription records a dedication to Hercules, Epona, and Silvanus, at these gods' bidding.[451] Silvanus was frequently honored with Hercules, especially by slaves and freedmen.[452] Epona, however, originates with Gauls as a horse-goddess; indeed, in northern Europe she, too, is honored with Silvanus.[453]

Thus the shepherds' apparition at the Rubicon represented the local Silvanus, to whom Caesar consecrated a herd of tame horses as one might have offered to Epona.[454] In any case, one of the few references to local festivals recorded in the inscribed calendars contains notice of rites for Epona on 18 December in the territory of Brixia.[455] It may not be coincidence that Epona's festival falls a day after the Saturnalia, festival of a god in whose Roman precinct was a statue of Silvanus. Moreover, on 31 December was fixed the feast of Saint Sylvester, whose beginning can be traced to Sanctus Silvanus Silvestris.

The most illustrious Christian Sylvester occupied the see of Rome from 1 January 314 to 31 December 335. According to the *Liber Pontificalis*, he performed two acts of great importance to the history of Christendom. After the bishop cured the persecuting emperor's leprosy, he baptized Constantine the Great and founded the Vatican basilica of St. Peter. Upon Constantine's remission of the persecutions, Sylvester descended from Mt. Soracte, where he had spent his exile from martyrdom. Mt. Soracte held one of the most unusual pagan shrines of Italy. A race of people or priests called *hirpi*, meaning "wolves" in Sabine, kept the cult of a Nethergod variously named Apollo or Dis. They worshipped wolves by imitating them. This imitation embraced walking on live, burning coals. On account of their abnormal holy practice, the Roman senate exempted the *hirpi* from all public services. In the myth explaining their institution, some shepherds had followed harmful wolves which led them to caves from which noxious fumes came forth to kill them. An oracle had prompted the institution. It has long been recognized how similar this Apollo or Dis Soranus is to the Roman Vediovis, and how the *hirpi* approximate the Roman *luperci*.[456] Moreover, the wolf-cult, the foul or noisome fumes, and the oracle recall the Faunus of Grove Albunea. Deives and Mephitis of Hirpinian Ampsancti also parallel the god of Soracte. Caverns still pit Mt. Soracte. On the hill today is also found a tiny church of St. Sylvester, which claims a sixth-century beginning, commemorating Sylvester's sojourn and evasion of martyrdom. Soranus' capacity to bestow good health will have been assumed by Sylvester's curing Constantine's leprosy.

The other important episode in Sylvester's life was the bishop's foundation of the basilica of St. Peter's. The most remarkable detail of the account contradicts facts and terrain known even in the Middle Ages, when the *Liber Pontificalis* was compiled. On three occasions the burial and basilica of Peter are set at the temple of Apollo on the Via Aurelia. Even allowing that the Via Aurelia Nova, a spur of the Via Aurelia (Vetus), was meant, we cannot reconcile this with the position of St. Peter's basilica. However, we can reconcile it with the *ager Apollinis Argentei* "district of Silver Apollo," which is the modern section of Monte Mario, about 2.5 kilometers from Vatican St. Peter's. The legendary location of the burial and the burial itself seem to have origin in an identification of this Apollo, in whose field pagans buried their dead, with the putative Apollo of Mt. Soracte. Pope Sylvester's retreat to Mt. Soracte is paralleled by his devotion to Peter's tomb below Mte. Mario. In antiquity the Mons Vaticanus stretched from the Janiculum to Mte. Mario.[457] Sylvester's life had pagan associations, and his death confirmed them.

Sylvester died and was burried on 31 December 335. In contrast with another Christian custom of observing birthdays in the liturgical year, (for example, 25 December, at one time the birthday of the Unconquerable Sun), the anniversary of Sylvester's death is still kept. The day must be a pagan holy day for Sanctus Silvanus (Silvestris). In fact, early Christian churchmen inveighed against the rites of St. Sylvester's Eve, as well as the various ceremonies confused with Christian ritual on 25 December and 1 January. All in vain! The anniversary of his death falls in the dead of winter, the season for nearly every festival discussed in this chapter.[458]

For the sake of summarizing the character of the cults kept for the deities whom we have treated here, this scheme of holy days, starting from March, the oldest beginning of the year, is presented:

7 March	Vediovis on the Capitol
17 March	Agonalia
21 May	Agonalia Vediovi Vediovis on the Arx
15 October	Ludi Tarpei (Capitolini) for Jupiter Feretrius Equus October Dedication of the altar to Silvanus
? November	Burial of live Gaulish pair
5 December	Rites of Faunus
11 December	Agonalia Ind(igeti)
17 December	Saturnalia

18 December	Rites of Epona
25 December	Birthday of the Sun (solstice) Birthday of the Anointed
31 December	Deathday of Bishop Sylvester
1 January	New Year's Day Aesculapius on the Island Vediovis on the Island
9 January	Agonalia
13 February	Faunus on the Island
15 February	Lupercalia

The scope of this short survey was delineation of Celtic cults concerning the Netherworld and oracles, and identification of deities related to such rites and of deities who might have suggested to the Romans their own Vediovis and Faunus. Late antique authors preserve the avowedly Gaulish Dusii, who resembled Inui, Silvani, Fauni, and the Greek Pans. Knowledge of the Dusii goes back to Varro, who exhibited an interest in the Fauni, classed among the *di medioximi* with other demons susceptible of angelic character. A Gaulish influence in rearing temples to Vediovis and Faunus at Rome is shown by the nationality of Rome's enemies in the 190's, by the occasion of the vows for all three of Vediovis' temples, and by the presence of Caprina Galla on the Island with the two gods. She was a Gaulish goat-goddess, in kind like the horse-goddess Epona. Her Gaulish name was Fenta, one of several names of Faunus' incestuous wife. Another of her names was Fatua, a name borne by goddesses in Narbonese Gaul and attested with an explicit defini- tion in Justin's epitome of the history by Pompeius Trogus, a Romanized Vocon- tian Gaul of that province. Silvana and Silvanae probably also reflect the creature called Caprina Galla on the Island.

Vediovis and Faunus were principally concerned with the Netherworld oracles, fertility and birth. Their bestial associations tended toward the goat after whom Faunus was physically modelled. From the beginning of contemporary history, the Romans associated Gauls of every ilk with human sacrifice. The goat offered to Capitoline Vediovis was given *humano ritu*, which, I have explained, means live burial. For, since 225, the Romans buried live pairs of Gauls at the initial impetus of a Gaulish foe. Besides Dis, lord of the Netherworld, the civilized world knew the Celtic deities Esus, Taranis, and Teutates, who received human victims, and Ogmius, the Herculean lord of the dead. This same Ogmius was venerated for his fair words.

Like all ancient Europeans, the Gauls experienced apparitions. In this section the visions, dreams, and commands which brought offerings to Silvanus and the

Parcae have been noted. The apparition that appeared to the shepherds and Caesar's troops at the Rubicon is explained as a Silvanus or Dusius. Because the creature was returned thanks of a herd of horses, he may have been Epona's partner.

The only notable oracular shrine in northern Italy was Geryon's oracle at the hot sulphur-springs of Aponus. Although the explicit evidence points to an oracle of lots, the name Geryon suggests an association with cattle, and hence the use of hides to seek the future through prophecy. In any event, such incubation is attested for the medieval descendants of the Gauls. Further, Ogmius' cloak of a lion's pelt may have supplanted the skin of a victim at an incubation rite. Ogmius resembled Hercules, who was considered the discoverer of the springs at Geryon's oracle. The same Greek god was the sometime father of Latinus by the "Hyperborean" girl, who is to be identified as the goddess Fenta.

In discoursing on angels, Augustine felt apprehension over the wanton demons whom women believed they did indeed feel. The demons' female opposites were the fabulous Namnite women who worshipped Dionysus on the oceanic island at the mouth of the Loire. Such conduct was not restricted to Gaul. In Picenum, a root smelling like a goat was applied to women in order to avert the haunting Fatui.

18. CONCLUSIONS

Long before the Latins had heard of Greeks, and before they had learned to write, they kept an incubation shrine in the vicinity of sulphur-springs, where Faunus addressed petitioners who lay down to sleep on the crude skins of slaughtered victims. Faunus could appear, or merely speak, anywhere. Direct solicitation was limited to an incubation site. Men consulted him on marriages and on pestilence. His response on one occasion promoted Aeneas' marriage to his own granddaughter, and on another the institution of the Roman feast of the Fordicidia, "pregnant cow slaughter," for Earth.

Toward 300 B.C., offerings to Parca Maurtia, Neuna, Neuna Fata, and the Lares were set up in the confines of Faunus' incubation precinct. This precinct was called Albunea, a name also borne by the Sibyl of the Latin town of Tibur. The grove of Albunea, however, lay in Lavinian territory. Lavinium, putatively Aeneas' foundation, had begun to receive Greek cults centuries before the date of the four cippi put in the grove of Albunea. The offerings to the Parca and the Fata make it possible for us to refine our understanding of these deities of life and death. Although their total number was reduced to three through syncretism with the Greek Moirai, their original total stood at nine. The name Neuna "Ninth" clarifies the number of sheep and goat victims offered to the Moirai at the Roman Secular Games. The theophoric adjective Maurtia allows us better to view the foundations of Latin literature. Miss Guarducci's insightful treatment of the Parcae and Fatae led to our discussion of the Secular Games. Tentative suggestions and guesses by Miss Taylor can be substantiated, especially in regard to the formulation of the rites on the eve of the Latin War, when the Lavinians kept their loyalty to Rome. Lavinium's gods were rewarded at Rome, at least every 100 years.

The dedication to the Lares by Vesuvia has been brought into relation with two aspects of the cult at Tor Tignosa. The god Faunus was consulted on matters of marriage and pestilence. Roman brides offered a coin to the Lares of their new home and new neighborhood. In one instance, we meet a woman's *iuno* given statues of the Lares to thank her for good health. Otherwise, the Lares are known to have taken an interest in health, especially in the neighborhoods of Rome. By no means exclusively assigned to neighborhoods and intersections, the Lares are also met in the cult of woods. The new reading of the monument to the Lares has removed the Lar Aeneas from any treatment of the Aeneas who was believed by some to have been worshipped at the nearby Numicus River.

Ultimately, Aeneas' importation as a god must be traced to the identification of the goddess of the Lavinian and Ardeate Aphrodisia as Aphrodite Aineia. One of these Aphrodites was surely brought to her Latin home from Sicily. Lanuvium claimed kinship with Centuripe. Saguntum claimed to be a colony of Ardea. Since Saguntines also believed in their ancestry on Zakynthos, Ardea the mediating city must have reckoned a kinship with the people of that island where Aphrodite Aineia and Aineias were worshipped. These details tell us much about the workings of the Latin mind after contact with the Greeks, and suggest the reason for Aeneas' worship.

Aeneas, or his father Anchises who had the gift of prophecy from Aphrodite, was sometimes believed to have been the Pater Indiges of the Numicus River. Another name of this Indiges was Jupiter. Upon examination of all surviving details of the Di Indigetes, in conjunction with the character of the cult around Tor Tignosa, it was concluded that *indiges* is the generic name of a god of incubation. Two likely linguistic analyses of the word confirm their nature: from *ind* + *agyo* "speak within" or *ind* + *ago* "act within." In the former case, Aius Locutius, the Iguvine Ahtu, and Jupiter Dicamnus offer analogy. The Di Indigetes were involved in cults of the Netherworld. Indeed, such oracles by incubation belong to Nethergods of a sort.

The Julian clan claimed Aeneas for their founding father by descent from his son Iullus. The Julian clan's ancestral shrine was situated at Bovillae, where they venerated Vediovis in accordance with the Alban canon. Vediovis, too, was a god of the Netherworld who was invoked at the cursing of Carthage. When Poppaea Sabina gave Nero a daughter, he exhibited circus games at the ancestral shrine at Bovillae. Vediovis was also reckoned important in Julian fertility. Analogous to the Bovillan cult of the Julian clan is the now better-documented Lucerian cult of the Magian clan, who honored Deives. The circumstances of his cult, associated with that of Mephitis, resembled the environment of incubation at Faunus' grove of Albunea and of the wolfmen devoted to Dis or Apollo on Mt. Soracte. Even a Roman bishop was made to keep alive the healing tradition of these wolfmen shepherds.

In archaic Rome proper, no temple was reared and no regular public cult was tendered to the Parcae, Fatae, Faunus, Aeneas, and Vediovis. The Parcae (Fatae) were honored with a single state sacrifice every century. Aeneas never acquired any religious eminence at Rome. Between 200 and 192 B.C., three temples were vowed and dedicated to Vediovis and one to Faunus. Two other deities who shared in incubation rites had been there before them.

Aesculapius, openly Greek in origin and in cult, had been established on the Tiber Island around 290 B.C. His rites were followed mainly for working cures of men, as in his homeland. On the Capitol the Jupiter who was housed with Juno and Minerva evidently received nocturnal consultants before Vediovis came. In any event, he was already an incubation god when Plautus wrote and P. Cornelius Scipio, destined to be Africanus, was growing up. His consultations took place just before dawn. Therefore, Jupiter Summanus, who was considered an offshoot of Capitoline Jupiter, could have been the Jupiter consulted before dawn.

Another Jupiter on the Capitol was Jupiter Feretrius. Ennius commemorated the games given him upon Romulus' completion of the temple: boxing matches and footraces performed on the oiled skins of sacrificial goats. It would appear from the cumulative evidence that the contestants sought a more immediate contact with the honored god. Ennius' attention to these contests was probably suggested by the recent prominence of the temple in Roman military history. Jupiter Feretrius, a lord of oaths, kept the armor stripped by a Roman commander from a slain enemy commander in his temple. The last Roman general to win these *spolia opima*, Claudius Marcellus, presented a Gaulish panoply taken in 222 B.C. In the 220's, the Romans launched vigorous assaults upon the Gauls in the latter's Cisalpine homelands.

War with the Gauls was marked by periodical burial of pairs of live Gauls and of Greeks. In Roman eyes the most outstanding aspect of Gaulish religion consisted in their various modes of human sacrifice. Throughout classical history, the Gauls bid fair for the notoriety of sacrificers and eaters of their fellow men. Vediovis and Faunus received their Roman temples only at the height of Roman fighting across the Po River.

Vediovis possessed three temples. One was set on the Arx and had the god's statue carved in cypress wood. The second lay between Arx and Capitol. Its famous cult statue, like Apollo, was accompanied by the figure of a goat, for a goat was offered to Vediovis in accordance with a human ceremony. This *humanus ritus* required burial of a live victim, as was performed for live human pairs. In the vicinity of the temple of this Vediovis was set the altar of the Julian clan, the same clan who worshipped him at Bovillae.

Vediovis very probably shared his third temple with Faunus. Faunus had a temple with a "Jupiter," a common literary mistake for Vediovis. This joint temple was reared on the Island where Aesculapius had been brought a century earlier. It is the only temple of Faunus known in the Roman world. Its situation by the most renowned incubation god in the civilized world cannot have been fortuitous. Also on the Island, Caprina Galla, "Gaulish Goat-goddess," was honored. She must have shared in the cult of Vediovis or Faunus, who received temples only during war with the Gauls. All of Vediovis' temples were vowed by Furius Purpurio, member of a family that specialized in conquering Gauls for nearly 200 years—or so they thought.

Knowledge of Gaulish influence in making these unique temples to Vediovis and Faunus led our argument to an examination of the gods and cults of the Gauls. The Gaulish divinity that was equated with Faunus bore the name Dusius. The Gaulish Goat-goddess must have been Fenta, whom Hercules brought to Rome from the northlands and gave to Faunus for wife. As Fauna or Fatua, she bore a close physical resemblance to her spouse, that is, she was goatish. In Cisalpine Gaul as well as the Narbonese province, many indications of long-lived Gaulish belief in the goatlike deities survived antiquity. Especially called Silvanus and Silvana, they fill functions known in central Italy, even to putting in a divine appearance now and then. One such shepherd deity appeared at the Rubicon in 49 B.C. Caesar honored it with a herd of horses. The god Silvanus is sometimes associated with Epona "Horse-goddess." Although incubation oracles with animal skins are known among the Celts in later times, only one oracular shrine has come to our attention. Near Patavium, Geryon's oracle delivered lots especially to those petitioning against a wrong fate. Hercules founded this oracle when his plow uncovered the springs of Aponus. Also commonly met by Gallo-Romans were the Fatae, destined to reach us as fairies. Ordinarily beneficent, the Fata had congeners in the Fatui. When Fatui annoyed the good ladies of Picenum, they resorted to a goat-smelling root for relief.

The sources for our study cover centuries in time, and range from Mt. Garganus in Apulia to the Treveri. Despite its unevenness, the evidence yields a general aspect of deities in the wilderness who were made to convey prophecy by peculiar sacrifices. These untamed and wanton creatures belonged to a kind of divineness of the Earth and the Netherworld. The Romans rarely wrote of them with any articulation of respect and true adoration; they mostly people pretty poems on Arcadian existence. Their rarity in the authors as well as city cults suggests a positive shame in others' belief. But many did believe in them.

In his *Satires* Lucilius uttered his contempt for popular credulity, "He attaches importance to these bogeymen and vampires (*lamiae*) whom Fauns and Numas founded. What is more, he shakes at the mere thought of them. As toddlers believe that all brazen statues are alive and are real men, so they think that artificial dreams are true and they believe bronze statues have hearts. The sculptor's studios harbor no truth, just their own creations." [459] By quoting Lucilius, the Church Father tried to dispel the belief in the wraiths of this and other worlds. But Lactantius could merely hope. How could there be assurance of religious victory? Ausonius falls back on his already classical education when he writes of the Moselle River. On its banks and in its stream the satyrs, the Pans, the Wanton Fauns (*lascivos paganica numina Faunos*) disport with Naiads and Oreiads and nymphs where the rich land has already received the Mediterranean vine. [460] Reading Ausonius' description of the gathering darkness on the Moselle, one can seek the river's own Lorelei and give ear to the rustle made by the Bockbeine.

CHAPTER FOUR

SATURN AND THE SATURNIAN VERSE

Some recent studies in old Latin literature suggest that the time is ripe to propose a theory on the origin of the name of the Saturnian verse. This puzzling metrical scheme has elicited modern studies many times the small bulk of the remaining Saturnian lines and the paragraphs of ancient grammarians that treat the measure. In this chapter I shall review some aspects of the cult of the Roman god Saturn and offer a possible link between the verse and the cult. Moreover, since modern philologists have, strangely enough, not paid much attention to the origin of the Latin names of meters and styles of songs, I shall discuss the name of this verse form because of its intrinsic interest for the development of Roman philology.

Rome's first great literary innovator was a poet from the peninsula's heel who claimed mastery of three tongues, Greek, Oscan, and his chosen literary vehicle, Latin. Otto Skutsch has broadened our appreciation of Q. Ennius by publishing in a single volume his researches on the poet from Rudiae, and has provided new insights into Ennius' claim to primacy in Latin poetry.[1] The intricacy of his argument and his economy of words prompts me to leave to one side Skutsch's revealing remarks on the rearrangement, proper quotation, and fine appraisal of Ennius' literary criticism. Rather, I recapitulate his statements on the *versus Saturnius.* The ancients never explicitly told us how or why this atypical meter received the name Saturnian. Varro, *De Lingua Latina* 7.36, first cites the name by introducing a line of hexameter from Ennius' *Annals:*

> versibus quo<s> olim Fauni vatesque canebant
> Fauni dei Latinorum ita ut et Faunus et Fauna sit; hos versibus quos vocant Saturnios
> in silverstribus locis traditum est solitos fari <a> quo fando Faunos dictos.

Skutsch rightly stresses that the absence of the name from the Ennian line and Varro's imprecise *vocant* suggest that Ennius himself did not use the term *versus Saturnii.* He proceeds to another suggestion. The lost Ennian context may have discussed Saturn or the land of Saturn, which, as we all know well, belong to the Romans' hazy poetic and antiquarian vision of their dim past.[2]

Saturnian verse is a term applied to a certain metrical construction that was employed in epic before Ennius, and in other cases even after Ennius' introduction and development of the hexameter. The metrical structure of the Saturnian line has always attracted attention, required careful analysis, and eluded attempts to establish a theory acceptable to all scholars. Another recent scholarly work surveys the few scraps of Saturnian verse that are subjected to exhaustive metrical scrutiny. Thomas Cole's cautious exploration permits us dimly to perceive a primitive verse form, shared by Italic and Celtic, that was further developed separately in the two cultures. In this historical context perhaps stood the Latin *vates* and Celtic *faith*, whose function was at one time especially religious.[3] Moreover, Ennius' line and Varro's explanation have always indicated a religious context in which the Saturnian verse flourished.

At every turn the student of early Latin poetry faces Varro's statement that the verses once sung by Fauns and indigenous singers and seers are called Saturnian. Further, it is significant that, in the passage quoted above, Varro does not follow the pattern—used by himself and also by others—of reporting a commonly accepted nomenclature through a passive form of *dicere, appellare,* or *vocare.* Here the *vocant* indicates that he had in mind some definite persons or writings responsible for the establishment of the term "Saturnian." In the sentence following upon his etymology of Faunus, Varro says *antiqu<i> poetas vates appellabant a versibus viendis ut <de> poematis cum scribam ostendam.* The second etymology does not inspire more confidence than the first. The subject *antiqu<i>* seemed necessary to Canal, L. Spengel, and Kent, who so corrected the *antiquos* of the manuscript, which Goetz and Schoell kept. Even if we retain the reading of the manuscript, we do not have analogous statements, for Varro defined the verses *quos vocant Saturnios.* Varro could not have meant that the Fauns gave them the name, but he could have intended *vates* to be understood: "which singers call Saturnian." However, the present tense in contrast with Ennius' *canebant* does not support this interpretation. The proem of Book 5 of the *Latin Language* reads: "de his tris [*sc.* libros] ante hunc feci quos Septumio misi: in quibus est de disciplina quam vocant ἐτυμολογικήν." The subject of this *vocant* may be inferred from the statement a few lines later that the Greeks call one branch of linguistics etymology.[4] I do not find an exact parallel elsewhere in Varro to *quos vocant Saturnios,* where the subject of the verb is left to guess.[5] It is the subject of *vocant* we seek. As we shall see later in examining other passages, Cicero did not call the verse by the name Saturnian; after Varro, the name next appears in Horace. Even if it originated outside learned circles, the term was applied to the verse by some scholar, for it belonged to literary history.

Our concern is not meter but literary history, or more precisely, history of literary scholarship. Although Ennius was surely capable of asserting literary rules and of pronouncing judgments on modes of poetic expression, and was also at one time a teacher, his surviving words give no indication of his invention of terms such as "Saturnian meter." Moreover, Varro's statement very likely precludes that possibility, because *vocant* does not imply the poet whose words he has quoted. Rather, Varro points to a specific subject who named the verse.

Since Havet's pioneering study of the Saturnian, it has been normal to assign the origin of the name to literary conceit, perhaps from Ennius, referring to the god Saturnus whose great antiquity was especially appropriate to an old-fashioned song.[6] Although Ennius was proclaiming an innovation in Latin poetry and disparaging one kind of poetry for the sake of his kind, neither Ennius nor critics who might have applied *Saturnius* to the verse would have chosen an appropriate name if *Saturnius* merely referred to the antiquity of the verse. If the name was fitting, we must ascertain how it was fitting within the framework of early Latin scholarship.

The first task of every student of classical scholarship derives from the need to put a phenomenon into a context. In this case the phenomenon involves the character of verse named after a Roman god. Saturn represented to the Romans the golden age of a glittering happiness on earth, even in Ennius' work.[7] The entire notion of Saturn's land of plenty which the Romans fancied for their prehistory also implied the good old days rather than old-fashioned and outmoded customs.[8] Saturn was already equated with the Greek god Kronos in Livius Andronicus' rendition of Homer's *Odyssey*.[9]

No Greek verse or meter was named after Kronos. In both social and literary criticism, Kronos suggested old-fashioned ideas and senile silliness.[10] *Saturnius* could hardly have been intended to convey such aspersions on Fauns and *vates*. By the same token, Ennius was apologizing for his own poetry by calling attention to the old manner of song. Whoever applied the term *Saturnius* to *versus* cannot have failed to appreciate the fact that the poet held the old verse in contempt and did not find it worthy of praise. However, ancient scholars did not name measures on the basis of their own or others' contempt. Ennius' lines are made to introduce the subject of the First Punic War. The poet was calling attention to the manner in which Naevius had written. He needed no name for the meter or the style, because his readers recognized what he was rejecting. But subsequent students of Latin literature needed to invent terms to cover all occurrences, not merely the single use. So far as we know, Lucilius was the first to discuss Latin metrics,[11] but he did not leave to posterity the term Saturnian. Rather, the application of the name *Saturnius* seems to have appeared in the technical discussion, or the history, of metrics. The Romans enjoy no reputation for the invention of technical terms. Modern students of metrics usually go to the Greeks for their terminology, just as the Romans based their research on that of their Greek predecessors. Accordingly we must look to the Greeks for a norm of naming meters. In this respect the sense and use of *kronios* and *kronikos*, with the inherent pun on *khronos*, have no bearing on Latin *Saturnius*.

In naming meters, the Greeks might resort to several means of identification. For the purpose of this analysis only two are important. Meters could be named after a place or after a god. The application of such names is reasonably old—older, in any event, than Latin scholarship. Kratinos applied *kretikos* to a trochaic meter. Wilamowitz would assign to Aristoxenos or one of his pupils the term *bakkheios*, which we now call bacchiac.[12] In the latter instance, as well as in such terminology as "paean" and "priapean," the notion underlying the choice of names is the suitability to the cult of a certain god or, to put it another way, the surmise of a cult origin peculiar to one god. Thus, even Xenophon might refer to the *bakkheios rhythmos* of the flute.[13] A Greek theophoric designation of a kind of music or of a verse measure bore a significance far different from that which has been imputed to the Roman name Saturnian applied to Naevius' epic measure. Striving to transplant Greek intellectual habits or to develop their own scholarly tools and language, the Romans followed their Greek models. *Versus Saturnii* should be referred either to a place or to the god in his cult setting, not at all to the god who merely represents to the Romans the Greek Kronos. The Roman's pun on, not to say etymology of, Saturnus, made him a god of earthly blessings through sowing and seed (*sero*, *satum*, etc.)

For brevity's sake I shall summarize just three authorities on *Saturnius* as a place name. Varro reports that the Capitolium had once been called Mt. Saturnius, and the old fortress of Rome had been Saturnia. The indications of these names were three: the shrine of Saturn at the entrance to the hill, the old Saturnian Gate on the site of the Porta Pandana, and the walls of houses behind the temple of Saturn, which were described as Saturnian. Ennius also called Latium the Saturnian land. Varro gives Junius Gracchanus as his source for the *Porta Saturnia*, but does not cite an authority for the *muri Saturnii.* [14]

Dionysius of Halicarnassus proves most extravagant with his Saturnian lore. Saturnia was the native name of Italy which the Greeks called Ausonia and Hesperia. [15] Narrower is the designation of the Saturnian Hill, which saw Hercules institute the Greek cult of Kronos-Saturnus. [16] There the Albans planted a colony called Saturnia. [17] Nor could Dionysius omit mention of Saturn's blessed reign. [18] Most interesting is Dionysius' further statement to the effect that many temples of Saturn are found in the country (around Rome?) ,and that many Italian place-names bear witness to his prominence. [19] In fact, no Latin shrine other than the one Roman temple is known to us, and no known place, hill, or promontory bears his name, despite Dionysius' assertion. [20]

The lexicographer Festus makes two pertinent entries. The second, "*Saturno*," will be quoted and discussed later. The first, "*Saturnia*," informs the user that Italy was named Saturnia, and the Capitol was named Mt. Saturnius, because Saturn was its protector. Men called *Saturnii* once kept a stronghold at the base of the hill and had dedicated the god's altar on this site before the Trojan War. Festus' *Saturnii* must be Dionysius' colonists. [21]

Varro (citing Ennius and Junius), Dionysius, and Festus represent a tradition older than the naming of the Saturnian verse, which is not connected with the names of the peninsula, region, hill, or town. Dionysius tells us that Pelasgians had once occupied a town called Saturnia, which the Etruscans seized. [22] This "Etruscan" town seems to be the colony of 183 B.C., set down in the Ager Caletranus. [23] Moreover, this is the oldest colony to bear a theophoric name. Surely the choice of name augured the town's prosperity. In similar fashion were named the nearly contemporary and contemporary colonies of Bononia (189; rather than Boionia), Potentia (184), and Aquileia (183-181; from the augural bird?). Some earlier colonial names were Beneventum (to avoid Maleventum), Valentia, and Placentia. No real or legendary place named Saturnia enjoyed a reputation for poetry. The application of this name to a colony in 183 B.C. proves the good omen which the name brought upon the foundation. The poetry could not have been named for a place. Indeed, Ennius and his contemporaries ought to have reckoned the adjective a compliment if they had applied *Saturnius* to Naevius' epic meter in the sense of a place that was bountiful, or of a reign that was beneficent. The cause of the name must be sought in the god's real or imagined cult if it cannot be traced to the god's high antiquity or to a place called after him.

Before examining the possibility that *versus Saturnii* were named after matters in Saturn's cult, I wish to complete what I consider an interesting chapter in the history of Roman literary scholarship. As mentioned previously, the Greeks called some measures, such as the cretic and the molossus, after places. The Romans followed the Greek practice in naming the Fescennine verse.

Long before the term Fescennine verse appears for the first time, almost simultaneously in Livy and Horace, Cato the Censor spouted some invective: "in coloniam, mercules, scribere nolim, si trium virum sim, spatiatorem atque Fescenninum." [24] These words were spoken in an era of quickened colonization. Indeed, the speech was perhaps given the year before Saturnia was founded. The explanation of *spatiator* is *errator*, as if a wandering player or tramp. Further, other fragments of the same speech refer to pirouettes (*staticuli*), riding ponies, cracking jokes, performing Greek verses, doing voice imitations, and representing an animated dummy on a festival float. Presumably Cato attributed this conduct to Caelius, who was a Roman senator. In the mutilated context of the fragments, Cato points to the ethnic character of a *Fescenninus* by reference to enrollment in a colony and to the outrageous performances including the Greek verses (*versus Graeci = scaena Graeca?*). Some ancient authorities derived the adjective *Fescenninus* from *fascinum* rather than Fescennia/ium, an Etruscan-Faliscan town on the Tiber River. [25] Cato's audience was surely expected to associate the name with the town in the context of colonization.

In a justly famous chapter on the development of the drama at Rome, Livy alludes to the Fescennine verse, which he indirectly describes as extemporaneous, unworked, and uncouth exchanges of dialogue, in contrast with the dramatic *saturae* which are full of measure. [26] Livy truly had no place for the Fescennine verse in the history of Roman drama. Equal to Livy's chapter in fame is Horace's opening letter in the second book of *Epistles*:

> Fescennina per hunc inventa licentia morem
> versibus alternis opprobria rustica fudit,
> libertasque recurrentis accepta per annos
> lusit amabiliter, donec iam saevus apertam
> in rabiem coepit verti iocus et per honestas
> ira domos impune minax.[27]

Thence Horace passes to *Graecia capta* and the *horridus numerus Saturnius* a few lines below. His lines on the Fescennine verse are reminiscent not only of Livy's passing remark, but also of the scraps of Cato's moralizing on M. Caelius. The *versus Fescenninus* did not designate a meter. Indeed, the inference from Livy suggests that it was relatively free of *modi*. Livy and Horace agree that *versus Fescennini* were *alterni*, which is to say, an exchange, of raillery. Nevertheless, *versus* implies song. Apparently we have a genre of song which in its kind of name might be distinguished from the genre of farce called *Atellana (fabula)*, which also takes its name from a place. Livy clearly suggests that the *versus Fescennini* were recognized as metrically and musically deficient by later standards. They remained a kind of song.

We do not know when the name *versus Fescenninus* found its place in literary scholarship. To all appearances, the word was connected by Cato with the name of the town. The oldest surviving and explicit statement on the name of the verse is made by Servius on *Aeneid* 7.695: "Fescenninum oppidum est ubi nuptialia inventa sunt carmina. hi autem populi ab Atheniensibus ducunt originem." This comment is of considerable interest, because the Athenian origin of Fescennia smacks of the antiquarian research and literary history which are reflected in Livy and Horace's letter. Probably even older than Servius are two truncated entries in Paul's epitome of Festus' lexicon (p. 76 Lindsay): "Fescennini versus qui canebantur in nuptiis ex urbe Fescennina dicuntur allati sive ideo dicti quia fascinum putabantur arcere;" and "Fescemnoe vocabantur qui depellere fascinum credebantur." The derivation from *fascinum* "phallus" or "phallic amulet" very likely comes from a literary history in which the author traced the beginnings of Roman drama back to Athens and to satyr plays. Such a work was written by M. Terentius Varro. [28] Although *fescemnoe* has been emended *fesceninoe*, masculine nominative plural, the precise nature of these objects for warding off the evil-eye (also *fascinum*) is unknown. They seem to have no bearing on our problem.

The introduction of the Fescennine verse into literary scholarship is probably owed to Terentius Varro, who related this primitive banter in song to Athens. Regardless of his identity, the author responsible for finding a place for Fescennine verse in literary studies did not create the term; he merely borrowed it from the Romans' everyday vocabulary. In doing so, the Roman literary historian could refer his reader to the Greek use of such terms as cretic and molossus, or to the putative ethnic origins of the song. In sum, Roman scholars did follow Greek scholarly conventions in such matters as interest us here, and they also drew on existing Latin idiom.

The other alternative for the origin of the Saturnian name is a derivation from the cult of Saturn, or, at least, a belief that it was appropriate to that god. The line of Ennius' *Annales* (214 V^2) that Varro quotes with his identification of the *versus quos vocant Saturnios* appears three times in Cicero, who speaks of *nostri veteres versus* and of Ennius who scorned the *vetera (verba)*. [29] Cicero leaves no room to doubt that the "old verses" should be related to the works of Livius Andronicus and Naevius. Moreover, he is equally explicit that such verse was appropriate to oracular prophecy. [30] Dionysius of Halicarnassus tells us that the prophecies of the Sibyl and of other gods refer to Italy as Saturnia and to the Capitol as Mt. Saturnius. [31] Here, then, we meet one possible source for Saturnian verse. Quintilian quotes part of the Ennian line to illustrate that *ante enim carmen ortum est quam observatio carminis.* [32] Festus surely alludes to Ennius when he notices Saturnian verse. [33] For Cicero, Varro, Festus and Quintilian, "versibus quos olim Fauni vatesque canebant" was a milestone in the development of Latin. In no case does an authority attribute to Ennius the use of the term Saturnian. [34] After Varro and

Festus, the term finds its way into the grammarians, who attribute the name to Saturnia, which they identify with either Italy or Latium or Rome. Marius Victorinus offers *Faunius* as another name. [35]

Upon mention of captured Greece captivating Roman poetry and bestowing learning upon uncouth Latium, Horace wrote

> sic horridus ille
> defluxit numerus Saturnius, et grave virus
> munditiae pepulere; sed in longum tamen aevum
> manserunt hodieque manent vestigia ruris.[36]

The *grave virus* was the Fescennine lampoon, which the poet appears to connect with Saturnian meter. Indeed, here is our first instance of *numerus Saturnius.* Horace's reader was already expected to know what place the Saturnian had in literary history. Ennius' line was a commonplace illustration of the beginning of the new poetic mode. After Ennius and before Horace, Saturnian became the accepted name of the old poetic measure. Moreover, Varro, who reports the name Saturnian, attributes it to a source other than himself.

Before identifying Varro's source, the natural question to be asked and answered entails the divinity of Saturnus and his cult. Instead of assuming that *versus Saturnii* represents a literary cliché for saying "old-fashioned," a connection with Roman cult ought to be explored even if it is to be discarded. The normal route for ascertaining details of the cult would be through the December festival of Saturnalia, which is unusually well documented. At this festival slaves participated in a banquet served by their owners. The *ritus* was Greek. Token gifts were exchanged. Yet in all the details we find no mention of peculiarly Saturnian song.[37]

The clue to a positive religious source for the name of the Saturnian verse has long been available in Festus, p. 432 Lindsay:

> Saturno dies festus celebratur mense Decembre, quod eo aedis est dedicata: et is culturae agrorum praesidere videtur, quo etiam falx est ei insigne. versus quoque antiquissimi, quibus Faunus fata cecinisse hominibus videtur, Saturnii appellantur. quibus et a Naevio Bellum Punicum scriptum est, et a multis aliis plura composita sunt. qui deus in Saliaribus Sa<e>ternus[38] nominatur, videlicet a sationibus.

> "A festival day is kept for Saturn in the month of December because his temple was dedicated then: he seems to supervise agriculture, for which reason he has a scythe for a symbol. Saturnian is the name of the very old measure by which Faunus seems to have sung the fates to men. Naevius wrote his *Punic War* and many poets set other songs in Saturnians. This god is called Saeturnus in the Salian Hymns from the act of seeding."

This etymology of Saturnus was universal, but the explanation of the meter in which the god Faunus sang is hedged here by *videtur*, as it is by *traditum est* in Varro's *Latin Language.* The Salian Hymns supplied the ancient students of archaic Latin with the vocables for study. Festus' entry places the Saturnian verse squarely in a religious context, The Salian Hymns belong to the Martial rites of March. Festus took many citations of the Salian Hymns from the *explanatio* of the grammarian Aelius Stilo.[39] Moreover, Stilo's name is more than once coupled with

Ateius Philologus,[40] whose only work here cited by title is the *Liber glossematorum*.[41] Festus and perhaps Verrius Flaccus resorted to Stilo and Philologus as their standard references.

Aelius Stilo very likely imparted to Varro the name of the Saturnian verse: "Aelii hominis in primo in litteris Latinis exercitati interpretationem carminum Saliorum videbis et exili littera expedita<m> et praeterita obscura multa." So Varro opens Book 7 of the *Latin Language*.[42] Varro himself nowhere else links Aelius, whom he uses in other matters, with the Salian Hymns. But his exploitation of the Salian Hymns bespeaks his reliance on his teacher.[43]

Varro quotes Ennius' *Annals* for the invocation of the Muses and the Salian Hymns in support of his etymology of *Casmenae*.[44] The same linguistic rule of rhotacism is wrongly adduced by Varro for the religious title *casmilla*, when he quotes Pacuvius and cites the specialists in obsolete words.[45] Save for a brief notice on Ennius' use of the Etruscan word *subulo*, Varro passes immediately from *camilla* to the above-quoted line of Ennius on archaic verse, and his own statement that "they call it Saturnian." Who are responsible for the name of the verse? Only two answers are possible in this context: the writers of glosses, or the Salian Hymns and Salian priests reported and studied by Aelius Stilo. Supporting evidence in Varro and Festus admits of either source. We can safely reject the possibility that the glosses invented the term Saturnian verse, even if we should accept the possibility of their reference to the verse by that term. The glosses were intended to serve the function of a dictionary of arcane words, and did not supply literary history or elucidate metrical problems.

For a moment, let us return to Festus' entry on Saturnus, who had a different name in the Salian Hymns, Sa<e>turnus. The entry as a whole does not belong simply to the realm of lexicography; it is partly derived from religious antiquarianism. More particularly, Varro's books of *Antiquities of Divine and Human Matters* could have been Festus' ultimate source.[46] A full discussion of the Saturnian meter must have been undertaken by Varro elsewhere. Varro himself did not invent the name of the meter. Indeed, he does not call it a meter, but *versus Saturnii*, just as we read in Paul's epitome of Festus: "axamenta dicebantur carmina Saliaria, quae a Saliis sacerdotibus componebantur, in universos homines composita. nam in deos singulos versus ficti a nominibus eorum appellabantur ut Ianuli, Iunonii, Minervii."[47]

Of the Salian Hymns, the *axamenta* contain a variety of songs named after the gods to whom they were addressed. Thus the *versus Saturnii* could have been found among the Salian *axamenta*, which had such *versus ut Ianuli, Iunonii, Minervii*. Aelius Stilo very likely put forth the names of these *versus* in his study of the Hymns.[48] The *Ianuli* will have been sung for the Janus worshipped on 30 March, the *Iunonii* for Lucina on 1 March, and the *Minervii* for Minerva of the Aventine on 19 March. Unfortunately, a March day reserved for Saturnian worship is unknown to us. However, the worship of Janus is reported only by a half-line of Ovid (*F.* 3.881).

The antiquarian entry in Festus' lexicon assures us of Saturn's presence in the

Salian Hymns, and cites the Salian name of the god in connection with the Saturnian verse. Varro tells us that the accepted name of the verse to which Ennius had referred was Saturnian. Now Varro's *vocant* can easily be interpreted to mean the Salian Hymns researched by Aelius Stilo. Both the researcher and his research are exploited by Varro in Book 7 of the *Latin Language*. A few chapters before his quotation of Ennius' proem to Book 7 of the *Annals* and his citation of the term Saturnian verse, Varro quotes from Ennius' proem to Book 1 of the *Annals* and proceeds to the *Salian Hymns*. The designation of the Salian *versus* by the names of gods is attested in Paul's epitome of Festus, who acknowledges his dependence on Stilo's research.

Aelius Stilo edited the texts of Ennius and Lucilius.[49] His interest in establishing correct texts must have led him into metrical matters. No intelligent ancient comment on the music and measure of the Salian Hymns survives.[50] We cannot ascertain the character of Stilo's research on the Salian Hymns as song. All ancient authorities agree upon the point that the Salians sang their *carmina* or *versus*, but not one reliable authority puts a name to the measure of the *versus*. Cicero's appreciation of Stilo's contribution to Latin scholarship and of Varro's indebtedness to his teacher reinforces what is to be inferred from the *Latin Language*.[51] Stilo belonged to a new breed of Romans who successfully combined Greek scholarship with their native lore. He chose to name the meter of the earliest epic after the Salians' *versus Saturnii*. In all probability, relatively little of the Salian Hymns was devoted to Saturn. For all we know, only the *versus Saturnii* of all the Salian *versus* represented the same measure as was found in the early epic. At this juncture, antiquarian interest in Saturnia may have suggested the choice.

From the first annals written in Latin, not a few Romans considered Saturn the human founder of their stock.[52] In legend Saturn was Saturnia's eponym, just as Romulus was Rome's. However, the Romans did not desire a primitive site for pre-Roman "Rome;" they already had the Palatine Hill to fill this historical function. Today it is clear to us that the use of *Saturnius* to describe structures on the Capitol, and the Capitol itself, stemmed from the location of Saturn's temple at the beginning of the main ascent to the Capitol. While the word Saturnus is full of good omen, the regular cult of Saturn was principally servile, and hardly lent itself to fancies on the Golden Age of pre-Roman "Rome."

In the context of the human Saturn must be discussed the unique notice in a fragment of Charisius.[53] After a discussion of some lines of the poet Laevius, which are not pertinent,[54] Charisius concludes with two explanations of the name Saturnian:

> hos Saturnios non nulli vocitatos existimant, quod eius temporis imperiti adhuc mortales huius modi usi versibus videantur suas sententias clusisse vocibusque pro modo temporum modulatis sollemnibus diebus cecinisse, vel quod eodem defuncto apotheosis eius hac dictione sit celebrata; cuius exemplum adhuc linteis libris reperitur.

> "Some men consider these verses to have been called Saturnian because the as yet unsophisticated men of that era seemed to end their periods by resort to verses of that measure and to sing hymns on holy days with words harmonized in proportion to the

measure of quantities, or because when Saturn died his deification was celebrated in this manner of speaking. An example of it is still to be found in the linen rolls."

So far as I can ascertain, this sentence has not been subjected to investigation since 1858, simply because Havet explicitly excluded it from his book on the grounds that the metrical examples were not Saturnian.[55]

In 1858, Keil recognized some similarity in this passage to a few insipid statements about Saturnus and Saturnia as possible sources of the name. However, Charisius' statement is much more informative than that of any grammarian except perhaps the remarks of Caesius Bassus (see below, n. 74). Charisius' two explanations are not at all mutually exclusive. Here the nameless authority expressly credits an origin in sacral hymns for certain feast days. Further, upon the death of Saturnus the man (he is the *eodem*), his deification was celebrated by this manner of speech, which was still to be found in contemporary linen books. Linen books in this instance must be a kind of prayerbook or hymnal; M. Aurelius remarked the existence of such holy relics at Anagnia,[56] and according to Symmachus, the Sibylline Books were kept on linen.[57] Neither the vague allusion to holy days nor the unusual mention of linen books gives us a clue as to the identity of the primitive hymns to which Charisius' authorities (*non nulli*) referred. The apotheosis or deification leads us straight to the Salian Hymns. The Senate decreed that the Salian Hymns should contain the names of the living and the dead C. and L. Caesares, Augustus, Germanicus, Drusus, Verus, and Caracalla.[58] Naturally, some precedent must have existed for the inclusion of the emperors in the Salian litanies. Two instances might have been adduced. First and famous, Mamurius Veturius was immortalized by the hymns for his fabrication of the Martial *ancilia.*[59] Equally appropriate was Lucia Volumnia, or Volaminia, who may have been Coriolanus' wife of legend.[60] Perhaps some Romans recognized these and other names as divine, but others thought them human names. Among the deified dead I put Saeturnus. As an eponym of Saturnia, Saturnus enjoyed a reputation like Romulus' and partook of divinity. In his own lifetime, Augustus' name was set beside the names of the gods. We can imagine no fitter companion than Saturn, who connoted much that inhered in *augustus* and *pater patriae*.

Dionysius did not merely emphasize Saturnia's priority over Rome; he believed the name was applied to several places, and that it was used especially by the Sibylline Books and other divine prophecies.[61] We have no control for the oracles, but we can surmise from the accumulated evidence that Dionysius did not check his source on the common Saturnian toponyms. Except for the single Roman colony, no town or place is known to have borne the name Saturnia. In every likelihood the Sibylline Books share some of the responsibility for Dionysius' assertion. The oldest attested religious incident that connects Saturn with the Sibylline Books occurred during the war hysteria of 217 B.C. Among the rites urged by the books was a *lectisternium* at Saturn's temple, and a public banquet.[62] This seems an unusual method of averting the hostility of the gods, nature, and Hannibal.

Insofar as the evidence permits us to make assumptions, Saturn's cult enjoyed no great interest anywhere beyond the one Roman temple. Its prominence is Roman. Although we know a good deal about the Saturnalia of 17 December, we are mostly ignorant of it before its hellenization in 217, and we have no certain knowledge of Saeturnus in the Salian cult of Mars beyond his name. Nevertheless, we can find an answer to the question of what connection Saeturnus had with the Salian priests of Mars.

Two ceremonial words that concerns some Saturnian cult survive to us. Varro uses *Luam Saturni* to illustrate the similarity of accusative *Luam* and fut. first sing. *luam*.[63] This incidental example presupposed his readers' familiarity with *Lua Saturni*. Centuries later, Aulus Gellius cites *Lua Saturni*: "conprecationes deum immortalium, quae ritu Romano fiunt, expositae sunt in libris sacerdotum populi Romani et in plerisque antiquis orationibus. In his scriptum est: Luam Saturni, etc." [64]

Vergil hints at Lua when he writes:

> miserandaque venit
> arboribusque satisque lues et letifer annus.[65]

Servius Danielis understood Vergil's intent and commented: "quidam dicunt diversis numinibus vel bene vel male faciendi potestatem dicatam, ut . . . sterilitatem horum (sc. liberorum) tam Saturno quam Luae; hanc enim sicut Saturnum orbandi potestatem habere." [66] Along with Jupiter, Angerona, and Ops Consiva, Lua was thought to be the ineffable name of Rome's secret patron deity.[67] This secret and ineffable divinity who protected the city was quite old:

> Roma ipsa, cuius nomen alterum dicere <nisi> arcanis caerimoniarum nefas habetur optimaque et salutari fide abolitum enuntiavit Valerius Soranus luitque mox poenas. non alienum videtur inserere hoc loco exemplum religionis antiquae ob hoc maxime silentium institutae. namque diva Angerona, cui sacrificatur a. d. XII Kal. Ian., ore obligato obsignatoque simulacrum habet."[68]

> "[There is] Rome itself whose other name is considered unutterable except at the secret rites of ceremonies. Valerius Soranus uttered it even though it was religiously kept for the weal of the state and soon thereafter he paid the penalty. At this point it seems appropriate to mention an example of the old religion instituted especially for this silence. For the goddess Angerona, to whom sacrifice is made on 21 December, has an idol which represents her with a finger to her sealed lips as an admonition of silence."

The careful reader will remark that Pliny's piety is quite superficial, for his *luit poenas* conveys Soranus' published name to us (cf. Varro's *Luam* and *luam*).

The reasons why a Roman did not speak the name of Lua are patent. Saeturnus protected the ascent to the Capitol and Citadel, the Romans' securest refuge. His protection depended upon his warding off *lua* or *lues*. The former word suggested the latter, and was still ill-omened to Vergil (*Aen.* 3.139, above). Accordingly a Roman did not speak of Saturn's "consort," Lua who was also thought to watch over the people. *Lua* and *lues* are the same word (cf. *materia* and *materies*).[69] Lua deifies not mere destruction but just such blight as the Arval Brethren annually prayed to Mars to ward off. Thus we can safely assume that Saeturnus was addressed by the Martial Salians to keep Roman welfare during the ceremonies of the month of Mars.[70] Lua, at first, appertained to the crops, which she could harm; concern for damage to the crops explains the popular change of Saeturnus to Saturnus. The latter word suggested the seed and supplanted the correct name kept by the Salians of Mars. And so Lua twice appears in Roman history. In 341 B.C. the consul C. Plautius defeated the Volscian Antiates at Satricum and dedicated to Lua Mater the many arms found in the camp and on the battlefield. In 167 Aemilius Paullus prayed to Mars, Minerva, Lua Mater, and the rest of the gods to whom it was meet and just to offer the spoils of the enemy, and then put a torch to the pile of captured arms. His military tribunes circled the heap and threw their own fire upon it.[71] In neither case is Lua associated with Saturn, although Mars is named in the second instance. However, in the earlier instance the consul's choice of deity will have been prompted by the namesake deity of Satricum. At some early date this town, held sometimes by Volscians and sometimes by Latins, will have taken its name from Satres, the Etruscan form of Saturn's name.[72]

The dedication of weapons to a goddess named Lua points to a thank-offering for victory over enemies destroyed; the destruction of the weapons by a fire-ceremony, in which the commander and his official staff participated, points to a thank-offering in the manner of the deity's power. Saturn's control of Lua must have rendered the special Saturnalia of 217 B.C. particularly appropriate to that catastrophic moment. Then Romans besought protection against their own destruction by placating Saturn, who was perhaps doubly relevant by virtue of an identification with a Punic god.[73]

Cicero makes clear Ennius' intention of supplanting the measures of Fauns and seers, in which Naevius wrote his *Punic War*, with the Greek hexameter. The same old measure was employed by triumphant generals upon the tablets they had engraved and set up on the Capitol.[74] When the Romans properly worshipped them, Saeturnus and his Lua returned them victory, and to their enemies destruction. The triumphant Romans adapted the kind of song sung to Saeturnus by the Salians to the commemoration of their triumphs. The archaic prayer of the Arval Brethren in which Mars is invoked against *lues* ends with the fivefold shout "Triumph." Lords of life-giving fields, Mars and Saeturnus marched to battle with the Romans. So great was their power that the Salians dared not neglect their prayers. Accordingly, the Salians were forbidden to march during the month of March, when Mars' shields were carried, and not even Scipio Africanus could then join his dull brother to engage Antiochus' armed force.[75]

Saturn as Saeturnus was first invoked in the Salian Hymns which were sung for the cult of Mars in Mars' month of March. Like Mars, Saeturnus began with an oversight of Roman tilthland. Like Mars, again, he extended his power to the Romans at war. After the season of growth had commenced and passed, Saeturnus was worshipped at his own feast, toward the winter solstice. His Saturnalia underwent considerable change after 217 B.C. Ennius attributed a kind of measure to Fauns and singing seers, and gave it a religious scent. When the occasion arose in the history of Latin letters to give a name to the measure, Greek learned practice allowed a name derived from a god and his worship. Aelius Stilo laid the foundation for the study of archaic Latin by his research into the Salian Hymns. The *axamenta* were hymns composed by the Salians for all men (or gods). The special *versus* took their names from the gods to whom they were addressed. Our single source gives but three names *exempli gratia*. A fourth name was, I have argued here, *Saturnii*. The Romans latterly considered Saturn the object of veneration owed to his deification. This interpretation of the Salian evidence must have been published before Augustus' regime, which the *felicitas saeculi* gave to the civilized world. The secular origin of the *versus Saturnii* must be traced to songs of military destruction and victory. In this measure boys will have sung at dinner the praises of their ancestors' brave deeds, Naevius composed his *Punic War*,[76] and triumphant generals posted record of triumph over destroyed foes.

CHAPTER FIVE

ON MUTINUS TITINUS
A STUDY IN ETRUSCO-ROMAN RELIGION AND TOPOGRAPHY

Aside from brief mention in general handbooks, Mutinus Titinus rarely occurs in discussions of Roman religion. No doubt a feeling of modesty has saved his phallic worship from keen inquiry. Three stages of knowledge of the god Mutinus Titinus survive from ancient times. In the later second century B.C., the Latin satirist Lucilius jests with the archaic form *moetinus* (without *titinus*). Some 300 years later Pompeius Festus, in his epitomized Latin lexicon derived from Verrius Flaccus, compiled an entry which reports modifications in the Roman cult of Mutinus Titinus worked in Augustus' regime, and the existence of a non-Roman cult. The last stage of our knowledge is met in several Church Fathers who drew on the encyclopedist M. Terentius Varro and obliquely disclose the actual cult of a phallic deity whose precise names vary slightly from those in former records and, indeed, could be separated. From the Fathers' writings it appears that the cult was no longer practiced.

This chapter discusses the names of the deity, the nature of his cult, two locations of his regular worship, and his survival at Rome beyond the Augustan era in a more acceptable guise. Further, the possibility of his connection with the Roman state religion as conducted by the Vestals is explored. In the course of the paper the important and mutilated entry in Pompeius Festus is fully, if tentatively, healed, and our knowledge of the Ager Veiens is thereby extended.

In the second book of his satires Gaius Lucilius recorded a jibe T. Albucius directed at Q. Mucius Scaevola Augur (cos. 117). In commenting on the verb *lurcare* Nonius has preserved two full lines:

> nam quid moetino subrectoque huic opus signo?
> ut lurcaretur lardum et carnaria fartim
> conficeret? [1]

Marx, attracting Cichorius' praise, recognized a double word-play in the first line. *Mucius* and *moetinus* (*mutinus*) are punning, while *moetinus*, the penis, invites attention to *scaevola*, the phallic charm or amulet that wards off the evil-eye.[2] Several deductions are to be drawn from the Lucillian fragment.

Marx and Warmington (see note 3) correctly take the word *moetinus* as an adjective modifying *signo* and in coordination with *subrecto*. Accordingly, our oldest reference to the word or god *Mutinus (Tutinus)* shows the first of his names to be a common adjective which is to be related to *mutto* and *mutunium*, similar genital designations. Moreover, the word *moetinus* has failed to call forth any comment from Nonius, who was concerned only with *lurcare*. *Moetinus* was evidently a common word. The Epicurean Albucius asks of the Stoic Mucius Scaevola, "For why did he need the raised penis image? Was it so that he could stuff himself with bacon and strip the larder of meat?"[3] The loss of the satire prevents us from recreating the context in which a *moetinum subrectumque signum* would help in gluttony. Nothing in the later evidence on the god points to a connection with food consumption. Possibly Albucius suggested how Mucius Scaevola used the image to embarras and expel diners, whose dinners he then consumed. Although special powers might reside in a phallus, there is no hint of the deity in Lucilius' lines. A presumptive efficacy in any phallic cult rests with the allurement of fertility of all kinds. Such a feeling for fertility might extend to plenty of food.

We do not meet another mention of Mutinus until the publication of Festus' lexicon, but the subsequent patristic discussions of the god ultimately go back to M. Terentius Varro. In Festus the whole, or nearly sound, part of the entry contains this information: "There was a shrine of Mutinus Titinus on the Velian Hill against Weasel Wall in that alleyway from which the altars were removed and where the baths of the mansion of Gnaeus Domitius Calvinus were built although it had lasted from the founding of the city to the principate of Augustus."[4] Mutinus is joined by Titinus and accurately located in Rome. Festus appears to have modified Verrius' statement, which very probably recorded the removal in the latter's day. The cult comprised a plurality of altars, but we cannot surmise a double god—that is, one god for each name—because the mutilated part of the entry refers to a single deity having been worshipped. The high antiquity of the deity, noticed by Festus, will be shown to be an inference from the name Titinus. Nothing in the surviving entry or in the mutilated part indicates the character of the cult. The house of Calvinus had presumably stood beside the shrine well before the removal, and the presence of Calvinus is perhaps incidental. However, in 36 B.C., Calvinus was responsible for rebuilding the Regia, or chief pontiff's headquarters, and obtained statues from Octavian by ruse to embellish it. Calvinus was a pontiff.[5] The Regia could have stood scarcely more than 200 meters from Calvinus' house and the shrine (see below).

Contemporary to Festus was the Latin Father Tertullian, whose knowledge of the deity is derived from Terentius Varro, as is that of all the Fathers.[6] In two pieces Tertullian sarcastically holds up Sterculus (Stercutus), Mutunus (without Tutunus), and Larentina as model gods who spread the Roman empire, and he contrasts these native gods with foreign ones.[7] Stercutus was a god of dung, and Larentina was a deified whore. More specifically, the same author introduces the god in other appropriate company: "There is a Juventa for the young who have just donned men's clothing, and already a Bearded Luck for the men. If I were to discourse on the wedding, there is Afferenda adjusted from the bringing of dowries; for shame! there is Mutunus and Tutunus and goddess Pertunda and Subigus and mother Prema."[8] Pertunda means the piercer, Subigus the forcer, Prema the presser. Too great emphasis cannot be given to the company gods keep in Varronian theology, because the associations often provide a key to open many closed doors on knowledge of Roman religion.

About a century later, Lactantius provides the oldest record of the god's cult: "and Cunina (is worshipped) who watches over infants in the cradle and keeps off the evil-eye, and Stercutus (is worshipped) who first imported the system of manuring the land, and Tutinus (is worshipped) in whose shameless embrace brides set themselves so that the god seems to have the first taste of their modesty."[9] Later on we shall have occasion to remark another connection of the god to infants' danger from the evil-eye. Arnobius supplies a most interesting list of divinities indirectly taken, in alphabetical order, from Varro. After Perfica and Pertunda and before Puta, Peta, Patellana, Noduterensis he writes, "Is there also (a god of the people) Tutunus whose gigantic genitals and scary penis you desire your ladies to straddle and consider auspicious?" Arnobius goes on to ask the fathers of new religions more rhetorical questions, "Do you shout and complain that such gods as these are violated and overlooked by us in sacrilegious contempt for Lateranus spirit of the hearth, Limentinus keeper of thresholds, Pertunda, Perfica and Noduterensis? And because we do not lie down and adore Mutunus and Tutunus, do you say that everything has gone to ruin and the world itself has changed its laws and statutes?"[10]

Finally, Augustine of Hippo explicitly cites the god. In a famous chapter of the *City of God* entitled "The many gods who heathen wisemen argue are the same as Jupiter," Augustine mentions *inter alios* gods we have just met elsewhere, Juventas, Fortuna Barbata or Barbatus, and Nodutus, and adds another Jupiter, "Mutunus or Tutunus who is Priapus among the Greeks."[11] In a later section where he cites the now-familiar Subigus, mother Prema, and Pertunda, whose names he clearly analyzes, he introduces the Priapus "on whose enormous and wanton penis the bride was bidden to sit."[12] Augustine's Priapus served the same purpose as Lactantius' Tutinus and Arnobius' Tutunus. Augustine's Priapus, in this second case, must be the Mutunus or Tutunus whom he identified a few chapters earlier.

We are immediately faced with two goals in attempting to assess Varro's lost account. What was the name or names of the god? And, second, in what relation did Varro view him besides the role of a Jupiter? Mutunus and Tutunus in Tertullian were double and obscene. Besides other deities interpreted with acts of the wedding night, he is associated with Stercutus. Tutinus (alone) is associated by Lactantius with a cradle deity against the evil-eye (*fascinum*) and Stercutus. Arnobius, too, associates the double Mutunus and Tutunus with a group of divinities of the wedding night. Augustine considers the double names as alternatives, relates the single god, like Priapus, to a host of divinities, and recalls the remarks of Lactantius and Arnobius on the cult function in equally graphic terms while, in applying the word *fascinum* in its other sense, he reminds us of Lactantius' Cunina and the evil-eye. Varro made a distinction between the names Mutunus and Tutunus. The former he very probably connected linguistically to *mutto*, *mutunium*, and their variant forms. His etymology accounts for the divergence from Lucilius' and Festus' name. Further, Varro confirmed the singleness of Lucilius' *moetinus*, if not its adjectival nature. Since Lucilius had the *scaevola* in mind when he wrote, Varro cannot be held accountable for inventing the phallic character of the god. However,

Varro bequeathed to the Fathers of the Church knowledge of a past private cult in which the god's image played a unique role. It is highly unlikely that Varro could have believed such practices occurred in an alleyway within easy reach of the Forum. Although the deity of the Velian Hill was identical with the one discussed by Varro, the Velian public cult can hardly have been identical with that described by Lactantius, Arnobius, and Augustine. Indeed, no author depending on Varro acknowledges the existence of a public cult.

A generation before Varro's research, the moneyer Q. Titius issued two denarii with the same reverse showing Pegasus. One obverse displays the god Bacchus wearing his common ivy wreath. The other obverse has the aged and bearded god with a winged diadem, who is recognized as the Priapos of Lampsakos. Accordingly, Roman numismatists have identified this god as Mutinus Titinus, whose second name was thought to have been derived from Titius' clan name.[13] Thus we are reasonably certain that Varro inherited the identification of Mutinus Titinus with Bacchus and with Lampsacene Priapus, as well as the putative association of Titinus with the Titii. The Jovian nature of Priapus may have been first demonstrated by Varro himself. The Titian coin of *ca.* 88 B.C. supplies a link between Lucilius and Varro whose account is preserved to us by the Christian authors. This link nowise strengthens the folk etymology of the word *titinus*, while it does indeed certify the early phallic character of the Roman Priapus and his similarity to Bacchus.

Putting aside the question of the private cult, we are still left with several important problems. First of all, there is the question of the precise nature of the two names. Second, we wish to know something of the public cult of Mutinus Titinus. Also of interest is the situation of the public shrines of the god.

The problem of the nature of the names can be resolved at once. Both *mutinus* and *titinus* are adjectives. Lucilius used the former to describe a statue or figure (*signum*) of some sort. In Varro's discussion of the many gods identical with Jupiter this deity was included. It follows that he had evidence of these words as Jovian epithets, or that he conjectured such a relation. The meaning of the first name *mutinus* can hardly be divorced from vulgar words for the male organ. The second name is controversial and must now be examined.

In Festus' lexicon it is written that the shrine of Mutinus Titinus had stood since the founding of Rome. Because no certain or plausible ancient evidence for any institution of such antiquity existed, we are compelled to ask why Festus (or Verrius Flaccus) believed in such antiquity. The lexicographer must have analyzed Titinus as a derivative of Titus Tatius, Romulus' royal colleague, or of the Curia Titia, one of many civil subdivisions or of the *tribus* of the Titienses, another civil division. The ancients usually related the last two names to Titus Tatius, so that we need not trouble ourselves in choosing one or the other implicit etymology.[14] Suffice it to say that our sources based their assertion of high antiquity upon an etymology of the second name. If *mutinus* is an adjective, from the word formation it follows that *titinus* is also an adjective. However, Jupiter, or for that matter a Mutinus, is not a likely bearer of an epithet derived from public organizations because of the religious context.

In regard to the Jovian connections of the names *mutinus* and *titinus*, the divinity of the Italic god Liber supplies us with most apposite analogues. The similarity of the Italic cult of Liber, as opposed to the latinized Bacchus/Dionysus, to Mutinus Titinus is quite strong.[15] Liber Pater, too, was considered another phenomenon of Jupiter.

The unusual general portrait of Liber found in Augustine's *City of God* is drawn from Varro, who recognized Liber as a seed god of fertility, *emissor seminum*, and derived his name from *liberamentum seminum*.[16] Liber appears in several Varronian chapters in a loose connection with Mutunus Tutunus, or Priapus, particularly because, to Varro's mind, they are reflexes of Jupiter.[17] Augustine's lengthiest treatment of Liber provides the analogous and unique cult practice. Liber watches over the seeds of vegetables and animals. His rites are conducted in the crossroads (*compita*) of Italy, where male genitals are worshipped. On his holy days the phallus is hauled on small carts through the country crossroads and then brought into the city. At the Latin town of Lavinium a month is named after Liber, because at that season the phallus is carried across the forum and brought to rest in its own place while the people resort to obscene words. A lady of good family then wreathes the phallus in order to elicit the good results from the seeds.[18] Augustine recurs to the same theme of the well-born lady reduced to draping Liber's phallus with a garland, but joins a later example to his criticism of the Magna Mater and the Priapus, who is implicitly the Mutunus Tutunus of the wedding night.[19] The association of Liber and Magna Mater can be detected in Roman religion (see below). Worship of Liber in crossroads of the country was accompanied by stage plays of some sort.[20] This Liber, who belongs to an old Italic religious stratum, resembles Mutinus Titinus. At Lavinium Liber was installed by the forum, while at Rome Mutinus Titinus was situated just above the forum. Both Liber and Mutinus can be reckoned reflexes of Jupiter. In regard to cult, Mutinus' known phallic cult was private and could have hardly become a public matter, while the matronly wreaths on Liber's phallus to elicit growth from seeds can be adduced to illustrate the character of the Roman public cult of Mutinus Titinus. The latter was surely performed by women, and perhaps also by the Vestal Virgins (see below). Moreover, the survival of the cult beyond the Augustan Age can be attached only to a Bacchic cult in the same vicinity of Rome.

The second of the god's names, *titinus*, has also been brought into connection with an Italic cult of fertility by function of the phallus.[21] The nearly unique evidence stems from the scholiast on a word in Persius' first *Satire*:

> tunc neque more probo rideas nec voce serena
> ingentis trepidare Titos, cum carmina lumbum
> intrant et tremulo scalpunter ubi intima versu.[22]

The comment runs: "ingentes Titos dicit Romanos senatores aut a Tito Tatio rege Sabinorum aut certe a membri virilis magnitudine dicti titi. titos scholasticos quod sint vagi neque uno magistro contenti et in libidinem proni sicut aves quibus comparantur, nam titi columbae sunt agrestes." The first explanation can be attributed to the fact that in some way the three ancient tribes of the Ramnes, Luceres, and

Titienses still served as senatorial divisions,[23] and that this division was thought to have descended from the followers of Tatius. The second explanation, appropriate to Persius' intent, uniquely provides knowledge of the word *titus* "penis." The afterthought on the wandering scholars and the wild dove is not applied to Persius' words. Nevertheless, the bird called *titus* is more important than all the lexical items because it is the oldest from the viewpoint of semantics and of the surviving evidence. In etymologizing the names of various priesthoods, Varro wrote: "sodales Titii <ab avibus titis> dicti quas in auguriis certis observare solent."[24] Elsewhere the writer has argued that the Sodales Titii took their name from the Curia Titia and that the Curia Titia took its name from the wild dove.[25] In a word, both the priests and the political division derive their names from the dove. Certain authors would combine Titinus with *titus* "penis," and thus extend the phallic cult. Moreover, the Sodales Titii are brought into the same combination in order to provide a priesthood for Mutinus Titinus and, not so incidentally, to recreate the history of the obscure priesthood.[26] The premisses of the arguments are slight. As Poucet points out, several animals in many languages yield names for genital parts, and not all such genital names yield the titles of priesthoods.[27] It is quite possible that Titinus is derived directly from *titus* "dove."

The name of the bird precedes the name of the penis. Italian offers the best parallel with *uccello*, defined even in dictionaries for Italian high school students as "penis" after the original "bird" (a diminutive of L. *avis*).[28] No one should reasonably argue for the priority of the former meaning. The bird *titus* is the same as the Latin praenomen *Titus* and, like *Gaius* "jay," was a bird of good omen who could supply a primitive personal name. Besides their function as auspicious praenomens bestowed at birth, Gaius and Gaia were spoken at the Roman wedding ceremony. On her way to her new husband's house the bride was prompted to say, "I am *gaia* where you are *gaius*." The utterance comports with the practice of augury and auspices at the wedding ceremony and invites the good fortune of the marriage. Most of our ancient sources cite only the brides by the name *gaiae*.[29] This ancient choice of emphasis was made because of the legal usage of *Gaia* in the texts of all periods when designating the slave or freedman of the otherwise anonymous married women, e.g. *G(aiae) l(ibertus)*. The oral utterance of the appropriate words and the choice of the wellboding name belong to Roman adherence to the omen (see above, ch. 1, sect. 3).

The name *titinus* is derived from *titus*. The question remains which sense of *titus* can be isolated in an analysis of *titinus*. There are many "gods" whose names are formed by the same -*nus* suffix. Here are those whose etymologies are reasonably certain, with the modern etymology which need not coincide with any ancient etymon: Aesculanus < aesculus, Silvanus < silva, Cunina < cunae, Lucina < lucus, Montinus < mons, Rumina < Roma, Tiberinus < Tiber, Nemestrinus < *nemester < nemus (cf. Campestres dei), Bellona < bellum, Bubona < bos, Mellona < mel, Orbona < orbus, Pomona < pomum, Populona < populus, Picumnus < picus, Vesperna < vesper, Nocturnus < nox (or < noctua), Volturnus < voltur(ius), Fortuna < *fortus, Portunus < portus. Among these divinities Volturnus certainly, Picumnus probably, and Nocturnus perhaps, represent respectively the ominous vulture, woodpecker, and night owl. Although none is formed in *-unus*, there are several non-divine derivatives analogous to *titinus*: anserinus, aquilinus, columbinus, Corvinus, hirundininus, noctuinus, palumbinus, passerinus, volturinus. Besides the famed divine association of the *picus Martius*, we know that the Divae Corniscae were related to the raven (*cornix*) and to the cult of Juno.[30] The osprey (*ossifraga*) takes its augural name *Sanqualis* from the god Semo Sancus. The divine Titinus can be derived from *titus* "dove" on both linguistic and religious grounds. From the Varronian analysis of the name of the Sodales Titii, we know that the *titi* had augural importance. Therefore, on purely religious grounds, a sense of phallic character in the name Titinus can be excluded or rendered secondary. Even Arnobius (above, n. 10) reports that a bride's contact with Mutinus Titinus was reckoned auspicious. Further, a direct relation to the Curia Titia, the Tribus Titiensis, and Titus Tatius need not be considered, although such a relation was implicitly invoked to assert the great antiquity of the Velian cult.

There can be little doubt that Mutinus Titinus was a god of fertility. That *titinus* principally betokens good omen should not occasion surprise. A more accurate solution to the semantical problem of *titinus* from "dove" can be found in the ancient lore on doves. The ancients attributed to doves (*columbae*) certain human feelings and behavior. They are chaste birds who kiss before intercourse; their fertility was extraordinary.[31] The lore of the dove is joined even to that of the weasel. The Roman shrine of Mutinus Tutinus was situated near Weasel Wall (see below). Ash of weasel brain in cheese prevented its consumption by mice. If ash of weasel is added to chicken and dove feed, the fowl will be immune to a weasel's predation.[32] The reader here can be spared elaboration of folk remedies calling for parts of doves or pigeons and weasel.[33] The bird *titus* was ominous and observed in augury. The Romans had apparently not always considered *Titinus* an indication of high antiquity. They saw in *titinus* the *titus*, the prey of the *mustella*, which named the *murus mustellinus*. Besides the native enmity of the two animals, another and more appropriate source of the wall's name is the folk-belief in the weasel's efficacy in human fertility. A unique inscription on the base of a golden figure of a weasel runs "Assist Lucia Cornelia daughter of Lucius" (*fove L. Corneliae L. f.*). If Cornelia addressed her prayer to the weasel to elicit fertility, the piece probably belonged to the religion of a happy marriage. The figure itself was perhaps donated to a deity like Mutinus Titinus.[34] On any interpretation, this kind of weasel offering could have been conjoined with the cult of some fertility deity.

When Titius issued his denarius with Lampsacene Priapus on the obverse, by accident or design he recalled the bird nature of Mutinus Titinus in reproducing the winged diadem worn by Priapus. Although Varro does not seem to have drawn attention to this aspect of Priapean iconography, the wings may have indicated to the Romans another reason to identify their native god, related to the dove, with the Eastern deity.

The only document in the history of the cult of Mutinus Titinus is the mutilated entry in Festus' lexicon. The following text is heavily restored in respect to the situation of the second shrine of the god. First the restored text is given, and then a commentary with justification of the restorations and explanations of the whole text is added: [35]

```
20                              Mutini Titini sa-
21   cellum fuit in Veliis, adversus murum Mustellinum
22   in angi<portu>, de quo aris sublatis balnearia
23   sunt <f>acta domus Cn. D<omitii> Calvini, cum man-
24   sisset ab urbe condita <ad pri>ncipatum Augusti
25   <sed deum placatum pro seminibus> et sancte cultum
26   <ab mulieribus velatis praetextatis> manifestum est.
27   <item sacellum via Cassia ad lapidem s>extum et
28   vicensimum, dextra v<ia propter id diver>ticulum
29   <ad Aras Mutias> ubi et colitur et <placatur> in e-
30   <odem more sub Ian>ula.
```

General comment. Similar entries in Festus provide immediate parallels:

1. P. 282. Pudicitiae signum in foro Bovario est ubi Aemiliana aedis est Herculis. eam quidam Fortunae esse existimant. item via Latina ad milliarium IIII Fortunae Muliebris, nefas est attingi nisi ab ea quae semel nupsit.[36]

2. P. 296. Pomonal est in agro Solonio, via Ostiensi ad duodecimum lapidem diverticulo a miliario octavo.

3. P. 298. Puilia saxa esse ad portum qui sit secundum Tiberim, ait Fabius Pictor. quem locum putat Labeo dici ubi fuerit Ficana, via Ostiensi ad lapidem undecimum.[37]

20. *Mutini Titini.* Festus appears to have made only this single entry under *M.* However, today the section on *T* is by no means complete. Therefore the equivocation of the Church Fathers suggests caution in believing the name Titinus was inseparable from *mutinus.* This entry is the only place we find the spelling *titinus* (cf. *latrones Titini* of Festus p. 496 L). The patristic *tutinus* and *tutunus* are assonant with *mutunus,* which, as suggested above, is a later form derived from *mutto,* *mutunium* etc.

20. *sacellum.* This is a generic term for an open-air shrine; see Festus p.422 L.

21. *in Veliis.* The Velian Hill was frequently altered in antiquity. It later bore the name Summa Sacra Via, or Clivus Sacer (in Martial only). The archaic shrines and the topography of this vicinity are discussed below.

21. *adversus murum Mustellinam.* Cf. Livy 43.16.4: clientem libertinum parietem in Sacra Via adversus aedes publicas demoliri iusserant (*sc.* censores) quod publico inaedificatus esset. The name of the wall has been discussed above in relation to the folklore of the dove and the weasel. Other conjectures are to hand, although there is no other analogously named wall in Rome.

22. *in angi<portu>.* Such an alleyway as this need not have been open to the public; cf. Festus p. 466 L: stercus ex aede Vestae XVII kal. Iul. defertur in angiportum medium fere clivi Capitolini, qui locus clauditur porta stercoraria.

22. *aris sublatis.* The plurality of altars is not especially significant, since a single shrine could contain more than one altar. On the other hand, see below on *ad*

Aras Mutias. Presumably any altar was holy. For this and other reasons given below, *sublatis* should be taken to mean "removed" and not "destroyed."

22. *balnearia* signifies the bath-house of, or bathing wing added to, Calvinus' house, which very likely had stood in its place for some time (Platner-Ashby, *TDAR*, p. 179, err on this point).

23. *domus Cn. D<omitii> Calvini.* Several houses of Republican date lie beneath the so-called Basilica of Constantine on the Velian Hill, where the shrine of Mutinus Titinus was situated (see below). Calvinus was the pontiff who elegantly re-built the Regia. Valerius Maximus (8.11.2) reports that Caesar went to the house of Calvinus on the ides of March, 44 B.C., in conformance with duty *(ad officium)*, and there met the haruspex Spurinna, who had predicted his death within the month ending on that day. Suetonius *(Jul. 81.4)* puts the meeting in the Curia after Caesar's famous sacrifices. Besides the Regia on the edge of the Forum, the house of the priest-king stood on the Velia by the Sacra Via.[38] Calvinus' house stood in the same locality and offered religious hospitality to Julius Caesar, the chief pontiff before or after his sacrifice.[39]

24. *ab urbe condita.* This early date was inferred from a connection with Titus Tatius, the Curia Titia, and the Tribus Titiensis, both "Romulean" founda-tions (see above).

24. *<ad pri>ncipatum Augusti.* Verrius Flaccus' lexicon would have been the basis of Festus' entry. Verrius doubtless referred to changes wrought in his own day.

25. *<placatum pro seminibus>.* On the assumption that Mutinus Titinus re-sembled Liber, I have restored a reference to the character of the public cult from Augustine's language: et Liber et Libera seminum commotores vel emissores;[40] sic... Liber deus placandus fuerat pro eventibus seminum, sic ab agris fascinatio repellenda ut matrona facere cogeretur in publico, quod nec meretrix, si matronae spectarent, permitti debuit in theatro.[41] A present infinitive is governed by *mani-festum esse* in Festus p. 260 L, "pedulla" (cf. p. 478 L, "Terentum"). Although the entry "scenam," p. 444 L, is corrupt, the use of *manifestum est* in contrast with *ambigitur* is preserved. Festus is implicitly contrasting present knowledge with a defunct cult.

26. *<ab mulieribus velatis praetextatis>.* Paul's epitome of Festus' entry runs: Mutini Titini sacellum Romae fuit cui mulieres velatae togis praetextatis solebunt sacrificare. There is not sufficient space to hold *togis.* Female worshippers ought not to surprise, since the defunct rites of Liber which disgusted Augustine were female. The handling of the ceremonial objects of the deity need not have invited fertility only upon the handlers. In discoursing on the phallic amulet *(fascinus)* worn by infants to keep off the evil-eye, Pliny the Elder reports that the same amulet guarded generals when it was hung from the triumphal cars. The encyclope-dist identifies the amulet as that guardian "which the Vestals worship as a god among the Roman rites."[42] This "guardian of generals and infants" recalls the fact that Lactantius spoke of Cunina and Tutinus in the same breath, and that Cunina kept the evil-eye from the cradled child.[43] The Vestals, whose headquarters stood

near the shrine of Mutinus Titinus, performed their appointed rites in many places
in the City. Their habitual sacrificial garb was an oblong white garment, with
embroidered edge (*praetextum*) that was pulled over the head and clasped beneath
the chin with a pin.[44] This peculiar dress, resembling a medieval nun's habit, is
figured on Roman monuments.[45] The *suffibulum* could have been the garment of
the women sacrificing to Mutinus Titinus which Paul's epitome yields. Possible
identification of Mutinus Titinus with the Vestals' divine *fascinus* and the trium-
phators' undercarriage companion is discussed below.

26. *manifestum est* close the notice of the Roman shrine and distinguish the
defunct Roman shrine of Mutinus Titinus from the god's other shrine, situated
elsewhere. See above, on *placatum.*

27. <*item*> begins the notice of the other shrine, as in the entry "Pudicitiae,"
quoted above (cf. Festus pp. 474/6, "Septimontio").

27. *sacellum* is restored from lines 20-21.

28–29. <*Via Cassia ad lapidem s*>*extum et vicensimum.* Ursinus and Müller
restored *s*>*extum* and believed there was a notice of a second urban shrine. But
Jordan correctly saw that the other shrine was designated by the appropriate reference to the twenty-sixth milestone from Rome.[46] Other examples of like directions
in Festus are fully quoted at the beginning of this treatment. On account of space
lapidem is preferred to *mil(l)iarium.* The *Via Cassia* is here conjectured because of
the equally conjectured *ad Aras Mutias* at line 29 and the partly restored *Ian*>*ula*
in line 30. Of course, many roads led from Rome. The "Mutian Altars" was in the
territory of Veii. About 21 miles from Rome, on the Cassian Way in Veientine
territory, was the site of Baccanae (mod. Baccano).[47] The name of the village can
be related to the Greek *Bakkhos,* who was variously *Fufluns* or *Pacha-* among
Etruscans.[48] The bad wine of the country may have prompted the special cult of
Bacchus.[49] Beyond Baccanae the Cassian Way verges northwest, whereas toward the
northeast ran the Via Amerina. Just south of the modern village of Monterosi and the
lake of Monterosi, a byroad leaves the Cassian Way and runs east to the Ame-
rine Way.[50] Here, roughly 26 miles from Rome, may be situated the other shrine of
Mutinus.

28. *dextra v* <*ia propter id diver*>*ticulum.* Müller and Ursinus restored *v*<*ia
iuxta diver*>*ticulum.* The preposition *propter* locates the shrine approximate to the
crossroads, a kind of site appropriate to the cult of Liber, according to Augustine's
report.[51] Left-hand and right-hand indications in itineraries are legal usage. For
comparison are these directions, all from Rome: via Flaminia inter miliar(ia) II et
III euntibus ab urbe parte laeva; via Appia inter miliarium secundum et III euntibus
ab Roma e parte dexteriori; via Ostiensi parte l[a]eva inter mil(iarium) I et II;
via Labi[cana inter miliarium II et III] euntibus ab urbe laeva ad viam; via Salaria in
agro Volusi Basilid<i>s ientubus (*sic*) ab urbe parte sinistra; via Triumphale inter
miliarium secundum et tertium euntibus ab urbe parte laeva in clivo Cinnae etc.; via
Tiburtina clivo Bassilli parte laeva.[52]

29. <*ad Aras Mutias*>. This location is known only from one citation by
Pliny, who says that in the Veientine territory and in two other districts there are

places where objects driven into the ground cannot be withdrawn.[53] Most of the Plinian manuscripts give *mucias*, one *mutias*, and an early printed edition *murtias*. The first reading is the easier and thus, perhaps, wrong. A dedication to Hercules Musinus has been brought into relation with the ancient Arae Mutiae and modern Mte. Musino. Monte Musino lies 6 miles north of Veii, not near Monterosi.[54] Some scholars would connect the place with the Mucii Scaevolae.[55] Among Etruscans the root *mut(t)*- is commonly met in family names.[56] The Etruscan ceremonial text written on the Zagreb mummycloth preserves the words *mutince* and *mutinum*. The former is twice met in a long formula with the words *thun mutince thezine*; this last word is not too dissimilar from *titinus*.[57] Such soil as Pliny described at Arae Mutiae would have required the attention of a fertility god. The territory of Veii was full of strange and holy places: the *Rementem* where it rained stones,[58] and the *locus Obscus* which the Roman augurs exploited.[59] The site at Monterosi suggested here is near the territories of Nepet and Sutrium, which the ancients did distinguish from Veientine territory.[60] Prodigies and similar wonders were regularly reported by the name of the countryside.[61] Rarely, a prodigy might be recorded by the territory of a long-defunct community.[62] Although the Ager Veiens embraced several extraordinary places, a precise location of Arae Mutiae remains unknown. However, if the name of the god is to be connected with the place, and if the actual *diverticulum* at the twenty-sixth mile on the Cassian Way is to be identified with that in Festus' mutilated entry, the Mutian Altars were altars to Mutinus Titinus, who was worshipped by the crossroads much as Liber received worship. The place called Arae Mutiae recalls the plurality of altars which belonged to Mutinus Titinus in the Velian alleyway.

29. *et colitur et <placatur>* is conjoined with another verb presumably identical with that restored in line 25. The contrast in tenses *cultum* (*esse*) and *colitur* demonstrates the longevity of the rural cult.

29/30. *in e<odem more>*. In the second instance, *sancte* was surely omitted, and very likely also *ab mulieribus*, etc. Therefore, the lexicographer probably asserted the sameness of the rite. For *mos* in this context, compare Ovid *F.* 2.533, Livy 7.2; *CIL* V 7906, 7909, IX 4185, and *BC* 1904, p. 286.

30. *<sub Ian>ula*. Many words could be restored consonant with *-ula*. The modern Lake of Monterosi was called Janula in the Middle Ages. It was here that Frederick Barbarossa refused to hold the stirrup of Pope Adrian IV (Nicholas Breakspear) in 1155. In all likelihood this toponym of the lake recurs to antiquity. Vergil calls the entrance to the underworld at Lake Avernus a *ianua*. Accordingly, this small volcanic lake may have been thought the gateway to the underworld.[63]

From the restored entry in Festus can be taken for certain the existence of a shrine of Mutinus 26 miles from Rome. The location of the rural shrine by an intersection suggests a similarity to the cult of Liber, which, Augustine reports, was widespread in Italy. By combination with the place called Arae Mutiae and the restoration of the toponym Janula, formerly known only from medieval texts, this shrine can be situated in the Ager Veiens on the Cassian Way. The nature of the soil, which made Arae Mutiae notorious, would have invited the protection of a fertility god. The presence of Liber can be easily assumed from the fact that the Greek Bacchanalia, which blighted the Roman religious world in the early second century B.C., were introduced from Etruria. Indeed, one of the ringleaders of the religious fanaticism came from Faliscan country, which neighbors the pertinent sector of the Ager Veiens. [64] According to the restoration made here, the Veientine Mutinus was worshipped in the same way as that god of Rome. From Paul's epitome is restored the worship by women especially garbed and veiled. The description of the female worshippers' ceremonial attire suggests the special costume, *suffibulum*, of the Vestals, who worshipped a divine phallic image which was like the amulet protecting children and may have been identical with the very tool suspended beneath the triumphal car. The conduct of the cult by women demonstrates yet another coincidence with the Italic cult of Liber, as well as the more familiar Bacchanalian orgy. Returning to the Velian Hill, where the erstwhile shrine of Mutinus Titinus stood, we ascertain from a survey of its cults that the religion of Mutinus Titinus survived the principate of Augustus.

Festus' entry makes clear that Mutinus Titinus' altars were removed to make room for the baths of Cn. Domitius Calvinus, and that his worship was in time past (*cultum . . . manifestum est*). Toward the beginning of the Christian era, several important religious buildings or centers stood on the Velian Hill or, as it was sometimes called, Summa Sacra Via.[65] Three major temples in this area are known. The Penates had a Velian temple. The two youthful gods were sometimes considered the deities brought from Troy to Italy by Aeneas.[66] Augustus lists this temple and that of the Lares among his restorations.[67] Of the latter Velian temple, little is known. The third temple of the area belonged to Jupiter Stator. Lesser deities were Vica Pota and Orbona. We learn nothing for certain about Vica Pota (see below). Orbona, a name formed as Mutinus Titinus, was thought to be goddess of persons bereft of their nearest kin. However, the cult of none of the aforementioned Velian deities can be ascertained.

Finally, we come to the single literary reference to Mutinus Titinus' successor god. In one of his by no means unusual epigrams in which Martial sent his first book in search of a well-to-do patron survives a precious description of this area, whose street he calls *clivus sacer*:

> flecte vias hac qua madidi sunt tecta Lyaei
> et Cybeles picto stato Corybante tholus.[68]

"Drunken Lyaeus" is Bacchus or Liber; Cybele, Magna Mater. It is Augustine who, we have seen, lumps together Liber, Magna Mater, and the Priapus who is Mutinus Titinus.[69] Dio Cassius probably refers to this less famous shrine of Cybele.[70] Indeed, a part of Bacchus' circular shrine or cupola (*tholus*) has been uncovered (see Figure 17).[71] Also, it is fully figured on a medallion (see Figure 18). The Magna Mater is represented on the Haterii relief (see Figure 19).[72] Indeed, Lugli argues that a single *tholus* held both Bacchus and Cybele. This conclusion will be refuted below.

Antoninus Pius minted a medallion bearing the shrine of Bacchus and thereby recording its restoration by him.[73] In an open circular tabernacle stands the erect and solitary statue of Bacchus with his Hellenic accoutrements; on the left a *victimarius* leads the traditional goat victim; on the right stands an attendant with a platter of fruits. Behind the tabernacle is a hemicyclic colonnade (see Figure 18). Ryberg believes the type reflects rustic landscapes, and assigns the scene to private cult.[74] Her feeling may be taken to support the notion of an ideal site in the Italian crossroads where Liber was worshipped.

The shrines of Lyaeus and Cybele stood on the Velia, west of the later temple of Venus and Rome (Eternal City) and south-east of the even later basilica of Constantine. It was within a few yards of the remains of houses datable to the republic.[75] The age of Martial's shrine of Lyaeus, which preceded that on Antoninus Pius' medallion, is unknown.

Speculation comes easy. In the era of Octavian, Cn. Domitius Calvinus expanded his real estate at the expense of the grounds of Mutinus Titinus, whose altars were removed from an alleyway. In 36 B.C. Calvinus rebuilt the Regia with funds won in his Spanish campaign. In it were set statues he had "borrowed" from Octavian. As pontiff, Calvinus could justifiably indulge in such activities. To his house Caesar had officially resorted on 15 March 44.[76] Although Caesar observed the tradition of the chief pontiff to occupy the *domus publica* beside the Vestals' *atrium*, in 12 B.C. Augustus transferred the headquarters of that priest to the Palatine.[77] Thereafter the complex of buildings kept by the Vestals underwent modification. Indeed, from 36 onwards the Sacra Via and Velia witnessed prominent architectural reconstruction under the impetus of the so-called Augustan restoration. To a degree, the Augustan restorations coincided with marked alteration in tradition, not to mention an outright revolution in religion. In this period, I conjecture, the cult of Mutinus Titinus was transferred from an alleyway to the Sacra Via itself and installed in a circular tabernacle in the company of the "Trojan" Magna Mater. Martial mentions this later shrine and attributes it to Lyaeus. The god himself underwent a double change: from Mutinus Titinus to Italic Liber to Hellenic Bacchus Lyaeus.

Terentius Varro bequeathed to Augustine information conjoining Magna Mater, Liber, and Priapus (Mutunus Tutunus). The Varronian discussion could have influenced Calvinus and Augustus to work the hellenization of the primitive god. With hellenization perhaps came the loss of phallic ceremonial tools. In any event, Antoninus Pius' commemorative medallion lacks any indication of a phallic cult. From Pliny, however, come the details on the phallic god which the Vestals worshipped with the Roman *sacra.*[78] Since Festus records the end of the archaic cult of Mutinus in Verrius Flaccus' day, the keeping of whatever old implements survived may have been entrusted to the Vestals. Pliny writes of their divine *fascinus* as if it were the same piece which travelled under the triumphal car and protected it and its occupant from the evil-eye. If the triumphator's amulet belonged to Mutinus Titinus, its preservation after the removal of the god's altars seems assured. The total lapse of an archaic cult and the repudiation of one of Rome's oldest gods hardly seem consonant with the public religious policy of Augustus and his fellow pontiff Calvinus. Instead of abolition, the worship was converted to the religion of

Liber. Indeed, on the Capitol Liber's statue was tolerated within sight of an altar of the Gens Julia.[79] Since Mutinus Titinus' rites were still performed at one country shrine, at least, and a common private cult was known to Varro, there is no reason not to assume that the Roman god was relocated and transformed. If we can trust the mended notice in Festus, the old cult was also changed. The spirit of the god lived on in Bacchic guise.

Gaius Julius Caesar was murdered on the ides of March. Various ancient accounts record the religious circumstances prevailing before his death.[80] Marked *NP* in the Roman calendars, this day was given over to the delightfully bawdy fertility festival of Anna Perenna.[81] All ides were dedicated to Jupiter. This day was no exception, and the ancient sources remark the devotion. As we have seen, Varro argued that Mutinus Titinus was Jupiter. March 15 also witnessed a procession for the Magna Mater that initiated a series of oriental rites for the goddess on subsequent days. Martial reports Lyaeus' proximity to Cybele on the Sacred Slope. Ovid emphasizes the slain Julius' priesthood of the chief pontificate and his superintendence of Vesta's worship.[82] Ovidian emphasis reinforces the suggestion of a relation of Mutinus Titinus to the Vestals' *fascinus* if the sacrifices of Caesar on this day can be related to the phallic god.

On 17 March the Romans kept the festival of Liber called the Liberalia. Basing himself on the Liberian character of this day, Degrassi identifies the Lavinian month of Liber as that of the season when spring commences.[83] This coincidence of the season of Mars and Liber and their worship is also met in October, and also falls on the ides.[84] The frequently mentioned prodigies attendant upon Caesar's death give no consistent picture. Valerius Maximus alone tells us that Caesar was at the house of Gnaeus Domitius Calvinus *ad officium*, where a sacrifice is implied by the presence of the haruspex Spurinna, also in the house *ad officium*. (In the various telling of the warnings given Caesar, Spurinna plays the haruspex on the Lupercalia and the day after, and is reported to have answered Caesar that the ides of March had not passed in Calvinus' house and upon the dictator's entry to the senate.)

On the ides of March the chief pontiff went from his official residence, the *domus publica*, to the neighboring house of Calvinus, by which he sacrificed to Mutinus Titinus. There he met with inauspicious victims. Thence he returned home, but D. Brutus Albinus urged him to reject the omens and to quit his house. Now he went to Pompey's theater and senate-chamber for his last meeting.[85] The previous day an auspicious bird called the "royal bird" (*regaliolus*) had brought laurel into the very chamber.[86] We at least wonder whether this otherwise unattested harbinger of doom was the wild dove. If the conjecture on the identity of the deity to whom Caesar sacrificed is correct, the reason for Calvinus' or Augustus' drastic change in the cult of Mutinus Titinus is apparent. The god had quit Caesar at the moment of the ultimate defeat. His heir saw to the dismantlement of the god's old shrine, and at a neighboring site to the installation of an altered divinity patterned after the hellenized Liber.

Every year on 9 June, the Vestal Virgins kept the feast of the Vestalia. They were attended by asses garlanded with loaves of bread. The ass was sacred to the Lampsacene god Priapus. It was this strange god who usurped the place of Mutinus Titinus in Latin authors. A single calendar painted in the reign of Tiberius informs us that the sacrifice took place at a *ianus*.[87] This *ianus* can be identified with an arch set up by Marius in close proximity to the Vestals' house (see below). Belief that the Vestal Virgins kept the asses of Priapus, a notorious and notoriously foreign god, arose from their veneration of Mutinus Titinus and his phallus. Whereas Mutinus Titinus was venerated by the chief pontiff and Vestals on 15 March, the ides sacred to Jupiter, Vesta was worshipped on 9 June by the Vestals, who also honored the phallus on this same day.

No little irony clings to Martial's conjunction of Cybele with Lyaeus, whose shrine is virtually located by the discovery of a sculptured fragment, and by Antoninus' inscribed record of restoration. The goddess Cybele is figured on the Haterii relief, whereon her cult statue stands at the top of a flight of stairs looking through the side openings of a *ianus* bearing a triumphal car. Before the shrine is an altar at the foot of the stairs (Figure 9). The nature of her shrine, the often discussed identity of that arch, and their relation to Gaius Julius Caesar can now be ascertained,

In 102 B.C. Gaius Marius faced the Teutons at Aquae Sextiae, and with Lutatius Catulus, in 101 at Vercellae the Cimbrians. Rome's destiny seemed weighed upon another Gaulish balance. From Pessinum in Asia came Battaces, a priest of the Great Mother of the Gods, who reported that the goddess foretold a Roman victory. Elated with the news coming at a time of untoward prodigies, the senate decreed a temple of Victory to Magna Mater. The plebeian tribune Aulus Pompeius denounced the report at the assembly summoned to hear such heartening divine news. Almost at once he dropped dead on the Capitol, where he had made his address to the gods. His death lent great corroboration to the Asiatic reporter.[88]

Upon the occasion of his triumph over the Gauls and Germans, Marius reared the temple of Honor and Courage, as well as trophies in two different quarters. Sulla destroyed the trophies, which Gaius Julius Caesar restored. One set stood on the Capitol. The second set's situation has remained unknown until this day.[89]

One of the temples of the Velia was that of Vica Pota. In antiquity it was confused with a temple of Victory, which was believed to explain the name Vica.[90] This temple of Victory can be no other than that vowed in 102 and related to the oracle of the Magna Mater. The senate chose the site on the Velia for three reasons. The name Vica already suggested victory, the Penates would stand by their ancestral associate from Troy, and, finally, the phallic amulet for triumphs was lodged with Mutinus Titinus who was quartered in the vicinity. As curule aedile in 65 B.C., Caesar restored the second set of trophies which his aunt's husband had set up by the senate's temple of Victory. In the temple stood a statue of the Magna Mater which looked through the side openings of a triumphal arch (Figure 19). Whose triumph was commemorated by the arch? It was Marius' triumph. No arch for a Marian victory is mentioned by an ancient source. However, the likelihood of this identity is considerable, for after 121 B.C. Q. Fabius Maximus Allobrogicus had set up the Fornix Fabianus illuminating his victory over the Gaulish Allobroges. Marius' idea for the arch would have come from the Fabian *fornix*, which was erected on the Sacra Via by the Regia, at the beginning of its ascent to the Velia. Further, eight years after Caesar restored the Marian trophies, Fabius Allobrogicus' grandson restored the *fornix* and honored the triumphs of his grandfather's natural clansmen, the grandfather Aemilius Paullus and the uncle Scipio Aemilianus.[91] Marius strove to emulate the great patrician generals. Sulla strove to eradicate the fame of his enemy. Caesar revived the glory of his relation.

A miracle took place on the battlefield where Q. Fabius Maximus met the Allobroges. After 130 enemy soldiers were slain, Fabius was released from a quartan fever. For what reason was this fact recorded so that it reached Pliny? Evidently Fabius recompensed the gods for his delivery. Valerius Maximus situates one of the three Roman precincts of Fever in the *area Marianorum monumentorum*.[92] From these two notices it seems likely that Fabius set aside land for Fever near the Fornix Fabianus. Some twenty years later Marius, too, set aside land for a complex of commemorative structures that embraced this precinct of Fabian Fever.

A further word on the Fabian Fever will demonstrate her presence in Latin literature, in order to ridicule the emperor Claudius' patronage of Gaulish senators, a patronage that outraged certain members of the established Roman aristocracy. The goddess Fever, whom Fabius Maximus Allobrogicus honored, appears in a little understood passage of Seneca's *Apocolocyntosis*, the Menippean satire written on Claudius' advent to heaven. In heaven Fever, the officially published cause of Claudius' death, identifies Claudius for Hercules, whom the freshly dead emperor has accosted: "He was born at Lugdunum. You are looking upon the fellow townsman of Maximus. What I'm telling you is that he was born sixteen miles from Vienna and is a Gaulish cousin (*germanus*). Consequently he seized Rome because a Gaul had to do so." Hercules is being doubly doltish because Fabius Maximus had reared a temple to him and another to Mars at the confluence of the Isar and Rhodanus rivers, where the Roman had defeated the Allobroges whose tribal center was Vienna. Since Vienna does not appertain to a report of Claudius' birthplace, its introduction suggests the Allobroges, Maximus' conquest, and the general's award to Hercules. Thus the troubled text of Seneca, *Marci municipem*, should now be corrected *Ma<xim>i municipem*, an allusion Hercules can understand. After being made an honorary Latin colony by Julius Caesar, Vienna became a Roman colony under Gaius Caligula or Claudius himself. What Fever conveys to Hercules is that before its colonial status the Allobroges' capital town had been reduced to the condition of Maximus' *municipium*. By way of illustration of this odd municipal status, we point to one Q. Fabius Sanga, who served the Allobroges as patron at Rome in 63 B.C. Claudius himself refers to Allobrogicus' descendant Paullus Fabius Persicus (cos. A.D. 34) as his friend, immediately after mentioning the Viennenses, in his famous speech to the senate in 48 when he advocated the admission of Gauls to that body.[93] Let us return to the tale of Marius' victory over the Gauls.

By two *quinarii* issued about 100 B.C., Roman moneyers spread Marius' fame. With Jupiter's head on the obverse, Gaius Fundanius and Titus Cloulius struck reverses on which a Victory crowns a trophy where a Gaulish captive is bowed in submission. The second moneyer also figured a peculiarly Gaulish battle-horn that is found on a contemporary coin of Gaius Egnatuleius, who has a horned helmet surmount the trophy without the captive.[94] After the battle of Vercellae, the soldiers of Lutatius Catulus had taken most of the Gaulish horns to their camps, and based the claim of their superiority upon these horns. Marius and his consular colleague quarreled over their several contributions to the defeat of the Cimbrians.[95] The attachment of the trumpets to the trophy reasserts Marius' claim of total responsibility for the victory. All three coin types reflect the character of the Marian trophies. Moreover, their peculiarity recalls the Gaulish monument of Fabius Allobrogicus, whom Marius imitated and whose Fever he appropriated.

The commemorative site which held Marius' trophies, the temple of Victory (Vica Pota), the triumphal arch, and a shrine of the Magna Mater as well as a precinct of Fever, was that place called *area Marianorum monumentorum*. Most of the terrain had formerly been occupied by the modest domestic establishment of sixteen members of the Aelian clan.[96] On the Haterian relief, the Flavian amphitheater (Colosseum) and the arch inscribed *in Sacra Via Summa* flank an archway topped by a triumphal car, which must represent a Flavian restoration. Through the *ianus* can be seen the Magna Mater standing in a shrine raised by fourteen steps. At the foot of the steps, the altar (see Figure 19).[97] On the reverse of a contorniate of Diva Augusta Faustina is figured the *tholos* of the Mater Deum Salutaris (see Figure 20).[98] The epithet *salutaris* reinforces the suggestion of an association with the precinct of Fever. Since Antoninus Pius restored the shrine of Bacchus (see Figures 17 & 18), his wife Faustina will have chosen to commemorate a like restoration of the *tholos* of Cybele.

After Caesar's death the shrine of Liber, formerly Mutinus Titinus, was planted in or beside the *area*, where he joined Caesar's restorations of the year 65 B.C. The last object of Caesar's devotion kept company with one of his ancestral goddesses and those concrete objects which family piety and political ambition had refurbished in his aedileship. Meanwhile on the Capitol, where the other Marian trophies were preserved, Liber's statue stood by the altar of the Julian Clan. Indeed, Liber at the altar of the Julian Clan and in the Marian precinct of victory on the Velia presented an auspicious aspect. In antiquity Marius was said to have regularly drunk from a cup, decorated with Bacchus leading the first triumph, after he had defeated the Cimbrians and Teutons, and to have compared his triumphs with that of the god.[99] From the Greek side, Bacchus represented the first triumphator; from the Roman side, Liber promoted the worship of the *fascinus*, a cult object applied to the triumphator's car to keep off the evil-eye. Indeed, Caesar converted the Liberalia of 17 March into a victory celebration commemorating the civil-war battle of Munda,[100] because protocol did not admit a proper celebration or perpetual commemoration of the defeat of fellow Romans. Liber supplied Caesar with a surrogate for a triumph, and thus came to attract the cult at the altar of the Julian Clan, which was located by this Capitoline statue.

Marius' triumphal arch opened the Sacra Via Summa to the later triumphal arch of Titus. Indeed, the Marian arch of the Haterian relief is surely a Flavian restoration, done when those emperors concerned themselves with the approaches to their new amphitheater, and Domitian especially assumed the task of rebuilding the burnt city. The market and stores for eastern spices were built by Domitian on the land that would later hold the so-called basilica of Constantine. It was destroyed in a fire under Commodus and rebuilt under Severus.[101] The ground for this store was that on which, it was suggested here, the house of Domitius Calvinus stood. If the Marian arch survived Hadrian's ambitiously conceived temple of Venus and Rome (Eternal City) and the destruction of the Spice Market, it probably did not endure the damage to Hadrian's temple by a fire in 307.[102]

In any event, Domitian is the likeliest candidate for having restored Marius' arch. Marius had won the first Roman victory over Germans, a bested enemy whom Domitian, too, could single out as his own. According to his biographer, Domitian's megalomania impelled him to build so many ponderous *ianos arcusque* in several urban regions that someone wrote on an arch the punning Greek word "enough" (*arci*).[103]

At the beginning of the second century, Trajan reissued several old republican coin types that fittingly reminded his subjects of past deeds. Among the revived types was the then 200-year-old coin of Q. Titius with Mutinus Titinus cast as Priapus of Lampsacus.[104] The reappearance of Mutinus Titinus perhaps reflects some Trajanic renovation of the shrine of Bacchus on the Velian Hill, which had been necessitated by Domitian's rebuilding of the neighboring arch of Marius. Trajan's choice of the obverse of Mutinus Titinus over Titius' other obverse of Bacchus will have been dictated by his program of encouraging the repopulation of Rome and Italy.[105] The revived type, then, would have masked allusion to the antique fertility cult of a phallic character.

Let us summarize the history of the Marian *area*. After his victory over the Allobroges in 121, Q. Fabius Maximus erected the Fornix Fabianus on the Sacra Via near the Regia and created a precinct for Fever on the Velia on the Sacra Via Summa. A few years later, an envoy from Asia Minor brought good news from the Magna Mater, to whom the senate promised a victory temple if the Romans should defeat the Teutons and Cimbrians. When Marius returned to Rome after delivering the two defeats upon the northern enemies, he set up trophies and a *ianus*, or triumphal arch, on the Velia where Fabius had laid out a precinct for Fever and the senate had converted the worship of Vica Pota to Victory for the Magna Mater. Sulla attempted to suppress these commemorative structures insofar as he was permitted. In 65 B.C. Julius Caesar took the occasion of his aedileship to refurbish the monuments of his aunt's husband. Soon thereafter, one of Fabius Allobrogicus' descendants rebuilt the Fornix Fabianus. After Caesar's death the god formerly known as Mutinus Titinus was moved to the Sacra Via Summa from an alley and placed beside the Magna Mater and the Marian arch. It was this *ianus* where the Vestals kept the Vestalia, and perhaps venerated the phallus employed in triumphal processions. Martial mentions the temples of Lyaeus and Cybele in the same breath. On the Haterian relief the four-way arch or *ianus* represents the restoration, which we propose is Domitianic. Fragments of the inscription, with a Maenad in relief, record the restoration of the Bacchic shrine by Antoninus Pius. This emperor also minted a medallion which preserves a view of the shrine, while for Faustina was issued a contorniate showing the *tholos* of Mater Deum Salutaris (Figures 17-20). After the Antonines, no mention of the shrines or monuments in the Marian complex survives.

In conclusion, four cults of Mutinus Titinus are discernible: a domestic cult subsequent to a wedding, public worship by women at altars in an alleyway on the Velian Hill, a presumably remodelled cult of Liber-Bacchus on the Sacra Via, which replaced the cult in the alleyway, and, finally, the rural observances in Veientine country by the twenty-sixth milestone on the Cassian Way.

The god Mutinus Titinus was worshipped for the fertility which he brought to the land and to its living things. The first name reflected his phallic nature; the second, the auspicious bird *titus.* His cult was associated with the god of manuring, whose rural function also bestowed fertility on the land, and with the goddess of cradles who protected babies against the evil-eye by virtue of a phallic amulet. Mutinus Titinus enjoyed two shrines. As late as Festus' day he was worshipped at the twenty-sixth mile from Rome. Here we have demonstrated the likely site on the Cassian Way, at a place called Arae Mutiae beneath the small lake Janula, where whatever was stuck into the ground could not be withdrawn.

At Rome the god was venerated by women in an unusual habit. By intricate combination of the details in the death of Julius Caesar, the date of 15 March for the god's annual rites is indicated. Two days before the Liberalia, the chief pontiff and the Vestal Virgins in their special garb perhaps venerated Mutinus Titinus with sacrifice. The Jovian observances on this day and all other ides suggested to Varro Mutinus Titinus' identification as Jupiter. Liber Pater, whose old Italic cult very closely resembled our slight knowledge of Mutinus Titinus' cult, was also considered a *Iovis pater* by the same Varro. Moreover, Caesar had rendered Liber responsible for the memory of his victory at Munda instead of a triumph. Sometime during Augustus' rule, Mutinus Titinus' altars were removed to make way for the bathing facilities of Cn. Domitius Calvinus, pontiff and associate of the two Caesars. In consequence of its removal from an alleyway, the cult of Mutinus Titinus was transformed into a hellenized Liber, or Bacchus Lyaeus, and made the neighbor of the Great Phrygian Mother, whose one feast also fell on the ides of March. Further, the reformed Mutinus Titinus was situated in, or beside, a precinct called *area Marianorum monumentorum* that Julius Caesar had restored to glorify his aunt's spouse. Domitian rebuilt Marius' triumphal arch, and perhaps only recorded his own name upon the monument as was his habit. Domitian's contemporary Martial speaks of the shrines of Lyaeus and Cybele side by side. The latter's temple looked upon the Marian arch. Antoninus Pius and Faustina restored the two unusual shrines of Bacchus Liber and the Great Mother. The emperor Trajan chose to remint a coin of the early first century B.C., on which was figured the bust of Mutinus Titinus in the Lampsacene guise of Priapus. This revival has been brought here into relation with the emperor's program for the increase in Italian population, which is otherwise well attested.

Finally, the "Trojan" setting recalls the origins of the neighboring Penates, which Augustus' ancestor had brought from Troy. Among Rome's *sacra*, also legacies of Troy, the Vestal Virgins kept a divine phallus like that which watched over babies and the cars of triumphant generals. Mutinus Titinus may well have been the very tool for the triumphant, for Augustine himself authenticates the phallic Liber's travel about the countryside in little carts.

Key to the Illustrations

Figure 1. The denarius (rev.) of C. Renius; ch. 1, sect. 3.

Juno Caprotina rides in a car drawn by two galloping goats, variants from the normal horses drawing war-chariots (see Figure 5). In her right hand Caprotina holds a whip, and in her left the scepter of dominion. The moneyer, C. RENI(*us*), intends to suggest his name's connection with a Greek word for sheep *(rhēn)* and a Celto-Latin word for a peculiar mantle of shaggy fleece (*reno*), and thereby to recall Caprotina's unusual Roman garb.

Figure 2. The denarius (obv.) of L. Thorius Balbus; ch. 1, sect. 8.

The head of I(*uno*) S(*ispes*) M(*ater*) R(*egina*) is shown with the goatskin headdress tied beneath the chin. The goddess was the principal deity of Lanuvium, where the moneyer originated.

Figure 3. The denarius (rev.) of the same; ch. 1, n. 195.

L. THORIVS BALBVS came from Lanuvium (*RE* 6A1 (1936) no. 4). He figures the charging bull (*torus*, i.e. *taurus*) to represent his family name. Both obverse and reverse play on the animal theme, with which compare the coins of Cornificius (above, ch. 3, sect. 8).

Figure 4. The denarius (obv.) of L. Procilius F.; ch. 1, sect. 8.

Another obverse with the head of Juno Sispes Mater Regina wearing the goatskin headdress was coined in accordance with a senate decree, S(*enatus*) C(*onsulto*).

Figure 5. The denarius (rev.) of the same.

L. PROCILI(*us*) F. (his cognomen is not spelled out) shows Juno Sispes riding in a war-chariot drawn by two horses. Head covered with the goat head, the goddess brandishes a spear in her right hand and with her left holds a figure-eight shield (*scutulum*, according to Cicero). The horses' forelegs rise above the erect serpent belonging to her Lanuvian cult (see Figure 7).

Figure 6. The denarius (obv.) of L. Roscius; ch. 1, sect. 8.

Behind a third head of Juno Sispes covered by the goatskin dress is represented a fixed circular altar peculiar to her Lanuvian cult. This symbol is always minted on this coin with that on the reverse (Figure 7), although the moneyer chose many other symbols for the same issue. L. ROSCI(*us*) Fabatus is one of several Roscii known to have originated in Lanuvium (*RE* 1A1 (1914) nos. 5, 15, 16), and is the second Roman moneyer from that town to issue a coin with this Juno (Figures 2, 3).

Figure 7. The denarius (rev.) of the same.

On the obverse FABAT(*us*) has chosen to represent the famous ordeal of the maid of Lanuvium who once a year descended blindfolded into Juno Sispes' cavern, where a hungry snake was expected to eat the cakes she bore in a basket. If it ate the cakes, this coin's symbol behind the maid, she was known to be virginal and the coming year to be fruitful. (See Prop. 4.8; Aelian *NA* 11.16). Perhaps Fabatus commemorates the successful ordeal of some Roscia. The same snake is met in Figure 5.

Figure 8. *Inscriptiones Italiae* 4.1.73; ch. 2.

This inscription from Tibur is now preserved in the Terme Museum, inv. no. 115643.

Figure 9. Plan of Lavinium and Environs; ch. 3.

Figure 10.   Belvedere Altar, Vatican Museum; ch. 3, sect. 15.

This side of the sculptured altar was set up after 12 B.C. and marked Augustus' assumption of the chief pontificate. The sides not illustrated here represent a winged victory, the apotheosis of Julius Caesar, and events in the compital cult of the Lares. In this illustration bearded Aeneas, leaning on his staff, stands on the right. He listens attentively to the now headless, heavily clothed god Faunus who reads from the Book of Fate concerning the omen of the white sow. The sow herself stands between the two persons, amid some of her thirty piglets. The rock ledge, the stone seat of Faunus, and the mutilated tree betoken the wildness of the place.

Figure 11.   The denarius (obv.) of P. Cornelius Lentulus Marcellinus; ch. 3, sect 11.

MARCELLINVS has chosen the realistic bust of his illustrious ancestor M. Claudius Marcellus, which may have been copied from the ancestral mask. Behind the gaunt face is the triskeles, a symbol of three running legs that betokens Sicily, where Marcellus conquered Syracuse during the second Punic War.

Figure 12.   The denarius (rev.) of the same.

MARCELLVS CO(*n*)S(*ul*) QUINQ(*ies*), i.e. consul five times, carries the uniform stripped by himself from the corpse of the Gaulish chieftain, slain at the battle of Clastidium in 222. Called *spolia opima*, these clothes and bodily accoutrements are displayed on a small cross which is to be installed in the temple of Jupiter Feretrius. Wearing a toga which is brought over his head in order to represent the ceremonial attitude of dedication, Marcellus begins to mount the steps to the tetrastyle temple of Feretrius, in whose honor were given games performed on the oiled skins of sacrificial goats. This coin probably also commemorates Marcellus' rebuilding of the temple that was thought to have been founded by Romulus.

Figure 13.   The denarius (obv.) of L. Caesius; ch. 3, sect. 12.

The diademed head and back of the god Vediovis are finely turned toward the viewer. Over the left shoulder is draped a cloak, and the right is bare. The god holds his thunderbolt in his right hand. Beside the head is an uncommon monogram of ROMA, also visible on Figure 15.

Figure 14.   The denarius (rev.) of the same.

L. CAESI(*us*) portrays the two Lares sitting on rocks. (The Lares are often elsewhere shown dancing on rocks.) While they are bare above the waist, they seem to wear dogskins on their laps. They pet a dog standing between them. The dog and the Lares are watchful guardians. Both Lares hold spears in their left hands, recalling the Lares Praestites "Guardians," or Militares. Above and between their heads is a small bust of Vulcan and the tongs mintmasters wielded. The god Vulcan's fire was needed to mint. It should also be remembered that the Lares kept watch against fire in their neighborhoods (cf. CIL VI 801, 802). The inscription on the reverse is a matter of some discussion. On the left are LA (*res*) in ligature, which assures the identification of the two gods. On the right are RE or ER in ligature, which may be the end of the word Lares or the beginning of another word. Some have thought of a reference to the Lares of Rhegium, for which no evidence exists. Very likely the second word, if it is a second word, is RE(*gionum*) since the Lares of the neigborhoods were supervised according to the administration of the four regions of Republican Rome.

Figure 15.   The denarius (obv.) of Manius Fonteius, son of Gaius; ch. 3, sect. 12.

This head of Vediovis sports lovely curled locks. The thunderbolt is set beneath the bust and the monogram of ROMA to the right. The same uncommon monogram is found on the other coin of Vediovis (Figure 13). The family of M(*anius*) FONTEI(*us*) C(*ai*) F(*ilius*) came from Tusculum and had connections with the Gauls through warfare.

Figure 16. The denarius (rev.) of the same.

Within Apollo's bay wreath are set several objects. The female goat, pertinent to Vediovis' Roman cult, here reflects the Cretan legend of Amalthea, who gave nourishment to baby Zeus. Vediovis was the Romans' "little Jupiter." The coin's infant is winged like an Eros, for no very good reason. Beneath the goat is a Bacchic thyrsus, with ribbons, making a pendant to the thunderbolt on the obverse, and reminding the viewer of one of Zeus' sons. Above the goat are the caps of the Dioskouroi, the twin sons of Zeus. Not unlike the bust of Vulcan and the tongs in Figure 14, the caps remind us not only of other sons of Zeus, but also of their prominent cult at the moneyer's hometown of Tusculum. The artisan who designed this coin has attempted to comprehend allusions to several gods as well as to the moneyer's family.

Figure 17. Inscribed portion of carved marble epistyle; see ch. 5.

The inscription recorded Antoninus Pius' restoration of the circular shrine of Bacchus on the Upper Sacred Way. Gilt bronze letters were once set in the carved grooves (*CIL* VI 36920). On the right was sculptured a whirling Maenad, devotee of Bacchus, carrying a ribboned thyrsus in her left hand.

Figure 18. Medallion of Antoninus Pius; ch. 5.

The circular shrine of Bacchus accommodates only the cult statue of the god and the drapery above. The statue is represented in an archaistic style. The god's left hand holds the thyrsus and his right a small object, perhaps a wine saucer. Before the tabernacle a *victimarius* escorts a sacrificial goat by the horns from the left, while another attendant bears a platter or flat basket of fruits to the god's altar from the right. The entire group is backed by a hemicyclic colonnade.

Figure 19. Relief from the tomb of the Haterii, detail, Vatican Museum, Lateran Collection; ch. 5.

The order of monuments in which this detail is arrayed is from left to right: the arch to the temple of Isis, facing front; an unidentified triumphal arch, perhaps that of Titus, sideview; the Flavian amphitheater, partly visible in this detail; the detail illustrated here; the arch in Upper Sacred Way, facing front, partly visible in this detail; and the temple of Jupiter Stator, facing front. The detail shows the left side of a triumphal arch topped by a horsedrawn car, in which the triumphant general stands with whip and a cluster of bay leaves in hand. Behind and slightly above him hovers winged Victory. The four horses are escorted by a half-naked, partly concealed god with a shield in his right hand. This arch was rebuilt by Domitian after his German "victory" and replaced Marius' arch commemorating his victory over Germans and Gauls. Pierced in both directions, the arch comprehends a *ianus*, perhaps the very *ianus* at which the Vestal Virgins performed certain rites. The Vestals also kept the state's phallic talisman, like that which was hung from the triumphator's undercarriage. On the right side of the arch and looking through the *ianus* is the small temple of the Magna Mater, whose cult statue, apparently in a seated posture, with its lion at the right of the feet, gazes at the viewer of the relief through the *ianus*. At the foot of the temple steps the goddess' altar is set. The senate erected this victory shrine to the Great Mother after she notified the Romans of Marius' future triumphs in the north.

Figure 20. Contorniate of Faustina; ch. 5.

Faustina, the wife of Antoninus Pius who restored Bacchus' neighboring shrine (Figures 17 and 18), issued this token MATRI DEVM SALVTARI. The idol of the Healing Mother of the Gods, in a seated posture, looks down the flight of steps. Her lion sits by her left foot and faces left. To the right of the shrine stands her alien cult partner Attis beneath some branches of his evergreen pine.

Illustrations

FIG. 1

FIG. 2

FIG. 3

FIG. 4

FIG. 5

FIG. 6

FIG. 7

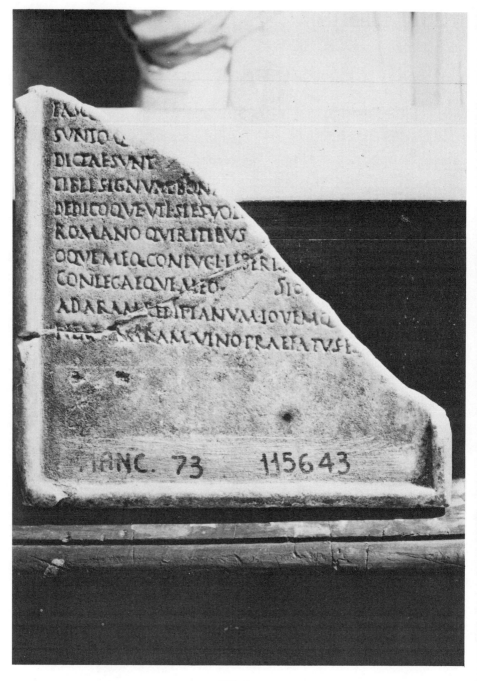

FIG. 8

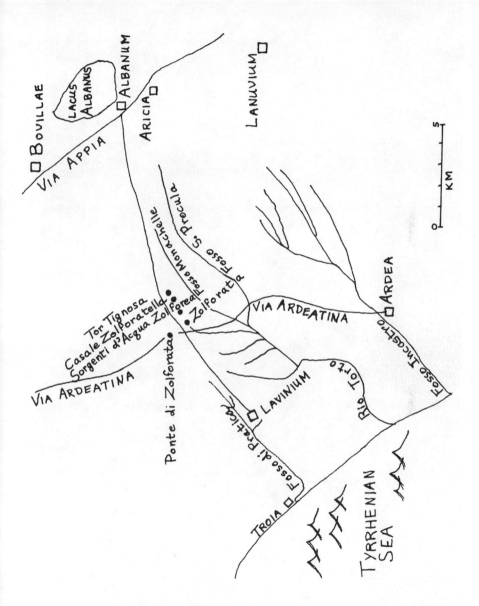

FIG. 9

FIG. 10

FIG. 11

FIG. 12

FIG. 13

FIG. 14

FIG. 15

FIG. 16

FIG. 17

FIG. 18

FIG. 19

218

FIG. 20

Notes

Foreword

[1] Pol. 6.56.6–12.
[2] Dion. Hal. *AR* 2.23.5–6.
[3] Cf. the remarks of Livy, 43.13, against the thought of his contemporaries and predecessors.
[4] See ch. 3, sect. 4.

CHAPTER 1

[1] Roscher, *Lex. gr. röm. Mythol.* 2.1 (Leipzig 1890–97). Cols. 574–605 are by Roscher on Juno; of these, 578–94 are devoted to her supervision of female functions. Vogel wrote on Juno in art (cols. 605–12). Roscher on Juno Caelestis of N. Africa (612–15), and Ihm on women's *iunones* (615–17).
[2] *Ibid.*, cols. 578 ff.
[3] "Iuno", *Philol.* 64 (1905), pp. 161–223, esp. 177–78, 221–23.
[4] *Religion und Kultus der Römer* (Munich, 1912), pp. 181–82. In the first edition (1902), Wissowa had analyzed her name of *Iovino* from *Iov-*; see pp. 113–14.
[5] "Was the Flaminica Dialis Priestess of Juno?" *CR* 9 (1895), pp. 474–76, reprinted in *Rom. Essays and Interpretations* (Oxford, 1920), pp. 52–55.
[6] E.g., in *Ancient Roman Religion* (1948), pp. 63, 68–69, Juno is merely "capable of becoming a war-goddess;" for Rose this function is quite secondary. In his article in the *OCD* (1949 and 1970), s.v. Juno, she "became a great goddess of the State."
[7] P. Noailles, *Fas et jus* (Paris, 1948), pp. 29–43.
[8] For the Etruscan forms see below, sect. 14, and Ernout-Meillet, *Dictionnaire étymologique*,[4] s.v. Juno; G. Radke, *Die Götter Altitaliens*, pp. 152–55; and below, n. 122. On the Piacenza Liver we meet *Uni* (i.e., Juno) and *Ani* (i.e., Janus); see Mart. Cap. 1.45 ff. and below, n. 192. Both divine names were borrowed from Latin speakers.
[9] *Loc. cit.*, nn. 3, 4.
[10] Agahd, pp. 121–22, 215–17.
[11] *LL* 5.67, 69, *ARD* frr. 16.52, 16.53 Ag., in Aug. *CD* 4.10, 7.3, 7.6.
[12] *LL* 5.67, 69.
[13] *ARD* fr. 16.53 Ag.
[14] Cf. Cicero *ND* 2.27.68, on which see Pease, and below, n. 127.
[15] *LL* 5.74.
[16] *AR* 2.50; cf. 2.21–23, and Festus 43, 55, 56, 302/304 L., Plut. *Rom.* 29.1. See A. Alföldi, "Hasta–Summa Imperii: The Spear as Embodiment of Sovereignty in Rome," *AJA* 63 (1959), pp. 18–20. On Juno Quiritis see J.A. Ambrosch, *De sacerdotibus curialibus* (Bratislava, 1840); Roscher, cols. 596–98; Otto, "Juno," pp. 197–203; De Sanctis, *Storia dei Romani*, 4.2.1, p. 139, n. 49; Eisenhut, *RE* 24 (1963), cols. 1324–33; Radke, p. 102; Palmer, *The Archaic Community of the Romans* (Cambridge, 1970), *passim*. The relationships of all these words have been most recently and fully developed by J. Poucet, "Recherches sur la légende sabine des origines de Rome," *Univ. Louvain Recueil de Trav. Hist. Philol.* ser. 4, fasc. 37, pp. 59–67, 320–22, and *passim*.
[17] *CIL* XI 3125–3126 =*ILS* 3111, 5374; see below, nn. 272, 278); Tert. *Apol.* 24.8: Faliscorum in honorem patris Curr < it > es et accepit cognomen Iuno (cf. Varro in *Ad Nat.* 2.8.6). On the extended life of Juno Quiritis of Falerii, see below.
[18] *CIL* I² 396 = IX 1547 =*ILS* 3096 =*ILLRP* 169.

19   Serv. Dan. on *Aen.* 1.17: Iuno Curitis, tuo curru clipeoque meos curiae vernulas. Note the primitive alliteration. See Latte, pp. 105–106, n. 2.; Palmer, pp. 61–62.

20   *AR* 2.23, 2.50.3; Festus 18, 59 L. Cf. Tertullian's outrageous exaggerations in *Anim.* 39.2, *Apol.* 39.15. See Ambrosch (above, n. 16); Palmer, pp. 97–122.

21   See, e.g., H.J. Rose, "Two Roman Rites," *CQ* 28 (1934), pp. 157–58; U. Coli, "Regnum," *SDHI* 17 (1951) pp. 160–61; Walde-Hoffman, *LEW*³ s.v. populor; Latte, p. 166; A. Momigliano, "L'ascesa della plebe nella storia arcaica di Roma," *Riv. St. Ital.* 69 (1967), pp. 304–305, and "Osservazioni sulla distinzione fra patrizi e plebei," *Fondation Hardt, Entretiens* 13: *Les origines de la république romaine*, pp. 199–221; Palmer, pp. 158–59, 215–20, 230–31. For one example of *populus* as "army" see below, n. 318, and cf. Livy 1.32.11–13, 8.9.5–8, 22.10.2–6 for a comparable sense in the phrase *populus Romanus Quiritium.*

22   Collected by Bremer, *Iurisprudentiae Antehadrianae* I (Leipzig, 1906), pp. 132–38, and Riccobono *FIRA* I², pp. 4–18.

23   Macr. *Sat.* 3.10.5–6 (on *Aen.* 1.736): ut in templo, inquit, Iunonis Populoniae augusta mensa est. *Augusta* might also have meant "bringing increase," were it not for the fact that the dedicated tables are being discussed. Bremer (1.261) assigns the fragment to Granius Flaccus' *De iure Papiriano*, not mentioned here by Macrobius (but see *Sat.* 1.18.4, 5.19.13), although Macrobius also cites a Tertius. Otherwise unknown, Tertius may be Titius, according to Bremer (2.9; cf. 1.131). A corrector of Macrobius suggests Terentius, to which Willis in his new edition objects. The quotation is usually assigned to the *Ius Papirianum* (see Latte, p. 166 n. 4), for Macrobius is adducing Papirius' collection against Tertius. On the Papirian collection, see below, n. 215. The ancient inscriptions normally give *Populona* while the authors exhibit both *Populonia* and *Poplona* as well as the spelling adopted in this text.

24   Macr. *Sat.* 3.10.5–7. The pulvinar (i.e., dining couch with bolster) and dining-room of Juno at Lanuvium are discussed below at n. 185.

25   In Aug. *CD* 6.10.

26   Mart. Cap. 2.149. Cf. Arn. 3.30.

27   *CIL* IX 2630 (Iuno Regina Populona), a title perhaps recurring to Capitoline Juno.

28   *CIL* I² 1573 = X 4780 = *ILS* 3105 = *ILLRP* 168; *CIL* X 4789 = *ILS* 3112; *CIL* X 4790; *CIL* X 4791 = *ILS* 3113.

29   *CIL* III 1074–76 = *ILS* 3085–87. The spelling Populonia is unimportant.

30   *LL* 6.18. For the Varronian usage of *adhibere* in cult cf. Charisius (p. 144 K., 183 B.): Varro in Aetiis, "fax ex spinu, alba praefertur quod purgationis causa adhibetur."

31   See A. Degrassi, *Inscriptiones Italiae* 13.2 (Fasti anni Numani et Iuliani) (Rome, 1963), pp. 477–81. On the oldest calendar the Ludi Apollinares are marked only on 13 July, but the games had already expanded beyond that one day years before the calendar (Ant. mai.) was inscribed. Other calendars (Maff., Amit., Ant. min.) mark 6 July the first day of Apollo's games. Thus Caprotine nones was the second day of the games, that were made permanent in 208, many years after any date when Juno Caprotina was first worshipped. See A.K. Michels, *The Calendar of the Roman Republic* (Princeton, 1967), pp. 133–34.

32   Degrassi, pp. 476–77. The notation *feriae Iovi* may refer either to a separate ceremony or to the Poplifugia. See C. Koch, *Der römische Juppiter = Frankfurter Studien zur Religion und Kultur der Antike* 14 (1937), pp. 93–97, 105, 115–16.

33   *SHA* 7.2.1–2. Cf. Sol. 1.20.

34   Commodus' devotion to Hercules is abundantly attested by inscriptions and *SHA* 7. As the Roman Hercules, he slew beasts in the Lanuvian amphitheater (7.8.5). His choice of town was excellent, for at Lanuvium was the great shrine of Juno Sispes dressed in a goatskin. She took on oriental affinities in the late republic; see below at nn. 195–98. Commodus' female attire (*SHA* 7.11.9, 13.1–4, 17.10) came in for latter-day criticism, but its Herculean function is indubitable.

35   *Rom.* 27 and 29; cf. Dion. Hal. *AR* 2.56.5–6. The variant *capratina* is discussed below in connection with the etymology of the epithet.

36 *Numa* 2. Recall that the nones fell on the seventh day only in March, May, July and October, and otherwise on the fifth.

37 For Nonae Caprotinae see Weinstock, *RE* 17.1 (1936), cols. 849–59; and for Poplifugia, Kraus, *RE* 22.1 (1953), cols. 74–78; Degrassi's commentary, pp. 476–81; Palmer, pp. 230–32.

38 *Tab. Iguv.* Ib 10–22, 40–44, VIb 48–65, VIIa 6–VIIb 2, on which see Poultney and Ernout. ¯

39 Livy 1.27. No shrines to these gods are known. Ogilvie, *ad loc.*, attributes them to Homeric epic. They belong, I propose, to the rites of the Poplifugia. See Poultney on Tursa; the Umbrian verb *tursitu* etc. is regularly employed in the imprecations against the foreigners. On Jupiter Deimatias see Palmer, pp. 186–87. On the feasts written on the calendar in small letters, see Michels, op. cit., pp. 27, 31–34.

40 Fr. 15.2 Ag. The book was entitled *de dis incertis*.

41 *Sat.* 1.3.2, 4.

42 1.4.14, 1.13.20–21, 1.15.18, 1.16.27, 1.16.33.

43 *Sat.* 1.12.16–29.

44 *Sat.* 1.12.13. On Cincius' debated dates and work, see J. Heurgon, "L. Cincius et la loi du *clavus annalis*" *Athenaeum* 42 (1964), pp. 432–37. It seems clear that both antiquarians lived and wrote at roughly the same time.

45 *LL* 5.148–49, 165.

46 Cf. Plut. *Rom.* 9 and 12 with Solin. 1.16–20. See Palmer, pp. 20–21, 26 ff.

47 Only in Fast. Ant. Mai., on which see Degrassi, p. 478.

48 *RR* 3.2.1–2. See L.R. Taylor, *Roman Voting Assemblies* (Ann Arbor, 1966), pp. 55–56 with n. 58.

49 *RR* 2.5.1.

50 *RR* 2.6.1.

51 See n. 48.

52 See Platner-Ashby *TDAR* s.v. Caprae Palus. Cf. *SHA* 4.13.6: de caprifici arbore in Campo Martio contionabundus.

53 Plut. *Cam.* 33.5.

54 Plut. *Cam.* 10, *Brut.* 17, *Cor.* 14. Cf. Ausonius, p. 104 P., *stola dempta.*

55 *LL* 6.19. Cf. Commodus' conduct at nn. 33, 34.

56 See F. Courby in Daremberg-Saglio 5.349 and Goethert, *RE* 6A2 cols. 1651–60. Cf. Livy 7.1, and below at nn. 160, 302.

57 See Nisbet on Cic. *Pis.* 4.8; Festus pp. 428/430 as restored by Scaliger; cf. Plut. *QR* 53. On the Capitoline games, see below, ch. 3, sect. 11.

58 *F.* 1.55–57. See Degrassi, p. 328, and below, at n. 151.

59 See Degrassi, p. 475.

60 See Degrassi, pp. 405–406, 418–19, 421, 475, 515–16, 518. For the *dies februatus*, which concerns Juno and the Lupercalia, see Varro *LL* 6.13, and below, sect. 4.

61 See Degrassi, p. 518. For reasons given below, I cannot hold that she was the evoked tutelary deity of Falerii.

62 *CIL* I² 2439–40 = Vetter no. 510 = *ILLRP* 167.

63 In Degrassi's *Imagines* p. 57, no. 84.

64 See Dessau, *ILS*, index 3.1, p. 521.

65 On the *Iunonarium* at Praeneste, see below at nn. 365–66.

66 See De Sanctis, *SR²* 2.128–31, Beloch, *RG*, pp. 299–302, Talor, *VD* p. 37. The Latin attack on the Romans under Livius Postumius cannot have taken place in the fourth century; see De Sanctis, *SR²* 2.229–30.

67 See Macr. *Sat.* 3.9, and below on Regina of Veii and Juno of Carthage. Livy 4.33–34 recounts the fall of Fidenae and includes *infert pavidos fuga in mediam caedem*, and the sale of its population. In the formula of *devotio*, note *fuga formidine terrore* in n. 318.

68 See Weinstock (above, n. 37), esp. cols. 854–57.

[69] Plut. *Rom.* 29, *Cam.* 33; *CIL* IV 1555.

[70] Aug. *CD* 4.8 derives it from *collis.* See Otto, "Römische Sondergötter", *RhM* 64 (1909), p. 456, and Wissowa's baseless objection in *RKR*,[2] p. 33 n. 3.

[71] Diana Tifatina is well known. For *tifata* "grove of oaks" see Festus 503 L and Tifata, a town, Pliny *NH* 3.68.

[72] Hesychius s.v.

[73] Pliny *NH* 3.120.

[74] *CIE* 3832; cf. 3833–34. On Etruscan names built upon ethnics see H. Rix, *Das etruskische Cognomen* (Wiesbaden, 1963), pp. 232–36.

[75] Sydenham *CRR* no. 432, dated to 135–126 B.C.; Grueber 1.885, pl. 25.14; see Figure 1. The moneyer is C. Renius, who chose to figure Caprotina because his name alluded to the Greek word *rhēn* "sheep" and the Celto-Latin *reno* "shaggy fleece mantle" (see Walde-Hoffmann, *LEW*[3], s.v.).

[76] Varro *LL* 6.18, Macr. *Sat.* 1.11.36–40, Arn. 3.30.

[77] See Weinstock (above, n. 37), cols. 849–50, Walde-Hoffmann *LEW*[3], and Ernout-Meillet[4] s.v. caper.

[78] Cf. the divine epithets Aesculanus, Querquetulani, Tifatina, and the usually solitary Silvanus.

[79] Radke, pp. 80–81, 304–305.

[80] Weinstock (above, n. 37), cols. 853–54.

[81] *Sat.* 1.11.38. See below, n. 318.

[82] The Greek name is borne by an Etruscan *lautnita*; *CIE* 870, 871. On this social class see Rix, pp. 356–76.

[83] Cf. Festus *Epit.* p. 57 L, where the text reads: Capralia appellatur ager, qui vulgo ad Caprae Paludes dici solet. The mss. read *cupruli* or *cuproli*, which are emended *capralia*, although it is a unique word and type of name. (Better *caprilia* "goat pens;" cf. the nearby Ovile.) Another possible emendation is *caproti*, i.e., Caproti(i), masc. pl., like Tarquinii, Veii, etc.

[84] *RR* 2.11.4–5; Varro in Non. 246 L.; Aug. *CD* 4.11, 4.21, 4.34. See Agahd on *ARD* fr. 14.24.

[85] Wissowa, p. 242; K. Latte, *Römische Religionsgeschichte* (Munich, 1960), pp. 111, 148.

[86] See Rix, p. 232. Of course the most telling evidence against Schulze's view has always been *CIE* 5275 Cneve Tarchunies Rumach, i.e., Cn. Tarquinius "of Rome" or "the Roman." Also in the François tomb we meet *Velznach* and *Sveamach* both of which are demotics. See *ILLRP* 1288 for the form *Ruma.*

[87] See the most recent articulation of this interpretation, which to my mind is correct: P. Mingazzini, "L'origine del nome di Roma ecc.," *BC* 78 (1961–62), pp. 3–7.

[88] In Aug. *CD* 6.10.

[89] *CD* 7.11.

[90] *Ibid.*

[91] Dion. Hal. *AR* 4.49.3 and Cic. *Div.* 1.11.18; cf. Festus p. 212 L. At the Parilia Pales also received milk with his dinner; Ovid *F.* 4.745–46.

[92] Varro in Serv. Dan. on *Ecl.* 7.21.

[93] As if derived from *ruma* "breast" and *rumĭnare* "chew" Ovid, *F* 2.412, calls the *ficus Ruminalis rumĭna,* but Ovid changed vowel quantities for the sake of folk etymologies. Cf. *fēralis* in *F* 2.569, as if from *ferre!*

[94] See *TDAR* s.v. Ficus Ruminalis.

[95] See Mingazzini (above, n. 87).

[96] Livy 10.23.12.

[97] Enn. *Ann.* 82 V.[2] in Cic. *Div.* 1.48.107; Dion. Hal. *AR* 1.85–87; Festus 345 L.; *OGR* 23.1.

[98] See *CIL* I[2] 971 = VI 566, 30794 = *ILS* 2985 = *ILLRP* 252.

[99] See Varro *LL* 6.13, 34, *ARH* fr. 17 Mir. in Cens. *DN* 22.13, *VPR* fr. 22 Rip. in Non.

p. 164 L.; Festus *Epit.* pp. 75–76 L.; Arn. 4.7.8; Mart. Cap. 2.149; *Myth. Vat.* 3.4.3. See Agahd, above n. 10, and n. 102.
¹⁰⁰ E.g., Arn. 3.25, 7.21; Mart. Cap. 2.149; *Myth. Vat.* 3.4.3. See below at nn. 236–37. Before reciting their famous hymn, the Arval Brethern anointed their goddesses (*deas unguentaverunt*: *CIL* VI 2104 =*ILS* 5039).
¹⁰¹ *LL* 6.13.
¹⁰² *LL* 6.34, Varro in *DN* 22.9–15. In *LL* 6.13 Varro acknowledges his earlier treatment in the *Antiquities*. Cf. Dion. Hal. *AR* 1.32, 1.80. If *sal februus* is "cleansing salt," a Juno Februa is "cleansing Juno."
¹⁰³ See below, at n. 158.
¹⁰⁴ Varro and Fabius Pictor in Non. 330 L, Serv. Dan. on *Ecl.* 8.82 and Fest. *Epit.*153 L.
¹⁰⁵ See Degrassi, pp. 409–11, on Lupercalia, 15 February; S. Weinstock, *Divus Julius* (Oxford, 1971), pp. 331–40.
¹⁰⁶ Well elucidated by F. Bömer's commentary on Ovid's *Fasti*, Book II.
¹⁰⁷ See Degrassi, pp. 405–406.
¹⁰⁸ Fest. *Epit.* 82 L., Arn. 3.30, Mart. Cap. 2.149; cf. Tert. *Ad Nat.* 2.11.3. See Agahd, pp. 216–17.
¹⁰⁹ Aug. *CD* 4.8; see Weinstock, *RE* 8A1 col. 288.
¹¹⁰ Cic. *ND* 3.20.52; cf. Luc. *BC* 1.600.
¹¹¹ See Bömer on *F.* 4.337. Serv. Dan. on *Aen.* 8.33 discourses on the efficacy and necessity of *aqua fluvialis* for purification.
¹¹² Serv. on *Aen.* 8.63, 8.90.
¹¹³ See Wissowa, p. 185 n. 4.
¹¹⁴ Cf. Fest. *Epit.* 50 L.
¹¹⁵ Cf. Ovid, *F.* 2.435–36, on which see Bömer.
¹¹⁶ See M. Leumann, *Lateinische Laut- und Formenlehre* (Munich, 1963), pp. 201, 224, *Glotta* 42 (1964), p. 112, and Radke, pp. 188–89.
¹¹⁷ *LL* 5.69, 5.74. See above.
¹¹⁸ See Degrassi, pp. 417–19; Palmer, pp. 162–64. Religiously and ritually, 1 March was a very full day that retained many ceremonies belonging to the beginning of the old liturgical year. The women's dedication is not only unparalleled but rendered highly improbable by the aetiological story of the foundation and dedication of the temple of Fortuna Muliebris four miles from Rome. Both the senate and the pontiffs were involved, according to the tradition, and the consul performed the dedicatory ceremony; see Dion. Hal. *AR* 8.55.3–5, Degrassi, pp. 479, 533.
¹¹⁹ *ILLRP* 160.
¹²⁰ Varro *LL* 5.50. See Palmer, pp. 84–97.
¹²¹ *CIL* I² 361 =*ILS* 3101 =*ILLRP* 161.
¹²² *CIL* I² 360 =*ILS* 9230a =*ILLRP* 163. On both see Degrassi. The spellings *Iun-* beside *Diov-* further militate against any linguistic relation of these two names.
¹²³ See Naevius *BP* and Varro *ARD* in Non., pp. 289–90 L.; *ILLRP* 67, Fest. p. 144, and Degrassi on 4 Oct., p. 517, (Ceres); Tert. *Iei.* 16.7 (Isis and Cybele); Arn. 5.16 (Ceres and Magna Mater?). Gellius *NA* 10.15.1 refers to the many *castus* of the flamen Dialis; cf. Varro *loc. cit.* On the adj. *castus* see below, at n. 217.
¹²⁴ See Degrassi on *ILLRP* 163. Only the scholia on Hor. *Carm.* 3.8.1 connect men with the cult; see below.
¹²⁵ See below, nn. 157, 299.
¹²⁶ *NA* 10.15, Fest. *Epit.* 77 L., Plut. *QR* 109–11. See above, n. 123, and Palmer "Ivy and Jupiter's Priest," *Homenaje a A. Tovar* (Madrid, 1972), pp. 341–47.
¹²⁷ Pl. *Aul.* 691–92: Opsecro te, uterum dolet, Iuno Lucina, tuam fidem; *Truc.* 476: date mi huc stactam atque ignem in aram ut venerem Lucinam meam; Ter. *Andr.* 473: Iuno Lucina, fer opem, serva me obsecro; cf. *Ad.* 487. Piso *Ann.* fr. 14 P. in Dion. Hal. *AR* 4.15.5. The idiom is

not reserved to Juno even in older authors; see Jocelyn on Ennius *Alexander*, line 42.

[128]   *CIL* X 3807 = I² 1581 = *ILS* 3099 = *ILLRP* 165 and *CIL* X 3808 = I² 1582 = *ILS* 3099a = *ILLRP* 139 are the Capuan dedications. Documents of the Tusculan priests are: *CIL* V 27, 5036, VI 2177, IX 2565, XIV 2580, 2603 (cf. *ILS* 902, 3152, 5016–18). For other alien *sacra*, see below ch. 2. On the annexation of Tusculum see De Sanctis² 2.231–32; on evocation of Junos and the curias, Palmer, *Archaic Community*, pp. 167–69, 180–81, and below.

[129]   De Sanctis *SR* 2.249; Weinstock, *Divus Julius*, p. 58.

[130]   Livy 5.21–23.7.

[131]   V. Basanoff, *Evocatio: Etude d'un rituel militaire romain* (Paris, 1947), pp. 42–49; S. Ferri, "La 'Iuno Regina' di Veii" *St. Etr.* 24 (1955), pp. 106–13; M. Sordi, *I rapporti romano-ceriti e l'origine della civitas sine suffragio* (Rome, 1960), pp. 1–23. Ogilvie on Livy 5.1.3 doubts the tradition because monarchy and impiety are "too schematic and too Roman" reasons for the neutrality of Veii's Etruscan neighbors. What is the source of the scheme? Livy, himself, as Ogilvie remarks, records the revival of the kingship. Livy or his predecessors could have explained the kingship as a revival, but are its unlikely inventors. Veii was either more conservative in retaining a political kingship or more reactionary in reviving it. So Livy interprets the case. Or the king was a priestly official who tried unsuccessfully to forestall the city's fall to Rome. See, further, H.H. Scullard, *The Etruscan Cities and Rome* (Ithaca, 1967), pp. 104–10 on Veii, 225–26 on her king, and 258–69 on her fall to the Romans.

[132]   On *reginus* (not to be starred; cf. Charisius 61 B and the cognomen Reginus), see Ernout-Meillet *Dict. étym.*⁴ *s. vv.* rex, gallus, M. Leumann (above, n. 116), pp. 204, 224, 269. The exact formation of the adjective is in doubt, but *regina*, as adjective, is as sure as any analysis can be.

[133]   E.g., Aemilius Paullus in Val. Max. 5.10.2 (*ORF*² p. 101); Cic. *Scaur.* 47; Livy 3.17.3; and in the *acta* of the secular games (below, n. 168).

[134]   Varro *LL* 5.158, our only reference except for the Regionaries.

[135]   See Platner-Ashby, pp. 293–302, for references.

[136]   See above, n. 23.

[137]   See n. 27.

[138]   See n. 29.

[139]   See below, n. 157. J.H. Oliver, *Demokratia, the Gods and the Free World* (Baltimore, 1960), chs. I–II, has some very pertinent remarks on Zeus, Athena, and Jupiter in the role of civic patrons (on Capitoline Jupiter see esp. p. 75 ff.). Curiously enough, it was in fact the third member of the triad, Minerva, identified with the Greek Athena, whom the Roman Juno resembled in the politico-religious sphere much more than her religiously pallid step-daughter. Minerva was included in the Capitoline temple because an identification with Athena had already been made in Etruria (see Radke, pp. 217–19). The Italic Juno, however, truly displayed the divine qualities of an Athena Polias.

[140]   Livy 5.54.7, Dion. Hal. *AR* 3.69.5–6, Pliny *NH* 35.108.

[141]   See Henzen *AFA*, p. 144. Cf. Pliny *NH* 2.16: quam ob rem maior caelitum populus etiam quam hominum intellegi potest cum singuli quoque ex semet ipsis totidem deos faciant Iunones Geniosque adoptando sibi; Sen. *Ep. Mor.* 110.1: singulis enim et Genium et Iunonem dederunt (*sc.* maiores nostri).

[142]   For the coin see Sydenham, *CRR* no. 561, p. 19; Grueber, 2.620 ff., pl. 94.16–17, 95.1–4. The moneyer was Cornelius Blasio whose coins Sydenham dates to 119–91 B.C. For the evidence of Jupiter Rex and Juno Regina, see Weinstock, *op. cit.*, p. 339 n. 6.

[143]   Macr. *Sat.* 1.15.19 (see below). The king's queen is the only known priest of Juno, which means that her husband served the same deity; see Fowler (above, n. 5).

[144]   Varro *LL* 6.27–28. The passage is corrupt but reparable from Macrobius *Sat.* 1.15.10 f., and is so restored in the text of the Spengels, and Goetz and Schoell. Kent's text in the Loeb Classical Library, like others of his textual emendations, is as unwarranted as his suggestion that

"... *Sat.* 1.15.10 ... may rest on a corrupted form of this passage which was in the copy used by Macrobius," because Macrobius nowhere cites the *De lingua Latina* (see Willis' edition vol. 2, p. 179), and in *Sat.* 1.15.18 cites Varro and *pontificalis auctoritas* for this whole discussion, only a very little of which is parallelled in *LL.*

145 Wissowa, pp. 184–87; E.L. Shields, *Juno: A Study in Early Roman Religion* (Northampton, 1926), pp. 13–18. Radke, pp. 99–100, sums up another view.

146 *Sat.* 1.15.4–22, in which Varro is cited twice and Verrius Flaccus once by Varro.

147 Cf. Varro *LL* 6.28. The king in turn issued the news to the people. Cf. Serv. Dan. on *Aen.* 8.654.

148 See Münzer, *RE* 6.2 cols. 2526–28. Michels, pp. 18–21 (cf. pp. 130–132), points out that the ceremony of Varro's day had deteriorated into a mere token.

149 Ms F (Laurentianus li) is lacking Varro's *LL* here. The suggestion of *novella* was made long ago by Scaliger; see Shield's fruitless discussion, pp. 13–15. If *novellam* is rejected, Varro's etymology of *nonae < nova* is left without linguistic support! Our oldest prose author Cato (*Agr.* 33.2, 4) attests *novellus*, which he applies to a grapevine and vineyards to describe their youngness. His contrast is with *vetus*, but he does not use *novus*. In the other writers on agriculture, *novellus* describes the newborn farm animals. The word seems to belong to the vocabulary of the most basic aspect of Roman life. The diminutive ending (see Leumann, *op. cit.*, p. 216) is old in Latin, as is perhaps evidenced on the cippus of the Lapis Niger (see Palmer, *The King and the Comitium = Historia Einzelsch.* 11, p. 24) and the word *sacellum* in Livy 4.30.11, for the year 428 (see Ogilvie's note). The word *bellus* shows a long history. Besides the defunct Aequian town Vitellia (Pliny *NH* 3.69 and Livy 2.39.4, with Ogilvie's note), there is the comparable Oscan town of *Nuvl-*, or Novella (cf. neighboring Neapolis), which the Romans knew as Nola.

150 *Sat.* 1.15.18–20: cum enim initia mensium maiores nostri ab exortu lunae servaverunt, iure Iunoni addixerunt kalendas, lunam ac Iunonem eandem putantes, etc. Cf. Varro *LL* 5.69, in *Sat.* 3.4.7–8 and in Aug. *CD* 7.2; Cic. *ND* 2.27.68–69; Plut. *QR* 77. On Varro and Luna see Agahd, p. 218. The Varronian and Ciceronian views that Juno was the moon depend on the etymology of *lucina* from *lux*, which is wrong, and the latter's true etymological connection with *luna*. Other identifications of Juno with a natural phenomenon were surely propounded, e.g., with air because of the similarity of *aer* and *Hera*. No such explanation applies to, or accounts for, the origins and nature of the goddess Juno in primitive Roman religion. While Jupiter was indeed a god of the sky or daylight in the first place, Juno as a name does not admit an etymological analysis connecting it with a natural phenomenon. On the other hand, the cults of such abstractions as *salus* are no less old at Rome, and the deities no less real for all their apparent irreality. Compare, for instance, Fortuna, Mercurius, Ceres, and Venus.

151 For a list see Wissowa *RKR*² pp. 594–97, wherein Juno's temples are dedicated on calends in 392(?), 375, 344, 194, but not the Capitolium in 509 nor the temple of 179 with other temples. Furthermore, the shrines of other gods were also dedicated on the calends in the years 388, 294, 291, 259, 258, 194, 193, 114, 91, 22 and 1 B.C. Only five months have ceremonies for Juno on the calends. Four celebrations were instituted after 400. The fifth, on 1 July, cannot be dated. The Junonian possession of all the calends was presumably an inference from the ceremony we are now describing.

152 *Sat.* 1.15.18.

153 *Sat.* 1.15.21–22.

154 *Sat.* 1.15.19.

155 Varro *LL* 6.28; *Sat.* 1.15.9–12. The statement that the minor pontiff *rem divinam facit* to Juno on the calends (*Sat.* 1.15.19) seems but a Varronian inference from the *calo lunam novellam*. It is a grave mistake to assert that the sex of a victim reflected the sex of a divinity. How can we speak of the sex of *salus, fortuna,* or pre-anthropomorphic *venus* and *cerus/ceres*? The niceties of anthropomorphic religion dictated certain rules that could not have been observed before anthropomorphism.

[156]   Festus 92 L; Placidus 58 D, who, of course, believed that she united in matrimony. The adj. *iugus* is attested only once and its meaning is none too clear (Cato *Agr.* 10.2), but *iugis* is common, especially in describing running (constant) water; cf. Cic. *Div.* 1.50.112, Serv. on *Aen.* 4.16. For the woman's marital status, see below.

[157]   See Degrassi, p. 509: epulum Iovi, Iunoni, Minervae in Capitolio. On 13 September the Capitolium was dedicated. Although it does not issue from an official voice, this curious text, written partly in Saturnian verse and cast in Faliscan evidently imitating Latin, was inscribed on a bronze plaque that was set up in Falerii in the second half of the third century. *CIL* I² 364 = X 3078, 7483 = *CIE* 834 = *ILS* 3083 = *ILLRP* 192: "To Jupiter, Juno and Minerva the Faliscans who are on Sardinia gave the gift. The masters (of the association), L. Latrius, son of Kaeso, C. Savena, son of Volta, oversaw (the business). The association that has been formed for their livelihood is well-endowed for enjoying life and feast-days. The cooks who very often have richly enhanced dinner parties and games, with their own cleverness and Vulcan's beneficence [*opid*] gave in this place [a gift] to the mighty commanders that they might gladly help them fulfill their desires." Evidently the "mighty commanders" (*imperatores summi*) are Jupiter, Juno, and Minerva. Perhaps this guild of cooks was accustomed to prepare the banquets of the triad who can hardly be construed as the patrons of cooks (cf. *opid Volgani* in reference to their patron and Plaut. *Aul.* 359). The style "commanders" applied to Juno and Minerva is unique but not inconsistent with their political role as members of the triad. See *ILLRP* 104, 105 ab, 106 for dedications to Praenestine Fortune by cooks, butchers, and cattle merchants.

[158]   Tac. *Ann.* 15.44.

[159]   Livy 22.1.17–18. On the political purposes of these and other ceremonies in 217, see below, sect. 17.

[160]   Macr. *Sat.* 1.6.12–14. Cf. Gellius *NA* 4.5, who reports on boys singing at the urging of Etruscan haruspices.

[161]   Above, sect. 3.

[162]   This Livius is Andronicus; see below, ch. 3, sect. 4.

[163]   On statues of cypress see Pliny *NH* 16.213–16 (cf. 236), and below, ch. 3, at n. 298.

[164]   Livy 27.37.6–15.

[165]   Livy 31.12.8–10.

[166]   On the place see F. Castagnoli, "Il Campo Marzio nell'Antichità," *Atti Acc. Naz. d. Lincei, Mem. Cl. Sci., mor., stor., filol.*, ser. 8, vol. 1, fasc. 4, pp. 99–112.

[167]   See below, ch. 3, sect. 4.

[168]   See Zos. 2.6; the *acta* in *CIL* VI 32323 (cf. *ILS* 5050); and Hor. *CS.* E. Fraenkel, *Horace* (Oxford, 1957), ch. 7 has a splendid study of ceremonies. Also see I.B. Pighi, *De ludis saecularibus populi Romani Quiritium = Pubbl. Univ. Catt. S. Cuore*, ser. 5, vol. 35 (1941), pp. 107–19, 201–21.

[169]   *Acta* lines 107, 132. See Ernout-Meillet⁴ s.v. *atalla*.

[170]   Livy 5.22.3–8. Dion. Hal. *AR* 13.3 reports that the soldiers were the most distinguished horsemen. On *evocatio* in general, see V. Basanoff—to be consulted with caution—and M. Van Doren, "Peregrina Sacra," *Historia* 3 (1954), pp. 488–97. Evocation was also employed in a simple transfer of gods from one shrine to another; Dion. Hal. *AR* 3.69, Festus 180/182 L.

[171]   See A. Ernout, *Le dialecte ombrien* (Paris, 1961), pp. 23, 25, 87, on *Tab. Ig.* IIb 23, III 28. The *iuventus* also performed the Atellan farces and Etruscan theater, which had a religious origin (Livy 7.2, in which *solutus iocus* and *iuventus inconditis inter se iocularia fundentes versibus*); cf. Val. Max. 2.4.4, wherein *iuventus iocabunda* at Consualia. The meaning "joke" is derivative. Caesar Augustus' assumption of the *toga virilis* (i.e., becoming a *iuvenis*) was celebrated with a *supplicatio* to Hope and Youth (*Feriale Cumanum*, Degrassi, pp. 278–80, 523) Cf. Fest. *Epit.* 92 L.: iuventutis sacra pro iuvenibus instituta. On the Vestals see Livy 4.44.11–12, with Ogilvie's comment; Sen. *Contr* 6.8 exc., apparently reflecting Livy's account, which generated school debates; Dion. Hal. *AR* 2.67; Plut. *Numa* 10; Broughton, *MRR, s. aa.* 230, 114.

172   Gellius 13.23.2. For one hymn of evocation, see below at n. 317.
173   Livy 5.22.5 (cf. 5.21 and Dion. Hal. *AR* 13.3). A similar identification may have been made through the *maia Vulcani*; see Gellius 13.23.2, Macr. *Sat.* 1.12.16–29. Cf. Festus 89 L. on Heres Martea; Degrassi, p. 502, on Hora Quirini; and Palmer, *Archaic Community*, pp. 108–109, 167–70.
174   Shields, pp. 59–62; Latte, p. 169. Livy 7.28.4–6 reports a war with the Aurunci. However, the dedication is better derived from a vow made by young Camillus when he was consul in 349 and fighting the Gauls in Latium; see De Sanctis, *SR* 2.260–61.
175   Livy 33.26.8: ad Monetae duarum hastarum spicula arserant. See below, sect. 10.
176   Cf. the town Corniculum and the Corniculan Mtns. On the formation of words in *-etum* see M. Leumann (above, n. 116), p. 228. The *-ē-* in *moneta* understood as a participle is unexampled as the *-o-* in Umbrian *Prestote* (*Tab. Ig., passim*). (See Ernout-Meillet, *Dict. étym.*⁴ s.vv. for analysis of the Latin words.) Compare the Capuan inscription of 71 B.C. (*CIL* I² 2.686 = X 3783 = *ILS* 6303 = *ILLRP* 722), which mentions a (public?) slave of Juno Gaura, whose name is connected with Mt. Gaurus near Naples (Pliny *NH* 14.64), outside the Ager Campanus. This Juno was perhaps introduced into Capua through a victory over the people of Juno Gaura, and her slave may be a legacy of war booty. Capuan Juno Gaura, from Mt. Gaurus, may have been associated with the appointed sacrifice for "all Campanians" at Hamae, which lay three miles from Cumae (Livy 23.35). Mt. Gaurus lay between Cumae and Naples; see Cic. *Agr.* 2.14.36; Pliny *NH* 3.60; Juv. 8.86 and 9.56–57 with the scholia; Florus 1.11.5, 1.22.28; and Servius on *Aen.* 3.571. See E.T. Salmon, *Samnium and the Samnites* (Cambridge, 1967), pp. 167, 201 for Juno Gaura, and pp. 177–79 for the shrine at Hamae. Compare the temple to Juno Moneta vowed by a Roman praetor fighting in Corsica and built on the Alban Mount (Livy 42.7.1, 45.15.10; Dio 48.14.5–6).
177   See Broughton, *MRR*, 1, pp. 128–29, and below sect. 8.
178   See Palmer, pp. 232–38, where I was hasty in accepting Livy's date for the vowing of the temple, better 349 than 345. On Moneta in Andronicus, see below, ch. 3, sect. 4.
179   Sydenham, 792 with pl. 22; Grueber, 1.3312 ff. with pl. 42.20–21. Sydenham dates these coins of L. Plaetorius to 78–55 B.C. The famous Caesarian moneyer T. Carisius put not only Moneta, in whose temple money was minted, but also the implements of coinage, on one of his issues ca. 45 B.C.; see Sydenham, 982 with pl. 26, Grueber, 1.4056 with pl. 52.1–2.
180   The site on the Arx where the temple was built was said to have held the houses of King Tatius and Manlius Capitolinus. Cicero, *Dom.* 38.101, tells his audience that they can see the remains of Capitolinus' house overgrown by two groves. See Platner-Ashby, *TDAR*, pp. 184, 191, 289–90.
181   Livy 8.14.2; Cic. *Mur.* 41.90.
182   Festus 388–89 and 462 L: sispitem Iunonem quam vulgo sospitem appellant, antiqui usurpabant, cum ea vox ex Graeco videtur sumpta, quod est σώξειν. *CIL* I² 2.1430 = XIV 2090 = *ILS* 3097 = *ILLRP* 170; *Eph. Epig.* 9.605 = *ILS* 9246. Cf. *ILS* 316, 5683.
183   Livy 8.14.2. See A.E. Gordon, "The Cults of Lanuvium," *Univ. Calif. Publ. Cl. Arch.* 2 (1938), pp. 24–37.
184   Gordon, pp. 27–28, who justly claims these are not offerings to a chthonic deity.
185   Varro *LL* 5.162; Livy 21.62.4. Jul. Obs. 46 reads "Lanuvii in aede Iunonis Sospitae in cubiculo deae sanguinis guttae visae," where the text should be *c <ena >culo.*
186   *CIL* XIV 2089 = *ILS* 6196: C. Agilleius C(ai) [f(ilius)] Mundus rex sacr(orum), aed[ilis], flamen Dial[is] I(unoni) S(ispiti) M(atri) R(eginae). Cf. *ILS* 4016. See Gordon, p. 49, on the priesthood.
187   *CIL* XIV 2120 = *ILS* 6199; XIV 2114 = *ILS* 6201 (*curia--amonalis*); XIV 2126 = *ILS* 6202 (*curia Clodia Firma*). See Palmer, *Archaic Community*, pp. 60–61.
188   Livy 32.30.10; 34.53.3 (where *Mututa* stands for *Sospita*); the latter passage sets the temple in the Forum Holitorium.
189   Ovid. *F.* 2.55-72. Its precise location has been made difficult to ascertain because

F 6.105–106 only mentions a temple of Carna near the same grove, which is, in turn, without certain siting. See De Sanctis, 4.2.1, pp. 139–40; Platner-Ashby, *TDAR*, p. 291; Bömer on *Fasti* 2.55, 6.37, 6.60, 6.101. On the grove of Helernus (Ovid's mss. provide variants) see R. Pettazzoni, "Carna," *St. Etr.* 14 (1940), pp. 163-72, who connects *lucus *Halernus* with **Falernus* and Carna with Juno. Noteworthy is the tradition that upon the expulsion of the kings Junius Brutus is said to have fulfilled a vow and offered to Carna on Mt. Caelius a sacrifice of meat (*caro* for *Carna*), bean porridge and lard, because Carna was a goddess of human strength. Accordingly, the calends of June were called bean-calends (Macr. *Sat.* 1.12.31–33). Tert. *Ad Nat.* 2.9.7 says that Carna's shrine *(fanum)* held newly imported gods *(adventicii)*, whereas the Palatium held the gods of the people *(publici)*. He learnt this from Varro (cf. *Ad Nat.* 2.9.3).

[190]   Cic. *Div.* 1.3.4 and 1.44.99, on which see Pease.

[191]   Jul. Obs. 55 (cf. Cic. *ibid.*). Only one temple *(aedis)* was restored, according to his notice, which fully bears out Ovid's report of a ruined *delubrum*.

[192]   These Latin words in *-es, -itis* form a class originally foreign to Latin. Lanuvian Sispes is without doubt a warrior. Radke, pp. 287–90, makes the attractive suggestion that *seispit-* etc. is related to the Greek *hepo* and *hoplon*. This accords well with Lakinian Hera's epithet Hoplosmia; see below, n. 254. Radke translates *Sispes* "Helferin." In Martianus Capella (1.45–62) stands the unique classical discussion of the division of the sky according to gods for religious purposes. The divisions are often related to the Etruscan liver made of bronze to describe the sky for divination; see H.L. Stoltenberg, *Etruskische Gottnamen* (Heidelberg, 1957). To Martianus' ninth region is assigned the *genius Iunonis Hospitae* (1.54). However Grotius and "perhaps" (so Dick) the wise corrector of Cod. Bamb. (cf. Dick, p. xvii) emend the otherwise unknown *Hospitae* to *Sospitae*, which is to say Sispes in archaic times. Hence the source of Sispes may have been Etruria. However, S. Weinstock, "Martianus Capella and the Cosmic System of the Etruscans," *JRS* 36 (1946), p. 127 accepts *Hospita* although he admits that, as epithets, *hospes* and *hospita* are found in the poets. He is overanxious about a Lanuvian deity's presence in Etruria, because Sispes is not by any means peculiar to Lanuvium. On the interrelation of *genius* and *iuno*, a possible semantic pair, see our nn. 141, 214, 227. Besides its *iuno*, each curia at Rome had its own *genius* (Dion. Hal. *AR* 2.23.1: *daimon*).

[193]   Above, n. 178.

[194]   *ND* 1.29.82.

[195]   Sydenham, *RCC* 598 with pl. 19 (Thorius, 119–91), 722 with pl. 22 (L. Procilius, 78–55), 773 with pl. 22 (L. Papius, 78–55), 915 with pl. 25 (L. Roscius Fabatus, 78–55), 964 (L. Papius, ca. 46), 1058 (M. Mettius, ca. 44). The Lanuvian Thorius figured a charging bull on the reverse to recall his name (*torus*, i.e., *taurus*), and thus imitated Renius (above, n. 75); see Figure 3. The goat and the bull are associated in the fable of Faunus and Vitellia; see below, ch. 3, n. 423.

[196]   Sydenham, *RCC* 772 with pl. 22 (L. Procilius, 78–55); Grueber, 1.3150 with pl. 41.18–19. See below at n. 200.

[197]   Sydenham, nos. 771, 772, 915 (cf. Prop. 4.8), 1058.

[198]   See Broughton, *MRR* 2.292, 327–28, 345, 360–61.

[199]   Sydenham, 1352–53 with pl. 30. Cf. Grueber, 2.pp. 577–78 with pls.121.15, 122.1.

[200]   Sydenham, 1354–55.

[201]   See Roscher, col. 602; Grueber, *loc. cit.* (above, n. 199).

[202]   Livy 21.62.4. A carnelian now in the British Museum has a carved scene of the ordeal of virginity undergone at the Lanuvian shrine of Juno Sispes. The raven views the ordeal on the gem. See E. Strong, *Art in Ancient Rome* (New York, 1928), vol. 1, p. 62.

[203]   Livy 24.10.6.

[204]   Fest. *Epit.* 56 L., where read *lucus* for *locus*, and Degrassi on *ILLRP* 69–70. See A. Ernout, "Numina Ignota. I: Devas Corniscas sacrum," *RPh* 39 (1965), pp. 189–94; Bailey on Lucr. 5.1084; Pliny *NH* 7.153; Pease on Cic. *Div.* 1.7.12; Poultney on *Tab. Ig.* VIa 1; Latte,

p. 139; and Symphosius' *Enigma* 27 with the comment of R.T. Ohl "The Enigmas of Symphosius," Univ. of Pennsylvania Diss. (Philadelphia, 1928), pp. 60–61. The *corvus* appearing to Valerius surely was not taken as a bad sign, for the Gauls were defeated by his commander, Furius Camillus, after the latter vowed a temple to Juno Moneta; see above, sect. 7.

205 Suet. *Aug.* 14, 96.2; Appian *BC* 5. 204–206; Dio 48.14.5–6; cf. Livy 5.21.8–9 and Ogilvie's comment, for the Perusine Juno. On Trebonianus Gallus: *CIL* XI 1926–31 with Bormann's major comments; T.L. Donaldson, *Architectura Numismatica or Architectural Medals of Classic Antiquity* (London, 1859) = *Anc. Arch. on Greek and Roman Coins and Medals* (Chicago, 1965), no. 17; H. Cohen *Description historique des monnaies etc.* 5.243–44; J. Heurgon, "Traditions etrusco-italiques dans le monnayage de Trebonien Galle," *SE* 24 (1955–56), pp. 91–105, esp. pp. 93–98, from whose interpretation I dissent. On Arruns Veltumnus: *Röm. Feldmesser*, p. 350 L.; J. Heurgon, "The Date of Vegoia's Prophecy," *JRS* 49 (1959), pp. 41–45; A.J. Pfiffig, "Eine etr. Prophezeiung," *Gymnasium* 68 (1961), pp. 55–64. For Martial's cognomen see 9.52; 10.24; 12.60. Cf. Ausonius' usage, p. 101 P.: Iunonius Mavors. Jeep wrongly condemns as unparalleled the title *Iunonalia* given to a mutilated poem in Claudian, *App.* 5. For Veltymnus and the status of Perusia see W.V. Harris, *Rome in Etruria and Umbria* (Oxford, 1971), pp. 33, 299–303, 309.

206 Above at nn. 75, 142.

207 Macr. *Sat.* 1.12.23.

208 Besides the coins, see Cic. *ND* 1.29.82, describing Lanuvian Sispes, on which see Gordon (above, n. 183), pp. 32–35; Jul. Obs. 27, a prodigy evidently in the temple of the Regina dedicated during the Ligurian war (cf. Livy 39.2.11, 40.52.1); Servius (next note); Plut. *QR* 87 ultimately depending on Varro, and 92 on the *corona* (cf. Gellius 5.6.11–15). In Macrobius' discussion of the table of Juno Populona (see above, at n. 24), shields and garlands are included among a temple's decoration. The details are too loosely given in this connection to warrant a certain association with Populona.

209 Serv. Dan. on *Aen.* 1.8, 1.16, 1.17, and 2.614 (hence a derivation of Curritis from *currus*), and the coins of Caprotina and Sispes.

210 So Juno Lucina and Moneta at Rome; Juno Quiritis of Falerii (*CIL* XI 3126 = *ILS* 5374; Ovid *Amor.* 3.113); Sispes at Lanuvium (above, n. 183); and Juno at Nuceria (Pliny *NH* 16.132). See also n. 189.

211 So Juno on the Capitoline, Arx, Aventine (who came from Veii's *arx*), and Esquiline (Lucina on Mt. Cespius according to Varro *LL* 5.50), and at Lanuvium.

212 E.g. Tac. *Hist.* 4.53; Vitr. 1.7.1; Plut. *QR* 92.

213 Charisius (258 B) errs in attributing *edepol* (or *pol*, for that matter) to women. In one Plautine play alone these two oaths by Pollux are spoken by men fifteen times (*Bacch.* 40, 78, 156, 166, 254, 293, 321, 394, 515, 545, 678, 1047, 1055, 1100, 1162). On Castor and Pollux see Dion. Hal. *AR* 6.13.4–5. The source of Charisius' error on the oath by Pollux seems to be Varro; see Gellius *NA* 11.6. On the Junonian oath see Palmer, *Archaic Community*, pp. 185–86.

214 *Amph.* 831–36: *Alcmene*. per supremi regis regnum iuro et matrem familias Iunonem, quam me vereri et metuere est par maxume, ut me extra unum te mortalis nemo corpus corpore contigit, quo me inpudicam faceret. *Amphitruo*. vera istaec velim. *Al.* vera dico, sed nequiquam, quoniam non vis credere. *Am.* mulier es, audacter iuras. Plautus' *vera dico* may reflect the cult of a prophetic Juno Veridica (*ILS* 3110) which, in turn, influenced the notion of Juno the Warner. Cf. *Cas.* 230–34. For other oaths by Juno see, e.g., Prop. 2.5.17, Tib. 3.19.15 and Juv. 2.98 (the Juno of a homosexual); cf. Tib. 3.12, an invocation of a girl's *iuno natalis*; above, n. 141, H. Wagenvoort, *Roman Dynamism* (Oxford, 1947), pp. 192–93.

215 Festus *Epit.* 248 L.; Gellius 4.3.3 has *aedem*, not *aram*. See Erdman, *RE* 18.2 (1943) cols. 2225–27. On Numan law see E. Gabba, 'Considerazioni sulla tradizione letteraria sulle origine della Repubblica," *Fondation Hardt, Entretiens* 13 (1967), pp. 135–74, who also discusses the Jus Papirianum (above, n. 23).

[216]   See Wagenvoort, pp. 48–58, 138 ff. The touching of the altar may refer to a prohibition against an oath by Juno where a *paelex* was concerned. Unlike the Vestals, for instance, a *paelex* would have been ritually unclean in the sight of any god because of her peculiar condition. Lastly, *paelex* may be referred to sacral prostitution, see below, n. 370.

[217]   See, e.g., Bömer on Ovid *F.* 1.587, and above at n. 123.

[218]   E.g., *Cist.* 36–40, *Merc.* 685–90 (coupled with Juno); *Rud.* 1047.

[219]   *Dig.* 50.16.144.

[220]   Gellius *NA* 4.3.3.

[221]   Fest. *Epit.* 248 L.

[222]   See above, nn. 23 and 215.

[223]   Cf. Erdmann (above, n. 215).

[224]   H. Le Bonniec, *Le culte de Cérès à Rome* (Paris, 1958), pp. 77–88.

[225]   See Degrassi, pp. 515–16.

[226]   For references and discussion of the ancient sources and the series of articles by Rose, see Latte, pp. 97–98, 133, Degrassi, pp. 468–69, 515–16, and the author's "Cupra, Matuta, and Venilia Pyrgensis," *Illinois Studies in Language and Literature* 58 (Urbana, 1969), pp. 292–309. Rose retains the oversight of girls only. However, once we accept the end of a linguistic relation with *soror*, introduce Janus Curiatius and curial institution, and acknowledge the purification of the male Horatius, we must abandon the specialization and open the ceremony to both sexes. On the curial business see Palmer, *Archaic Community*, p. 137.

[227]   Ernout-Meillet, *Dict. étym.*[4] *s.v.* ops, takes *opigena* as "born of Ops," whom the Romans identified with Rhea in their Hellenic mythology (cf. Varro *LL* 5.57, 64; Macr. *Sat.* 1.10. 18–21). The determinative compound is of the type *agricola, interduca* (below). See W.W. Fowler, "Fortuna Primigenia," *Roman Essays and Interpretations* (Oxford, 1920), pp. 64–70. Opigena is so badly attested (Fest. *Epit.* 221 L., Mart. Cap. 2.149) that *opigenia* is possibly the primitive epithet that can be set beside the *genius*, which is paired with Juno, nn. 141, 192, 214.

[228]   Varro *LL* 6.21; Festus 202 L.; Macr. *Sat.* 1.12.21–23. On Juno in the Regia and her scepter, see above.

[229]   Fest. *Epit.* 3 L. Juno was also worshipped in this month on the calends (Feriae Marti) as Lucina and the nones at Junonalia. On the *axamenta* see below, ch. 4.

[230]   Cato *Agr.* 134.

[231]   See Le Bonniec (above, n. 224), pp. 148–57, and below, ch. 2.

[232]   See above at n. 20.

[233]   See Degrassi, pp. 499–500, 502–503, 538, 541. Cf. Le Bonniec (above, n. 224), pp. 180–84, 193–95.

[234]   See Ernout-Meillet[4] *s.v.* epulum, and Le Bonniec, p. 194–95.

[235]   Cf. Ter. *loc. cit.* (above, n. 127): fer opem.

[236]   Fest. *Epit.* 55 L.; Arn. 3.25, 3.30; Mart. Cap. 2.149.

[237]   A *cinctus* was for men, *cingillum* and *cingulum* for women (Varro *LL* 5.114; Festus 55). However see Isidore *Etym.* 19.33.1–2. Compare the old military idioms *classis procinta* and *in procinctu*. On a probable Umbrian usage see Poultney on *Tab. Ig.* VIb 59. Cf. Serv. on *Aen.* 1.16: "arma" instructam armis Iunonem in alio loco testatur ut ferro accincta vocat. See Radke, p. 92. We have already analyzed her name Unxia "anointed" above, at n. 100. Of course, there is no evidence that these epithets are any older than the first century B.C.

[238]   Aug. *CD* 7.3 (cf. *CD* 6.9 Domiducus) and Mart. Cap. 2.149. The *-duca*, like *opi-gena*, is not necessarily a feminine agent; cf. *agricola*. Mercury is *viarum atque itinerum dux* (Caes. *BG* 6.17), and Neptune who guided the Roman attack on New Carthage's walls facing the lagoon is *dux itineris* (Livy 26.45.9). Also see Pease's note on *domum itionem* in Cic. *Div.* 1.32.68.

[239]   Cf. the incantations for bone-setting in Cato *Agr.* 160 and Pliny *NH* 28.227, 30.119.

[240]   See Agahd, pp. 121–22, 215–16, Bonniec (above, n. 224), and above all the works of

Noailles on ancient marriage collected in *Fas et jus*, and R.G. Austin, *P.V.M. Aeneidos Liber Quartus*, on lines 166ff.

241   Cf. Varro in Cens. *DN* 14.2 and Gellius *NA* 10.28.1.

242   See nn. 158, 168.

243   Livy 7.28, and above, sect. 9. Compare the temple of Juno Moneta on the Alban Mount, which was vowed under like circumstances; above, n. 176.

244   Livy 32.30.10, 34.53.3. On other votive temples originating in Gaulish wars see below, ch. 3, sects. 12–13.

245   Livy 39.2, 40.52.1–2.

246   See Platner-Ashby, *TDAR* pp. 304–305, Degrassi, 508, 512. Cf. the temple of Jupiter Stator vowed in a war with the Samnites (Livy 10.36–37). Probably in this temple the twenty-seven maidens rehearsed their hymn for Regina in 207.

247   On the Roman psychology in promising temples in wartime and in their choice of deity, see below sect. 17.

248   For a collection of the evidence and discussion see G. Giannelli, "Culti e miti della Magna Grecia: Contributo alla storia più antica delle colonie greche in occidente," *Univ. di Napoli, Centro di Studi per la M.G.* 2 (1963), pp. 135–51.

249   Livy 9.30.4 (the creation of the fleet). De Sanctis, *SR*² 2.346–47, puts the treaty's date at the time of Cleonymus (*ca.* 303), whereas Frank, *CAH* 7.640, suggests a treaty made by Romans and Tarentines under the influence of Alexander of Epirus (ca. 334). See the discussion of R.E. Mitchell, "Roman-Carthaginian Treaties: 306 and 279/8 B.C.," *Historia* 20 (1971), pp. 633–55.

250   Giannelli (above, n. 248), pp. 143–44; J. Bérard, *La colonisation grecque*² (Paris, 1957), pp. 156–62. There is a tradition that Thetis was the former occupant of the shrine (Tzetzes and Schol. on Lyc. *Alex.* 856–58; Serv. Dan. on *Aen.* 3.552). G. Pugliese-Carratelli, "Santuari extramurani in Magna Grecia," *Par. Pass.* 17 (1962), pp. 241–46, holds the view that such shrines as that of Hera Lakinia go back to Mycenaean settlements.

251   [Arist.] *Mir. Ausc.* 96 (838); Livy 24.3.3–7, 30.20.6. See Giannelli, p. 136, and Bérard, *ibid.*

252   Strabo 6.1.11; Serv. Dan on *Aen.* 3.552. Called today Cape Colonna after the remains of the ancient temple, the promontory rises about sixty-eight feet above the sea.

253   Lyc. *Alex.* 856–58; Livy 24.3.3–7.

254   *Alex.* 856–58, 614. See Tzetzes *ad* 858, who says Hera of Elis bore the same epithet, and Giannelli pp. 137, 144–45. Zeus also was called Hoplosmios (Arist. *Part. Anim.* 673a, 19; *IG* V 2.344 = Ditt. *SIG*³ 490; cf. the Mantinean tribe Hoplodmia in *IG* V 2.271). A precise analysis of the suffix eludes us. For a possible etymological connection with J. Sispes, see above, n. 192.

255   Philostratos *Vita. App.* 4.28; Giannelli, pp. 138, 144–47.

256   Paus. 6.13.1.

257   Lyc. *Alex.* 859–65; Justin 20.4.11–12; Iamb. *Pyth. Vita* 9.50.

258   Cic. *Div.* 1.24.48; Livy 28.46.16, 42.3.

259   Dion. Hal. *AR* 1.5.3; cf. Verg. *Aen.* 3.552. See Giannelli, p. 157. The inscription of Lakinion recorded the name of the recipient, not the donor's.

260   Conon *Narrat.* 3; Lyc. *Alex.* 1007. See Giannelli, p. 143, Bérard (above, n. 250), p. 409, and previous notes. Unfortunately, we cannot ascertain the age of these legends.

261   Although the historical incidents reported by Livy 10.2.9–15 may be doubted (cf. De Sanctis, *SR*² 2.346–47), the temple, its deity, and the offerings were old and authentic. For the dedication of maritime spoils to the Hera of Samos by Polycrates' father, see Tod *GHI* I² 7.

262   Above, n. 17.

263   Pol. 1.65.2, Livy *Per.* 20, Val. Max. 6.5.1, Eutr. *Brev.* 2.28, Zon. 8.18, Oros 4.11.10. See Scullard, pp. 112–15, and M. Frederiksen and J.W. Perkins, *PBSR* 25 (1957) p. 190, for the valley site of Juno's precinct.

[264] *AR* 1.21.

[265] Above, sect. 6.

[266] *AR* 2.22.

[267] *AR* 1.21. See Scullard, pp. 35–38.

[268] Cf. Varro *LL* 7.34, Macr. *Sat.* 3.8.5–7, Serv. on *Aen.* 11.543.

[269] See above, at n. 20.

[270] *AR* 2.23.5. The basket was perhaps a *sporta* (see Varro *VPR* in Non. p. 261 L), or a *cumera* (see Varro *LL* 7.34 and Festus 55 L).

[271] On the Triad and banquets at Falerii see above, n. 157.

[272] Cf. Ovid *Amor.* 3.13, *F.* 6.49; *ILS* 3111 *(pontifex sacrarius Iunonis Quiritis); ILS* 5374 *(lucus Iunonis Curritis).*

[273] In *Röm. Feldmesser* p. 217 L. See Huelsen *RE* 6.2 cols. 1970–71, and Harris, *op. cit.*, p. 307. A fresh analysis has been offered by I. di Stefano Manzella, "Un'iscrizione di Falerii sul mercato antiquario romano," *Acc. Naz. dei Lineci, Rend. Cl. Sci. mor., stor., filol.*, ser. 8, vol. 26 (1971), pp. 1–15.

[274] Eutr. 2.28.

[275] Vell. Pat. 1.15 and below, n. 320; Livy 39.55.9 for Saturnia, on which see below, ch. 4.

[276] Her festival was 7 October. See Degrassi, p. 518.

[277] *F.* 3.835–46, on which see Bömer. Cf. Platner-Ashby, *TDAR* pp. 343–44; Radke, p. 81.

[278] *CIL* I² 365 = XI 3081 = *ILS* 3124 = Vetter no. 320 = *ILLRP* 238 records an early offering to Minerva by the local praetor at the senate's behest. *ILS* 5374 records the repaving of the Sacred Way from the Chalcidicum to the grove of Juno Curritis. See above, n. 263. Cf. the temple of Minerva Chalcidica and the Chalcidicum at Rome *(TDAR s.vv.).* These two Faliscan goddesses were not the members of the Triad (above, n. 157).

[279] Val. Max. 6.5.1.

[280] R. Mengarelli, "Il luogo e i metariali del tempio di ' 'HPA a Caere," *SE* 10 (1936), pp. 83–86, who suggests the Greek dedications were owed to commercial ties. For a shrine with much older dedications to Hera in the same neighborhood, see now M. Torelli, "Il santuario di Hera a Gravisca," *PP* fasc. 136 (1971), pp. 44–67.

[281] Mengarelli, p. 76 and pl. xxvii nos. 1,2. See above, n. 192.

[282] *Ibid.*, pp. 80–81, pl. xxvi no. 3, xxix nos. 6 and 8. The outer shield bears a lion's head. See further Q.F. Maule and H.R.W. Smith, "Votive Religion at Caere: Prolegomena," *Univ. of Calif. Publ. Cl. Arch.* 4 (1959), p. 65.

[283] Diod. 15.14.3–4; [Arist.] *Oec.* 1349b33; Polyaen. 5.2.21; Aelian *Var. Hist.* 1.20. On the incident see Sordi (above, n. 131) pp. 64–68.

[284] Livy 5.19.6, 23.7; Ovid *F* 6.479–80; Plut. *Cam.* 5. This reconstruction is discussed by the author elsewhere (see above, n. 226).

[285] The rapid publication of the Italians, who issued a preliminary report within the year, is commendable: "Scavi nel santuario etrusco di Pyrgi," *Arch. Cl.* 16 (1964), pp. 49–117. The archaeologist digging at the site, G. Colonna, wrote on the situation of the plaques, pp. 49–57; G. Garbini published, translated, and commented on the "Punic" inscription, pp. 66–76; M. Pallottino published, attempted a translation of, and commented on the two Etruscan plaques (A and B), and appended a discussion of the general importance of the discovery, pp. 76–117. The inscriptions indeed have a significance that reaches much further than the scope of this study, and will be the subject of discussion for many years to come. The problem of the dating is critical. Garbini (pp. 75–76) dates the "Punic" inscription to the fifth cent.; Pallottino (pp. 79–81), the Etruscan inscriptions to the late sixth cent. Since the dedicant of all three is the same, no considerable latitude in dating is allowed for the several plaques. Pallotino wants to bring the date close to the Roman treaty with Carthage in 509 (Polyb. 3.22–25, on which see Walbank), and at the same time make Roman ties with Caere much earlier than those attested for the late fifth and early fourth cent. (see Sordi above, n. 131 *passim*). In my view, there is at this time no firm evidence for dating the three inscriptions, and, moreover, they bear

no immediate contemporary relation to Rome. (See also M. Pallottino, "Nuova luce sulla storia di Roma arcaica dalle lamine d'oro di Pyrgi," *SR* 13 (1965), pp. 1–13.) G. Radke, "Punicum," *Gymnasium* 73 (1966), pp. 241–44, argues that the place named Punicum was not on the Tyrrhenian coast, but in ore-bearing mountains, and that there is no relation of the toponym to the Phoenicians. Following A.J. Pfiffig. "Uni-Hera-Astarte," *Oestr. Akad. Wiss. Philos.-hist. Denkschr.* 88.2 (1965), p. 39, Radke also holds that Pallottino and others date the inscriptions too early; he prefers a fourth-century date. Pfiffig has been partly seconded by M. Cristofani, "Sulla paleografia delle iscrizioni etrusche di Pyrgi," *Arch. Cl.* 18 (1966), pp. 103–109. Also Fitzmyer (next note) holds to a data *ca.* 500 for the Semitic. The language of the Semitic inscription seems now to be Phoenician rather than Punic, and to bear resemblance to the Phoenician of Cyprus; G. Levi Della Vida, *Oriens Antiquus* 4 (1965), pp. 49–52; J. Ferron, "Quelques remarques à propos de l'inscription phénicienne de Pyrgi," *Oriens Antiquus* 4 (1965), pp. 181–98; J.A. Fitzmyer (below, n. 286); G. Pugliese Carratelli, "Intorno alle lamine di Pyrgi," *SE* 33 (1965), pp. 221–35. A text of the Etr. inscriptions may also be found in *SE* 33 (1965), pp. 511–13 with pl. cxviii; in Fowler and Wolfe (below, n. 294) no. 9021, although the texts reached them too late for inclusion in their splendid analytical indices; Pallottino, *TLE*² 874–75; *CIE* 6314–16. K. Olzscha, "Die punisch-etruskischen Inschriften von Pyrgi," *Glotta* 44 (1966), pp. 60–108, discusses all three inscriptions and offers a translation of A (p. 95) and B (p. 105). See also the lucid summary of J. Heurgon, "The Inscriptions of Pyrgi," *JRS* 56 (1966), pp. 1–15; M. Pallottino, "I frammenti di lamina di bronzo con iscrizione etrusca scoperta a Pyrgi," *SE* 34 (1966), pp. 175–209; W. Fischer and H. Rix, "Forschungsbericht: Die phönizisch-etruskischen Texten der Goldplättchen von Pyrgi,"*Götting. Gel. Anz.* 220 (1968), pp. 64–94; Scullard, pp. 102–104.

²⁸⁶ J.A. Fitzmyer, S.J., "The Phoenician Inscription from Pyrgi," *JAOS* 86 (1966), pp. 286–87. Italicized translations indicate for Fr. Fitzmyer uncertain renderings. His article offers a text with commentary and draws our attention to the linguistic affinities of the Pyrgan inscription with the Phoenician attested on Cyprus. Cf. Heurgon, n. 285, pp. 10–11.

²⁸⁷ See above, n. 226. We have already remarked the Junos installed in other gods' shrines; see above at nn. 140, 141. The Junonarium in the Praenestine temple of Fortune is another example; below at n. 366.

²⁸⁸ See G. Colonna, "The Sanctuary at Pyrgi in Etruria," *Archaeology* (U.S.A) 19 (1966), pp. 11–23, esp. 21, on the time of the temple's destruction. Colonna, "Il santuario di Pyrgi alla luce delle recenti scoperte," *SE* 33 (1965), pp. 201–203, identifies Temple B as the site of the "holy place" and its tablets. Pfiffig (above n. 285) commenced the discussion of Eileithyia's temple in this regard. On the relation of Astarte's shrine and the temple or precinct, see Pfiffig, p. 42, and Heurgon (above, n. 285), pp. 6–7. R. Bloch, "Un mode d'interpretation à deux degrés: de l'Uni de Pyrgi à Ilithye et Leucothée," *Arch. Cl.* 21 (1969), pp. 58–65, further pursues the connections of these goddesses.

²⁸⁹ *CIE* 3415, 3426. See Rix, pp. 176 and 309 n. 17.

·²⁹⁰ Pallottino, *Arch. Cl.*, 106–109, suggests Velianas' Caeretane title was *zilath*, even though the Etr. word from which L. *lucumo* is derived is usually considered the equivalent of L. *rex*. However, *zilacal* of Inscr. A refers to the magistracy, not necessarily that of Velianas. See also Olzscha (above, n. 285), p. 86. On the office of *zilath*, previously unattested at Caere, see R. Lambrechts, "Essai sur les magistrates des républiques étrusques," *Et. Phil. Arch. Hist. Anc. Publ. Inst. Hist. Belge de Rome* 7 (1959), *passim*, esp. pp. 89–108, and Scullard pp. 221–31. G. Pugliese Carratelli, *op. cit.* (above, n. 285), p. 221–35, explores Greek, Carthaginian,and Etruscan relations bearing on the Pyrgan finds and canvasses the possible sense of the Semitic "king" at Caere. The king's praenomen is discussed by M.G. Tibilletti Bruno, *SE* 33 (1965), pp. 545–46; at pp. 547–48 she treats the Semitic rendition of the name of Caere, which Fitzmyer (above, n. 286), p. 290, remarks on.

²⁹¹ *Tab. Ig.* Va 2–3, 15 which Poultney renders "during the *auctorship* of Titus Castrucius son of Titus" and "during the *auctorship* of C. Cluvius son of Titus." Note that all the Iguvine

records and the two epigraphs cited in the next note are sacral.
292   Buck no. 84 = Vetter no. 236 = Ernout no. 6. Cf. *su maronato V.L. Varie T.C. Fulonie*
(Buck 83 = Vetter 233 = Ernout 4), where the slightly different formula of *su* with ablative is
followed by the two personal names in the genitive. For the originally Etruscan office of *maru*
(L. *maro*) see Lambrechts (above, n. 290), pp. 108–14 and *passim*. Olzscha (above, n. 285),
pp. 77–79, believes that *tamers-ca* in A may be "tyrant," as Pfiffig (above, no. 285) suggests, or
is a priest, and at pp. 88 ff. suggests that *atranes* is related to the Etr. word for "father." With
the former suggestion I agree, for *tamers-ca*, Velianas' apparent title, could represent the notion
of king who was a priest, i.e., a *rex sacrorum*. On *atranes* I hold a different view from Olzscha's
and from G. Devoto's "Considerazioni sulle lamine auree di Pyrgi," *SE* 34 (1966), p. 218,
which argues that *atranes* means "day." Cf. Heurgon (above, n. 285), pp. 11–14. On the
Etruscan month see M. Durante, "Masan" *SE* 36 (1968), pp. 67–69.
293   *Arch. Cl.* 16 (1964), pp. 96–100, 102–104. "Annual" is a rendition of Etr. *avil* in A 15
and *avilchval* in B 6–7. The suffix *-chva*, in Pallottino's view, is comparable with substantives of
Latin festivals in *-alia*.
294   I am indebted to Professor Murray Fowler for supplying me with a list of Etr. words in
-um and *-chva* prior to the publication of his and R.G. Wolfe's *Materials for the Study of the
Etruscan Language*, 2 vols. (Madison, 1965), a fundamental ancillary to the enucleation of
proximate sense from Etruscan texts. The suffix *-um* is not in question here because the word
cannot be *pul* (a preposition) +*-um* (a conjunction "and" or "but") +*chva* (substantival suffix): *pulumchva* is the last word in A and last but one in B. Besides Pallottino's view, the suffix
-chva is subject to other interpretations: K. Olzscha, "Interpretation der agramer Mumien-
binde," *Klio* Beiheft 40 (1939), p. 154 n. 1, calls it a possessive suffix; A.J. Pfiffig, "Studien zu
den agramer Mumienbinden," *Oestr. Ak. d. Wissensch. Phil. -hist. Kl. Denkschr.* 81 (1963),
pp. 75–77, calls words compounded *-chva*, *-cva*, and *-va* "Repletivadejecktiva," which I cannot
follow if we accept the generally acknowledged meaning of Etr. *caper* (cf. L. *capis*) as "cup,"
since in context *caperchva* (Mummy VII 10, which Pfiffig does not adduce) makes no sense as
"full of cups." Cf. Pfiffig's explanation of *pulumchva*, *op. cit.* above, n. 285, pp. 34, 39.
M. Durante, "Le formule conclusive dei testi etruschi di Pyrgi," *Rendic. Accad. Naz. Lincei* 20
(1965), pp. 308–21, argues that *pulumchva* means "borchie," and that *pul-* = L. *bulla*. In
response to this argument G. Pugliese Carratelli, "Le stelle di Pyrgi," *Par. Pass.* 20 (1965),
pp. 303–305, draws our attention to Festus 476 L: stellam significare ait Ateius Capito laetum
et prosperum, auctoritatem secutus P. Servili auguris [stellam], quae ex lamella aerea adsimilis
stellae locis inauguratis infigatur. (The present writer had already noted this connection between the stars of the Phoenician inscription and the inaugural practice, and concurs in Pugliese
Carratelli's view.) This agreement of customs notwithstanding, *pulumchva* can be related to
another Italic practice, and need not be an Etr. word for "star," "boss," "buckle," or "nail."
(Colonna, *SE* 33 (1965), pp. 203–209 with pl. lvii, discusses the significance of the nails from
the site and opts for a location of the inscriptions "ai battenti della porta della cella" of
Temple B and its *adyton*.) If Latin and Phoenician intend the same thing when they refer to the
"stars," why does Etruscan call them *bullae* (i.e., "borchie")? Furthermore, "annual stars,"
which would have indicated the age of the foundation, could hardly have been in sufficient
number to flatter Astarte with the wish "And may the years of the statue of the deity in her
temple be years like *the stars of El* [or: *like these stars*]." We assume that there were many stars.
Olzscha (above, n. 285), p. 93, and M. Torelli, "Le formule conclusive delle tre lamine di
Pyrgi," *SE* 35 (1967), pp. 175–78 accept the suggestion that *pulumchva* reflects a word concerning the heavens.
295   The *pulum* of Fab. *CII* 2033 is badly attested; see E. Goldman, *Beiträge zur Lehre vom
indogermanischen Character der etruskischen Sprache* 2 (Heidelberg, 1930), p. 127 n. 1. It may
be the preposition *pul* (next note) and conjunction *-um* (on which see Olzscha, above, n. 294,
pp. 153–54, and Pfiffig, above, n. 294, p. 11).
296   An excellent parallel is the Etr. preposition *pul* and *epl* with prothetic *e-*. A. Trombetti,

La lingua etrusca (Florence, 1928), p. 136, makes an attractive comparison of it with its L. equivalent *apud, apur*. See also Goldman, pp. 71–73, 126–27 and Olzscha (above, n. 294), p. 84 n. 1. Furthermore, a consonant cluster *pl*, regardless of etymology, would be susceptible to the addition or subtraction of *e-*; cf. *Tusci/Etrusci*. The Etruscans may have treated the *e* of *epulum* as prothetic by analogy with the prothetic *e-* (demonstrative?) in *e-dio, e-iuno, e-quirine, e-castor*, and *e-de-pol* in oaths, and the *e-nos* of the Arval hymn. On the Etr. borrowing of Gk. names in which π is pronounced φ (f), see E. Fiesel, "Namen des griechischen Mythos im Etruskischen," *ZVZ* Erganz, hft. 5 (1928), in the Gk. index *s. vv.* Persephone, Perseus, Polyxene, and Polyneikes, and pp. 33–35. Notable parallels with Latin are Populonia for Etr. Fufluna/Pupluna (see below, n. 332) and Etr. *nefts* with Latin **nepots*.

[297]   See M. Pallottino, *The Etruscans* (Hammondsworth-Baltimore, 1955), pp. 269–70; Goldman, pp. 84–87; and Trombetti, pp. 166–67, with translation on p. 206, "ricchezza" rendering what he thinks is a word related to Gk. φυλ-.

[298]   E.g. Cic. *Vat.* 30–32 (*epulum, epulae, cenare*); *CIL* VI 10297, V 7906, VIII 11813; *ILS* 7235, 8374, 8375 (*epulum* or *epulari*); cf. *ILS* 6468 (*cena*), 6711, 8372 (*cibi*), 8371, 8369 (*escae*).

[299]   Fest. *Epit.* 68 L.: epolonos dicebant quos nunc epulones dicimus. datum est autem his nomen quod epulas indicendi Iovi ceterisque dis potestatem haberent. Cf. *idem* 72 *s.v.* epulam, 76 *s.v.* ferias, and above, n. 157. The references to banquets of Juno, e.g., Val. Max. 2.1.2, 6.1, Tac. *Ann.* 15.44, draw the distinction between *lectisternia* for gods and *sellisternia* for goddesses. This is a nicety of polite society which does not tell us what the Romans called the meal itself, but only how the cult statue was arranged on the furniture. The clay drinking cup dedicated to Juno (*CIL* I² 444 = XI 6708.5 = *ILS* 2962 = *ILLRP* 173) may have come from any kind of supper set for her. Cf. the cups from Caere with Hera's name on them; above, n. 280.

[300]   See Olzscha (above, n. 294), p. 151 on *pruchum*, and Fiesel, pp. 95, 99–101. Olzscha generalizes his remarks on these forms as accusatives at pp. 104–105 and 194–95, where he discusses *cletram*, an Umbrian accusative.

[301]   Above, n. 294. Cicero (*Div.* 1.34.75, on which see Pease) mentions the Spartan dedication of golden stars to Castor and Pollux in the gods' Delphic temple after Lysander's victory over Athens. A. Neppi Modona, " 'Queste stelle' o 'stelle di el' nella lamina punica di Pyrgi?," *SE* 36 (1969), pp. 65–66, rejects the views of Pugliese Carratelli and Torelli on Festus' inaugural stars, but allows that the stars were visible in the temple. Heurgon (above, n. 285), p. 11 n. 71a, follows Dupont–Sommer and holds that the "stars" are the familiar real stars of the heavens. When the author of the Phoenician text wrote "these stars" did he mean "the stars"?

[302]   Apul. *Meta.* 11.4, cf. 24. On the *toga picta*, R. Eisler, *Weltenmantel und Himmelzelt* vol. 1 (Munich, 1910), pp. 40–45 (cf. pp. 63, 66–69); Ehlers, *RE* 7A1, cols. 504–505; L.B. Warren, "Roman Triumphs and Etruscan Kings: The Changing Face of the Triumph," *JRS* 60 (1970), pp. 64–65. The starred cloak may be a late republican innovation or borrowing (so Ehlers). Since, however, the Roman triumph and perhaps the *toga picta* (Macr. *Sat.* 1.6.7) originated in their Roman form with the Etruscans (Ehlers, *ibid.*, cols. 493–95), and since the triumphator's garb was the same as that of Jupiter O.M. (Wagenvoort, pp. 164–68), the possibility of an archaic starred cloak worn by an Etruscan deity cannot be ruled out. For Juno Caprotina's *toga praetexta* see sect. 3. Juno Caelestis in Africa later wore some kind of cloak. *SHA* 24.29.1: Celsum imperatorem appellaverunt peplo deae Caelestis ornatum. Cf. Eisler *ibid.* pp. 43–48. A similar cape of Sybarite origin, for a long time on display at Hera's temple at Lakinion, was sold to a Carthaginian by Dionysius for 120 talents ([Arist.] *Mir. Ausc.* 96 (838)); its embroidery suggests a religious purpose. Caelestis Augusta wore a corselet (*thorax*), befitting attire for a war-goddess attached to the ruler-cult in Africa (*ILS* 4433 from the vicinity of Tunis). On the antiquity of such garments in archaic Greece and the Near East, see M.-Th. Picard, "La thoraké d'Amasis," (Hommages à W. Deonna) *Coll. Latomus* 28 (1957),

pp. 363–70. Juno Caelestis is discussed below. On the star as a divine attribute see S. Weinstock, *Divus Julius* (Oxford, 1971), pp. 370–84.

[303]   In M. Buffa, *Nuova raccolta di iscrizioni etrusche* (Florence, 1935), no. 1021, and Vetter's reading in F. Slotty, *Beiträge zur Etruskolgie: I. Silbenpunktierung und Silbenbildung im Altetruskischen* (Heidelberg, 1952), pp. 5–6.

[304]   Lines 12–13, in whose interpretation and rendition I partly follow Trombetti, pp. 146–47 and 204, and Olzscha (above, n. 294), p. 163.

[305]   Trombetti, p. 139, who translates *in Iunonis Orsminiae atrio.*

[306]   Olzscha (above, n. 294), pp. 162–63.

[307]   Cf. *CIE* 471: tinścvil mi unial curtun, "... I belong to Juno Cortona." For Etruscan curias see Festus 358 L. *s.v.* rituales, and *CIL* XI 3593; Palmer, *Archaic Community,* pp. 59–60. The Etruscan family name *ursimini* is attested in *CIE* 3033 and restored in *CIE* 5457. The Etr. name *ursme* may originally have been foreign to the Etruscans; see Rix, p. 365 (cf. p. 155 n. 7).

[308]   Cf. I *Sam.* 31.10, I *Kings* 11.5, and the Chaldaean prayer to Ishtar, "Lady of Conflict and of All Battles ... most powerful of all princes who holdest the reins [over] kings," translated by F.J. Stephens in J.B. Pritchard's *ANET,* pp. 383–85. Ishtar, in fact, had many of those attributes which the Romans claimed for Juno.

[309]   See G. Charles-Picard, *Les religions de l'Afrique antique* (Paris, 1954), ch. 3 and passim; Preisendanz, *RE* 4A2, cols. 2178–2215. Cf. the dedication at our n. 370.

[310]   For the latter, Cic. *ND* 3.23.59 and Charles-Picard, pp. 115–18.

[311]   Charles-Picard, p. 108; cf. Herodian 5.6.4, who says that Dido had brought the moon goddess whom the Libyans called the Ourania, the Carthaginians Astroarche (= Astarte?). See above, n. 150, and below, n. 371.

[312]   Cf. Charles-Picard on Venus and Caelestis, pp. 114–18.

[313]   Polyb. 7.9.

[314]   See Charles-Picard, pp. 83–85.

[315]   *Idem,* p. 84. n. 2. Caelestis, in any event, was the *genius* or *daimon* according to Tertullian, *Apol.* 24.8. Curiously enough, the shield of the Caeritane warriors, painted for the mural of Uni's temple, bears a Lion's head on the escutcheon; above, n. 282.

[316]   So the Chaldean prayer (above, n. 308).

[317]   Recorded by a "certain Furius" and excerpted from the *Res Reconditae* of Sammonicus Serenus by Macr. *Sat.* 3.9.7–12. On Furius see below, ch. 3, at n. 284.

[318]   "si deus si dea est, cui populus civitasque Carthaginiensis est in tutela." Cf. *Sat.* 3.9.2–3. That *populus* should be translated "army" at this late date is indicated in the subsequent formula of the town's *devotio,* wherein *omnes illam urbem Carthaginem exercitumque quem ego me sentio dicere fuga formidine terrore compleatis* and the repetitive *pro populo Romano exercitibus legionibusque.* See above, n. 21. Four republican inscriptions affirm the formula *sei deus sei dea* (*ILLRP* 291–93); *one*: at the beginning of the first century the praetor restored at the senate's behest the altar to the Nameless Deity on the Palatine near the Steps of Cacus; *two* and *three*: at Tibur and Spoletium, similar dedications without details; *four*: a newly uncovered inscription from near 'Old Isaura. In 1970 A. Hall of the University of Keele found at Bozkir in Turkey a document recording the campaign of 75–74. He has generously shared with me the text which he will soon publish. I render the complete inscription: "After conquering the enemy, taking Old Isaura and selling the captives, the *imperator* Servilius, son of Gaius, kept his vow if god, if goddess be in whose care was the town of Old Isaura." The application of this formula to an evocation anticipated any eventuality, whereas these final dedications suggest a continued doubt as to a positive identity of a foreign divinity – foreign at least in the certain case of Old Isaura. Success against both Old and New Isaura bestowed upon Servilius and his clan the name Isauricus. A thank-offering of the same character was reared by Fabius Allobrogicus in Gaul after he had won his honorific cognomen. Allobrogicus, however, recognized the gods whom he was rewarding; see below, ch. 3 at n. 419, ch. 5, n. 91.

[319] Dion. Hal. *AR.* 4.58, Verg. *Aen.* 7.682-84 and Servius on 682. For the same Vergilian expression see *Aen.* 7.739 and Servius thereon. On Gabii and S<ol>onii, see Palmer, *Archaic Community,* pp, 180–81. The section of Rome called Fregellae (Festus *Epit.* p. 80 L.) may have housed the evoked deity from that destroyed colony.

[320] Plut. *CG* 11, Solinus 27.11.

[321] See above at nn. 273–75

[322] Nor does Juno's protection of Carthage come to Roman attention only in 146: see Serv. on *Aen.* 1.281 = Ennius *Ann.* 291 V².

[323] *ILS* 4438 (dated by consuls to 259 A.D.); cf. Ovid *F.* 6.33–34.

[324] Gatti, *Diss. Pont. Accad. Arch.* ser. 2, 6 (1896), pp. 329–52.

[325] See Charles-Picard (above, n. 309), p. 84. Augustine (*Quaest. in Heptat.* 7.16) says unequivocally that Juno was Astarte, and he was in a better position to discuss Punic religion than many ancients: solet dici Baal nomen esse apud gentes illarum partium Iovis, Astarte autem Iunonis quod et lingua Punica putatur ostendere . . . . Iuno autem sine dubitatione ab illis [*sc.* Punicis] Astarte vocatur, etc.

[326] Basanoff, pp. 141–50, esp. p. 147.

[327] *Aen.* 1.16–17; *Fasti* 6.45–46.

[328] *F.* 6.37–38. This was Regina, which is further proof of her being the king's *iuno,* since royal scepters do not belong to ancient queens unless they are divine.

[329] *Aen.* 7.544–51; *F.* 6.91–100.

[330] *Aen.* 8.81–85; cf. 12.134–35.

[331] Cf. Albana (Tert. *Ad Nat.* 2.11.7).

[332] *Aen.* 10.172–73. The *mater Populonia* must be reminiscent of Juno Populona as well as referring to the town. On the town see C. Battisti, "Sul nome di Populonia," *St. Etr.* 27 (1959), pp. 385–412, in answer to G. Devoto, "Nomi di divinità etrusche: I. Fufluns," *St. Etr.* 6 (1932), pp. 243–60.

[333] *Aen.* 10.180–84; cf. Macr. *Sat.* 5.15.4. The Vergilian numbers of men in the units reflect the archaic Roman army: 300 and 600 horsemen, 1000 foot-soldiers. For Hera of Graviscae see above, n. 280.

[334] Fr. Fitzmyer draws my attention to the Near Eastern vacillation on the sex of Ishtar, and to A. Caquot, "Le dieu 'Athor et les textes de Ras Shamra," *Syria* 35 (1958), pp. 45–60. At Pyrgi both Uni and Astarte are decidedly female, so that the likelihood of a similar confusion of sex seems remote. Folk legend about a deity once honored at Pyrgi and long lost from view preserved the name till Vergil's *Aeneid.*

[335] *Aen.* 10.198–200; Serv. Dan. on 198.

[336] *Aen.* 10.75 and Serv. Dan. thereon.

[337] *Aen.* 10.544 and Serv. Dan. on 7.678.

[338] Serv. Dan. on *Aen.* 10.145.

[339] *Loc. cit.*, above, n. 268. Cf. Salius (*Aen.* 10.753) and Sacrator (*Aen.* 10.747).

[340] See below, n. 349 and ch. 3, sect. 7.

[341] Nissen, *Ital. Landesk.*, vol. 2.2 pp. 629–30.

[342] Strabo 5.3.5 (cf. Suet. *Aug.* 97.2). For Carthaginian trading-posts' usual site see B.H. Warmington, *Carthage* (Baltimore, 1964), p. 65. One thinks at once of the site of Tyre.

[343] Polyb. 3.22, on which see Walbank.

[344] See M. Cary and E.H. Warmington, *The Ancient Explorers* (Baltimore, 1963), pp. 61–71. This voyage took place around 500 or shortly thereafter; Warmington (above, n. 342), pp. 73–80. Pliny calls the shrine of Juno a *templum.* Hanno's record of the voyage was placed in the *temenos* of Kronos (his *Periplus* in Müller *GGM* vol. 1). Warmington (n. 342), pp. 74, 142 points out that this was Baal's temple, which may also be related to Tin(n)it's shrine. The gorillas are mentioned by Hanno, ch. 18, who says he brought home two pelts. It is worth noting that when the Carthaginians were defeated in 480/79 they were compelled to pay an indemnity of 2000 talents and to build two temples for housing two copies of their treaty with

Gelon (Diod. 11.25.2–3). Presumably one temple was in Carthage, the other somewhere in Carthaginian Sicily. It is remarkable that there was no temple for such a purpose. Both Hanno's Greek *temenos* and Pliny's *templum* perhaps bear out the lack of a proper temple at Carthage ca. 500.

[345]   Cf. Festus 418 L.: Stura flumen in agro Laurenti est quod quidam Asturam vo<cant>. The entry itself proves this variant was the less usual. Note that the Astura is in Laurentine territory according to Festus, but in Antiate territory according to Pliny, below, n. 347. The variant orthography is illuminating: Astyr/Astur/Astor, Stora/Stura/Astura. Etruscan had no *o*. With Astura/Stura compare Aphrodite/Frutis.

[346]   Mela 2.71: Circeia, Antium, Aphrodisium, Ardea, Laurentum, Ostia.

[347]   Pliny *NH* 3.57: dein quondam Aphrodisium Antium colonia, Astura flumen et insula. This follows upon mention of Ardea, so that we can be sure that he and Mela refer to the Ardeate shrine, not that at Lavinium. Cf. *NH* 3.81 (on islands): ab eis ultra Tiberina ostia in Antiano Astura, mox Palmaria, Sinonia, adversum Formias Pontiae. Servius on *Aen.* 7.801 is alone in saying there was a town called Astura.

[348]   Cassius Hemina fr. 7 P. in Solinus 2.14: nec omissum sit, Aeneam aestate ab Ilio capto secunda Italicis litoribus adpulsum, ut Hemina tradit, sociis non amplius sexcentis in agro Laurenti posuisse castra. ubi dum simulacrum, quod secum ex Sicilia advexerat, dedicat Veneri matri, quae Frutis dicitur . . . .

[349]   This is not the place to discuss the cult's role in the Aeneas legend. See R. Schilling, "La religion romaine de Venus," *Bibl. Ecoles Franç. Ath. Rome* 178 (1954), pp. 95–98, 233–54, and Tümpel, *RE* 6.1, cols. 604–606; G.K. Galinsky, *Aeneas, Sicily, and Rome* (Princeton, 1969) pp. 115–19, 148–49. Cf. Diod. Sic. 4.83, Dion. Hal. *AR* 1.63–65, and Serv. Dan. on *Aen.* 1.720. A. Alföldi, *Early Rome and the Latins* (Ann Arbor, 1965), p. 256 n. 1, insists that there was but one Aphrodisium, which "Strabo erroneously duplicated." His statement does not bear close scrutiny.

[350]   E.g., Wissowa, *RKR*² pp. 289–90, De Sanctis, *SR*² 2.200. See C. Koch, *RE* 8A1 (1955), cols. 845–46.

[351]   See Latte, p. 188, n. 4 (cf. p. 184), Alföldi (note 349), and our notes 345, 352. Galinsky, *loc. cit.*, holds different views. Cf. Weinstock, *op. cit.*, pp. 15–16.

[352]   *Op. cit.* (note 349), pp. 75–89, 246. Schilling believes the Ardeate supervision at Lavinium and the Ardeates' own temple-precinct are later than the original cult institution at Lavinium. In a single case the Etruscans' counterpart of Aphrodite was *Turan*, which has every likelihood of being a feminine of the Anatolian ancestor of the Greek *tyrannos* and of meaning "sovereign lady;" see Schilling, pp. 161–65. The Etruscans would have imposed the name Aphrodite rather than Turan upon the goddess because she was known to them some time after the Elymian communities, such as Segesta, had been hellenized. Astura, on the other hand, points to Phoenician recognition of a like goddess. Given the paucity of evidence, it cannot be said who first brought the goddess or cult to the central Tyrrhenian coast and on what occasions she was introduced. Indeed, the deity may be indigenous. The words *Astura, Frutis* and *Frutinal*, and *Aphrodisium* point to different eras of the cult of the same deity in different places; a chronological sequence is not hazarded here.

[353]   Livy 22.1.19, connected by Wissowa (note 350) with this Venus' cult.

[354]   Livy 22.9.7–11 (cf. 22.10.10, 23.31.9). Schilling (above, n. 349) draws attention to the Fabian worship of Erycina.

[355]   Livy 22.10.1–7 (cf. 33.44.1–2, 34.44.1–3).

[356]   Serv. on *Aen.* 7.796 (cf. Festus 424 L.). The custom is not peculiar to Venus' cult. Vergil's *sacranae acies* (*Aen.* 7.796) certainly refers to some Latian people.

[357]   See below, n. 376.

[358]   The "deification" of *venus* is dated by Schilling, pp. 9 and 86, to the sixth and fifth centuries.

[359]   See above, n. 285. In the *Aeneid* Cyprian Idalium is mentioned at 1.681, 693, 5.960, and

10.52 (with Amathus, Paphos, and Cythera) in connection with Venus of Eryx. Schilling, pp. 236–39, draws our attention to the Cyprian relations of Astarte and Venus Erycina.

[360]   Naevius *Bellum Punicum* fr. 9 Str.; Ennius *Ann.* 18–19 V^2.

[361]   E. Marmorale, *Naevius Poeta*[2] (Florence, 1950), pp. 26–39.

[362]   W.F. Albright, "The Role of the Canaanites in the History of Civilization" in *The Bible and the Ancient Near East* (New York, 1965), p. 467.

[363]   See above, n. 285. Colonna, *op. cit.* (above, n. 288), pp. 209–12, prefers a relation of the Pyrgan Phoenician text to W. Sicily and to Erycina.

[364]   Livy 21.62.

[365]   Cic. *Div.* 2.41.85–86, on which see Pease's commentary.

[366]   *CIL* XIV 2867 = *ILS* 3687 (*bis*). See above, at nn. 62–65.

[367]   Livy 22.1.19, 22.9.10, 22.10.10.

[368]   Livy 22.1.10, 22.36.7.

[369]   See above, sect. 13. For another prophetic Juno, see above, n. 214.

[370]   These officials are thought to be Elymians despite the title; see Warmington (above, n. 342), p. 84. The Astarte of Eryx also received a dedication at Sardinian Caralis (*CIS* I 140). Colonna, *op. cit.* (note 288), p. 212, tries to make something of Lucilius' *scorta Pyrgenisa* (in Serv. on *Aen.* 10.184). But most ports still cater to the needs supplied by prostitutes, religion notwithstanding. For what it is worth, we note that L. *paelex* bears an affinity to Gr. *pallake*, the generic word for concubine also applied to ritual prostitutes. The prohibition against a *paelex* touching Juno's altar (above, sect. 10) perhaps suggests exclusion of religious prostitutes. A hint of similar Roman practice of prostitution may be discerned at the beginning of the third century. In 295 B.C., Fabius Gurges exacted from matrons convicted of *stuprum* money fines with which he built a temple to Venus (Livy 10.31.9). She was commonly known as V. Obsequens; see Schilling, pp. 27–30, 93–95, 147–48 (cf. 242–43). Since a Fabius was involved in the foundation, we assume that this goddess and the source of her building fund had a connection with Erycina. Cf. n. 354 above. It is clear from the necessity to gloss the word *paelex*, as Festus, Gellius, Granius Flaccus, and Masurius Sabinus (in the *Digest*) did, that the sense of the word as found in the Jus Papirianum (so the *Digest*) was under suspicion when antiquarians researched old records. On the religious practice of prostitution see F. Cumont, *Les religions orientales dans le paganisme romain*[4] (Paris, 1929), p. 258 n. 58.

[371]   Justin 18.5.1–5, on which see Warmington, *ibid.*, p. 157. See above, n. 311.

[372]   Cic. *In Caec.* 55–56; Strabo 6.2.6 Cf. Vergil *Aen.* 1.335 and Servius *ad loc.* The Locrians of S. Italy were also willing to prostitute their women for Venus (Justin 21.3).

[373]   Tac. *Hist.* 2.2–3, and above, nn. 359–60.

[374]   See nn. 285 and 363.

[375]   See above, n. 359.

[376]   *CIL* X 6430 = *ILS* 5984: ad promuntur(ium) Veneris public(um) Circeiens(ium) usq(ue) ad mare a termino LXXX long(o) pedes L, |la|t(o) pe(des) CCXXV. Recall that the people of Circeii were included in Rome's first treaty with Carthage. Unfortunately, we lack precise information on the goddess Circe whom the Roman colonists of Circeii worshipped in her own temple; see Cic. *ND* 3.19.48, with Pease's note; Strabo 5.3.6; *CIL* X 6422 = *ILS* 4037 (her altar restored in 213 A.D.); and Bethe, *RE* 11.1 (1921), cols. 501–505. Portus Veneris, mod. Portovenere near Spezia, is a natural haven on a promontory; Nissen, *Ital. Landesk.* 2.147. It may also have been a temporary Carthaginian station when, for instance, they operated in Liguria at the end of the second Punic War. It could have been the port for taking off the Ligurian mercenaries at the outset of the first Punic War (Polyb. 1.17.4).

[377]   Serv. on *Aen.* 7.47. Augustine, *CD* 2.23, connects her name with Marius, who hid in her swampland. Marica = Pontia; see Palmer (above, n. 226). Servius is explaining Vergil's *Laurente Marica* since no goddess of that name was known at Lavinium. Marica could have been the original native name of the deity worshipped at the Frutinal/Aphrodisium. According to Lactantius, *DI* 1.21.22, Circe's divine name was also Marica.

378   See above at n. 344.
379   See n. 287.
380   *CIS* I 135, the dedication to Astarte at Mt Eryx, styles her the giver of long life, an idea
not too distant from that of *iuno*.

CHAPTER TWO

1   I. Mancini, *Inscriptiones Italiae* 4, fasc. 1, 2nd ed. (Rome, 1952). The first edition was
withdrawn from sale on account of keen critical attacks. See A. Degrassi, *Scritti vari di antichità*
(Rome, 1962), 1.604, 610.
2   See Reimer's end map in *CIL* XIV and Cozza's map (tab. 1) in Mancini *II* 4.1. The stone
now bears the inventory no. 115643 at the Museo Nazionale delle Terme in Rome. See Figure 8.
I am grateful to S. Panciera and H.-G. Kolbe for their assistance in obtaining this new photograph, and for reply to my inquiry; see below, n. 35.
3   Marcellina lies in a direction opposite that of the famous villa of Hadrian, but could have
been a suitable location for such a sumptuous country house as those famed resorts mentioned in
various authors.
4   See G. Tibiletti in his and G. Barbieri's entry "Lex" in E. De Ruggiero, *Dizionario epigrafico* etc. (Rome, 1957), 4.775−76, 781−82. See below for Latte's judgment. Heretofore no one
has published a study of this document.
5   K. Latte, *Römische Religionsgeschichte* (Munich, 1960), p. 206, n. 3. See below, and above,
ch. 1, sect. 10.
6   A. Mazzarino, *M. Porci Catonis de agri cultura ad fidem Florentini codicis deperditi* (Leipzig, 1962). It is quoted below in full and with all its orthograhical variants.
7   Lex Narbonensis: *CIL* XII 4333 = *ILS* 112 = Bruns[7] no. 106 = *FIRA III*² no. 73.
8   Lex Salonitana: *CIL* III 1933 = *ILS* 4907 = Bruns[7] no. 107 = *FIRA* III² no. 74.
9   *CIL* XI 361. See below, on lines 3−5:
10   Lex Mactaritana: *CIL* VIII 620 = S 11796 and p. 2372 = *ILS* 4908. The *Corpus* contains
the text of the fragment of the left side of the base.
11   Lex Furfensis: *CIL* IX 3513 = I² 756 = *ILS* 4906 = Bruns[7] no. 105 = *FIRA* III²
no. 72 = *ILLRP* 508.
12   The inscribed laws of holy groves belong to a different class, since they themselves record
the rule of the grove without reference to a canonical rule at Rome. See R.E.A. Palmer, *The
King and the Comitium = Historia Einzelschr.* 11 (1969), pp. 47−53. Latte (see below) holds a
view that the Lex Tiburtina is quite late.
13   *AR* 4.26. Besides Dionysius' explicit statement on its asylum, Festus, p. 460 L., s.v. "ser-
vorum dies festus," implies the asylum, as do all authorities that claim a relation of this Diana
to Aricine Diana; see below. A gloss on an old word from some document in the shrine is found
in Festus, p. 164 L., s.v. "nesi." If it does not come from the bronze pillar of Servius, it may
come from the so-called plebiscite of Icilius dating to 456 B.C.; see Dionysius *AR* 10.31−32
and Livy 3.31−32. Secession to the Aventine Hill also applies to asylum; see Palmer, above,
n. 12. In 121 Gaius Gracchus first sought sanctuary with Diana, but drew his last breath at the
asylum in the grove of Furrina; see Plut. *C. Gr.* 16 and Palmer, *op. cit.*, p. 27. On the Latins'
Diana the reader will find a recent general discussion in A. Alföldi, *Early Rome and The Latins*
(Ann Arbor, n.d. [1965]), pp. 85−89, and will be forewarned of its unreliability.
14   *CIL* XIV 2892 = I² 62 = *ILS* 3419 = *ILLRP* 132 and *add.* See Platner-Ashby *TDAR*,
p. 462, for references to the Roman shrine of Salus. We encounter *-a* for *-ae* on *ILLRP* 1149.
The other dedications to Hercules are *CIL* XIV 2891, 2893 = I² 61, 63.
15   *CIL* XIV 2387 = I² 1439 = *ILS* 2988 = *ILLRP* 270. See below, ch. 3, sect. 10 on this cult.

16 Lex Brixiana: E. Pais, *CIL V Suppl. Italicum* 1273 = *ILS* 4910 and *add.* = Bruns[7] no. 108.

17 Indeed Schmidt suggests (*CIL* VIII S 11796) that the very temple was Apollo's. See G. Charles-Picard, *Civitas Mactaritana* = *Karthago* 8 (1957), p. 39, and below.

18 *CIL* XI 361.

19 See above, at n. 14.

20 *CIL* XI 379, 417–19, 421; cf. *ILS* 6661–6664. There is no reason to doubt the foundation of the *vici* at the time when the colony was founded. Here the *vicus Esquelinus* of Cales (*CIL* I² 416 = *ILS* 8567 = *ILLRP* 1217) is relevant, for it is surely as old as Cales itself.

21 Cf. Roman Fregellae in Festus, p. 80 L.

22 See G. Wissowa, *Religion und Kultus der Römer* (Munich, 1912), pp. 249–50, Platner-Ashby *TDAR*, pp. 149–50; K. Latte (above, n. 5), p. 173. G. De Sanctis, *Storia dei Romani*, vol. 4, part 2, tome 1, (Florence, 1953), pp. 158–62, holds a different view. Also see Alföldi, *loc. cit.* (above, n. 13), who never answers the objections of his critics: see A. Momigliano, "Sul *dies natalis* del santuario federale di Diana sull' Aventino," *Rend. Acc. Lincei. Cl. Sc. mor., st., filol.*, ser. 8, 17 (1962), pp. 387–92 = *Terzo contributo alla storia degli studi classici e del mondo antico* (Rome, 1966), pp. 641–48 (with appendix pp. 647–48), partially in response to an earlier article by Alföldi. On a possible Greek precedent for the league see below.

23 The only other instance of Bona Dea in the Ager Tiburtinus is the Bona Dea Sanctissima Caelestis *sub monte Aeflano*, whose temple was rebuilt and dedicated on the nones of July in 88 A.D. (*II* 4.1.611). Cicero, *Mil.* 31.86, makes a point of the irony in Clodius' death at the shrine of Bona Dea in a private estate (*fundus*) between Aricia and Bovillae (see Asconius, p. 31 Clark).

24 *CIL* X 3138 = I² 1793 = *ILLRP* 57.

25 *CIL* VI 68 = *ILS* 3513.

26 *CIL* V 762 = *ILS* 3498; V 761 = *ILS* 3499. Also Magna Mater is called Cereria at Aquileia; see *CIL* V 796. Cf. A. Degrassi, *Scritti vari di antichità* (Rome, 1962), 2.962. Similar derivatives from the same root are found at Iguvium. Whereas *Cerfus* is always modified by *Martius*, the adjective *Cerfiar* modifies a number of deities. See J.W. Poultney, *The Bronze Tables of Iguvium* (Baltimore, 1959), p. 326 (index) and A. Ernout, *Le dialecte ombrien* (Paris, 1961), p. 73.

27 Macr. *Sat.* 1.12.21–29, citing the discussions of Cornelius Labeo and Terentius Varro among others. Cf. Cic. *Leg.* 2.9.21. See G. De Sanctis, *op. cit.* (above, n. 22), pp. 279–80.

28 See A. Degrassi *II* 13.2, p. 493, and Macrobius, n. 27. This Ceres is styled "Mater," which is not an unusual Roman cult title. Since Ceres does not usually bear an epithet, however, I have restored none to line 5, although there very likely was a cult title like "Mater."

29 *CIL* X 6640 = *ILS* 3338: in sacrario Cereris Antiatinae deos sua impensa posuit.

30 See above, n. 17.

31 Twice in *Agr.* 134. For the full context see below.

32 *Agr.* 139 and 141. Compare in the second prayer: "duis bonam salutem valetudinemque mihi domo familiaeque nostrae."

33 *CIL* VI 32323, lines 96–7, 99, 129–30; 17 B.C. See below, ch. 3, sect. 4.

34 *CIL* VI 32328, line 80; cf. mutilated lines 53–56 and 78; 204 A.D.

35 In reply to my inquiry, Prof. Silvio Panciera of the University of Rome provided me with results of the recent reading of the stone by H.-G. Kolbe, who remarked the trace of an *M* at line 8 and confirmed the same letter at the end of the line.

36 See Mancini's index to *II* 4.1, pp. 240–41.

37 Varro *LL* 6.86; see Palmer, *The Archaic Community of the Romans* (Cambridge, 1970) pp. 158–95, and below, ch. 3, sect. 9.

38 See Wissowa, *op. cit.* (above, n. 22), p. 217, and H. Le Bonniec, *Le culte de Cérès à Rome* (Paris, 1958), pp. 91–107, 148–56.

39 Le Bonniec, *op. cit.*, pp. 148–56. This matter is treated above, ch. 1, sect. 10. An analogous preliminary prayer is attested at Iguvium. See *Tab. Iguv.* IIb 17–18 and the verb *prepesnimu.*

[40]   Latte, *op. cit.* (above, n. 5), p. 206, n. 3. Such conclusions were not reached by Mancini or G. Tibiletti (above, n. 4).

[41]   1. *Lex XII Tab.* 8.12; 2. *CIL XI* 4766 = I² 366 = *ILS* 4911 = Bruns⁷ no. 104b = *FIRA* III² no. 71a = *ILLRP* 505; 3. *CIL* IX 782 = I² 401 = *ILS* 4912 = Bruns⁷ no. 104a = *FIRA* III² no. 71b = *ILLRP* 504; ex. 4 is quite a common legal idiom, for which see Simbeck in *TLL* s.v. damnas; 5. *Lex Col. Gen. Urs.* ch. 66 lines 42–43, *CIL* II 5439 = I² 594 = Bruns⁷ no. 28 = *ILS* 6087 = *FIRA* I² no. 21.

[42]   Lex Narbonensis, lines 15–17 of side; Lex Salonitana, line 8.

[43]   See Varro *LL* 5.112 and Marquardt-Wissowa, *Römische Staatsverwaltung* 3², pp. 181–85.

[44]   Val. Maximus 1.1.4: consimili ratione P. Cloelius <Siculus>, M. Cornelius Cethegus, C. Claudius propter exta parum curiose admota flaminio abire iussi sunt coactique etiam. Flamens handle *exta* in Varro *LL* 6.16 (see below, n. 55) and Ovid *Fasti* 4.901–42.

[45]   Varro *LL* 6.31 (cf. *LL* 6.16); Ovid *Fasti* 1. 49–52; Macr. *Sat.* 1.16.3; *Fasti Praenestini*; see A. Degrassi *II* 13.2, p. 334.

[46]   Varro *LL* 5.98, 5.104; Festus *Epit.* pp. 21–22 L.; see Marquardt-Wissowa, *loc. cit.*, (above, n. 43).

[47]   *ILLRP* 509 with Degrassi's full comment. Also see below for the evidence of the Arval Brothers.

[48]   Above, n. 45.

[49]   Livy 41.14. 7–15.4. The apparent cause of these unusual proceedings' being preserved in the histories was Cornelius' untimely death. He was also a pontiff (Livy 41.16. 1–4).

[50]   *Fasti* 2.373–75.

[51]   See G. Henzen, *Acta fratrum Arvalium* etc. (Berlin, 1874), pp. 92–95.

[52]   *CIL* VI 2065 = *ILS* 5034 (87 A.D.). 2. *CIL* VI 2104 = *ILS* 5039 (this is the famous record of 218 A.D. containing the Arval Hymn). Also recorded in this document is the procedure: "deinde reversi in mensa sacrum fecerunt o<ll>is . . . ad aram reversi." 3. *CIL* VI 2086 = *ILS* 5041 (213 A.D.). Cf. *CIL* VI 2067 = *ILS* 5040.

[53]   *Tab. Iguv.* Ib 8–9, Ib 36–39, IIa 39–40, VIb 47 and VIIa 40–. The Iguvine verb is the exact cognate of Latin *converto*

[54]   Verg. *Georg.* 2.193–94: inflavit cum pinguis ebur Tyrrhenus ad aras / lancibus et pandis fumantia reddimus exta. Servius on 194: "reddimus exta" sacerdotum usus est verbo; reddi enim dicebantur exta, cum probata et elixa arae superponebantur. Statius *Theb.* 4.463–67 (a sacrifice to Ceres *profunda*): tunc innuba Manto / exceptum pateris praelibat sanguen, et omnis / ter circum acta pyras sancti de more parentis / semineces fibras et adhuc spirantia reddit / viscera. Tac *Hist.* 4.53: tum Helvidius Priscus praetor, praeeunte Plautio Aeliano pontifice, lustrata suovetaurilibus area et super caespitem redditis extis, Iovem, Iunonem, Minervam praesidesque imperii deos precatus uti coepta prosperarent . . . .

[55]   E.g., Varro *LL* 6.31, *RR* 1.29.3; Macr. *Sat.* 1.16.3. *Porricere* was defined as *dare.* I quote two examples that illustrate our text. Varro, *LL* 6.16, describes part of the ceremony of Vinalia: nam flamen Dialis auspicatur vindemiam et ut iussit vinum legere, agna Iovi facit, inter cuius exta caesa et porrecta flamen pr<im>us vinum legit. In an extended discussion of *Aeneid* 5.235–38, Macrobius, *Sat.* 3.2.3–4, quotes Veranius on the first book of Pictor: exta porriciunto, dis danto, in altaria aramve focumve eove quo exta dari debebunt. Plautus preserves several examples of religious usage with respect to the *exta.* The inwards of lamb are offered (*porricere*) in the *Pseudolus* 265–69, 326–34 (cf. *Stichus* 250–52). In the *Poenulus* (449–65, 491, 615–18, cf. 1205–1206, 803–804), an haruspex finds doom portending in lamb inwards sacrificed to Venus; apparently the ceremonial interval between sacrifice and presentation are reflected in these lines: dum exta referuntur, volo narrare tibi etiam unam pugnam; ego . . . revortar . . . interibi attulerint exta. Another such offering to Venus is implicit in the materials borrowed by sacrificants coming to the goddess' shrine: fire, water, pots, knife, spit and an *aula extaris* (*Rudens* 131–35).

56 See Val. Ant. fr. 6 Peter; Ovid *Fasti* 3.295–356 with Bömer's comment on 3.340; Plut. *Numa* 15.
57 Strabo 4.1.5, 8; Dion. Hal. *AR* 4.25; Livy 1.45 with Ogilvie's comment; cf. Pliny *NH* 36.32. See De Sanctis, *loc. cit.* (above, n. 22); below, ch. 3, at n. 197; C. Ampolo, "L'Artemide di Marsiglia e la Diana dell'Aventino," *PP* fasc. 130–33 (1970), pp. 200–210.
58 *CIG* II 2737 = Bruns[7] no. 43 = Dittenberger *OGIS* nos. 453–455 = *FIRA* I[2] no. 38 = R.K. Sherk, *Roman Documents from the Greek East* (Baltimore, 1969), no. 28. The last edition is the most complete but does not contain discussion of Daube's theory (see n. 61) or, for that matter, touch on the Aventine canon. The pertinent passage stands in the senatorial degree (*OGIS* no. 455; Sherk B), lines 10–13. See D. Magie, *Roman Rule in Asia Minor* (Princeton, 1950), 2.1271, n. 43; L. Robert, "Inscriptions d'Aphrodisias" *AC* 35 (1966), pp. 408–13, who remarks that Plarasa and Aphrodisias were combined in sympolity.
59 Strabo 14.1.23. See *SIG*[3] 989 = F. Sokolowski, *Lois sacrées de l'Asie Mineure* (Paris, 1955), no. 85.
60 Tacitus *Ann.* 3.60–63. See below. On Tiberius and a Romanized priest of Aphrodite of Aphrodisias, see S. Panciera, "Miscellanea epigrafica IV," *Epigraphica* 31 (1969), pp. 112–20.
61 D. Daube, *Forms of Roman Legislation* (Oxford, 1956), pp. 88–91. On the Aventine right of asylum see above, n. 13.
62 See Dittenberger's note 18. Daube, too, calls the form of the decree Latin. Cf. Sherk (above, n. 58) no. 32, which may be a senatorial decree, wherein is partly restored *deisidaimonia*. For other Latin terminology, see below.
63 Caeser *BC* 3.33, 105–106; Dittenberger *SIG*[3] 760. See M. Gelzer, *Caesar, Politician and Statesman* (Cambridge, Mass., 1968), pp. 244–46, and Magie (above, n. 58) 1.405–407, 2.1258–61. Some portents attendant upon the victory at Pharsalus are also mentioned in Val. Max. 1.6.12; Pliny *NH*17.244; Plut.*Caes.* 47; Dio Cass. 41.61.3. See S. Weinstock, *Divus Julius* (Oxford, 1971), pp. 166,296.
64 *CIL* IX 34 = I[2] 789 = *ILS* 71 = *ILLRP* 407 (Brundisium); IX 2563 = I[2] 787 = *ILS* 70 = *ILLRP* 406 (Bovianum); V 4305 = I[2] 794 = *ILS* 75 = *ILLRP* 415 (Brixia, perhaps to Octavian); *ILLRP* 408 (by the Roman citizens on Cos); *SIG*[3] 759 (Athens). See Weinstock, *op. cit.*, pp. 30–34.
65 *Ann.* 3.58–63. Tiberius later delivered the decree of the pontifical college on the Dial flamen, in which he cited the judgment (*arbitrium*) of the chief pontiff (3.71).
66 In general see Wissowa, *op cit.* (above, n. 22), pp. 477–79 and F. Schulz, *History of Roman Legal Science* (Oxford, 1946), esp. pp. 16–19. For a statement on pontifical jurisdiction see Aelius Gallus in Festus p. 424 L. Macrobius, *Sat.* 3.3, recapitulates the definitions found in pontifical decrees by applying details from Trebatius' books on religion to Vergil's *Aeneid*. Definitions of the character of *loci* are found in Gaius *Inst.* 2.2–8 (cf. Trajan to Pliny in *Ep.* 10.50) and *Dig.* 1.8.6–9 (Ulpian and Marcian).
67 E.g., *CIL* X 2015 = *ILS* 8235: locus sacer et religiosus. See esp. E. De Ruggiero's *Diz. epigr.* vol. 4, s.v. *locus*, pp. 1586–87 and 1649–1716 ("Locus nel diritto sacrale"). The *locus* and *topos asylos* of the *SC de Aphrodisiensibus* are discussed on p. 1704. Cf. Robert, *loc. cit.* (above, n. 57).
68 *CIL* X 8259 = *ILS* 8381 = Bruns[7] no. 76 = *FIRA* I[2] no. 63. See above, n. 64.
69 *CIL* VI 1884; VI 2963 = *ILS* 8382; VI 22120 = *ILS* 8383; IX 1729 = *ILS* 8110; IX 4881 = *ILS* 8390.
70 *CIL* VI 10675 = *ILS* 8386. Cf. VI 10812 = *ILS* 8387: *ex arka pontificum.*
71 *CIL* VI 35987 = *ILS* 8392: quisq(ue) autem secus ara(m) igne(m) fecer(unt) sciat se ad pontifices disputaturu(m).
72 Livy 27.25.7–8; 31.9.5–10; 34.44.1–3. See above, n. 65.
73 Cicero *Domo* 53.136.
74 *Ad Att.* 4.2.3–6.

[75] Tac. *Ann.* 3.64.

[76] Suet. *Claud.* 25.3: Iliensibus, quasi Romanae gentis auctoribus, tributa in perpetuum remisit, recitata vetere epistula Graeca senatus populique Romani Seleuco regi amicitiam et societatem ita demum pollicentis si consanguineos suos Ilienses ab omni onere immunes praestitisset. Under Greek diplomatic influence first exerted in the third century B.C., the Romans sought recognition of kinship through treaty (*cognatio*). In some instances these ties assumed great importance; see below, ch. 3, nn. 177, 187, 196–97, 216.

[77] Pliny *Ep.* 10.50; Gaius *Inst.* 2.7, 7a. Cf. Weinstock, *op. cit.*, pp. 83, 140, 297.

[78] Ampolo, *op. cit.* (above, n. 57). I am not persuaded by Alföldi's arguments on the identification of the statue of Aricine Diana and the relation of the two Dianas' leagues (see above, nn. 13 and 22). The purported image of Aricine Diana is on a single coin whose traditional interpretation I have reinforced in *The Archaic Community of the Romans*, pp. 109, 118–20. Saserna's coin may show the cult figure of Massilia. However, its age cannot be proved and its likeness to that of Aventine Diana remains undemonstrated.

[79] See above. It is not certain that at African Mactar the Aventine canon is being cited or quoted. On the status of the town, which became a colony only under the joint reign of Aurelius and Commodus, and the date of *CIL* VIII S 11796, see Leo Teutsch "Gab es 'Doppelgemeinden' in römischen Afrika?" *RIDA* ser. 3, 8 (1961), pp. 349–352, in answer to a work of Charles-Picard (above, n. 17); and G. Charles-Picard, "Postumus et Vetranion," *Atti del terzo congresso internazionale di epigrafia greca e latina* (Rome, 1959), pp. 263–70.

[80] Appian *BC* 1.294.

[81] Cato *Orig.* book 2, fr. 58 P.²: lucum Dianium in nemore Aricino Egerius Laevius Tusculanus dedicavit dicator Latinus. hi populi communiter: Tusculanus, Aricinus, Lanuvinus, Laurens, Coranus, Tiburtis, Pometinus, Ardeatis Rutulus, On Mt. Corne the Tusculans kept a Latin grove of Diana (Pliny *NH* 16.242).

[82] *CIL* XIV 3537 = I² 1480 = *ILS* 3238 = *II* 4.1.7 = *ILLRP* 85. See St. Weinstock *RE* 6A1 (1936) col. 835.

[83] *IG* XIV 1124 = *II* 4.1.32.

[84] Martial 7.28.1: silva Dianae Tiburtinae.

[85] See above.

[86] *CIL* XIV 4269 = I² 40 = *ILS* 6128 = *ILLRP* 77.

[87] E.T. Salmon, *Roman Colonization under the Republic* (Ithaca, 1970), pp. 95–111. The last Latin colony was founded in 181 B.C.

[88] *AR* 4.25–26.

[89] Livy 7.9.1–2, 7.19.1–2, 8.12–14.

[90] See below, ch. 3, sect. 4.

[91] See above, on lines 5–10.

[92] Momigliano, *loc. cit.* (above, n. 22), rightly stresses the universal acceptance of the Aventine Diana in Italy, rather than the universal acceptance of the Aricine Diana, whom Alföldi wrongly champions.

[93] Tac. *Ann.* 3.71.

CHAPTER THREE

[1] See Stefan Weinstock, "Two Archaic Inscriptions from Latium," *JRS* 50 (1960), pp. 112–14. More recently Greek wares, datable to the sixth century, have been uncovered at the site of Troia near the mouth of the Fosso di Pratica; see F. Castagnoli, "I luoghi connessi con l'arrivo di Enea nel Lazio (Troia, Sol Indiges, Numicus)," *Arch. Cl.* 19 (1967), pp. 235–47.

[2] M. Guarducci, "Tre cippi latini arcaici con iscrizioni votive," *BC* 72 (1946–48), pp. 1–10; "Cippo latino arcaico con dedica ad Enea," *Bullettino del Museo della Civiltà Romana* (published with *BC* 76) 19 (1956–58), pp. 3–13. Hereafter I refer to these articles as Guarducci *BC* and *BMCR*, respectively. H.-G. Kolbe, "Lare Aineia?," *Röm. Mitt.* 77 (1970), pp. 1–9, has shown that the fourth monument was misread and never contained Aeneas' name. He retains the single Lar, but did not consider that, once Aeneas has been removed, we must assume that *Lare* stands for *Lare(bus)*. Of course, the cult of Aeneas is known from other sources referring to this area. Miss Guarducci, "Enea e Vesta," *Röm. Mitt.* 78 (1971), pp. 73–89, pls. 57–63, has very strongly reasserted her earlier contention and has noted that a single, unidentified Lar would be an anomaly (p. 77). Further, she has modified her reading to *Lare Aenia d.* Finally, she reports some recent discoveries on the site of Tor Tignosa which include the remains of a building that presumably housed one of the cults (pp. 87–89). See below, n. 143.

[3] See n. 2. All these places are recorded on Foglio 150 of the ordnance map published by the Instituto Geografico Militare in 1970, which I have used. See G.M. DeRossi, *Apiolae (Forma Italiae* I. 9) (Rome, 1970), pp. 95–97.

[4] B. Tilly, "The Identification of the Numicus," *JRS* 26 (1936), pp. 1–11 and *Vergil's Latium* (Oxford, 1947), pp. 103–11. Beside many implicit and one explicit (below, n. 19) ancient notices situating the Faunian center in the territory of Lavinium at this place, Vergil's language clearly gives the name Albunea to the grove itself. The adjective *alta* refers to the height of the trees (cf. Vergil *G.* 1.173, 2.431; *E.* 8.86; *A.* 3.681, 11.456, 11.739–40), and *sub* to a position beneath the trees (cf. Vergil *E.* 1.1, *G.* 4.566; *Cat.* 9.17; *A.* 6.11); the two usages are combined in *Aen.* 7.107–108, following the Faunian oracle, "Aeneas primique duces et pulcher Iullus / corpora sub ramis deponunt arboris altae." *Alta Albunea* may also refer to the hillock above the road along which the dedications were found. Tor Tignosa itself is at the crest of a slope. The Vergilian usage in this instance is exemplified by *Aen.* 6.179 (cf. 9.386–88). Seneca, *Ep.* 41.3, supplies an apposite statement on the divine presence in high dense woods: "si tibi occurrit vetustis arboribus et solitam altitudinem egressis frequens lucus et conspectum caeli ramorum aliorum alios protegentium summovens obtentu, illa proceritas silvae et secretum loci et admiratio umbrae in aperto tam densae atque continuae fidem tibi numinis facit." In any case, Tibur itself cannot have been the home of the Faunian oracle; see below, n. 40.

[5] See esp. Fabius Pictor in Gellius 10.15. The present writer treats some of the prohibitions in "Ivy and Jupiter's Priest." The ceremony is described by Servius Dan. on *Aen.* 4.374: mos enim apud veteres fuit flamini ac flaminicae, dum per ferreationem in nuptias convenirent, sellas duas iugatas ovilla pelle superiniecta poni eius ovis quae hostia fuisset, ut ibi nubentes velatis capitibus in confarreatione flamen ac flaminica resiederent. Also see Servius on 4.103 and 646.

[6] Pliny *NH* 36.151.

[7] See above, ch. 2.

[8] L. Deubner, *De incubatione capita quattuor* (Leipzig, 1900), esp. pp. 8, 10, 16–19, 23, 26–27, and 41.

[9] Livy 2.6–7.4, on which we see Ogilvie, who has references to similar accounts. Ogilvie holds that Dionysius gave the name Faunus to one whom the Latin accounts called Silvanus. Why not Pan? See below on another instance of Livy's avoiding the name Faunus. In 137 B.C. the Laurentine forest still stood and filled the Romans with awe, as this notice in Julius Obsequens 24 testifies: cum Lavinii auspicarentur, pulli e cavea in silvam Laurentinam evolarunt neque inventi sunt.

[10] See above, ch. 1, sect. 4.

[11] Ovid *Fasti* 2.267 ff.

[12] Livy 1.5.1–2, on which see Ogilvie. Degrassi *II*, 13.2, pp. 409–11, cites the major evidence on the Lupercalia and gives some bibliography. There survive very many ancient allusions to this feast and to Pan Lycaeus' involvement.

[13] Ennius *Ann.* 213–216 V.², which must be understood along lines of argument presented by O. Skutsch, *CQ* 42 (1948), pp. 94–96 = *Studia Enniana* (London, 1968), pp. 30–34;

St. Enn. pp. 119–29; and below, n. 77. Next after Ennius in the surviving literature, Lucilius (fr. 484-89 M.) mentions the Fauni, who spread belief in bogeymen and witches (*terriculae, Lamiae*), in connection with men who consider the fictions of dreams the truth (*somnia ficta vera putant*); see below, at n. 459. The Fauns' connection with Saturnian verse is preserved by Serv. Dan. on *Georg.*. 1.11; also see below, ch. 4.

14   *LL* 6.51–55, 7.36; see below, sects. 5, 16.

15   *Sat.* 1.12.21–29. See R. Agahd, "M. Terentii Varronis Antiquitatum Rerum Divinarum libri I XIV XV XVI," *Jahrb. cl. Phil.* Supplbd. 24 (1898), pp. 79–83, 191–94, and below, sect. 5, 7, 9, 16.

16   *Epit.* 43.3–8, discussed below, sect. 17.

17   *Dict. étym.*⁴ s.vv. Fatuus, fatuus.

18   *NH* 27.107.

19   [Probus] on Vergil *Georg.* 1.10. For a *silva Laurentina*, see above, n. 9; on *for, faunus, fanum*, Varro *LL*. 6.51–55.

20   See above, n. 12; cf. Macr. *Sat.* 1.22.2–7, Arn. 3.23.

21   *Aen.* 6.775. Latian Castrum Inui was sometimes confused with the Etruscan Castrum, as in the *De reditu suo* 227–36 of the late senator Rutilius Namatianus, who set it by Caere. Namatianus identifies Inuus with Pan and Faunus and preserves the learned etymology by *incola Faunus init.* However, he makes the god enter his native gulfport , not women!

22   *Alex.* 1253–58 and Steph. Byz. s.v.

23   See below, sect. 7.

24   See Ernout-Meillet, *Dict. étym.* s.v. Faunus.

25   *Aen.* 8.146; 10.616, 688; 12.22, 90, 723, 785, and 934.

26   *Meta.* 15.727–28.

27   *Pun.* 8.356–61.

28   See Ogilvie on Livy 1.1.3, where he rightly emphasizes the probability that *troia = castrum*, i.e. a fort. Cf. Lycophron's thirty *pyrgoi* (above, n. 22). On the two Castra see Tilly, *Vergil's Latium*, pp. 1–30, and Castagnoli, *op. cit*, (above, n. 1).

29   On *Aen.* 6.775, discussed below, sect. 17; cf. Mart. Cap. 5.425.

30   *CD* 15.23 (2.108 D.).

31   *Etym.* 8.11.103–104, which Isidore closes with the opening lines of Horace's *Ode* 3.18, discussed above; see below, sect. 17.

32   See Agahd's frs. 1.22e, 39a, 15.15, 16a–c; and, below, sect. 17.

33   References to *incubare* in Deubner, *op. cit.*, p. 8.

34   Hor. *Carm.* 3.18.1–4. Ausonius in his *Mosella* 175–77 (p. 126 Peiper) imitates Vergil's *Georgics* 1.10 and this poem of Horace:
     saepe etiam mediis furata e collibus uvas
     inter Oreidas Panope fluvialis amicas
     fugit lascivos paganica numina Faunos.
Indeed, he also refers to Panes and Satyri in a Gallic setting.

35   *Etym.* 8.8; *DI* 1.6.7–17; cf. Tib. 2.5.67–70.

36   *AR* 4.62.

37   *Od.* 10.503 ff., and much of book 11.

38   *Epit.* 37 L. Cf. Strabo 1.2.9; 5.4.5; 7.2.2, 4.5.

39   Only Ammianus Marcellinus, 28.4.19, mentions this name. The properties of the site support a connection with a deity like the Faunus of Albunea. On the place see J.H. D'Arms, *Romans on the Bay of Naples* (Cambridge, Mass., 1970), pp. 107, 118, 120, 139, and 141. Besides being the name of the builder or owner, Silvanus might have designated the men's bath, a less likely possibility if the variant was *lavacrum Mammaea.* The initial cause of naming the male baths after Silvanus stems from the exclusiveness of his cult and shrines; see below, sect. 17. Ammianus acidly reports the sighs of the jaded suffering from the hot sun: "Oh to be a Cimmerian!"

[40] *Carm.* 1.7.12; *Aen.* 7.83–84. For references to Aquae Albulae near Tibur see *CIL* XIV 3534 and 3909 (= *II* 4.1, 34, 595 = *ILS* 6227, 3862), as well as XIV 3911 = *II* 4.1.596, a poem to the Lympha of the *gurges Albuleus* who cured a man with her waters. Besides other occasional references to these curative waters compare Martial 4.60, which mentions a summer holiday at Ardea, *Castrana rura* (i.e. Castrum Inui; see above), and Tibur. In the last case the epigrammatist seems to be playing with the notion of a death met anywhere, and the relation of such sulphur springs to the Netherworld: inter laudatas ad Styga missus aquas. The name Albunea also seems to represent the sulphuric qualities of the water. Thus Vitruvius (8.3.2) reports that the river Albula on the Via Tiburtina and the coldsprings in Ardeate country (on the Via Ardeatina?) emit the same sulphuric smell. It would further seem that the Sibyl Albunea came to Tibur from another place, since there are no sulphuric waters at the town itself. Cf. T. Ashby, *The Roman Campagna in Classical Times* repr. ed. (London, 1970), pp. 98–100, 209. On the virtues of soil and climate with respect to divination, see Cic. *Div.* 1.36.79 with Pease's comment.

[41] *Opp. citt.*, above, n. 1.

[42] *ILLRP* 10–12, with the measurements of the stones.

[43] Fr. 11 Morel.

[44] *NA* 3.16.9–11.

[45] *ARD* pp. 14.12a; cf. 12b Agahd, and Varro's *Tubero de origine humana* in Cens. *DN* 9.

[46] *LL* 6.52. Varro's reference to himself is on the section concerning Fauni and the Saturnian measures discussed below, ch. 4.

[47] Tert. *Anim.* 39.2 = *ARD* 14.15. For the form of the name Scribunda, compare the Arvals' Adolenda, Coinquenda, Commolenda, and Deferunda, which J. Bayet, "Les 'Feriae Sementivae' et les Indigitations dans le culte de Cérès et de Tellus," *Revue d'Histoire des Religions* 137 (1950), pp. 172–206 = *Croyances et rites dans la Rome antique* (Paris, 1971), pp. 177–205, believes are no more than modes of address (*indigitamenta*).

[48] Guarducci, *BC*, p. 8; St. Weinstock, "Parca Maurtia und Neuna Fata," *Festschr. A. Rumpf* (Krefeld, 1952), pp. 152, 156. Only G. Radke, *Die Götter Altitaliens* (Münster, 1965), p. 103, now wishes to retain Decima, which he derives from *decet*. But he also has a different interpretation of Neuna from others; see below, n. 128.

[49] *NA* 6.2, 11.15.1–3, 18.11. Sulpicius Apollinaris believed that Caesellius also did not understand Vergil; cf. *NA* 2.16.

[50] Servius on *Aen.* 3.63. In his quoted case of *bellum* we are to understand that it is not pretty (*bellus*), and of *lucus* that it is not full of light (*lux*); Isid. *Etym* 8.11.93 and 100 (with a citation of Apuleius).

[51] Weinstock, *op. cit.* (above, n. 48), pp. 151–60, relies so heavily on this ancient derivation of the word that, when he had to abandon it in *JRS* 1960, p. 115 n. 38, in favor of "Merciful" from *parco*, he left his first argument virtually in shambles. Miss Guarducci, *Röm. Mitt.* 78 (1971) p. 84 ff., has observed the extent to which one may not rely on Weinstock's argument.

[52] *Parca*, like *Fata*, is not an unusual Latin word formation, although most such nouns are compounds; e.g., those in *-cola*, *-vena*. See above, ch. 1, sect. 10, on Juno Domiduca. Simples are the deities Panda Cela, Genita Mana, Vica Pota (see below, ch. 5).

[53] Festus *Epit.* 249 L.; see Ernout-Meillet, *Dict. étym.*⁴ s.v. parco.

[54] See Bömer on Ovid *F.* 2.451.

[55] *CIL* XIV 2578 = I² 49 = *ILS* 3142 = *ILLRP* 221 from Tusculum. Dissent from Guarducci's and Weinstock's view of *Maurtia* < *Mavort*- is registered by G. De Sanctis *SR* 4.2.1, p. 149, and K. Latte *RRG* p. 53 n. 1.

[56] Guarducci, *op. cit.* (above, n. 1), and Weinstock, *op. cit.* (above, n. 48).

[57] *CIL* I² 2 = *ILS* 5039 = *ILLRP* 4. I have followed Degrassi's lucid commentary. I take *lue rue* as accusatives without the diacritical *-m*; by *in pleores* for *in ploeres*, i.e. *plures*, I understand that *lues rues* have already arrived and halt is called (otherwise, it may be understood "upon the many" people or fields); the vocative *fere* I relate to *ferax* and *fertilis* from *ferre*;

advocapit I do not take as an apocopated second plural (future ind.) but rather third sg., Mars being its subject. On *lues* see below, ch. 4.

58   *Agr.* 83. I do not take these two words as asyndetically conjoined deities.

59   *Agr.* 141; on some of the formulas, see above, ch. 2.

60   See sects. 1, 6, 17.

61   Guarducci *BC*, p. 7; Dion. Hal. *AR* 1.14.5, and cf. Plut. *QR* 21, citing Nigidius Figulus. On the doves or pigeons at Dodona see H.W. Parke, *The Oracles of Zeus: Dodona, Olympia, Ammon* (Cambridge, Mass., 1967), pp. 34–45, 64 ff. On the Latin wild dove, see below, ch. 5.

62   See Poultney on *Tab. Ig. Vb* 9 *agre tlatie piquier martier* and 14 *agre casiler p. m.*

63   *Brut.* 18.72–73, on which see further below. A.E. Douglas' comment on this section does not clarify any ambiguities in the ancient statements, and omits to mention H.B. Mattingly, "The Date of Livius Andronicus," *CQ* 51 (1957), pp. 159–63, which has little worthwhile argument beneath the rhetoric. The still useful work on his career is H. de la Ville de Mirmont, "Livius Andronicus," *Rev. Univ. du Midi* (1896–97), which is to be more easily consulted in his *Etudes sur l'ancienne poésie latine* (Paris, 1903), pp. 5–218. In spite of a great burden of citations and obviously extensive reading, G. Marconi, "La cronologia di Livio Andronico," *Atti Acc. Naz. Lincei. Mem. Cl. Sc. mor. stor. filol.* ser. 8, vol. 12 (1966), pp. 123–214, does not submit convincing arguments to his readers. E.J. Jory, "Associations of Actors in Rome," *Hermes* 98 (1970), pp. 223–36, offers important observations on Andronicus' career in regard to the guild of writers and playwrights. Mattingly, whom Marconi ignores, would have Andronicus dead before Marconi would bring him to Rome.

64   *Gram.* 1.

65   See Broughton *MRR*, s. aa., for the references to these and subsequent Livii in public offices.

66   Livy 27.34.

67   Marconi, *op. cit.*, accepts the Accian tradition that was rightly rejected 2000 years ago (see below), and he is not the first to reject a capture at Tarentum in or before 272 B.C. Let it be stressed that no one had to capture a slave to own one.

68   Cic. *Brut.* 18.71–73 (Varro's *Antiquities* cited in 15.60 and 56.205), *TD* 1.1.3, *Sen.* 14.50; Gellius *NA* 17.21.42, where Varro's *Poets* is cited; cf. Livy 7.2. See Fr. Leo, *Geschichte d. röm. Literatur* 1 (Berlin, 1913), p. 55.

69   Livy 7.2. The nature of the ancient records available to Varro and others can be briefly described. The Roman annals (cf. Livy 6.42, 7.1–2) contained notices on plagues, and their religiously inspired remedies through special (often imported) rites on behalf of the gods with whom the Romans made a formal agreement (*pax*). Some priesthoods, but most often the pontiffs, kept accounts of the state religious proceedings and transactions that varied from the normal. Moreover, any institution, such as a new magistracy like the curule aedileship, that had to be enacted by legislation, was duly recorded. Many, but by no means all, new institutions are remarked in the surviving authors. On the other hand, private details (e.g., Ennius' birthdate) will have become part of a reliable tradition only if the individual himself conveyed it through his writings.

70   Livy 27.37, a fine example of the preservation of a notice of a religious act.

71   For the list of pontiffs see Broughton *MRR s.a.* 210. Livy 27.37.7 mentions the pontiffs, the hymn, and Livius; cf. Festus, pp. 446/8 L.

72   Livy 31.12.8–10. Contrast the Latin cognomen *Tegula* (tile) with the Greek personal name Andronicus.

73   Cic. *Brut.* 18.71–73. For Cicero's use of *commentarii* in this work, cf. *ex pontificum commentariis* on T. Coruncanius (14.55) and *in veteribus commentariis* on the date of Naevius' death, where Cicero (15.60) faults Varro's date in the *Antiquities.*

74   Livy 36.36.4–6. The confusion in dates arose from the fact that in 197 and 191 a consul Cornelius fought the Gauls in northern Italy.

[75] Livy 33.42.1. Unfortunately, we cannot know whether he was related to P. Licinius Tegula.

[76] See above, ch. 1, sect. 7.

[77] On the site see Platner-Ashby, *TDAR*, pp. 89–90; and on the method of translation Leo (above, n. 68), pp. 73–74; on Ennius and Fulvius, O. Skutsch, *Studia Enniana* (London, 1968), pp. 3–9, 18–29 (= *CQ* 38(1944), pp. 79–86); and above, n. 13.

[78] See Skutsch, above nn. 13 and 77. *Pace* Marconi, the unanimous ancient tradition that makes Livius Andronicus Rome's first poet in the universally accepted sense of the word "poet" is sound and indubitable.

[79] *Od.* 2.99–100, 3.236–38, 19.144–45, 24.133–34.

[80] *BC*, pp. 7–8.

[81] See Degrassi on *ILLRP* 10–12, Ernout-Meillet, *Dict. étym.*[4] s.v. Morta; A. Giacolone-Ramat, "Studi intorno ai nomi del dio Marte," *Archivio Glottologico Italiano* 47 (1962), p. 116.

[82] *BC*, p. 8; *BMCR*, p. 12.

[83] L.R. Taylor, "New Light on the History of the Secular Games," *AJP* 55 (1934), pp. 106–107.

[84] Dion. Hal. *AR* 6.17, 6.94.3. See Platner-Ashby *TDAR*, pp. 109–10 for further references.

[85] *AR* 7.71–72.

[86] See Platner-Ashby *TDAR*, p. 539, and next note. The medieval evidence is discussed by R. Valentini and G. Zucchetti, *Codice topografico della città di Roma* vol. 2 (= R. Istituto Storico Italiano per il Medio Evo, *Fonti per la storia d'Italia* 88, 1942), p. 126 n. 1, p. 274 n. 2.

[87] Pliny *NH* 34.22, cf. 29. Degrassi (above, n. 81) draws our attention to the Tria Fata but gives a wrong reference to the *NH*. For Messalinus and the Sibyls, cf. Tib. 2.5.

[88] *NH* 34.26. The time is probably that when the Romans imported Asclepius; see below. The Curia Hostilia stood in the Comitium. Accordingly, the statues of the three Sibyls and the two Greeks belonged to the same museum.

[89] See above, sect. 1. Ausonius in an occasional piece, *Gryphus Ternarii Numeri*, 85–87 (p. 204 Peiper), obviously has in mind a traditional triad of priestesses:

et tris fatidicae, nomen commune, Sibyllae,

quarum tergemini fatalia carmina libri,

quos ter quinorum servat cultura virorum.

In his prose preface, line 51 (p. 199 P), he refers to Varro, who must be his authority for the three Sibyls.

[90] Macr. *Sat.* 1.12.35. See M. Hofmann *RE* 18.2 (1942), cols. 2174–75. Pacuvius engaged in some very un-Roman conduct with respect to Augustus; see Dio 53.20.

[91] Val. Max. 2.4.5 and Zosimus 2.1 ff. Other references in Platner-Ashby *TDAR*, pp. 152, 508–509, Taylor (above, n. 83), pp. 101–20, Nilsson *RE* 1A2 (1920), cols. 1696–1705. Insofar as it concerns the Sibylline Books, H. Diel's *Sibyllinische Blätter* (Berlin, 1890) has collected, indexed, and discussed the Greek authorities. The only lengthy work devoted entirely to these rites is I.B. Pighi *De Ludis saecularibus populi Romani Quiritium libri sex = Pubblicazioni dell' Università Cattolica del S. Cuore* ser. 5 (Scienze Filol.), vol. 35. Most copies of this book were destroyed during the second World War. A reprinted (second) edition with additions and corrections up to 1964 (pp. 407–19), was published by Schippers, Amsterdam, 1965. Pighi collects all the literary testimonia and also brings together the quindecemviral transactions and proceedings, coin legends, and so forth. His commentary and synthetic chapters leave something to be desired. H. Erkell, "Ludi saeculares und ludi latini saeculares: Ein Beitrag zur römischen Theaterkunde und Religionsgeschichte," *Eranos* 67 (1969), pp. 166–74, repeats the putative connection of the games with the Italian Greek city and does not seem to know F. Castagnoli's major work on the topography of the Tarentum, "Il Campo Marzio nell' antichità," *Atti dell' Accademia Nazionale dei Lincei, Mem. Cl. sci. mor. stor. filol.* ser. 8, vol. 1,

(1947), pp. 93–193. In his addenda Pighi, too, ignores this study, as well as other necessary changes in charts of the topography of Campus Martius. For a major subsequent advance in our knowledge see F. Coarelli, "Navalia, Tarentum e la topografia ecc.," in F. Castagnoli ed., *Studi di topografia romana*, (Rome, 1968), pp. 33–37.

⁹² Castagnoli, *ibid.*, pp. 99–112.

⁹³ Suet. *Claud.* 21.2; cf. *Dom.* 4.3. For a table of dates see Pighi, *op. cit.*, 101–103.

⁹⁴ *Aen.* 6.792–93. Much earlier the games were due and postponed, very probably because of civil turmoil; see below on Vergil's fourth eclogue in sect. 15.

⁹⁵ *AJP* 55 (1934), 101–20. For the prayer, see below.

⁹⁶ *Loc. cit.*, pp. 105–106, 119. See Degrassi, "Fasti consulares et triumphales" *II* 13.1, pp. 62–63 and 142. Miss Taylor modified her views on the debt to Valerius Antias for the "glorification of the early Valerii" in regard to *AJP* 55 (1934), pp. 115 f.; see *AJP* 90 (1969), p. 226, n. 2.

⁹⁷ Cens. *DN* 17.9, Augustus' edict; Hor. *CS* 21–22.

⁹⁸ *CD* 3.18 (pp. 126–27 D).

⁹⁹ Taylor, *op. cit.*, pp. 113, 116 n. 49. See above, nn. 35, 36, 89 and Pighi, *op. cit.*, pp. 67–75.

¹⁰⁰ Compare *CD* 1.32 (p. 49 D), 2.8 (p. 62 D), with Livy 7.2.

¹⁰¹ I am not saying that Andronicus wrote a *carmen saeculare*, whether in 249, in 236, or, for that matter, in 207; see Marconi, *op. cit.*, pp. 147–78. We are dealing with games of 236 and *ludi Latini* and *ludi Graeci*, Latin and Greek stageplays. If indeed a *carmen saeculare* was composed for the celebration of 249 (*comm. Cruq.* on Hor. *CS* 8), Livius Andronicus might have written it (Pighi, *op. cit.*, pp. 4–8, 197–230, 292–94, records the evidence on the *carmina*), for only his first stageplay was dated to 240 or 239 B.C.

¹⁰² The Augustan *acta* are *CIL* VI 32323 = *ILS* 5050. Messalla Messalinus and Potitus Messalla are mentioned in lines 150, 152, and 154. Both had the praenomen Marcus. The former was evidently consul in 3 B.C., the latter suffect consul in 32 B.C. See Pighi, *op. cit.*, p. 236.

¹⁰³ Taylor, *op. cit.* pp. 106–107; see above.

¹⁰⁴ *Acta*, lines 90–99 (Pighi, *op. cit.*, pp. 113–14); all restorations are nearly certain. For the Moerae in the oracle, Zosimus 2.5.2 and *Oracle* lines 7–9 = Diels pp. 132, 134; Pighi, *op. cit.* pp. 43–58.

¹⁰⁵ *CIL* VI 32328, lines 52 ff.; Pighi, *op. cit.*, pp. 152–53.

¹⁰⁶ See I.S. Ryberg, *Rites of the State Religion in Roman Art* = *MAAR* 22 (1955), pp. 174–77 with pl. LXIII; cf. Pighi, *op. cit.*, pp. 79–87. There are two coins: Mattingly, *CREBM* Domitian 411 and 430; Mattingly and Sydenham, *RIC* Dom. 38.1.

¹⁰⁷ Livy 8.11.

¹⁰⁸ *Ibid.*

¹⁰⁹ *Acta* of 17 B.C., lines 134–37; *Oracle* lines 11–12 = Diels, p. 134.

¹¹⁰ *CS* 25–32. See E. Fraenkel's splendid seventh chapter in *Horace* (Oxford, 1957).

¹¹¹ See Fraenkel, pp. 379–82.

¹¹² *CS* 13–20; *acta* lines 115–118 (Ilithyiae and Ilithyia). The one Ilithyia receives nine offerings because she was originally plural; see the oracles in Diels, pp. 132, 134. Their reduction to one was apparently influenced by the one Juno Lucina, who was equated with *Eileithyia*.

¹¹³ Festus p. 446/8 L. See the interesting study of Jory, *op. cit.*, pp. 224–36. On the rites of this temple, see Degrassi *II* 13.2, pp. 426–28.

¹¹⁴ *BP* fr. 12 Str. = 18 Mo., from Varro in Lact. *DI* 1.6.9.

¹¹⁵ For the grotto see B. Tilly, *Vergil's Latium*, pp. 106–109 and pls. 32–35. The change of the site of the Cimmerian Sibyl is adduced by Strabo 5.4.5 (244–45 C).

¹¹⁶ Fr. *incertae sedis* 40 Morel, who acknowledges Ribbeck's assignment of the fragment to a Livian Tragedy *TRF*³ fr. 33.

¹¹⁷ *BC*, p. 6.

[118] Above, sect. 1.

[119] Above, sect. 3.

[120] See Ogilvie on Livy 4.25.3, 5.13.5.

[121] *Op. cit.* (above, n. 48).

[122] Tertullian, quoted above at n. 47. The seven-day week which Tertullian mentions may have been in Varro's mind on account of his attention to hebdomads, but the prior and very likely ritual "week" was the *nundinae* of eight days, counted inclusively. The Faunus of Calpurnius Siculus' first eclogue wrote on the bark of a living beech (cf. Ovid's Numa with beechen chaplet).

[123] See above, ch. 1, sect. 16.

[124] Fabius Pictor's *Iuris Pontificii Libri* (?) I fr. 1 Peter, in Gellius *NA* 1.12.14; cf. Fabius Pictor's *Latini Annales* (?) fr. 1 Peter, in Serv. on *Aen.* 12.603.

[125] Gellius *NA* 1.12.19.

[126] All of them are conveniently collected and discussed by J.A. Hanson, "Plautus as a Source Book for Roman Religion," *TAPA* 90 (1959), pp. 53–59, 72.

[127] On Vesta and the Numician waters, see below, n. 207.

[128] Radke, *op. cit.*, p. 232, refers the name to the root of *nuere* "nod."

[129] *CIL* I² 455 (and p. 714) = Vetter no. 364b.

[130] Vetter no. 364a. If the other receptacle contains the name of gods, then this object may have belonged to a divine Titus comparable with the birds *titi* or Titinus; see below, ch. 5.

[131] *Ibid.* and "Di Novensedes, di Indigetes," *IF* 62 (1956), pp. 1–16.

[132] Macr. *Sat.* 1.16.36; see Weinstock, *op. cit.* (above, n. 48). At that time Weinstock held the view that *parca* was derived from *pario*; see above, n. 51.

[133] *RKR*² *passim.* Wissowa's theory remains sheer speculation with slight support in ancient authorities.

[134] *CIL* XI 6297 = I² 375 = *ILS* 2977 = *ILLRP* 20. I resolve the dedication in the dative in agreement with Degrassi *ILLRP* 2, p. 380, *add.* to no. 20.

[135] *LL* 5.74. The name variants *Novensides* (*-sedes*) and *Novensiles* are thought to be neglible attempts at etymologizing spellings.

[136] *Adv. Nat.* 3.38.

[137] Livy 8.9.6–8.

[138] Furius, conveyed by Sammonicus Serenus to Macr. *Sat.* 3.9.10–12.

[139] Above, sect. 1 and n. 40, and below, sect. 7.

[140] See Priscian *GL* 2.257 K.; Macr. *Sat.* 1.17.62, 1.9.11.

[141] *Op. cit* (above, n. 131), pp. 11–16.

[142] *RKR*² pp. 18–23.

[143] H.-G. Kolbe, "Lare Aineia?," *Röm. Mitt.* 77 (1970) pp. 1–9 = *AE* 1969–70, no. 2; M. Guarducci, *BMCR* (above, n. 2); Weinstock, *JRS* (above, n. 1), pp. 114–18, and *Divus Julius* (Oxford, 1971) *passim.* Because Weinstock has so much to say on the nature of the Lares, I shall answer some of his arguments, mistaken in interpretation of existing evidence as well as in that of the purported Lar Aeneas, which Miss Guarducci first published. For the ending *-ebus/ -ebos* see Degrassi, *ILLRP* 2, p. 510. In his addendum to no. 20 (2, p. 380) Degrassi acknowledges the abbreviation *No[v]esede(bus)*; see above, n. 134. *CIL* VI 550 = I² 993 = *ILLRP* 236: Sex(tus) Q(uintus) Vesu(v)ies Q(uinti) Sex(ti) f(ilii) d(onum) d(ant). Kolbe discusses the rare name Vesuvius and cites this inscription, but he does not call attention to the two occurrences of the same praenomen. The document raises the question whether Vesuvia was a Roman of Rome. Her filiation assures her Roman citizenship even though the name is rare. M. Guarducci has replied to Kolbe in such a way that none of his discussion is acceptable to her; see above, n. 2. From the stone itself and from photographs one can be certain of the reading *Lare* and nothing else. Probability militates against Lar Aeneas. Even with Miss Guarducci's reading *Aenia*, very close to the *Annia* Kolbe discarded, we are left with serious doubts: first, the dipthong *ae* would lower the date very probably to the second century, a date improbable by

virtue of the archaeological and paleographical evidence; second, the word *Aenia* might conceal a personal name of a dedicant or a descriptive epithet (*Lares aenei*; cf. Petronius *Sat.* 29.8, *Lares argentei*; 60.8, *Lares bullati*) or dedicated object (*aeniad*; as *ture vino facere*). Although I cannot insist on any letter read after *Lare*, I can point out that the conjunction of Lar and the name of a mythological, divine or human being stands without parallel. In the dedication *Silvano Lari agresti* (*CIL* VI 646), itself unique, the latter god stands in apposition to the former unless *silvanus* describes Lar. In any case, we do not have an analogous Lar Silvanus, which also could be interpreted as adjectival epithet (cf. Mars Silvanus in Cato *Agr.* 83; *CIL* VI 36786 Iovi Silvano Salutari).

144   *JRS* pp. 114–18; cf. idem, *Divus Julius*, pp. 10, 177, 291–92; G.K. Galinsky, *Aeneas, Sicily, and Rome* (Princeton, 1969), pp. 158–61, treated the Lar Aeneas in passing. Like Weinstock, he makes too much of the cults at Lavinium, makes little of the relation to the Parcae, and mentions nothing about Faunus or the oracular character of the shrine. In fact, he confuses two cult centers, one of which he practically ignores. He puts the cult of Aeneas Indiges in Lavinium. We now see that Lar and Indiges cannot be equated or related.

145   W. Altmann, *Die römischen Grabaltäre der Kaiserzeit* (Berlin, 1905), esp. pp. 174–87.

146   Cassius Hem. fr. 11 P, Nonius p. 114 L, Prop. 4.1.21; representations on Lares' altars are: Vatican 1115 the white sow and 30 piglets (see our Figure 10); Ostia, altar of "Piazzetta dei Lari," *NdSc* 1916, pp. 145–48, *Arch. Cl.* 4 (1952) pp. 204–208, with pl. LI; W. Hermann, *Röm. Götteraltäre* (Kallmunz, 1961), pp. 97–99, no. 32; see M. Bulard, *Exploration archéologique de Délos* IX (1926), figs. 49, 54, plates V 1, VII 1 and 2, IX 1, XIII 1, XVII 2, XVIII, XIX, XXI, XXV 1. Figs. 49 and 54 and Plates XIII and XXI have the same dark pig. The other three pigs are light. The household Lares are also represented in receipt of a pig. Among the best preserved Pompeian examples is that now in the Naples Museum and available as Alinari photograph no. 12190 (mistitled). See M. Bulard, *La religion domestique dans . . . Délos* = *BEFAR* 131 (1926), pp. 57–96, who errs in attributing the material to the private cult. The shrines were situated on the streets. See *Inscr. Délos* nos. 1760–71.

147   Compitalia: Asc. p. 57 K.S.; Cic. *Pis.* 4.8–9, *ad Att.* 2.3.4; Dion. Hal. *AR* 4.14; Festus 55, 108, 213, 304/6L.; Gellius *NA* 10.24; Macr. *Sat.* 1.4.27, 1.7.34, 1.16.6, Pliny *NH* 3.204, 19.114, 36.104; Varro *LL* 6.23, 29; [Verg.] *Catal.* 13.27. Ludi Comp.: Asc. 6–7 K.-S.; Cic. *HR* 11–13 (?), *Pis.* 4.8–9; Diom. *Com. Gr.* in Kaibel *CGF* 1.57–58 (= Keil *GL* 1.488 = Varro fr. 305 Fun.); Don *Com.* in Kaibel *CGF* 1.67 (= Varro fr. 305 Fun.). Site of the Compitalia: Cato *Agr.* 5, 57; Festus 35 L; Macr. *Sat.* 1.7.34; Serv. on *Aen.* 8.717, on *Georg.* 2.382–83; Vergil *Aen.* 8.714, *Georg.* 2.380 ff. Cf. Festus 55 L. A rural *compitum* is recorded on *ILS* 5792 (Amiternine). Compare the description in the scholion on Persius 4.28.

148   See above at n. 57. For the Lares' *limen*, see *CIL* V 3257 = *ILS* 3610 (Verona) and *EE* 9.679 (Tusculum); cf. *CIL* I² 2661, set up by three *magistri*, perhaps of a *compitum*, in 171 B.C.

149   Plaut. *Aul.* 387; Varro in *Non.* p. 531 L; see below.

150   E.g., see Petron. *Sat.* 60.8 and the altar fragment in the Capitoline Museum garden (inv. no. 1276; see Pietrangeli *BC* 1942, pp. 127–30, and Hermann, *op. cit.*, pp. 89–90, no. 19); see below.

151   *CIL* I² 753 = V 4087 = *ILLRP* 200, with Degrassi's important comment.

152   E.g., *CIL* VI 443, 445–49, 451–55, 30768, 30954, 30956–60, 309562, 36809, X 1582, XIV 367, 3561; *ILS* 9388; *AE* 1960, no. 61; 1964 nos. 74, 151, 152, 155; *EE* 9.679; *II* 13.1.20. He was in fact borrowing an epithet from the gods.

153   Suet. *Aug.* 31.4; Serv. on *Georg.* 2.383; *ILS* 9252; *CIL* XI 4818; *CIL* XIV S 4297; *AE* 1945, no. 56, for example.

154   Arn. *Adv. Nat.* 1.28; Cass. Hem. fr. 11 P; Non. p. 114 L. They are to be construed as belonging to the thirty Roman curias; see Palmer, *The Archaic Community of the Romans*, pp. 9–10, 81.

155   Livy 40.52.5; Degrassi, *II* 13.2, p. 543; Ovid *F.* 5.129; Plut. *QR* 51; *CIL* VI 456; cf. Pliny

NH 21.10; *CIL* VI 459; *CIL* VI 36810–12 (for other Lares Viales see, for example, Plaut. *Merc.* 864; Varro *LL* 6.25); Varro *LL* 5.49.

[156] W. Amelung, *Die Skulpturen des Vatikanischen Museums*, 1.440–41, no. 185, pl. 46; E. Simon in W. Helbig, *Führer* etc., 4th ed., 1.281, no. 368. The Lares Militares are also met in dedications (*ILS* 3637–38) and in the rites of the Arval Brethren (*ILS* 451). Weinstock's interpretation of the various Lares in Capella, "Martianus Capella and the Cosmic System of the Etruscans," *JRS* 36 (1946), pp. 109–10, 114–15, is either inconclusive or unconvincing.

[157] *The King and the Comitium, Historia Einzelschr.* Heft 11 (1969), pp. 7–8.

[158] *CIL* VI 646 = *ILS* 3570, offered by A. Larcius Proculus, whose name may have suggested the denomination.

[159] *CIL* VI 582, 630 (= *ILS* 1699, 3541), 671 (= *ILS* 3543), 692; cf. *CIL* VI 10231 = *ILS* 7313 = *FIRA* III no. 93. The lowest classes and slaves were especially devoted to these gods; see F. Bömer, "Untersuchungen über die Religion der Sklaven in Griechenland und Rom, Erster Teil: Die wichtigsten Kulte und Religionen in Rom und im lateinischen Westen," *Akad. Wiss. Lit. Abh. Geistes- u. Sozialwiss. Kl. Mainz* (1957), pp. 406–72.

[160] *Expl. de Délos* IX (1926), pl. XVIII; and above, n. 146.

[161] *CIL* XI 2096 = *ILS* 3631, in payment for a vow.

[162] *CIL* VI 975. The Lares held special sway in the worship of all Roman neighborhoods.

[163] See Bömer, *loc. cit.*, and Kolbe, *op. cit.*, for a review of the question.

[164] In Naevius' *Tunicularia, CRF* 99–102 R³ = Marmorale pp. 224–25, a Greek artist is painting the *Lares ludentes*. The unrhotacized *Lases* of the Arval hymn strongly indicates that the cult was very old among the Romans.

[165] Schol. on Persius 4.28; see H. Bloch, "A Monument of the Lares Augusti," *HTR 55* (1962), p. 219.

[166] Nonius pp. 852, 863 L; cf. Plaut. *Aul.* 23–27, 382–87. For other objects hung at the *compitum*, see Festus pp. 108, 272, 273 L; Macr. *Sat.* 1.7.34, and above, n. 150.

[167] *CIL* XI 1324 = *ILS* 3645; see Bömer, *op. cit.*, p. 423.

[168] See above, ch. 1; cf. Ovid, *F.* 5.129, Cens. *DN.* 2.3, *CIL* VI 445, 449, 451, 452, 30958, 30961, for example.

[169] *CIL* VI 459, 31270 (Vicus Salutaris situated near the cult of Salus; cf. Symm. *Ep.* 5.54), and 975 in Regions X and XIV. Cf. Bömer, *op. cit.*, p. 424. No other name of a *vicus* is so frequent at Rome.

[170] *CIL* III 633, VI 10231, X 444 (cf. *FIRA* 3² nos. 37, 42, 93); Bömer, *op. cit.*, pp. 452–61; Cato *Agr.* 83; Cic. *Leg.* 2.8.19, 2.11.27.

[171] *CIL* VI 2099 = *ILS* 5047 (183 A.D.); VI 2107 = *ILS* 5048 (225 A.D.). In contrast the Lares Militares received a white steer from the Arvals; *CIL* VI 2086 = *ILS* 451.

[172] Livy 8.9.6; Mart. Cap. 1.45–61.

[173] Val. Ant. fr. 12 P.; Dion. Hal. *AR* 3.70.2, 4.2; Plut. *Rom.* 2, *FR* 10; cf. Pliny *NH* 36.204. See Stoll in *Roschers Lexikon* 2.1887–88.

[174] Verg. *Aen.* 1.378 and Servius' comment; Dion. Hal. *AR* 1.67–69; and many other authorities.

[175] Tib. 2.5. The four mentioned Sibyls are reminiscent of Varro's list of the canonical ten.

[176] *Pun.* 1.658–61, 665–69, reminiscent of the *Aeneid.* Cf. Livy 21.7.1–2.

[177] See the major document published by G. Manganaro, "Un senatus consultum in greco dei Lanuvini e il rinnovo della *cognatio* con i Centuripini," *Rend. Acc. Arch. Lett. Bell. Arti Napoli* n.s. 37 (1962), pp. 23–44. On other modes of similar federation, see above, ch. 2. On the relation of Saguntum to Zakynthos through Aeneas, below, nn. 196–97. Ardea's kinship with Saguntum may have promoted the special Roman sacrifices at Ardea after the outset of the second Punic War; see Livy 22.1.19, discussed above, ch. 1, sects. 6, 17. Less noticed kinships are that of the Samothracians, Trojans and Latins (Varro and others in Serv. on *Aen.* 1.378, 3.12, 8.679, in Macr. *Sat.* 3.4.6–11, Dion. Hal. *AR* 1.68–69, 2.66.5; cf. Varro *LL* 5.58, 7.34 and Aug. *CD* 7.28), and that of the Trojans, Latins and Gaulish Arverni (Lucan *BC* 1.427–28;

Sid. *Ep.* 7.7.2), and Aedui (Caes. *BG* 1.33.2, Cic. *Ad Att.* 1.19.2, Tac. *Ann.* 11.25.2).
[178]   *AR* 1.64.5. The trees are apparently the grove mentioned in Sil. *Pun.* 8.39.
[179]   *AR* 4.14.3. κατὰ πάντας ἐκέλευσε (ὁ Τύλλιος) τοὺς στενωπούς
ἐγκατασκευασθῆναι καλιάδας ὑπὸ τῶν γειτόνων ἥρωσι προνωπίοις κτλ. |
[180]   Cf. the sepulchral inscription, *CIL* I² 1596 = X 4255 = *ILS* 7999 = *ILLRP* 938: deis inferum parentum sacrum.
[181]   *NH* 3.56. Mss: locus solis, sometimes emended to *Iovis*. On Jupiter Indiges,, see below. Following Koch, Weinstock accepts the reading of *lucus Solis Indigetis.* C. Koch, *Gestirnverehrung im alten Italien: Sol Indiges und der Kreis der Di Indigetes* in *Frank. St. zur Rel. u. Kult d. Antike* 3 (1933), pp. 105–109, insists that the Sol, who had a "Trojan" shrine in Lavinian territory, was called Indiges and was the *pater Indiges* (i.e., Aeneas). This Sol does not bear the name Indiges; see below, sect. 8, *pontifex dei Solis.* Furthermore, Dionysius (*AR* 1.55.1–2), who visited the springs and altars of Helios as well as the *heroon* of Aeneas, would not have failed to notify us that they were somehow related. Sol Indiges is otherwise attested only at Rome.
[182]   See Tilly, *op. cit.,* pp. 66–82; Galinsky, *op. cit.,* p. 149, n. 26, wrongly reports Castagnoli, *loc. cit.,* (above, n. 1), pp. 244–45.
[183]   P. Sommella, "Heroon di Enea a Lavinium," *Pont. Acc. Rom. Arch. Rend.* 44 (1971–72), pp. 47–74; *idem* in *Roma medio-repubblicana: Aspetti culturali di Roma e del Lazio nei secoli IV e III a. C.* (SPQR, Rome, 1973), pp. 312–15.
[184]   *AR* 1.55.2, 1.64.5.
[185]   H.J. Rose, "The 'Oath of Philippus' and the *Di Indigetes,*" *HTR* 30 (1937), pp. 165–81, in response to C. Koch, *op. cit.* (above, n. 181). Moreover, Weinstock, *JRS* (1960), fails to take Rose's discussion into account.
[186]   Miss Tilly, *ibid,* favors a site near the sea where the land is marshy, because Vergil speaks of the *stagna.* But, of course, *stagna* are not necessarily *paludes.* One of the upper reaches of the Rio Torto, Fosso delle Monachelle, runs quite close to Tor Tignosa. See Figure 9.
[187]   *AR* 1.49–53. The Trojans and Zakynthians shared pre-war *syngeneia*; see nn. 196–97.
[188]   *AR* 1.53.3, 55.2. See Castagnoli, *op. cit.* (above, n. 1).
[189]   *AR* 1.56. See below, sect. 15, for a sculptured representation of Aeneas and Faunus.
[190]   *Aen.* 8.17–101; cf. 7.25–35.
[191]   See Tilly, *op. cit.,* pp. 72–75, 80–82.
[192]   See above, n. 40.
[193]   Strabo 5.3.5 (232 C). See above, ch. 1, sect. 17.
[194]   Mela 2.71; Pliny *NH* 3.57.
[195]   Hemina fr. 7 P., quoted above, ch. 1, n. 348.
[196]   On Saguntum and Zakynthos, see A. Schulten, *RE* 1A 2 (1920), cols. 1755–56, and below, nn. 197, 298, and Ardea, above, at n. 177.
[197]   Strabo 3.4.6 (159 C), 3.4.8 (160 C), 4.1.4–5 (179–80 C), 4.1.8 (184 C); see above, ch. 2: since Strabo considered Saguntum a Zakynthian settlement (3.4.6), he does not remark an Ephesian Artemis at Saguntum. Her Saguntine temple is known from Pliny *NH* 16.216, quoted and discussed below, at n. 298. On the *xoanon* see C. Ampolo, "L'Artemide di Marsiglia e la Diana dell' Aventino," *PP* fasc. 130–33 (1970), pp. 206–208.
[198]   Val. Max, 2.4.5; cf. Dion. Hal. *AR* 4.2.
[199]   Aeneas Indiges: Varro *ARD* 15.12 Agahd (= Tert. *Ad nat.* 2.9; see Agahd, pp. 80–81); Vergil *Aen.* 12.794–95; Tib. 2.5.44; Ovid *M.* 14.598–99, 607–608; Festus *Epit.* 94 L; Sil. Ital. 8.39; Sulpicius Apollinaris in A. Gellius *NA* 2.16.8–10; Schol. Veron. on *Aen.*1.259; cf. Arn. 1.36. Pater Indiges: Sol. 2.15; the inscribed elogium (*CIL* X 8348 = I² p. 189 = *ILS* 63 = *II* 13.3.85) calls the god Indigens Pater; *OGR* 14.4.
[200]   Livy 1.2.6; Serv. Dan. on *Aen.* 1.259.
[201]   Sulpicius Apollinaris in A. Gellius *NA* 2.16.8–10.

202   Lycophron 1047–61, with Tzetzes' comment; Strabo 6.3.9 (284 C); see Deubner, *op. cit.*, pp. 19, 27, 41.

203   Cf. Lycophron 1063, 1264, and Vergil, *locc. citt.*, above, n. 25.

204   See below, sects. 11–14, 17.

205   See Wörner in *Roschers Lexikon* 1.338–39, and above.

206   Festus p. 152 L; Plut. *Numa* 13.2; Serv. on *Aen.* 11.339. See L.A. Holland, *Janus and the Bridge* = *PMAAR* 21 (1961), p. 317. For an apparently like rule at Tibur, see C.F. Giuliani, "Note di topografia tiburtina," *Soc. Tib. Atti e Mem.* 41 (1968), pp. 101–103.

207   Serv. on *Aen.* 7.150. Miss Tilly, *op. cit.*, p. 80, thinks this was a local Vesta. However, the Roman pontiffs and consuls came to sacrifice at the Numician spring (Schol. Ver. on *Aen.* 1.259; see below, n. 246), perhaps on the tenth day after the Latin Festival, when the consuls made the annual renewal of the Roman treaty with Lavinium (Livy 8.11.15; see below, sect. 8). The waters of Juturna's spring near the Numicus River were carried to Rome (Serv. on *Aen.* 12.139; rejected by Tilly, p. 78, n. 5).

208   See Tilly, p. 76, and preceding note.

209   *CIL* XIV 2065, 2066 = *CLE* 212 = *ILS* 6181, 6182.

210   *Aen.* 9.3–4.

211   *Aen.* 10.75–76.

212   See above, ch. 2. Cf. the *devotio* of Decius: uti populo Romano Quiritium vim victoriam prosperetis (Livy 8.9.7).

213   Vergil *Aen.* 7.88, 7.92; Livy 8.9.7, controlling the clause quoted in n. 212; see above, sects. 1, 5.

214   *EE* 9.594 = *ILS* 6185, from *ca.* 300. See Junius Priscillianus Maximus in *PIR*² 4.800.

215   On *vates* and *vaticinatio*, see Cic. *Div.* 1.6.12, 1.11.18, 1.18.34; on Fauns and *vates*, see below, ch. 4. Dionysius, *AR* 5.54, gives the legendary account of two Laurentine conspirators who are troubled by *daimones* that appeared in their sleep. They consulted a *mantis* after the appropriate sacrifices. This *mantis* admonished them to uncover their Latin conspiracy to the righteous Roman. Not only can this *mantis* be considered a *vates* of Faunus (responsible for the dreams), but he must also be understood as a spokesman for a pro-roman policy at Lavinium. Perhaps this legendary incident contains the elements of Lavinian debate on the eve of the Latin War; cf. *Div.* 1.11.18.

216   *IGRRP* 4.199; Sherk no. 53. See Manganaro, *op. cit.*, and above, sect. 7.

217   *CIL* X 797 = *ILS* 5004 (Pompeii).

218   See above, n. 207.

219   The prayer is quoted and translated in sect. 5; the inscribed choliambs are quoted in sect. 8. Beneficent Jupiter and Tellus are met in Varro *RR* 1.1.5. Traces of the formula of *devotio* may be implicated in Ennius *Annales* 208–10 *V.*² See O. Skutsch, *Studia Enniana* (London, 1968) pp. 54–59.

220   *Sat.* 3.8–10. On the *evocatio* of Juno, see above, ch. 1; on the cursing of other cities, see Palmer, *The Archaic Community of the Romans*, p. 181.

221   On the meaning of *capita*, see Palmer, *The King and the Comitium*, p. 10.

222   On *populus* in this context, see Palmer, *The Archaic Community of the Romans*, pp. 158–59, 230, and above, ch. 1, sects. 2, 15.

223   *CIL* X 5779 = *ILS* 3071 from the putative territory of Cereatae Marianae (mod. Casamari), formerly a part of Arpinate land. See A. Degrassi, "Iuppiter Aeris?," *Epigraphica* 31 (1969), pp. 59–64 = *Scritti vari di antichità* 4 (Trieste, 1971), pp. 135–39, on whose quotation of A. Giannetti, *Cereatae Marianae (Casamari)* (Abbazia di Casamari, 1968) I rely. Also see *AE* 1969–70. no. 111. Before the latter's new reading was known to me, I had already guessed at a cognomen from the root *atr-*.

224   For the victims, see Wissowa, *op. cit.*, p. 413, with reference to Jupiter Summanus and the Di Manes, and Pighi, *op. cit.*, pp. 52, 57, 307–308, 310. The *devotio* of Carthage is accompanied by the sacrifice of three black sheep; see above. The name of Aternus, healed in

Festus p. 83 L, was probably researched when Aelius and Varro sought etymologies of *furvus*; see A. Gellius *NA* 1.18.3–6. The form *aternus* finds support in the gentilicial name Aternius; cf. Rubrius and Rufriis. However, W.F. Otto, "Römische 'Sondergötter,' " *RhM* 64 (1909), pp. 464–65, emends Festus to *Helerno* in conformity with Ovid *F.* 2.67, 6.105. In *Tab. Ig.* VIIa 6–40, red or black sows are offered to Prestota Cerfia of Cerfus Martius, with black libation vessels first and then white vessels set over the black vessels; the Umbrian root is *adr-*. Cf. M.E. Armstrong, *The Significance of Certain Colors in Roman Ritual* (Diss. Baltimore, 1917), pp. 32–38.

²²⁵   Cf. the early cognomens found in the consular lists: Amintinus, Caeliomontanus, Camerinus, Capitolinus, Cerretanus, Cicurinus, Collatinus, Coritinesanus, Esquilinus, Lateranus, Lactucinus, Macerinus, Medullinus, Mugillanus, Tolerinus, Tricipitinus, Vaticanus, Vecellinus, Vibulanus; Aventinensis, Inregillensis, Maluginensis, Regillensis. Some of these personal names certainly referred to places of origin, real or fancied.

²²⁶   Degrassi, *op. cit.*, proposed the restoration [*statuae*] *d(e)i* instead of Mommsen's [*et ae*]*di*. A statue is implicit in most cults, and certainly here on the *basis*. Vell. Pat. 2.83.2: caeruleatus et nudus; compare the women prepared for sacrifice in Plaut. *Rud.* 270: candidatas hostiatasque. *Carm. Priap.* 72.2: rubricato mutinio. Pliny *NH* 33.111–12: Iovem miniandum locari; 35.157: (effigiem Iovis in Capitolio) fictilem eum fuisse et ideo miniari solitum. *Atramentum*: Vitr. 7.10; Pliny *NH* 33.90, 35.30, 41–43, 50, 97; Isid. *Etym.* 19.17.17–18.

²²⁷   Fortuna Barbata and F. Viscata are discussed in the handbooks; for Hercules Barbatus and H. Bull(atus), see *ILS* 3447, 3460. Juno's epithet Caprotina is sometimes thought to refer to her garb; otherwise, she is known to have worn the *toga praetexta*; see above, ch. 1, sect. 3.

²²⁸   Cic. *Div.* 1.43.98 with Pease's note, 2.27.58. Cf. the Aternus R., dividing the Vestini and Marrucini and emptying into the Adriatic at Aternum.

²²⁹   *Ibid.* 1.47.105 with Pease's note.

²³⁰   Aug. *CD* 7.9 and 7.11, quoting Varro who quotes Valerius, fr. 4 Morel.

²³¹   See *CIL* XI 6138, where Mommsen's rejection of a relation with the last Atratinus is to be rejected.

²³²   See below, sects. 10, 17.

²³³   *Pun.* 8.39.

²³⁴   Symmachus 10.3.10 (= *Rel.* 3.10): ergo diis patriis, diis indigetibus pacem rogamus. This is a variation on *Georgics* 1.498.

²³⁵   *Bell. Gild.* 128–32.

²³⁶   *Comm. Somn. Scip.* 1.9.7; Hesiod *Op.* 122–24, 126.

²³⁷   *Adv. Nat.* 1.36.

²³⁸   See above, sect. 5.

²³⁹   Festus *Epit.* p. 94 L. See Rose, *op. cit.*, p. 181. Cf. *vos quo alio nomine fas est nominare* in the *devotio* of Carthage.

²⁴⁰   Schol. Bern. on Verg. *Georg.* 1.498 (p. 213 Hagen).

²⁴¹   *Ibid*; Serv. on *Georg.* 1.498, on *Aen.* 12.794.

²⁴²   *DN* 4.11, in imitation of Vergil's rendition of Evander (*Aen.* 8.314), "haec nemora indigenae Fauni Nymphaeque tenebant, etc."

²⁴³   *Tab. Ig. IIa* 6–14. The translation is Poultney's.

²⁴⁴   See Poultney on this passage. A. Ernout, *Le dialecte ombrien* (Paris, 1961), pp. 69–70, 73, casts doubt on certainty in analyzing both *ahtu* and *tikamne*.

²⁴⁵   *Op. cit.*, p. 69.

²⁴⁶   Schol. Veron. on *Aen.* 1.259, referring to Aeneas Indiges' precinct at the Numicus; see above, n. 207. The Di Indigetes were also worshipped at Praeneste (Serv. on *Aen.* 7.678), and are mentioned in conjunction with Praenestine pontiffs. Servius' garbled comment relies upon Varro and Cato's *Origins* (see Schol. Veron. *ad. loc.*), but the role of the Indigetes in the foundation legend of Praeneste is not made clear.

²⁴⁷   The most recent general treatment of the Julian clan, its Trojan ancestry, and the extrav-

agant claims of the Caesars is that of G.K. Galinsky, *op. cit., passim.* For the late republican interest in Trojan clans at Rome, see also Palmer, *The Archaic Community of the Romans*, pp. 136, 290–91.

[248]   See C. Koch, *Der römische Juppiter = Frankfurter Studien zur Religion und Kultur der Antike* 14 (1937), pp. 67–90 and *passim*; Radke, *op. cit.*, pp. 306–10; Weinstock, *Divus Julius*, pp. 4–12. The last author can reject (p. 8) Vediovis of the underworld because he does not examine the origin of the god's cult at Rome (see below), and avoids a connection between the Julian offerings at births and the religious nature of the god. On the other hand, Weinstock's discussion of Iul(l)us as youthful Jupiter and the Julian clan's ties with the Bovillan priesthood is very informative. For Weinstock, Vediovis can only be youthful Jupiter. However, *ve-* is privative as well as diminutive, a fact acknowledged by him. The infantile aspect of Vediovis (see below) is omitted by Weinstock. His analysis of Iullus interpreted "little Jove" helps to explain how the Romans came frequently to confuse Vediovis and Jupiter.

[249]   For citations and discussion of the *lex Albana*, see above, ch. 2. The form Vediovis is epigraphic, Veiovis literary.

[250]   *Ann.* 2.41; see Weinstock, *loc. cit.* The relation of the family religion to Germanicus' triumph will be apparent. Details of the archaic religion of patrician clans are lacking. Not every clan was involved only in Alban cults. A pertinent fragment from Cato's speech against L. Veturius, who lost his public horse because of the wrongful performance of sacrifice, tells of a *sacrarium* into which the water of the River Anio had to be carried at the distance of some fifteen miles (*ORF²* Cato fr. 74; see P. Fraccaro, "La *tribus Veturia* e i Veturi Sabini," *Athenaeum* 2 (1924), pp. 54–57 = *Opusc.* 2.1–3, and L.R. Taylor, *The Voting Districts of the Roman Republic = PMAAR* 20 (1960), p. 42). The *sacrarium* surely held the instruments of sacrifice; the word is used in its proper sense. The need for a "sacristy" at the Veturian shrine suggests that Tiberius saw the same need. However, in his day *sacrarium* was confused with *sacellum* (cf. Ulpian on the Edict in *Dig.* 1.8.9). On the requisition of holy waters, see above, n. 207. The only other patrician family of Trojan ancestry that purportedly kept rites of high antiquity was the Nautian clan. The Nautii observed the cult of Minerva, whose palladium was carried from Troy to Italy (Varro *de familiis Troianis* in Serv. on *Aen.* 2.166 and 5.704 = fr. 1 Peter). Some Romans seemed astonished that a Trojan deity was not in the charge of the Julii. Cf. *opp. citt.* (above, n. 247). For another *sacrarium*, see Cic. *Ad fam.* 13.2, with Tyrrell and Purser's comment on no. 259, which misses the point since it was a storehouse and not a shrine; cf. S. Treggiari, *Roman Freedmen During the Late Republic* (Oxford, 1969), pp. 136–38.

[251]   *Ann.* 15.23.

[252]   Tac. *Ann.* 1.54; *Hist* 2.95. On the archaic sodality, see below, ch. 5; Weinstock, *Divus Julius*, p. 7.

[253]   See Weinstock, pp. 11, 87. These sites are remarked on the military diplomas which preserve notice of the place of record at Rome; see *CIL* XVI 7–19, 21, 23, 24, 31–33. On Liber and the Caesars, see below, ch. 5. The oldest diploma citing the Julian altar is dated 22 December 68.

[254]   Plut. *Rom.* 20; Sol. 1.21. This was on the Arx, the site of another shrine to Vediovis.

[255]   L. Gasperini, "La più antica dedica a Dite," *Epigraphica* 32 (1970), pp. 35–49. The shrine would have lain not too distant from the incubation center of the heroes of Mt. Garganus, which resembled in cult the center of Faunus; see above, sect. 7.

[256]   *Ibid.*

[257]   Buck, no. 21.

[258]   See below, sect. 17.

[259]   *ILLRP* 504, cf. Palmer, *The King and the Comitium*, pp. 26 ff., and Gasperini, *op. cit.*

[260]   Gasperini, *op. cit.*, collects the references and deals with the site to be discussed now.

[261]   Cic. *Div.* 1.36.79, with Pease's important comments, which include modern descriptions of the black waters and deadly exhalations from the earth; Verg. *Aen.* 7.563–71 and Servius' complementary material *ad loc.*; Pliny *NH* 2. 207–208, with mention of other comparable

sites evidently drawn from the work of Varro cited by Servius on *Aen.* 7.563. For Dis and Pluto, see Cicero *ND* 2.26.66, with Pease's comment.

262   See below, sect. 17.

263   See above, sects. 1, 7.

264   See above, sect. 4. At Rome, Mephitis had an Esquiline shrine and grove; see *TDAR*, p. 338, and Wissowa, *RKR*[2], p. 246.

265   See above, n. 248.

266   See sect. 9.

267   *AR* 2.10.3.

268   *Lex XII Tab.* 8.21 with Riccobono's comment (*FIRA* I[2] p. 62, cf. p. 5).

269   See Platner-Ashby, pp. 293–94, and Walbank on Pol. 3.25.6–9.

270   Schol. Bern. on Verg. *Georg.* 2.384 (p. 242 Hagen); the source of the skin is inferred from the forepart of the comment and Vergil. Enn. *Ann LI* Vahlen[2]. For the coin, see T.L. Donaldson, *Architectura Numismatica or Architectural Medals of Classic Antiquity* (London, 1859), no. 11 (reprinted as *Ancient Architecture on Greek and Roman Coins and Medals* [Chicago, 1965]); Grueber *CRRBM*, vol. 1, p. 567, 4206–4208; Sydenham *RCC*, no. 1147. G. Fuchs, *Architekturdarstellung auf römischen Münzen der Republik und frühen Kaiserzeit = Deut. Arch. Inst. Antike Münzen und geschnittene Steine* 1 (Berlin, 1969), pp. 33, 67–68 and pl. 4.49, 50. Romulus cannot be held responsible for the temple shown on Marcellinus' coin. On the character of Marcellus' victory, see below, sects. 12, 17.

271   *II* 13.2, p. 522. The same day was observed as the feast of the October Horse; see below, nn. 382, 451.

272   Livy 2.36, on which see Ogilvie's comment; Dion. Hal. *AR* 7.68 and Macr. *Sat.* 1.11.2–5, probably from Varro.

273   *Curc.* 260–72.

274   The consequences of the cumulative evidence on Scipio's religious sentiments are denied by R.M. Haywood, *Studies on Scipio Africanus = Johns Hopkins Univ. St. Hist. Pol. Sci.* ser. 51, vol. 1, pp. 23–32. For purposes of Roman religion the following accounts certify Roman belief in the efficacy of incubation at Jupiter's temple. There is no compelling reason to suppose Scipio did not receive divine counsel. It is still received in Rome.

275   Polybius 10.2, 4–5, who asserts that Scipio either instilled belief in his divine guidance or took advantage of popular beliefs at home and abroad; he reports one of his dreams. Livy 26.19.3–9, who took the story from Polybius, *pace* Haywood; Appian *Ib.* 23; A. Gellius *NA* 6.1, citing Oppius and Hyginus; Dio 16.38–39. Scipio's adversary Hannibal was the earlier of the two generals to see Jupiter in his dreams (Silenus in Cic. *Div.* 1.24.49).

276   Val. Max. 8.15.1; Appian *Ib.* 23. The *spolia opima*, taken by his ancestor Cornelius Cossus and exhibited in the near temple of Jupiter Feretrius, should also be remembered when one remarks the religious practices of the Cornelii.

277   *CIL* XVI 21, 31.

278   Tac. *Ann.* 15.36.

279   Cic. *Div* 1.10.16; Livy *Per.* 14; Ovid *F.* 6.731–32. The time of this incident falls close to that of Jupiter Optimus Maximus' dream apparitions.

280   *LL* 5.74.

281   Degrassi *II* 13.2, p. 472.

282   Festus 66, 254 L; Pliny *NH* 2.138; Aug. *CD* 4.23 (pp. 175–76 D). See De Sanctis, *op. cit.*, 4.2.1, p. 284; Radke, *op. cit.*, p. 295.

283   Above, sect. 9.

284   See Teuffels *Röm. Lit.*[6] vol. 1, p. 237. Toward the end of the second century, L. Philus' son Marcus issued a denarius which commemorated either his ancestor's consular victory over Gauls in 223 or the recent victory over Bituitus in 121, in which no Furius is known to have taken part; see Sydenham, *RCC* 529.

285   See Broughton *MRR, s. aa.,* for references.

[286] See Degrassi *II* 13.2, p. 421. The calendars, Vitruvius 4.8.4, and Ovid (*F.* 3.429–48) have the name Vediovis. For a full account of the literary evidence and the real remains, see A.M. Colini, "Aedes Veiovis inter Arcem et Capitolium," *BC* 70 (1942), pp. 5–56, with 5 drawings and 4 plates.

[287] *NA* 5.12: immolatur ritu humano capra.

[288] *F.* 3.429–48.

[289] See Colini, *op. cit.*, and E. Nash *PDAR*² 2.490–95. With respect to the cult statue Weinstock, *Divus Julius*, pp. 10–11, has invented a relationship between the Julii and the cult of Roman Vediovis which has no support in the sources.

[290] Grueber, *CRRBM*, vol. 2, p. 290, 585–89; Sydenham, *RRC* no. 564. The arguments of T.J. Luce, *AJA* 72 (1968), pp. 25–39, do not convince me in regard to these coins and cult matters.

[291] *QR* 51; cf. Ovid *F.* 5.135–42.

[292] Grueber, *CRRBM*, vol. 1, pp. 333–35, 2606–24; Sydenham, *RRC*, no. 721. The moneyers were Gargilius, Ogulnius and Vergilius.

[293] Grueber, *CRRBM*, vol. 1, pp. 322–23, nos. 2476–83; Sydenham *RRC*, 724, 726.

[294] See Broughton, *MRR* vol. 2, pp. 104, 109 n. 6; Cic. *Pro Fonteio, passim*, esp. 31–32. Possibly the moneyer and the governor were closely related or identical; see F. Münzer *RE* 6.2 (1909), cols. 2842–46. The moneyer may have commemorated the governor's victory over Gauls by representing the Vediovis whom Purpurio had honored. In this case, the coin must be dated at least eight years later. Conversely, Marcus Fonteius could have received a command over the Gauls because he or his family had previously gained experience in that sector.

[295] A.B. Cook, *Zeus: A Study in Ancient Religion*, (repr. New York, 1964), pp. 710–17, 1109–10. On Jupiter Puer, see Cic. *Div.* 2.41.85 with Pease's lengthy note. For the Furfensian cult, see *CIL* IX 3513 = *FIRA* 3 no. 72 = *ILLRP* 508. For a discussion of Puer and Liber, see Koch, *Der röm. Juppiter*, pp. 47–49, 82–84.

[296] Grueber, *CRRBM*, vol. 1, p. 320, 2467–69; Sydenham, *RRC*, no. 732. For a Gaulish Minerva with whom the figure on the reverse might be identified, see sect. 17.

[297] *CIL* XVI S 158.

[298] *NH* 16.215–16. I have no certain confidence in the correct transmission of the numbers, but have adopted one of several readings because Pliny appears to refer to the dedication of the statue alone, not to the dedication of the temple. See Colini, p. 40.

[299] See above, sects. 6–8. In Rome, where molded statuary was normal and stonework the unusual, wooden images aroused curiosity. At the famous purification for which Livius Andronicus composed the poem, the Romans bestowed two cypress statues of Juno Regina on that goddess at the bidding of the Sibylline Books (Livy 27.37; Jul. Obs. 46; oracle in Diels, *op. cit.*, pp. 114–15, lines 56 and 64). Regina enjoyed Veientine origin; see above, ch. 1, sect. 6.

[300] See Degrassi *II* 13.2, p. 460. Here I am developing the suggestion of Colini, *ibid.*

[301] Degrassi *II* 13.2, pp. 393–94, 425, 534, 535–36; Weinstock, *Divus Julius*, p. 8. The solar identity depends upon Lydus. The authors insist on Janus' receiving the sacrifice of 9 January. Sol Indiges was venerated on 9 August, but his festival differed from those *agonalia*, in that it is not marked on the calendars as one of the oldest celebrations. See Degrassi *II* 13.2, p. 493.

[302] See Platner-Ashby, *TDAR*, pp. 2–3; Degrassi *II* 13.2, p. 388.

[303] See Deubner, *op. cit., passim;* M. Hamilton, *Incubation: Or the Cure of Diseases in Pagan Temples and Christian Churches* (London, 1906), pp. 63–73.

[304] Livy 10.23.11–12.

[305] Pliny *NH* 34.26.

[306] Livy 31.21.12: aedemque Diiovi vovit, si eo die hostes fudisset; 34.53.7: et in Insula Iovis aedem C. Servilius duumvir dedicavit: vota erat sex annis ante Gallico bello a L. Furio Purpurione praetore, ab eodem postea consule locata. The calendars yield *Vediovi*; see Degrassi *II* 13.2, p. 388.

[307] Livy 30.1.8, 19.6–8.

[308] See above, n. 286.

[309] *F.* 1.293–94.

[310] *CIL* VI 379 = I² 990 = *ILLRP* 186, with Degrassi's notes.

[311] E.g. *CIL* VI 7 = I² 800 = *ILS* 3836 = *ILLRP* 39.

[312] M. Besnier, *L'Ile tibérine dans l'antiquité* = *BEFAR* 87 (1902), pp. 247–72, is perverse in denying the existence of Vediovis' temple on the Island. Such perversity has merely clouded any balanced treatment of the god, because no one took the pains to disentangle the Livian statements on the total number of his temples at Rome or how they came to be vowed.

[313] Livy 33.42.10; 34.53.4.

[314] Degrassi *II* 13.2, p. 409.

See Platner-Ashby *TDAR*, pp. 258–59. The most important texts are Cic. *ND* 2.61, Livy 25.40.3, 27.25.7–9, Val. Max. 1.1.8, and Symm. *Ep.* 1.20. The Romans had long memories: Gaius Marius also built a temple for Honor and Virtus after his victory over the Cimbrians and Teutons.

[316] Livy 35.20.2, 22.3–4, 40.2–4, 36.37.6.

[317] See Degrassi *II* 13.2, pp. 409–11. Cf. Livy 1.5.1–2, with Ogilvie's comment; Serv. on *Aen.* 8.343.

[318] See preceding note and above, ch. 1, sect. 4, on *amiclum Iunonis*, and Palmer, *The Archaic Community of the Romans*, pp. 135–36, on the Luperci.

[319] See below, ch. 4.

[320] Fronto p. 146 Naber = 2.66 *LCL*.

[321] Livy 2.7; Ogilvie distinguishes Silvanus from Faunus. However, Livy also avoids the former name in rendering the Pan Lycaeus of the Lupercalia.

[322] *AR* 5.16.

[323] Val. Ant. fr. 6 Peter = Arn. *Adv. Nat.* 5.1; Ovid *F.* 3.285 ff; Plut. *Numa* 15. See above, ch. 2.

[324] On Verg. *Aen* 8.314; see above, sect. 1.

[325] Serv. Dan. on *Aen.* 8.275. The *Res humanae* of Varro are explicitly cited in the next lemma.

[326] *Carm.* 1.4.11–12: nunc et in umbrosis Fauno decet immolare lucis, / seu poscat agna sive malit haedo. This festival is to be distinguished from another on 5 December, for which Horace and his commentators are our sole source. Horace apparently associates it linguistically with the wind Favonius, which, not so coincidentally, rises on 11 March *natalis Favoni*; see Degrassi *II* 13.2, p. 421.

[327] *Carm.* 3.18; see above, sect. 1; and below, sect. 17. Favonius was also thought to rise on 7 February; see Degrassi *II* 13.2, p. 407, and C.L. Babcock, "The Role of Faunus in Horace, *Carmina* 1.4," *TAPA* 92 (1961), pp. 13–19.

[328] *Ecl.* 5.25–29.

[329] *Ecl.* 1, esp. lines 8–15, 33–35. On the Writing Fates, see above, sect. 5.

[330] *Leg.* 2.8.19 (cf. 2.11.27): lucos in agris habento, et Larum sedes.

[331] Pighi, *op. cit.*, pp. 302 (Ilithyiae, Juno), 303–304 (Apollo); cf. Hor. *CS.* For the games needed in 49 or 46, see Weinstock, *Divus Julius*, pp. 195–96.

[332] *Acta, c* (witness at writing the senatus consultum), lines 107, 151, [168]; see Pighi, pp. 233–34.

[333] See above, sect. 4.

[334] See Schanz-Hosius, *Rom. Lit.* 2⁴, pp. 42–46.

[335] Festus *Epit.* 519 L.

[336] Ovid *F.* 3.429–45.

[337] Dio 47.18. See Syme *RR*, p. 203. The date of official divinity depends in part on the contents of the Lex Rufrena; see A. Degrassi, "Epigraphica III," *Atti Acc. N. Lincei. Mem. Cl. mor. st. filol.*, ser. 8, 13 (1967–68), pp. 12–15, and Weinstock, *Divus Julius,* pp. 386–91.

338 *CIL* XII 4333 = *ILS* 112. See above, ch. 2.

339 See I.S. Ryberg, *Rites of the State Religion in Roman Art* = *MAAR* 22 (1955), p. 58. The altar is now in the Vatican Museum's Gabinetto Apoxymenos and bears the inscription *CIL* VI 876. Before Mrs. Ryberg's book, its standard studies were W. Amelung, *Die Skulpturen des vatikanischen Museums* vol. 2 (Berlin, 1908), pp. 242–47, no. 87b, pl. 15, and H.C. Bowerman, *Roman Sacrificial Altars: An Archaeological Study of Monuments in Rome*, Bryn Mawr Coll. diss. 1913, pp. 45–47, no. 60. Writing after Mrs. Ryberg's work, W. Hermann, *Römische Götteraltäre* (Kallmunz, 1961), p. 154, judges it an uncertain altar.

340 E. Simon in W. Helbig, *Führer durch die off. Samml.* usw. I⁴ (Tübingen, 1963), pp. 198–201, no. 255.

341 Mart. Cap. 2.166; at 1.58, Capella assigns Vediovis and the *dii publici* to the fifteenth region of heaven.

342 See Diels, *op. cit.*, p. 56, n. 4, and above, sects. 1, 4.

343 *CIL* VI 10317 = I² 1005 = *ILLRP* 772.

344 W. Liebnam, *Zur Geschichte und Organisation der römischen Vereinwesens* (Leipzig, 1890), p. 64; cf. M. Cohn. *Zum römischen Vereinsrecht* (Berlin, 1873), p. 79.

345 Besnier, *op. cit.*, pp. 44–49, who has nothing to contribute on this dedication.

346 *CIL* VI 9231 = *ILCV* 688.

347 Although we frequently read the word *signum*, sometimes with the deity's name in the genitive (cf. *ILLRP* 562a, 625, 633, 665, and 717), I find only one relatively early example of the divine name in the accusative (*CIL* I² 2238 = *Inscr. Délos* 1750 = *ILLRP* 751): Maiam statuerunt; eisdem aaram. A comparable construction is used in the Greek version, which omits mention of the altar.

348 E.g., Varro *RR* 2.3.9 (goats and sheep), 2.4.10–11 (swine) and 2.5.9 (cattle).

349 See below, n. 444.

350 See above, sect. 12.

351 Serv. on *Georg.* 2.380.

352 *CIL* VI 567 = *ILS* 3474.

353 *CIL* XIV 2839 (Gallicano).

354 See above, sect. 12.

355 See Besnier, *op. cit.*, pp. 273–89.

356 *CIL* VI 568, 30994 = *ILS* 3472, 3473. For other evidence, see Besnier, *ibid.*

357 Cf. Festus *Epit.* p. 30; Schol. on Persius 2.27.

358 *CIL* VI 451, 821, 975 (reg. 14) = *ILS* 3619; cf. *ILS* 6073, for Vicus Censorius. The strife of the Fifties is reported with reference to *vici* and *decuriae*, which have every appearance of connection with the *vici.* (See Cic. *Sest* 15.34, *Dom.* 5.13, 21.54, *Ad QFr.* 2.3.5; S. Treggiari, *Roman Freedmen during the Late Republic* (Oxford, 1969), pp. 173–77.) However, no evidence of *decuriones* survives. Although *d(ecreto) d(ecuriae)* is not an impossible resolution, it does not conform with the normal usage. In a word, the record of the gift to Caprina Galla does not reflect ordinary documents of the *vici.* On the other hand, this inconsistency does not preclude Caprina Galla's having named a *vicus.*

359 *CIL* VI 451.

360 Caes. *BG* 2.4.7, 13.1; Suet. *Galba* 3; cf. Meillet-Ernout *Dict. étym.*⁴ s.v., and Conway, Whatmough, Johnson, *The Prae-Italic Dialects of Italy* 2, p. 196. Their freedmen usually styled themselves *Galbae liberti.*

361 Varro *LL* 5.157; Livy 5.48.3, on which see Ogilvie, 22.14.11. A *bustum* was a funeral pyre.

362 *CIL* VI 37043 = I² 809 = *ILLRP* 464: ab cleivo [infi]mo [Buste]is Galliceis ve[r]sus [ad su]mmum cleivom etc. This stretch of pavement is wrongly brought into relation with the *scaleis --- nieis*, which are mentioned after the heavy punctuation of a blank space.

363 G. Lugli, *Roma antica* (Rome, 1946), pp. 577–79.

[364] Oros. 4.13.3–10; Livy 22.57. A doctoral candidate, Bruce Macbain, suggests to me that the requirement of a pair of Greeks was inspired by the Etruscan influence inherent in decemviral innovations according to the Sibylline Books.

[365] Plut. *Marcellus* 3.3–4, cf. *QR* 83. He writes of "unspeakable and secret ceremonies."

[366] See Platner-Ashby, *TDAR*, pp. 293–94; and above, sect. 11.

[367] *Pun.* 8.641–42, which I have never seen cited on Busta Gallica. See below, n. 431.

[368] Jul. Obs. 21; Dio fr. 74.

[369] See below, ch. 5.

[370] Plut. *QR* 83.

[371] Jul. Obs. 44a.

[372] Plut. *Marius* 21 and 27.

[373] Sall. *Hist.* 1.29; Plut. *Marius* 43–44, *Sert.* 5; Appian *BC* 1.343–44 (cf. 308); Oros. 5.19. 24. Compare the *bardaicus iudex* in Juvenal 6.13–19 and its scholia. Among Spartacus' slave forces fourteen years later were both Gauls and Germans, evident remnants of the wars a quarter century earlier; Sall. *Hist.* 3.96 M, Plut. *Crassus* 8–11, Oros. 5.24.1.

[374] See Gabba on App. *BC* 1.341–42, and E. Badian, "Lucius Sulla the Deadly Reformer," *Todd Mem. Lect.* 7 (Sydney, 1970).

[375] See esp. Cic. *in toga cand.* and Asconius' comment, pp. 75, 78, 80–81 KS; Sall. *Hist.* frs. 1.43–46 M; Plut. *Sulla* 32.2; Schol. Bern. on Luc. 2. 173 (pp. 61–62 Usener). Q. Cicero, *Comm. Pet.* 3.10, and Lucan, *BC* 2.169–93, mention the *bustum* of Catulus, while other sources say the grave (e.g. Schol. Bern. *ad. loc.*, Val. Max. 9.2.1, Florus 2.9.26, Oros. 5.21.7). Since Seneca the Younger explicitly asserts the foreignness of Gratidianus' manner of execution (*Ira* 3.18), the word *bustum* could have conveyed the source of the foreignness by allusion to the Busta Gallica. For more detail see F. Münzer in *RE* 14.2 (1930), cols. 1825–27. In another slaughter Catiline commanded Sulla's Gauls (Q. Cic. *Comm. Pet.* 2.9). The story does not end with Gratidianus' murder. Catulus junior blocked his fellow censor's proposal to enfranchise the Transpadane Gauls in 65/4; Dio 37.9.3–4, Plut. *Crassus* 13.1–2.

[376] As in the case of other heroic exploits in early Roman history, the date of Torquatus' deed fluctuates; see Broughton *MRR s.a.* 361, for references.

[377] Pliny *NH* 28.12, 30.13. See Palmer, *The King and the Comitium*, pp. 16–17. In this context falls Caligula's boast (Suet. *Gaius* 29.2): Gallis Graecisque aliquot uno tempore condemnatis gloriabatur Gallograeciam se subegisse.

[378] *Pro Font.* 31, an attempt to discredit Gauls of the Narbonese province as witnesses against Fonteius.

[379] *BG* 6.16, 18.

[380] Livy 23.24.11–12.

[381] Diod. Sic. 5.29, Strabo 4.4.4–5 (197–98 C).

[382] Dio 43.24.3–4; Palmer, *op. cit.*, p. 16; see below, n. 451.

[383] Mentioned only by the *Notitia urbis Romae* etc.

[384] See Caesar *BG* 6.13–16; Diod. Sic. 5.28–32; Strabo 4.4.4–5 (197–98 C). Cf. Dion. Hal. *AR* 1.38.2, Livy 5.37.8, Tac. *Germ.* 3.1 with Anderson's note. For these aspects of Gaulish religion see J. De Vries, *Keltische Religion = Die Religionen der Menschkeit* 18 (Stuttgart, 1961), pp. 81–82, 203–17. A little music after murder has a soothing effect. So King David felt. Nero's conduct was exceptional inasmuch as it was not therapeutic.

[385] Cic. *Div.* 1.41.90; Ausonius, pp. 52 and 59 Peiper. On Belenus see De Vries, *op. cit.*, pp. 75–76.

[386] Lucan *BC* 1.441–58. The context fully supports a view that we are dealing with Transalpine Gauls (cf. Amm. Marc. 15.9.8). On Lactantius *DI* 1.21, see below. The Scholia Bernensia on Lucan offer varying Roman syncretism of the three gods. Moreover, Lucan's comparison of Taranis with the Diana (Artemis) who sought human victims seems to suggest that Taranis is a goddess. See De Vries, *op. cit.*, pp. 45–50, 63–64, 97–100; cf. Tac. *Ann.* 14.30, Suet. *Claud.* 25.5.

[387] *NH* 30.12–13; Tac. *Ann.* 2.36; Suet. *Tib.* 36, *Cl.* 25.5.

[388] See above, n. 386.

[389] *Marcellus* 3.3–4; *QR* 83.

[390] See J.H. Oliver and R.E.A. Palmer, "Minutes of an Act of the Roman Senate," *Hesperia* 24 (1955), pp. 320–49.

[391] Strabo 4.5.4. (201 C); Jerome *Adversus Jovinianum* book 2 (Migne *PL* 23, cols. 307–10). See R. Syme, *Ammianus and the Historia Augusta* (Oxford, 1968), pp. 18–23.

[392] Gellius *NA* 5.12.12. Cf. Fest. *Epit.* p. 91 L: humanum sacrificium dicebant quod mortui causa fiebat.

[393] See Radke, *op. cit.*, p. 310.

[394] Livy 31.10.1–2; 31.21; 33.36–37.

[395] Aug. *CD* 15.23 (2.108 D).

[396] Isid. *Etym.* 8.11.87 and 101–104; *Larvae* etc. are discussed by Aug. *CD* 9.11 (1.382 D). On *lamiae* see below.

[397] *Etym.* 7.5.

[398] Jer. *In Esaiam* 5.13.21: pilosi saltabunt ibi, vel incubones, vel satyros, vel silvestres quosdam homines, quos nonnulli fatuos ficarios vocant aut daemonum genera intellegunt.

[399] On Verg. *Aen.* 6.775; cf. on 7.47.

[400] Serv. on *Aen.* 7.47; Serv. Dan. on *Georg.* 1.11; Macrobius *Sat.* 1.12.21–25. See Agahd, *op. cit.*, pp. 193–94. Probably also Varronian in part is [Probus] on Verg. *Georg.* 1.10, who tells us of the monthly and yearly rites for Faunus as well as his oracle at Albunea, the Lavinian woods.

[401] *Ann.* 214 V.^{2}; see below, ch. 4.

[402] *Ann.* 605 V.^{2} See Conway, Whatmough, and Johnson *The Prae-Italic Dialects of Italy* 2, p. 181.

[403] See above, sect. 11.

[404] Plaut. *Cist.* 512, cf. 611; and Fest. *Epit.* 110 L.

[405] Varro *Modius* in Non. 205 L.

[406] Mart. Cap. 2.153–54.

[407] On Verg. *Aen.* 3.134, 8.275 (with mention of Faunus), in which is cited Apuleius *Dogma Plat.* 1.8 (= p. 95 Thomas).

[408] Strabo. 3.3.7 (155 C).

[409] Strabo 3.4.16 (164 C).

[410] Posidonius in Strabo 4.4.6 (198 C), where read *namniton*, for *samniton*.

[411] Strabo 5.1.9 (215 C).

[412] Suet. *Jul.* 32. According to Ovid, *F.* 2.277, the Pan who serves as Lupercalian Faunus was a *numen equarum*. Plutarch does not report any vision. Instead he offers us Caesar's dream of sexual intercourse with his mother (*Caes.* 32; cf. *Pomp.* 60.3), which Suetonius (*Jul.* 7) assigns to Caesar when quaestor in Spain, some twenty years earlier. Lucan (1.183–257), however, recreates the marvelous vision of the *Patria* or Fortuna, properly topped with the towers of a city-wall. This fearful apparition counsels the utmost in caution. Sallust, too, makes the Patria and Caesar's *parentes* address him (*Ep. de re pub.* 2.13; see now the writer's "Tre lettere in cerca di storico," *RFIC* 99 (1971), pp. 397–98). On the Gaulish war horn see below, ch.5. In Accius' *Brutus* a shepherd appears to Tarquinus Superbus in a dream (Cic. *Div.* 1.22.44).

[413] Suet. *Jul.* 81.2. Weinstock, *Divus Julius*, pp. 343–44, accepts the authenticity of the sacred horses, and denies the apparition and the prodigy of weeping.

[414] A. Tovar, *The Ancient Languages of Spain and Portugal* (New York, 1961), p. 128, identifies the god Aherbelste of Aquitanian Convenae as very similar to the Basque "black he-goat;" see *CIL* XIII 174.

[415] *BG* 6.18.1–2.

[416] Cicero *Div.* 1.45.101, 2.32.69; Varro *ARD* in Gellius *NA* 16.17, with the connection of Vaticanus Ager to the root of *vates*; Livy 5.32.6–7, on which see Ogilvie, 5.50.5 and 52.11;

Plut. *Cam.* 30, *FR* 5. Although it is often quoted, I find no authority who calls this voice *indiges.*

[417]   Lucian *Hercules* (entire) and *Bis Accusatus* 27.

[418]   See J. De Vries, *op. cit.*, pp. 65–71.

[419]   Strabo 4.1.11 (185 C), 4.6.3 (202 C); cf. Serv. on *Aen.* 6.830. Pliny *NH* 7.166 reports the miracle; see Degrassi *II* 13.2, p. 492, and below, ch. 5, on Fabius' Roman monuments, including a temple of Fever.

[420]   Lucan 7.192–200; Pliny *NH* 2.227; Martial 1.61.3, 6.42.4; Suet. *Tib.* 14; Claudian *Carm. Min.* 26 (*Aponus*). See C.B. Pascal, *The Cults of Cisalpine Gaul = Coll. Latomus* 75 (1964), pp. 95–96. The apparently Gaulish flavor of the shrine is assured by Ausonius' address to the spring of his native Burdigala (*Burd.* 29–34, pp. 153–54 Peiper). Here are lines 31–34: salve, urbis genius, medico potabilis haustu, / Divona Celtarum lingua, fons addite divis. / non Aponus potu, vitrea non luce Nemausus / purior, aequoreo non plenior amne Timavus. Lucan, *loc. cit.*, had already linked Aponus to Timavus. The cult of the Timavus is attested by *CIL* I² 2647 = *II* 10.4. 318 = *ILLRP* 261; *CIL* I² 2195 = *CIL* V *Suppl. Ital.* Pais 380 = *ILS* 3900 = *ILLRP* 262; *CIL* I² 652 = *ILS* 8885 = *II* 10.4.317 = *ILLRP* 335; Strabo 5.1.8–9; *AE* 1969–70, no. 200.

[421]   *LL* 7.36, with Ennius *Ann.* 214 V² (see below, ch. 4): "versibus quos olim Fauni vatesque canebant." Fauni dei Latinorum, ita ut et Faunus et Fauna sit; hos versibus quos vocant Saturnios in silvestribus locis traditum est solitos fari <a> quo fando Faunos dictos. antiqui poetas vates appellabant a versibus viendis, ut <de> poematis cum scribam ostendam.

[422]   Dion. Hal. *AR* 1.43.

[423]   Arnobius 1.36 (cf. 1.28, 5.18); Lactantius *DI* 1.22.9–11; Servius on *Aen* 7.47 and Serv. Dan. on 8.314; Macr. *Sat.* 1.12.21–29; Mart. Cap. 2.167. The notice in the last author suggests a derivation of Fenta from *for* as if Fantua: "Vedius ... id est Pluton, quem etiam Ditem Veiovemque dixere. ipsam quoque terram, qua hominibus invia est, referciunt longaevorum chori, qui habitant silvas, nemora, lucos, lacus, fontes ac fluvios appellanturque Panes, Fauni, Fon<ion>es, Satyri, Silvani, Nymphae, Fatui Fatuaeque vel Fantuae vel etiam Fanae, a quibus fana dicta, quod soleant divinare. hi omnes post prolixum aevum moriuntur ut homines, sed tamen et praesciendi et incursandi et nocendi habent praestantissimam potestatem." I have corrected the corrupt *fones* from the deity Fonio; see below, n. 442. A few chapters earlier Martianus mentions the *medioximi*, which constituted the Varronian classification; see above. At. *Sat.* 1.12.21, Macrobius indicates that some of the information comes from the pontifical archives which Cornelius Labeo (1.12.21) would have reported from Varro (1.12.27). Unfortunately, Macrobius or Labeo omitted mention of Fenta, who is explicitly named by Arnobius and Lactantius (also in the epitome of the *DI*) and implicitly by Martianus Capella. To complete the list of Faunus' wives I dare not omit Vitellia, who an enterprising "Elogius" believed was once a Latin goddess married to Faunus. She brought forth the line of the imperial Vitellii; see Suet. *Vit.* 1. With her may be compared Vitula (above, ch. 1, sect. 3) and the Aequian town of Vitellia (Livy 2.39.4, with Ogilvie's note). The bride and bridegroom are no other than Heifer and Goat, lovely ancestors for the emperor Vitellius. Cf. the coin of Thorius, above, ch. 1, n. 192, and the key to Figures 2 and 3.

[424]   *DI* 1.21–22. Lactantius attributes the foundation of the human sacrifice for Saturn to his grandson Faunus.

[425]   *AR* 1.19; R.M. Ogilvie brought this passage and the character of the oracle to my attention.

[426]   *AR* 1.37–44.

[427]   *Sat* 1.7.28–31.

[428]   Pliny *NH* 15.77. See A. von Domaszewski, "Silvanus auf lateinischen Inschriften," *Philologus* 61 (1902), pp. 1–2 = *Abhandlungen zur römischen Religion* (Leipzig, 1909), pp. 58–59, who follows Mommsen in suggesting devotion on the part of the bureau of public clerks. The fig tree recalls the scabrous Faunus or Fatuus *ficarius*. On the *caprificus* and Juno Populona, see above, ch. 1, sect. 2.

⁴²⁹ Justin 43.1.8–9; see above, sect. 1. In like vein , Hercules bids Claudius to stop *fatuari* in Sen. *Apoc.* 7.1, where the god plays on the two meanings of the verb. For the Gaulish connection see below, ch. 5.

⁴³⁰ Justin 43.5. See De Vries, *op. cit.*, pp. 230–33, 241. This Gaulish "Minerva" will have been the "Athena" whose temple housed Insubrian standards (Polyb. 2.32.6).

⁴³¹ See W.R. Halliday, *Greek Divination: A Study of its Methods and Principles* (London, 1913), pp. 128 ff. According to Nicander in Tert. *An.* 57.10, the Celts looked for dream visions of their dead by passing the night at the *virorum fortium busta*. When the elder Drusus died, the army raised for him an honorific mound around whose base the soldiers annually ran and the tribes of the three Gauls rendered public thanksgiving (Suet. *Claud.* 1).

⁴³² Halliday, *op. cit.*, pp. 131–33.

⁴³³ See above, n. 417.

⁴³⁴ *CIL* XII 5835, inscribed with a relief of a patera and cornucopia.

⁴³⁵ *CIL* XII 5890: [per] so[m]niu[m iuss]us Val(erius) Ta---Parcabu[s] v(otum) s(olvit) l(ibens) m(eritis).

⁴³⁶ *CIL* XII 174, a bilingual text wherein the Latin portion should be restored [*Silvano v(otum) s(olvit)*].

⁴³⁷ De Vries, *op. cit.*, pp. 91–96, esp. p. 93.

⁴³⁸ *CIL* XII 1102: [Silvano] Valerius [S]ecundinu[s e]x iussu v.s. l.m; 1335: Deo Silvano P. Iccius Veratianus ex iussu; 4103: Silvano Aug(usto) Q.C.R. — ex imperio; 5960: [Si]lvano Aug(usto) [sacr(um) — Plompeius Ingen[uus iu]ssum redd[idit].

⁴³⁹ *CIL* XII 1103; cf. *CIL* 3393 (Campana), 4441-42 (Carnumtum).

⁴⁴⁰ See Pascal, *op. cit.*, pp. 170–76, 193–94, and von Domaszewski, *passim*.

⁴⁴¹ *CIL* XI 3, 362 (cf. V 815), 555. Syncretism employing the Latin Silvanus could have been mediated by the Etruscans, who also worshipped the Latin god. See G. Colonna , "Selvans Sanchiuneta," *SE* 34 (1966), pp. 165–77.

⁴⁴² *CIL* V 757: Annia M(arci) f(ilia) Magna et Seia Ionis et Cornelia Ephyre magistrae B(onae) D(eae) porticum restituerunt et aediculam Fonionis; 758: Fonioni sac(rum) Seia Ionis mag(istra) d(onum) d(edit). See above, n. 423.

⁴⁴³ See above, and Pascal, *op. cit.*, pp. 75–76, 183–184.

⁴⁴⁴ *CIL* XIII 4142 = *ILS* 4673: in h(onorem) d(omus) d(ivinae) Deo Caprion[i] L. Teddiatius Primus.

⁴⁴⁵ *CIL* V 775 (Aquileia), 4208 (Brixia), 5002; 5005 (Riva); see Pascal, *op. cit.*, pp. 118–23. The Fatae Dervones are usually compared with the Matronae Dervonnae.

⁴⁴⁶ *CIL* V 3256, 5660.

⁴⁴⁷ *CIL* V 817, 3303. Pascal, *op. cit.*, p. 176, says that these female deities are "almost exclusively Illyrian." They are also met in Apta in Narbonese Gaul.

⁴⁴⁸ *CIL* VI 816: Silvano sacrum C(aius) Petronius Andronicus ex viso.

⁴⁴⁹ *Sat.* 6.447; *Epigr.* 10.92.

⁴⁵⁰ *CIL* VI 579: cf. IX 2447. See von Domaszewski, *op. cit.*, pp. 10–11 (68–69). For the *lavacrum Silvani* at Baiae, see above, n. 39. Women were excluded from the rural cult of Mars Silvanus described by Cato *Agr.* 83. Compare the dedication to Mars and Nemetona Silvinis (*CIL* XIII 6131 = *ILS* 4586).

⁴⁵¹ *CIL* VI 293. Platner-Ashby, *TDAR*, pp. 489–90, list the known shrines of Silvanus at Rome. All are of little account. The most recent important finds of Roman Deus Sanctus Silvanus are a marble altar, dedicated 15 October 170 by four priests, and a cippus given by three Sulpicii, two of whom have the alien cognomens *Ians.* and *Ianti.*, which are Venetic (see *CIL* V 746, Iantulla of Aquileia; 4506 Iantinus of Brixia). If the pieces are not compital, they belong to a shrine dedicated to the god on the Campus Martius near Ponte Umberto. This site approximates the Ciconiae Nixae, where the race of the October Horse was run on 15 October and whence the head of the winning right horse was taken for display in the City. It was this rite Caesar imitated during a mutiny, as far as it was humanly possible (see above). See

B.M. Felletti-Maj, *NdSc* 1957, pp. 329–31; *AE* 1960, nos. 251–52; *Carta Archeologica di Roma* tav. 1 (Ist. Geogr. Mil., Florence, 1962) I 89 b. Since we have no secure evidence on the situation of Ciconiae Nixae, other than its nearness to the Tiber in Region IX (cf. *CIL* VI 1785 = 31931), from the coincidence of this dedication to Silvanus with the festival of the October Horse, the newly uncovered shrine should be reckoned as an index to the site of Ciconiae Nixae and the horserace for Mars. S. Panciera, "Nuovi documenti epigrafici per la topografia di Roma antica," *Pont. Acc. Rom. Arch. Rend.* 43 (1970–71), pp. 125–34, edits a new inscription commemorating a statue of Silvanus, put up in accord with a vision at the temple of Diana Planciana.

⁴⁵²   See Bömer, *op. cit.*, pp. 452–61.

⁴⁵³   De Vries, *op. cit.*, pp. 123–27, esp. p. 125. See above, n. 412.

⁴⁵⁴   See above, n. 413.

⁴⁵⁵   Degrassi *II* 13.2, pp. 234–35, 380, 540. De Vries, *ibid.*, has the wrong calculation of the day.

⁴⁵⁶   See Vergil *Aen.* 11.784–93; Pliny *NH* 7.19; Silius *Pun.* 5.175–85, 7.662, 8.492; Varro in Servius on *Aen.* 11.785, 787. *CIL* XI 7485 = *ILS* 4034 (Falerii): C. Varius Herme[s] Sancto Sorano Apollini pro sal(ute) sua et fili sui et patroni sui et coniugis eius et filior(um) d(onum) d(edit); this dedication suggests that Soranus was a god of healing.

⁴⁵⁷   *CIL* VI 2233, 29967 (cf. 21861) for Apollo Argenteus; *CIL* XIII 7281 for a Vatican cult of an oriental nature, which can be related to the priestly office of the decedent in VI 2233, found on the land of the church of S. Maria in Vallicella of Mte. Mario. See R. Valentini and G. Zucchetti, *Codice topigrafico della città di Roma*, vol. 2 = R. Istituto Storico Italiano per il Medio Evo. Fonti per la Storia d'Italia, vol. 88, p. 221.

⁴⁵⁸   For the legend of St. Sylvester, see Duchesne's edition of the *Liber Pontificalis*, vol. 1, pp. *CIX–CXX, CXXXIX–CXL*, 170–201; J.J. Dollinger, *Fables Respecting the Popes of the Middle Ages*, tr. A. Plummer, (London, Oxford, Cambridge, 1871), pp. 89–103. Beyond the *Liber Pontificalis*, which bears traces of a legend *ca.* 500, lie many other legends about Sylvester. Sylvester's death on 31 December is recorded at the end of the life in the *LP* (whereas at the beginning of that life the date 1 January is given), and his burial on 31 December at the catacomb of Priscilla is recorded in the *depositio episcoporum*. On the pagan roots of certain Christian winter holidays, see M.P. Nilsson, "Studien zur Vorgeschichte des Weihnachtsfestes," *Archiv für Religionsw.* 19 (1916–19), pp. 50–150 (= *Opusc. Sel.* 1 [1951], pp. 214–311). This Compitalia for the Lares, a movable feast of candles, also underlies the various Christian rites of the season.

⁴⁵⁹   Lucilius 484–89 Marx, from Lactantius' discussion of Fauna, Fatua, Fenta, and so forth (*DI* 1.22); see above, sect. 17. A definition of a *lamia* is quoted above, at n. 396.

⁴⁶⁰   *Mos.* 169–99 (pp. 126–27 Peiper); see above, n. 34.

CHAPTER FOUR

¹   O. Skutsch, *Studia Enniana* (London, 1968). The new piece "On the Proems of Annals I and VII," pp. 119–29, complements and continues an older work, "Enniana II," *CQ* 42 (1948), pp. 94 ff., there reprinted on pp. 30–45.

²   *Studia Enniana*, 120–21.

³   T. Cole, "The Saturnian Verse," *Yale Classical Studies* 21 (1969), pp. 1–73, esp. 66–73. The work of B. Luiselli, *Il verso Saturnio = Studi di Metrica Classica* 3 (Rome, 1967), does not interest us here; even his rehearsal of ancient opinions on the origin and name of the meter, pp. 13–31, makes no new contribution. On the divine character of Fauns and the powers and function of *vates*, both Italic and Celtic, see above, ch. 3.

⁴   *LL* 5.1–2.

⁵   Cf. 5.68: quidam . . . vocant; 5.146: secundum Tiberim ad <Port>unium forum Piscarium

vocant. In the latter case Varro means the people of Rome. A general subject of this sort is ruled out because the Saturnian verse was not widespread. Indeed, Ennius had claimed it was outmoded (*canebant*) more than a century earlier.

[6] See L. Havet, *De Saturnio Latinorum versu* = *Bibl. d. Ecole d. Hautes Etudes* 43 (Paris, 1880), pp. 15–16. In 1838, Lersch had first attributed the choice of the name to Ennius.

[7] Cf. *Euhemerus*, fr. LX Vahlen[2]. What the Greeks called the *bios* of Kronos, the Romans later called the *regnum* of King Saturn.

[8] On the land of Saturn, see below.

[9] *Od.*, frs. 2 and 14 Morel.

[10] See Aristophanes *Nub.* 398 (with schol.), 929, 1070, *Vesp.* 1480 (with schol.), and *Plut.* 581; Plato *Lys.* 205c and *Euthyd.* 287b.

[11] In lines 1294–95 we encounter *numerus* for *metron*: servandi numeri et versus faciendi, / nos Caeli numeri numerum ut servemus modumque. See Marx *ad loc.* At lines 484–85 Lucilius may be following Ennius by his reference to the Fauni. Although from his fragments we detect Accius' interest in metrics, we know of no critical term developed by him. L. Mueller not only shows some awareness of the problem underlying the name of the meter, but also credits Accius with the earliest research on the Saturnian verse. There is no evidence of Accius' pursuit of Saturnian studies. See Mueller's *Der saturnische Vers und seine Denkmaeler* (Leipzig, 1885), pp. 1–2, 8–9. The only possible indication of Accius' interest in Saturn is a considerable fragment of his epic *Annales* (fr. 3 Morel, p. 34), which concerns the Athenian Cronia and evidently belonged to a discussion of the origin of the Saturnalia (Macr. *Sat.* 1.7.36). Accius, of course, was among Rome's earliest literary historians; he did not take the palm for accuracy; see above, ch. 3, sect. 4.

[12] U. von Wilamowitz-Moellendorf, *Griechische Verskunst* (Berlin, 1921), pp. 61–68.

[13] From *Symp.* 9 one could argue for this phrase as a technical term derived from cult.

[14] *LL* 5.42, with Enn. *Ann.* 25 Vahlen[2].

[15] *AR* 1.18.2, 1.34.5, 1.35.3.

[16] *AR* 1.34, 1.38.2, 1.44.2, 1.89.2, 2.1.4.

[17] *AR* 1.45.3, 1.85.4.

[18] *AR* 1.36.

[19] *AR* 1.34.5.

[20] See below for the possibility that Satricum was thought to be named for Saturn.

[21] Festus 430/2 Lindsay. (Cf. Isidore *Etym.* 9.2.84.) Another version made the man Saturn an eponymous founder; see below.

[22] *AR* 1.20.5.

[23] Livy 39.55.9. Pliny, *NH* 3.52, says the Saturnini used to be called Aurini. The latter name, of course, connotes the golden age and may have suggested the name of the new colony. But it seems more likely that the Aurini were invented to reinforce the idea of the golden age inherent in the name Saturnia, because the name of the *ager* in which the colony was settled evinces the name of the former, that is pre-colonial, community. The archaeological evidence seems to affirm the long-time vacancy of the site before the Roman settlement. See E.T. Salmon, *Roman Colonization under the Republic* (Ithaca, 1970), pp. 105, 119, 174 n. 68, 175 n. 77, 186 n. 181, 187 n. 184, and 188 n. 202. On the Etruscan Saturn, see below.

[24] The oration entitled *si se M. Caelius tribunus plebis appellasset* was perhaps delivered in 184 during Cato's censorship. This and other fragments are found in Malcovati *ORF*[2], pp. 46–48; this fragment is owed to the unusual word *spatiator*.

[25] For the *versus Fescenninus* see Teuffel's *Geschichte der römischen Literatur*[6] (Leipzig, 1916), pp. 5–6, and Fr. Leo, *Geschichte der römischen Literatur* I (1913), pp. 16–18.

[26] Livy 7.2: qui non, sicut ante, Fescennino versu similem incompositum temere ac rudem alternis iaciebant sed impletas modis saturas descripto iam ad tibicinem cantu motuque congruenti peragebant. On the dramatic *satura*, see the bibliography of W.S. Anderson, "Recent Work in Roman Satire (1962–68)," *CW* 63 (1969–70), pp. 181–82.

[27]   *Epist.* 2.1.145–50. Horace's account is more accurate than the attribution of the Fescennine verse to scurillity at a wedding party, which stems from Catullus 61.119–22. Augustus taunted Pollio in Fescennine verses (Macr. *Sat.* 2.4.21), and thus placed himself in the Catonian, not the Catullan, tradition. In response Pollio rendered the famous "*at ego taceo. non est enim facile in eum scribere qui potest proscribere.*"

[28]   See Diomedes, *De comedia Graeca*, in Kaibel's *CGF* 1.57–58 and Keil's *GL* 1.488. Funaioli makes it fr. 305 of Varro. I would attribute it to Varro's *De originibus scaenicis.* Varro, *LL* 7.36 quoted above, indicates a forthcoming work entitled *De poematis.* On such Varronian matters see these three articles by H. Dahlmann: "Vates," *Philologus* 97 (1948), pp. 337–53, "Varros Schrift 'de poematis' und die hellenistisch-römische Poetik," *Akad. Wiss. Lit. Mainz. Abh. Geistes- und Sozialwiss. Kl.* (1953), pp. 87–158, and "Studien zu Varro 'de poetis,' " *ibid.* (1962), pp. 553–676. The same Diomedes, *GL* 1.479, is unique in equating the *Fescenninus* with the metrical foot *amphimacrus.* See below, n. 50. For the ritual *fascinum*, see below, ch. 5.

[29]   *Brut.* 18.71 (cf. 19.75), *Orator* 51.171 (cf. 47.157), *Div.* 1.50.114.

[30]   *Div.* 1.50.114.

[31]   *AR* 1.34.5. The element of prophecy also has an important place in Varro's explanation (*LL* 7.36), quoted above.

[32]   *Inst.* 9.4.115.

[33]   P. 432 Lindsay, quoted below.

[34]   The line is also quoted in the *Origo gentis Rom.* 4.4–5; Servius on *Georg.* 1.11 quotes Varro *LL* 7.36 in part.

[35]   All these sources are quoted by Havet (above, n. 6) pp. 310–11, and Luiselli (above, n. 3), pp. 105–14. In addition, [Acro] on Horace *Epist.* 2.1.158 assigns the name to king Saturn's reign.

[36]   *Epist.* 2.1.157–60.

[37]   See G. Wissowa, *Religion und Kultus der Römer*[2] (Munich, 1912), pp. 204–08; K. Latte, *Römische Religionsgeschichte* (Munich, 1960), pp. 254–55; A. Degrassi, *Inscr. Ital.* 13.2 (Rome, 1963), pp. 538–40. The Greek origin of Saturnalia is the subject of the fragment of Accius' *Annales* (above, n. 11).

[38]   *Saturnus* is in the codex, but Paul's epitome has *Sateurnus*, which is usually taken as a mistake for *Saeturnus* (cf. *CIL* XI 6708 = I[2] 449 = *ILS* 2966 = *ILLRP* 255). See Wissowa (above, n. 37), p. 204, n. 8.

[39]   Pp. 124 Lindsay s.v. molucrum, 132 s.v. manuos, 230 s.v. pescia. See B. Maurenbrecher, "Carminum Saliarium reliquiae," *Jahrb. f. cl. Phil.* Suppl. 21 (1894), pp. 313–52.

[40]   Pp. 166 s.v. Naucum: Philologus, Cincius, Stilo, *scriptores glossematorum,* Verrius; 176 s.v. nuscitiosum: Philologus, Opillus Aurelius, Stilo; 512 s.v. vacerram: Stilo, *alii complures,* Philologus.

[41]   P. 192 s.v. ocrem.

[42]   *LL* 7.2; for other references to, and quotations from, the Salii and their songs cf. 5.85, 5.110, 6.14, 6.49, 7.3, 7.26, 7.27, 9.61.

[43]   Cic. *Brut.* 56.205–207; A. Gellius *NA* 16.8.2.

[44]   *LL* 7.26 with *Ann.* 2. Vahlen[2] .See Skutsch, *Studia Enniana*, pp. 20–21.

[45]   *LL* 7.34: qui glossemata interpretati. Among them may be Aurelius Opillus; see *LL* 7.50, 65, 67, 70, 79, 106. The fragments of early anonymous glosses are collected by Funaioli, pp. 111–13.

[46]   Festus cites this work on pp. 150/2, 290, 472, and 476. On Saturn in the *Antiquities*, see R. Agahd's index, pp. 378–79 of his text "M. Terenti Varronis Antiquitatum Rerum Divinarum libri I XIV XV XVI," *Jahrb. f. cl. Phil.* Suppl 24 (1898), pp. 1–220, 367–81.

[47]   Festus *Epit.* p. 3. Maurenbrecher (above, n. 39) pp. 319–20, 322, 328–29, discusses this passage and tries to divide the fragments according to the gods. He emends *in universos homines* to *in universos <deos> omnes.*

[48] See Teuffel (above, n. 25) pp. 127, 276–78, for Stilo's edition and his career. Stilo apparently wrote on antiquities, but direct knowledge of his treatment seems not to have survived Cicero and Varro. For Salian *versus*, see Cic. *de or.* 3.51.197, Varro *LL* 7.27, and Quintilian *Inst.* 1.10.20; cf. Maurenbrecher (above, n. 39), pp. 320–21.

[49] Stilo's attention to Ennius' text is attested by *Anecd. Par.* (Par. 7530) attributed to Suetonius = Aelius *test.* 21 Funaioli (pp. 54–56). See Teuffel (above, n. 25), pp. 73–74. Cf. Fronto, p. 20 Naber = 1.166 *LCL*.

[50] Diomedes, in Keil's *GL* 1.476, describes the Salian Hymns as *spondeum melos* and gives it the Latin name *pes pontificius.* Diomedes (*GL* 1.479) calls the *amphibrachys* a *pes Ianius*, and a *palinbacchius* a *pes Latius* or *Saturnius*. See above, n. 28.

[51] *Brutus* 56.205–207; *Acad. Post.* 1.8.

[52] Cassius Hemina *Ann.* fr. 1 Peter, with the testimonia.

[53] Keil's *GL* 1.288–89 = Barwick, p. 376.

[54] See H. Keil, "Fragmentum Charisii," *Philologus* 3 (1858), pp. 90–98, and Fr. Leo, "Die römische Poesie in der Sullanischen Zeit," *Hermes* 49 (1914), pp. 183–85, reprinted as an appendix to his *Geschichte der röm. Literatur* (Darmstadt, 1967).

[55] See Keil (above, n. 54), pp. 97–98, and Havet (above, n. 6), p. 5, n. 2. Luiselli (above, n. 3), pp. 41, 112, at least cites the passage.

[56] In the correspondence of Cornelius Fronto, p. 67 Naber = 1.174 *LCL*: praeterea multi libri lintei quod ad sacra adtinet.

[57] *EP.* 4.34.3: monitus Cumanos lintea texta sumpserunt. These were in Greek. In the *SHA (Aurel.)* 26.1.7 are cited the linen books of the Ulpia Bibliotheca. Perhaps the author alludes to Livy's early use of *libri lintei* of another kind (*idem*, 2.1). R. Syme, *Ammianus and the Historia Augusta* (Oxford, 1968), pp. 2–3, 98, suspects their very existence.

[58] Aug. *RG* 10 (cf. Dio 51.20.1); Tac. *Ann.* 2.83, *Ann.* 4.9; *SHA* 4.21.5, 13.11.6 (doubtful). For the honors accorded the young Caesares and Germanicus, see the Lex Tabulae Hebanae, lines 4–5, and its bibliography in J.H. Oliver and R.E.A. Palmer, "Text of the Tabula Hebana," *AJP* 75 (1954), pp. 225–27, and S. Weinstock, "The Posthumous Honours of Germanicus," *Mélanges d'archéologie et d'histoire offerts à A. Piganiol* 2 (1966), pp. 891–98.

[59] Fr. 8 Maurenbrecher, pp. 339–41.

[60] Fr. 5 Maurenbrecher, pp. 336–37.

[61] See above, nn. 15–20, 22–23, 57.

[62] Livy 22.1.

[63] Varro *LL* 8.36: . . . cum dico ab Saturni Lua Luam, et ab solvendo luo luam.

[64] *NA* 13.23.1–2.

[65] *Aen.* 3.138–39.

[66] On *Aen.* 3.139. The manuscripts read *Lunae*, which was corrected to *Luae*. This correction found its way into the reference works with the first edition of Wissowa's *Religion und Kultus der Römer* (Munich, 1902), but has not yet come to the attention of the editors of the Harvard Servius. Saturnus, who took on Kronos' legend, acquired the *potestas orbandi* by consuming his children, even though Lua might have promoted the attribution by her mere name.

[67] Macr. *Sat.* 3.9.4–5. The manuscripts also have *Lunam*, which was corrected in 1926. See G. Radke's new arguments in support of this second correction in *Die Götter Altitaliens = Fontes et Commentationes* 3 (Münster, 1965), p. 186. Willis has not noticed the necessary correction of Macrobius in his recent Teubner edition.

[68] Pliny *NH* 3.65 (cf. Plut. *QR* 61) = Soranus fr. 6 Morel, p. 41.

[69] K. Latte, "Ueber eine Eigentumlichkeit des italischen Gottesvorstellung," *Arch. f. Religionsw.* 24 (1926), pp. 252–53; P. Kretschmer, "Nochmals die Hypachäer und Alaksandus," *Glotta* 24 (1935), p. 228, who acutely draws attention to the words *robigus* and *Robigo*; E. Manni, "A proposito del culto di Saturno," *Athenaeum* 16 (1938), pp. 224–26; R.M. Ogilvie, "Some Cults of Early Rome," *Coll. Latomus* 102 (= *Homm. M. Renard*) 1969, p. 566, n. 2. Radke, *op. cit.*, forces the meaning "fresh green" for Lua.

[70]   For the Arval hymn see above, ch. 3, at n. 57. Manni, *loc. cit.*, sees the same connection between *lua* and *lues*, but does not develop it.

[71]   Livy 8.1.1–6; this story is doubted as a doublet of the campaign against Satricum in 346 (Livy 7.27), but the unusual dedication seems to authenticate the events. See Manni, *op. cit.*, pp. 227–28. Paullus' conduct is in Livy 45.33.1–2. For a comparable and explicable sacrificial burning of arms on behalf of Vulcan, see Livy 1.37.5, 8.10.13, 30.6.9, 41.12.6; on behalf of Jupiter Victor, Livy 10.29.14–18; and on behalf of an unnamed god, Plut. *Marius* 22. See Latte, *RRG*, pp. 55, 129.

[72]   It is so attested on the bronze liver of Piacenza. See C. Thulin, *Die Götter des Martianus Capella und der Bronzeleber von Piacenza = Religionsgeschichtliche Versuche und Vorarbeiten* 3 (1906–1907), pp. 29, 41, 74–75, and Manni, *op. cit.* The cult of Mater Matuta was prominent at Satricum (Livy 7.27).

[73]   Manni, *op. cit.*, pp. 228–32.

[74]   Caesius Bassus in *GLK* 6.265–66 = fr. 6, lines 292–300 Mazzarino, pp. 142–43. Cf. *ILLRP* 122 and 335, both triumphal tablets in Saturnians which are not from the Capitol.

[75]   Pol. 21.12.10–14, Livy 37.33.6–7.

[76]   Cato's *Origines* in Cic. *TD* 4.2.3, and *Brut.* 19.75–76, where Cicero goes on to refer to Naevius' epic and Ennius' poetic strictures. See F. Leo, *Geschichte der röm. Literatur*, 1, pp. 18–19.

CHAPTER FIVE

[1]   Lines 78–80 Marx. The text is that of C. Cichorius, *Untersuchungen zu Lucilius* (Berlin, 1908), pp. 240–41.

[2]   F. Marx, *C Lucilii carminum reliquiae* (Leipzig, 1905), vol. 2, *ad loc.*; Cichorius, *ibid.*

[3]   E.H. Warmington, *The Remains of Old Latin*, vol. 3, p. 25, in the "Loeb Classical Library" renders the first sentence, "For what need had he of a phallic emblem thus affixed?"

[4]   Festus p. 142 L. The full text and its restoration are treated below.

[5]   Dio 48.42; *EE* 1, p. 215 = *CIL* VI 1301 = *ILS* 42. In 36, Aemilius Lepidus was chief pontiff.

[6]   See R. Agahd, "M. Terenti Varronis Antiquitatum Rerum Divinarum libri I XIV XV XVI," *Jahrb. class. Philologie* Supplbd. 24 (1898), pp. 123, 158 (*ARD* 1.39c = Tert. *Ap.* 25), 176 (*ARD* 14.59 = Aug. *CD* 4.11, Tert. *ad Nat.* 2.11, Lact. *ID* 1.20.36). Varro died in 27 B.C., but this work, which was partly dedicated to Julius Caesar, was published many years before his death (Cic. *Acad.* 1.3.9–10).

[7]   Tert. *Apol.* 25.3, *ad Nat.* 2.17.3. He calls the one god Sterculus, who is variously called by the Fathers. See Aug. *CD* 18.15 and Lact. *DI* 1.20.30 (below).

[8]   *Ad Nat.* 2.11.11–12: <est et Iu>venta novorum togatorum, virorum iam Fortuna Barbata. <si de nu>ptialibus disseram, Afferenda est ab afferendis <d>otibus ordinata; <sunt, pro pu>dor, et Mutunus et Tutunus et de<a> Pertund<a et> Subigus et Pre<ma> mater.

[9]   Lact. *DI* 1.20.30: colitur . . . Cunina quae infantes tuetur in cunis ac fascinum submovet, et Stercutus qui stercorandi agri rationem primus induxit, et Titinus in cuius sinu pudendo nubentes praesident ut illarum pudicitia prior deus delibasse videatur. Latent wordplay on *cunus/cunae* cannot be ruled out of the discussion, in that Cunina may have suggested Tutinus to the writer or to Varro.

[10]   Arn. 4.7: etiamne Tutunus, cuius inmanibus pudendis horrentique fascino vestras inequitare matronas et auspicabile ducitis et optatis? *Idem.* 4.11: hoscine a nobis deos violari et neglegi sacrilego clamitatis queritaminique contemptu, Lateranum genium focorum, Limentinum praesidem liminum, Pertundam Perficam Noduterensem? et quia non supplices Mutuno procumbimus atque Tutuno, ad interitum res lapsas atque ipsum dicitis mundum leges suas et constituta mutasse? The alphabetical list is drawn on in 4.7–9. See L.W. Daly, *Contributions to a History of*

Alphabetization in Antiquity and the Middle Ages = Coll. Latomus 90 (1967), pp. 52–54.
[11]   *CD* 4.11 (p. 161 D): ipse (*sc.* Iuppiter) sit Mutunus vel Tutunus, qui est apud Graecos Priapus. In the Priapean collection Priapus is described as *mutuniatus* (*Carm. Priap.* 52.10; cf. Mart. 3.73) or armed with a *mutinium rubricatum* (*ibid.* 72). The tool was originally fertilizing and not frightening.
[12]   *CD* 6.9 (p. 265 D): sed quid hoc dicam, cum ibi sit et Priapus nimius masculus, super cuius inmanissimum et turpissimun fascinum sedere nova nupta iubebatur, more honestissimo et religiosissimo matronarum?
[13]   Grueber, *CRCBM* 1, p. 287, no. 2220 with note; Sydenham, *RCC* nos. 691, 692. For the revival of the Priapus type see below.
[14]   See. J. Poucet, *Recherches sur la légende sabine des origines de Rome = Université de Louvain Receuil de Travaux d'Histoire et de Philologie*, ser. 4, fasc. 37 (1967), esp. pp. 384–90; and R.E.A. Palmer, *The Archaic Community of the Romans* (Cambridge, 1970), for lengthy discussions of these antiquarian matters.
[15]   See A. Bruhl, *Liber Pater: Origine et expansion du culte Dionysiaque à Rome et dans le monde romain = Bibl. Ec. Franç. Ath. Rome*, fasc. 175 (1953), pp. 26–27.
[16]   *CD* 6.9, 7.2–3, 7.16, 7.19.
[17]   *CD* 4.11, 6.9, 7.24; see below.
[18]   *CD* 7.21 (pp. 299–300 D) = Varro *ARD* 16.42 Agahd.
[19]   *CD* 7.24 (pp. 305–306 D).
[20]   Verg. *Georg.* 2.371–96 with Servius' comment. Both poet and commentator probably rely on Varro's *Origins of the Theater*. K. Meuli, "Altrömischer Maskenbrauch," *Mus. Helv.* 12 (1955) pp. 206–32, followed by C.A. Van Rooy, *Studies in Classical Satire and Related Literary Theory* (Leiden, 1966), pp. 5–7, is quite wrong in removing Bacchus and substituting the Lares. He does not exploit the material in Augustine. The Lares were not the only deities kept at intersections, and not all the Lares are found there.
[21]   The principal discussions of the deity, besides Poucet's (above, n. 14) are K. Vahlert *RE* 16 (1933), cols. 979–87, G. Wissowa, *Religion und Kultus der Römer*² (Munich, 1912), pp. 169 and 243–44, K. Latte, *Römische Religionsgeschichte* (Munich, 1960), p. 69, G. Radke *Die Götter Altitaliens = Fontes et Commentationes* 3 (1965), pp. 225–26 and 305. Also, see S. Weinstock *RE* 6A2 (1937), cols. 1538–40 on the Sodales Titii.
[22]   Pers. *Sat.* 1.19–21.
[23]   Palmer, *op. cit.*, p. 217.
[24]   *LL* 5.85. The restoration of the text is as certain as can be. Cf, Serv. on Verg. *Ecl.* 1.57 (and Philarg. *ad loc.*): "palumbes." columbae quas vulgus tetas vocat.
[25]   Palmer, *op. cit.*, pp. 93–95.
[26]   See the works cited in note 21.
[27]   Poucet, *op. cit.*, pp. 386–87; see below.
[28]   Poucet amusingly lists a few modern usages. Without attempting to grace them with such lexical citation as Poucet gives, I can add the English "cock" and "pussy."
[29]   See Ernout-Meillet, *Dictionaire étymologique de la langue latine*⁴ *s. vv.* gaius, titus. These birds were presumably sighted at the moment of birth, just as the time of day or month was kept in other praenomens. H. Petersen, "The Numeral Praenomina of the Romans," *TAPA* 93 (1962), pp. 347–54, also points out that the praenomens from months' names were later applied as cognomens. In this vein can be remarked bird cognomina (e.g. Corvus, Aquilus, etc.), which, of course, may have originated as omens in a man's lifetime or as derisive nicknames from a man's aspect or habit. One of the pieces of grave pottery found with the piece given to the Nine Gods at Ardea (see above, ch. 3, sect. 5) bears the inscription *titoio(m)*, which Vetter, no. 364 a, interprets as a possessive adjective of the personal name Titus. However, it may be a divine name of the Ardeate Titinus, either in the dative or accusative case. For Gaius and Gaia, see Plut. *QR* 30; for Gaia, Cic. *Mur.* 12.27, Quint. 1.7.28, Festus *Epit.* 85 L, and [Val. Max.] *Praen.* 7. On the wedding auspices, see esp. Cic. *Div.* 1.16.28 and above, n. 10. For related

details see Marquardt-Mau, *Privatleben der Römer*[2], pp. 47–50. In his comment on Plut. *QR* 30, H.J. Rose remarks that "Gaius" is a stock name on charms.

[30]   See Degrassi on *ILLRP* 69, 70, and above, ch. 1, sect. 8. At Dodona doves were thought to utter the prophecies of Zeus, just as the woodpecker of Mars made oracular utterances in central Italy; see H.W. Parke, *The Oracles of Zeus: Dodona, Olympia, Ammon* (Cambridge, Mass., 1967), pp. 34–45, 64 ff; see above, ch. 3, sect. 3.

[31]   Pliny *NH* 10.104–105, 146–47, 158–59; cf. Isidore *Etym.* 12.7.60–62.

[32]   Pliny *NH* 30.144; cf. 18.160, 28.265.

[33]   *Ibid.* 30.76, 78, 109–10.

[34]   *CIL* XV 7065 = I[2] 573 = *ILLRP* 1252. See Steier *RE* 16.1 (1933), cols. 906–907.

[35]   The text is that of Lindsay, p. 142, with the lineation of that work.

[36]   Paulus' entry is a good example of his rather inaccurate method of epitome: Pudicitiae signum Romae colebatur, quod nefas erat attingi nisi ab ea quae semel nupsisset.

[37]   Similar examples in Festus are pp. 270 "Plebeiae Pudicitiae,"416 "Statae Matris," and, in Paulus' epitome, p. 52 "Clitellae."

[38]   Festus p. 372 L.

[39]   See Stein *RE* 5 (1903), cols. 1419–24, and R. Syme *RR* pp. 234–35, 411–12. On Caesar's sacrifices, see below.

[40]   *CD* 7.3 (p. 275 D); cf. *CD* 6.9, 7.2, 7.16, 7.19.

[41]   *CD* 7.21 (p. 299 D).

[42]   *NH* 28.39: cur non et haec credamus rite fieri, extranei interventu aut, si dormiens spectetur infans, a nutrice terna adspui in os? quamquam religione eum tutatur et fascinus, imperatorum quoque, non solum infantium, custos, qui deus inter sacra Romana Vestalibus colitur et currus triumphantium, sub his pendens, defendit medicus invidiae, iubetque eosdem respicere similis medicina linguae ut sit exorata a tergo Fortuna gloriae carnifex. This Vestal worship fits well their care to agricultural fertility (Radke, *op. cit.*, p. 329). Otherwise, it is neglected as insignificant; see Wissowa, *op. cit.*, p. 243 n. 6. Macrobius, *Sat.* 1.6.9–10, refers to the *bulla* which the triumphator wore against envy. On the appearance of this kind of amulet on triumphal monuments, see I.S. Ryberg, *Rites of the State Religion in Roman Art* = *MAAR* 22 (1955), pp. 21, 146.

[43]   *ID* 1.20.36, quoted in n. 9. See Varro *ARD* frs. 14.23 a b, 91 Agahd. Macrobius, *ibid.*, also refers to the *bulla* worn by children. Perhaps Pliny and Macrobius took their complementary information from a common authority where the *bulla* and *fascinus* were treated together.

[44]   It was called a *suffibulum* from the *fibula*; see Festus pp. 474, 475, and cf. Varro's false etymology, *LL* 6.21.

[45]   I.S. Ryberg, *op. cit.*, pp. 41, 52, 71, and figs. 26, 27, 36f.

[46]   H. Jordan, *Topographie der Stadt Rom im Alterthum*, vol. 1, pt. 2 (Berlin, 1885), p. 419.

[47]   H. Nissen, *Ital. Landeskunde* (Berlin, 1902) 2.356–57.

[48]   Cf. M. Pallottino *TLE* 336: Fuflunsul Pachies Velclthi. See C. Koch, *Gestirnverehrung im alten Italien: Sol Indiges und der Kreis der Di Indigetes* = *Frankfurter Srudien zur Religion und Kultur der Antike* 3 (1933), pp. 60–63, and Bruhl, *op. cit.*, pp. 70–81; cf. n. 64, below.

[49]   Hor. *Sat.* 2.3.143; Martial 1.104.9, 2.53.4, 3.49.1.

[50]   M.W. Frederiksen and J.B. Ward Perkins, "The Ancient Road Systems of the Central and Northern Ager Faliscus (Notes on Southern Etruria, 2)." *PBSR* 25 (1957), p. 80, discuss this *diverticulum*, which is drawn on Figure 1 of p. 68.

[51]   See above, n. 18.

[52]   *CIL* VI 2120, 10231, 10233, 10239, 10241, 10247, 36364. Cf. Front. *Aqu.* 5, 7, 8, 9, 11, 14.

[53]   *NH* 2.211: ad Aras Mutias in Veiente et apud Tusculanum et in silva Ciminia loca sunt in quibus in terram depacta non extrahuntur. in Crustumino natum faenum ibi noxium, extra salubre est. The second sentence illustrates that old topographical designations were retained to record prodigious happenings or conditions.

[54] See Nissen, *op. cit.*, p. 260, and vol. 2, p. 361, following Nibby; Bormann on *CIL* XI 3778; L.R. Taylor, *Local Cults in Etruria* = *PMAAR* 2 (1923), pp. 38–39, makes the same connection and prefers *Mutiae.*

[55] Ogilvie on Livy 2.13.5, following Pais.

[56] See W. Schulze *ZGLE*, pp. 193–94, on Mut(t)ii, Muttenus etc. Cf. *CIE* 1005, 3083.

[57] Col. 3, 14; 4, 5 and 18; 6, 1 (?) Runes.

[58] Livy 42.2.4: in Veienti apud Rementem lapidatum. This *hapax legomenon* may be a manuscript corruption of *Tromentum.* The *campus Tromentus* gave its name to the Roman Tribus Tromentina (Festus, *Epit.*, 505 L).

[59] Festus p. 204 L.

[60] Livy 26.34.10.

[61] Pliny *NH* 2.230 and 7.19. Julius Obsequens is a veritable mine of details in this respect; see his *Liber prodigiorum* 11, 12, 14, 27, 41, 43, 54.

[62] See Livy 41.9.5, 13.1, 13.3 for prodigies in the Ager Crustuminus of the defunct Crustumerium (cf. Pliny *NH* 2.211, 3.52, 54, and Livy 39.55.9).

[63] For the medieval sources and their criticism see H. Simonsfeld, *Jahrbücher d. deut. Reiches unter Friedrich I* (Leipzig, 1908), vol. 1, pp. 331, 679–82. The ancient and medieval history of this lake is summarized by J.B. Ward-Perkins and M.E. Mallett in G.E. Hutchinson *et al.,* "Ianula: An Account of the History and Development of the Lago di Monterosi, Latium, Italy," *Trans. Amer. Philos. Soc.* n.s. 60, 4, (1970), pp. 10–16; the poor land drainage even in times of settlement suggests why people of the area might have sought the aid of a fertility god. See Vergil *Aen.* 6.106–107, 126–27 for the *ianua* that served as entrance to the underworld by Lake Avernus. The adjective *Ianulus* referring to the god Janus is met in Paul's *Epitome* p. 3, s.v. *axamenta;* see above, ch. 4. On the *ianus* at which the Vestals kept the Vestalia, see below. The word *mentula* cannot be restored to Festus, because it means the physical penis whereas *fascinus* and the like are representations thereof.

[64] Livy 39.8.3–4, 9.1, 17.6. See Bruhl, *op. cit.*, pp. 82–87, 93.

[65] Besides consultation of Platner and Ashby, *TDAR*, under the appropriate entry, the reader will easily find full information and discussion in G. Lugli, *Monumenti minori del Foro Romano* (Rome, 1947), pp. 165–92, and F. Castagnoli, "Il tempio dei Penati e la Velia," *RFIC* 74 (1946), pp. 157–65.

[66] See esp. Dion. Hal. *AR* 1.68–69, 2.66, and below, n. 78. The Penates' cult was closely linked to the Vestal cult. In A.D. 59 the Fratres Arvales sacrificed to the Penates in front of the house of Cn. Domitius Ahenobarbus (*CIL* VI 2042 = *ILS* 230) which was situated on the Sacra Via (*CIL* VI 2041 = *ILS* 229; VI 32352; Sen. *Contr.* 9.4.18) and also contained its own baths (Sen. *loc. cit.*). Since the ancients could not distinguish between the Velian Hill and the Sacra Via (Summa) at this point, one must assume that the Sacred Way here ascended a part of the Velia.

[67] *Res Gestae* 19, 35.2.

[68] Martial 1.70.9–10. On this Bacchic shrine also see Bruhl, *op. cit.*, pp. 197–99.

[69] *CD* 7.4; see above. An inscription from Samnite Telesia of 13 B.C. records the erection of a statue group of Liber and Priapiscus (*CIL* IX 2197 = *ILS* 3372/3). Priapus and Liber are joined in a fragmentary and abbreviated text of unknown Roman provenience in which the *sigill. Priap. Liber.* finds mention (*CIL* VI 564). This document is not discussed by N. Turchi in the entry "Liber" of the *Diz. Epigr.* The Roman agricultural cult of Dionysus/Bacchus can be traced back at least to the fifth century B.C., when the Arval Hymn incorporated the already latinized *thriambos* as *triumpe* (*CIL* I² 2 = *ILS* 5039 = *ILLRP* 4).

[70] Dio 46.33.3.

[71] Lugli, *op. cit.* 174–79. The material document is a piece of the circular marble epistyle on which was carved a Maenad and the remains of an inscription (Figure 17): — An]toninus/ —imp(erator) II/— r]estituit (*CIL* VI 36920). For the two shrines and their remains, see E. Nash, *Pictorial Dictionary of Ancient Rome*, 2nd ed. (New York and Washington, 1968),

vol. 1, pp. 165–68 (Bacchus, sacellum), and vol. 2, pp. 34–35 (Magna Mater, tholos).
[72]   Lugli, *loc. cit.* It is discussed below.
[73]   T.L. Donaldson, *Architectura Numismatica or Architectural Medals of Classic Antiquity* (London, 1859), repr. as *Architecture on Greek and Roman Coins and Medals* (Chicago, 1965), treats the shrine (no. 37) as the "temple of Flora or Pomona," although he knew the view of Venuti that the god is Bacchus. See H. Cohen, *Description historique des monnaies frappées dans l'Empire romain* (Paris, 1880–92), vol. 2, p. 396, no. 1187; Lugli, *op. cit.*, p. 174, fig. 49; and *idem, Roma antica* (Rome, 1946) pp. 219–20, fig. 53.
[74]   Ryberg, *op. cit.*, p. 184 n. 46.
[75]   Lugli notes the remains of Bacchus' shrine by the number 42 on pl. 1 of *Monumenti minori* ecc., = pl. 4 of *Roma antica*, and the inset of his and I. Gismondi's *Forma Urbis Romae imperatorum aetate* (Novara, 1955). On the last map he has slightly altered its location. On the two earlier plans the houses are noted with a "P" but have no note on the *Forma*. Lugli locates the shrine of Tutunus Mutunus (*sic*) beside the Fornix Fabianus by guessing at the site of Calvinus' house (*Roma antica*, p. 88 and pl. 3). The two locations of the shrine on Lugli's maps can be explained by the fact that one marks the find site and the other its present situation. These are clearly marked on Nash's plan, *op. cit.*, vol. 1, p. 165 (cf. the plan, fig. 595, on p. 485).
[76]   See above and below.
[77]   Suet. *Jul.* 46; Dio 54.27.
[78]   See above n. 42. For the Trojan origins of the *sacra* and the Penates see F. Bömer, *Rom und Troja* (Baden-Baden, 1951), and A. Alföldi, *Die trojanischen Urahnen der Römer* (Rektoratsprogr., J. 1956, Basel, 1957), and above, n. 66.
[79]   See *CIL* XVI 10, 11 (=*ILS* 1989), 13, diplomas of 70 and 71 A.D., which record the Capitoline record of the document: in podio arae gentis Iuliae latere dextro ante signum Liberi Patris. Apparently this place of Liberian worship existed under the republic (Cic. *Ad Att.* 6.1.12; Ovid *F.* 3.713–90; see Turchi, *op. cit.*, p. 831).
[80]   S. Weinstock, *Divus Julius* (Oxford, 1971) pp. 342–46, would reject all the forebodings of Caesar's death as inventions after the fact, save for that on the Lupercalia which is reported by Cicero, *Div.* 1.52.119. Even Cicero has recorded an inauthentic omen according to Weinstock. In a word, Weinstock denies the authenticity of the ancient reports because they are not found in Cicero, or because, he says, Cicero is wrong in one instance. Resort to the argument from silence in Cicero is hazardous, especially in this case, as can be illustrated by the brevity of Cicero's account of Ateius and Crassus (*Div.* 1.16.29–30); see J. Bayet, "Les malédictions du tribun C. Ateius Capito," *Coll. Latomus* 1960 (*Mélanges Dumézil*), pp. 31–45 = *Croyances et rites dans la Rome antique* (Paris, 1971), pp. 353–65. Cicero does not claim to report a list of omens, prodigies, and dreams occurring before Caesar's death. Weinstock does not attempt to find a special religious occasion for Caesar's sacrifice on 15 March, other than the usual offerings ". . . when he left his house and before he entered the senate," because he holds that the entire story of that day's religious proceedings is a *post mortem* fabrication flawed (as indeed it is) with inconsistencies.
[81]   See A. Degrassi *II* 13.2, pp. 423–24 for quotation and discussion of the authorities; also see A.K. Michels, *The Calendar of the Roman Republic* (Princeton, 1967), p. 79.
[82]   *F.* 3.697–710.
[83]   Degrassi, *op. cit.*, pp. 425–26. See Censorinus *DN* 20.1 for mention of the Lavinian calendar different from the Roman.
[84]   Degrassi, *op. cit.*, pp. 521–22.
[85]   See above, n. 80. The chief sources are Cic. *Div.* 1.52.119, with Pease's commentary, Suet. *Jul.* 81, Appian *BC* 2.116, Plut. *Caes.* 63; and Val. Max. 8.11.2: "eo cum forte mane uterque (*sc.* Caesar et Spurinna) in domum Calvini Domitii ad officium convenisset . . . ." The chance of the meeting (*forte*) involves Spurinna assisting, too, at this sacrifice. Plutarch also mentions morning sacrifices and prophecies. Although doubts on the circumstances of the sacrifices on

15 March must be entertained, the occasion at Calvinus' house can be taken as legitimate. Since even Weinstock (above, n. 80) grants that all the reports ultimately reach back to sources contemporary with the murder, the heaven-sent signs will have commanded credence soon after the death. If what I have reconstructed was only believed to have truly happened, the transfer of Mutinus Titinus will have occurred under the influence of that belief. What is confused in the ancient stories is the locality of the sacrifice: Curia Pompeia or house of Calvinus. To this confusion is added the possible extension of Spurinna's role beyond the Lupercalia. The normal offering incumbent upon a senate president (Gellius *NA* 14.7.9) has been assumed by several authorities as the second occasion of Caesar's foreboding sacrifice. No doubt, Caesar sacrificed at the Lupercalia of 15 February (Cicero); other sources mention the thirty fatal days or imply them. The sacrifice at Calvinus' house took place in the morning (Val. Max); Caesar sacrificed before entering the senate after the fifth hour of 15 March (Suet. and Plut.). It is not surprising that the anxious murderers counted the hours Caesar kept them waiting. On the Etruscan Spurinnae see W.V. Harris, *Rome in Etruria and Umbria* (Oxford, 1971), pp. 28–30, 315.

[86] Suet. *Jul.* 81.3. The comparable formation is the augural *ardeola* (Pliny *NH* 10.164, 204, 207; 11.140; 30.140). Otherwise the name is variously attested in the bilingual glosses, sometimes as a translation of *basiliskos* "wren," *spinnos* (*spiza*) "chaffinch," or merely *ornuphion*; see Forcellini's *Lexicon*. The Latin word bears all the marks of an augural designation irrespective of species.

[87] See Degrassi, *op. cit.*, pp. 467–68. On Vesta and Janus, see L.A. Holland, *Janus and the Bridge* =*PMAAR* 21 (1961), pp. 283–84. For Vesta and her ass see Ryberg, *op. cit.*, p. 62 with fig. 33a.

[88] Diod. Sic. 36.13; Pliny *NH* 7.182; Plut. *Marius* 17.5–6. Diodorus mentions no temple or oracle, Pliny cites the tribune's sudden death. Plutarch records oracle and the senate's resolution συγκλήτου . . . τῆς θεῷ ναὸν ἐπινίκιον ἱδρύσασθαι ψηφισαμένης, as well as the tribune's conduct.

[89] Val. Max. 2.5.6; 4.4.8; 6.9.14; Suet. *Jul.* 11; Plut. *Caes.* 6.1–3; Vell. Pat. 2.43. For references to the several Marian buildings and their conjectured sites, see Platner-Ashby, *TDAR*, pp. 259–60, 541–42, to which should be added the allusion in Cic. *Font.* 5.12. These *tropaea* are not to be confused with the paintings commemorating Marius' northern victories, which were displayed in the Forum (Cic. *De orat.* 2.66.266; Pliny *NH* 35.25; Quint. 6.3.38). In general on the victory monuments of Marius, see J.-C. Richard, "La victoire de Marius," *Mél. Arch. Hist.* 77 (1965), pp. 69–86, and T. Hölscher, *Victoria Romana* (Mainz, 1967), pp. 140–42.

[90] Asc. p. 13 C; cf. Cic. *Leg.* 2.11.28. St. Weinstock, *RE* 8A2 (1958), cols. 2014–15, holds that Vica Pota was indeed a goddess of victory from the outset. All indications point to a shrine much older than *ca.* 100, whose precise identity was obscure even to learned Romans. Previously the Magna Mater was associated with Victory. In 205 B.C., when the sacred stone was brought from Asia, it was temporarily housed in the temple of Victory, from which it was moved to its own temple a year later (Livy 29.14.13–14). C. Hoeing, "Vica Pota," *AJP* 24 (1903), pp. 323–26, argues that the goddess' names intended "mistress of the people" or "mistress of towns," and hence that she was identified with the Cybele who wore the mural crown. At the same time, however, he rejects the earlier identification of Vica Pota with the Magna Mater found on the Haterii relief, and makes no mention of Marian connections with Vica Pota or of the passage in Martial.

[91] G. Lugli, *Monumenti minori* ecc., pp. 41–50. The inscription (*CIL* VI 1303, 1304 = I² 762, 763 =*ILS* 43, 43a =*II* 13.3.71 =*ILLRP* 392) falsely attributes a third triumph to Aemilius Paulus. For the remains see Nash, *op. cit.*, 1.398–400. Florus (1.37.6) makes this interesting observation on another monument of the Allobrogic war: . . . et Domitius Ahenobarbus et Fabius Maximus ipsis quibus dimicaverant locis saxeas erexere turres, et desuper exornata armis hostilibus tropaea fixerunt, cum hic mos inusitatus fuerit nostris. This memorial stood at the site of his victory (cf. Strabo 4.1.11 and Apollodorus in *FGH* 2B 1027 F 25); see above, ch. 3, sect. 17.

[92]   Pliny *NH* 7.166; Val. Max. 2.5.6. See above, ch. 3, sect. 17.

[93]   Seneca, *Apoc.* 6, with the critical comment of Buecheler-Heraeus; Strabo 4.1.11, *ILS* 212 (Claudius' speech), Pliny *NH* 3.36, Tac. *Hist.* 65–66; Sall. *CC* 41, cf. E. Badian, *FC*, p. 264. See above, ch. 3, sect. 17.

[94]   E.A. Sydenham, *The Coinage of the Roman Republic* (London, 1952) nos. 584, 586, 588. The horn is also figured on the Caesarian coinage; see C. Ampolo, "L'Artemide di Marsiglia e la Diana dell'Aventino," *PP* fasc. 130–133 (1970), pp. 200–201.

[95]   Plut. *Mar.* 27.4. For the strangeness of the trumpets, see Diod. Sic. 5.30. The din of the Gauls' battle music of horn and trumpet was known to Polybius (2.30.6), who thought it common to the barbarians of northern Italy in 225 B.C.

[96]   Val. Max. 4.4.8.

[97]   See Nash, *loc. cit.* (above, n. 71). The modern history of this relief, and of the entire burial plot with its buildings and furnishings, is treated by A. Giuliano, "Documenti per servire allo studio del monumento degli Haterii," *Atti Acc. Naz. Lincei Mem. Classe Sc. mor. stor. filol.* ser. 8, vol. 13 (1967–68), pp. 477–82, with 48 figs.

[98]   Nash, *ibid.*

[99]   Val. Max. 3.6.6; Pliny *NH* 33.150; cf. Macr. *Sat.* 1.19.4. See Richard, *op. cit.*, pp. 78–80, 84.

[100]   Degrassi *II* 13.2, p. 426.

[101]   Platner-Ashby, *TDAR* s.v. horrea piperataria; R. Valentini and G. Zucchetti, *Codice topografica della città di Roma* vol. 1 (= *R. Ist. Stor. Ital. per il Medio Evo. Fonti per la storia d'Italia* vol. 81) 1941, pp. 274–75; Nash, *op. cit.*, 1.485–87.

[102]   The colossus of Nero, later of the Sun, which Martial mentions before the shrines of Lyaeus and Cybele, was moved to make room for Hadrian's structure (*SHA Hadrian* 19.12–13).

[103]   Suet. *Dom.* 13; cf. Martial 8.65, Dio 68.1; see L.A. Holland, *op. cit.*, pp. 92–107. Mrs. Holland does not even remark the interesting design of Domitian's arch of Marius. On his coins Domitian records a single type of arch or gate surmounted by two elephant-drawn triumphal cars; see Donaldson, *op. cit.*, no. 57, and H. Mattingly, *Coins of the Roman Empire in the British Museum* 2 (London, 1930), p. xciii and Domitian nos. 303, 433, 476, with pl. 71.6 and 81.1. Domitian's selfishness in recording only his name on structures which he merely rebuilt or refurbished is noted by Suetonius (*Dom.* 5). For a full treatment of the problems concerning the triumphal monuments, see F. Coarelli, "La porta trionfale e la via dei trionfi," *Dialoghi di Archeologia* 2 (1968), pp. 55–103.

[104]   See above, n. 13, and Mattingly and Sydenham, *RIC* 2, pp. 306, 776, and Mattingly, *CREBM* 3, p. 132 n. 675.

[105]   See R.P. Longden, *CAH* 11.210–12.

Bibliography

Agahd, R., "M. Terentii Varronis Antiquitatum Rerum Divinarum libri I XIV XV XVI," *Jahrbücher für classische Philologie* Supplbd. 24. Leipzig, 1898, pp. 1–220 (with indices, pp. 367–81).

Alföldi, A., "Hasta–Summa Imperii: The Spear as Embodiment of Sovereignty in Rome," *AJA* 63 (1959) pp. 18–20.

Alföldi, A., *Early Rome and the Latins* (Ann Arbor, n.d. [1965]).

Altmann, W., *Die römischen Grabaltäre der Kaiserzeit* (Berlin, 1905).

Ambrosch, J.A., *De sacerdotibus curialibus* (Bratislava, 1840).

Ampolo, C., "L'Artemide di Marsiglia e la Diana dell'Aventino," *PP* fasc. 130–33 (1970) pp. 200–210.

Basanoff, V., "Evocatio: Étude d'un rituel militaire romain," *Bibliothèque de l'École des Hautes Etudes, Sciences Religieuses,* Vol. 61. Paris, 1947.

Beloch, K.J., *Römische Geschichte bis zum Beginn der punischen Kriege* (Berlin and Leipzig, 1926).

Bérard, J., *La colonisation grecque*, 2nd ed. (Paris, 1957).

Besnier, M., *L'Ile tibérine dans l'antiquité, BEFAR* 87 (1902).

Bömer, F., *Rom und Troja* (Baden-Baden, 1951).

Bömer, F., *P. Ovidius Naso: Die Fasten*, 2 vols. (Heidelberg, 1957).

Bömer, F., "Untersuchungen über die Religion der Sklaven in Griechenland und Rom. Erster Teil: Die wichtigsten Kulte und Religion in Rom und im lat. Westen," *Akad. Wiss. Lit. Abh. Geistes- u. Sozialwiss. Kl. Mainz* (1957), pp. 375–580.

Broughton, T.R.S., *The Magistrates of the Roman Republic, Philological Monograph of the Amer. Phil. Assn.* 15, 2 vols. and suppl. (1951–1960), usually here cited by year.

Bruhl, A., *Liber Pater: Origine et expansion du culte Dionysiaque à Rome et dans le monde romain, BEFAR* 175 (1953).

Bulard, M., *La religion dans . . . Délos, BEFAR* 131 (1926).

Cary, M., and Warmington, E.H., *The Ancient Explorers* (Baltimore, 1963).

Castagnoli, F., "Il Campo Marzio nell'antichità," *Atti Acc. Naz. dei Lincei, Mem. Cl. Sci. mor. stor. filol.* ser. 8, vol. 1, fasc. 4 (1947).

Castagnoli, F., "I luoghi connessi con l'arrivo di Enea nel Lazio (Troia, Sol Indiges, Numicus)," *Arch. Cl.* 19 (1967), pp. 235–47.

Charles-Picard, G., *Les religions de l'Afrique antique* (Paris, 1954).

Cohen, H., *Description historique des monnaies frappées dans l'Empire romain* (Paris, 1880–92).

Cole, T., "The Saturnian Verse," *YCS* 21 (1969), pp. 1–73.

Colini, A.M., "Aedes Veiovis inter Arcem et Capitolium," *BC* 70 (1942), pp. 5–56.

Colonna, G., Garbini, G., and Pallottino, M., "Scavi nel santuario etrusco di Pygri," *Arch. Cl.* 16 (1964), pp. 49–117.

Colonna, G., "Il santuario di Pygri alla luce delle recenti scoperte," *SE* 33 (1965), pp. 201–12.

Colonna, G., "The Sanctuary at Pygri in Etruria," *Archaeology* (U.S.A.) 19 (1966), pp. 11–23.

Conway, R.S., Whatmough, J., and Johnson, S.E., *The Prae-Italic Dialects of Italy*, 3 vols. (Cambridge, Mass., 1933).

Cook, A.B., *Zeus: A Study in Ancient Religion* (repr. New York, 1964).

Cristofani, M., "Sulla paleografia delle iscrizioni etrusche di Pygri," *Arch. Cl.* 18 (1966), pp. 103–109.

Daube, D., *Forms of Roman Legislation* (Oxford, 1956).

Degrassi, A., *Scritti vari di antichità*, 2 vols. (Rome, 1962).

Degrassi, A., *Inscriptiones Italiae*, vol. 13. fasc. 2 (Fasti anni Numani et Iuliani) Rome, 1963.

De Sanctis, G., *Storia dei Romani*, vols. 1–2, 2nd ed. (Florence, 1956, 1960), vol. 4, pt. 2, tome 1 (Florence, 1953).

Deubner, L., *De Incubatione capita quattuor* (Leipzig, 1900).

Devoto, G., "Considerazioni sulle lamine auree di Pyrgi," *SE* 34 (1966), p. 218.

De Vries, J., *Keltische Religion, Die Religionen der Menschkeit* 18 (Stuttgart, 1961).

Diels, H., *Sibyllinische Blätter* (Berlin, 1890).

Donaldson, T.L., *Architectura Numismatica or Architectural Medals of Classic Antiquity* (London, 1859), *Ancient Architecture on Greek and Roman Coins and Medals* (Chicago, 1965).

Durante, M., "Le formule conclusive dei testi etruschi di Pyrgi," *Rendic. Accad. Naz. Lincei* 20 (1965), pp. 308–21.

Ernout, A., and Meillet, A., *Dictionnaire étymologique de la langue latine*, 4th ed. (Paris, 1959).

Ernout, A., *Le dialecte ombrien: Lexique du vocabulaire des "Tables Eugubines" et des Inscriptions* (Paris, 1961).

Fiesel, E., "Namen des griechischen Mythos im Etruskischen," *ZVZ* Ergänzhft 5 (1928).

Fischer, W., und Rix, H., "Forschungsbericht: Die phönizisch-etruskischen Texten der Goldplättchen von Pyrgi," *Göttinger Gelehrten Anzeiger* 220 (1968), pp. 64–94.

Fitzmyer, J.A., S.J., "The Phoenician Inscription from Pyrgi," *JAOS* 86 (1966), pp. 285–97.

Fowler, M., and Wolfe, R.G., *Materials for the Study of the Etruscan Language*, 2 vols. (Madison, 1965).

Fowler, W.W., "Was the Flaminica Dialis Priestess of Juno?" *CR* 9 (1895), pp. 474–76, *Roman Essays and Interpretations* (Oxford, 1920), pp. 52–55.

Fraenkel, E., *Horace* (Oxford, 1957).

Gabba, E., "Considerazioni sulla tradizione letteraria sulle origini della Repubblica," *Fondation Hardt, Entretiens* 13 (1967), pp. 135–74.

Galinsky, G.K., *Aeneas, Sicily and Rome* (Princeton, 1969).

Gasperini, L., "La più antica dedica a Dite," *Epigraphica* 32 (1970), pp. 35–49.

Gelzer, M., *Caesar, Politician and Statesman*, Engl. tr. (Cambridge, Mass., 1968).

Giannelli, G., *Culti e miti della Magna Graecia: Contributo alla storia più antica delle colonie greche in occidente, Università di Napoli, Centro di Studi per la Magna Graecia* 2 (1963).

Goldmann, E., *Beiträge zur Lehre vom indogermanischen Character der etruskischen Sprache*, 2 vols. (Heidelberg, 1930).

Gordon, A.E., "The Cults of Lanuvium," *University of California Publications in Classical Archaeology* 2 (1938).

Grueber, H.A., *Coins of the Roman Republic in the British Museum*, 3 vols., (London, 1910).

Guarducci, M., "Tre cippi latini arcaici con iscrizioni votive," *BC* 72 (1946–48), pp. 1–10.

Guarducci, M., "Cippo latino con dedica ad Enea," *Bullettino del Museo della Civiltà Romana* (published with *BC* 76) 19 (1956–58), pp. 3–13.

Halliday, W.R., *Greek Divination: A Study of its Methods and Principles* (London, 1913).

Hamilton, M., *Incubation: Or the Cure of Diseases in Pagan Temples and Christian Churches* (London, 1906).

Harris, W.V., *Rome in Etruria and Umbria* (Oxford, 1971).

Henzen, G., *Acta Fratrum Arvalium* (Berlin, 1874).

Hermann, W., *Römische Götteraltäre* (Kallmunz, 1961).

Heurgon, J., "The Inscriptions of Pyrgi," *JRS* 56 (1966), pp. 1–15.

Holland, L.A., *Janus and the Bridge, Papers and Monographs of the American Academy in Rome* 21 (1961).

Jory, E.J., "Associations of Actors in Rome," *Hermes* 98 (1970), pp. 223–36.

Koch, C., *Gestirnverehrung im Alten Italien: Sol Indiges und der Kreis der Di Indigetes, Frankfurter Studien zur Religion und Kultur der Antike* 3 (1933).

Koch, C., *Der römische Juppiter, Frankfurter Studien zur Religion und Kultur der Antike* 14 (1937), repr. Darmstadt, 1968.

Kolbe, H.-G., "Lare Aineia?" *Röm. Mitt.* 77 (1970), pp. 1–9.

Lambrechts, R., "Essai sur les magistrates de républiques étrusques," *Et. Phil. Arch. Hist. Anc. Publ. Inst. Hist. Belge de Rome* 7 (1959).

Latte, K., *Römische Religionsgeschichte* (Munich, 1960).

Le Bonniec, H., *Le culte de Cérès à Rome* (Paris, 1958).

Leo, F., *Geschichte der römischen Literatur* 1 (Berlin, 1913), reprinted Darmstadt, 1967, with "Die römische Poesie in der sullanischen Zeit," *Hermes* 49 (1914), pp. 161–95, on pp. 499–532.

Leumann, M., *Lateinische Laut- und Formenlehre* (Munich, 1963).

Lugli, G., *Roma antica* (Rome, 1946).

Lugli, G., *Monumenti minori del Foro Romano* (Rome, 1947).

Manganaro, G., "Un senatus consultum in greco dei Lanuvini e il rinnovo della *cognatio* con i Centuripini," *Rend. Acc. Arch. Lett. Bell. Arti Napoli* n.s. 37 (1962), pp. 23–44.

Manni, E., "A proposito del culto di Saturno," *Athenaeum* 16 (1938), pp. 224–38.

Marconi, G., "La cronologia di Livio Andronico," *Atti Acc. Naz. Lincei. Mem. Cl. Sc. mor. stor. filol.* ser. 8, vol. 12 (1966), pp. 123–214.

Mattingly, H.B., "The Date of Livius Andronicus," *CQ* 51 (1957), pp. 159–63.

Maule, Q.F., and Smith, H.R.W., "Votive Religion at Caere: Prolegomena," *University of California Publications in Classical Archaeology* 4 (1959).

Maurenbrecher, B., "Carminum Saliarium reliquiae," *Jahrb. für Cl. Phil.* Supplbd. 21 (1894), pp. 313–52.

Mengarelli, R., "Il luogo e i materiali del tempio di '*HPA* a Caere," *SE* 10 (1936), pp. 80–86.

Nash, E., *Pictorial Dictionary of Ancient Rome*, 2nd ed., 2 vols., (New York and Washington, 1968).

Nilsson, M.P., "Studien zur Vorgeschichte des Weihnachtsfestes," *Archiv für Religionsw.* 19 (1916–19), pp. 50–150, *Opusc. Sel.* 1 (1951), pp. 214–311.

Nissen, H., *Italische Landeskunde*, 2 vols. (Berlin, 1902).

Noailles, P., *Fas et jus* (Paris, 1948).

Ogilvie, R.M., *A Commentary on Livy Books 1–5* (Oxford, 1965).

Oliver, J.H., *Demokratia, the Gods and the Free World* (Baltimore, 1960).

Olzscha, K., "Die punisch-etruskischen Inschriften von Pyrgi," *Glotta* 44 (1966), pp. 60–108.

Otto, W., "Juno," *Philologus* 64 (1905), pp. 161–223.

Otto, W.F., "Römische Sondergötter," *RhM* 64 (1909) pp. 449–68.

Pallottino, M., "Nuova luce sulla storia di Roma arcaica dalle lamine d'oro di Pyrgi," *SR* 13 (1965), pp. 1–13.

Pallottino, M., "I frammenti di lamina di bronzo con iscrizione etrusca scoperta a Pyrgi," *SE* 34 (1966) pp. 175–209.

Palmer, R.E.A., "Cupra, Matuta, and Venilia Pyrgensis," *Illinois Studies in Language and Literature* 58 (1969), pp. 292–309.

Palmer, R.E.A., *The King and the Comitium, Historia Einzelschrift* 11 (1969).

Palmer, R.E.A., *The Archaic Community of the Romans* (Cambridge, 1970).

Palmer, R.E.A., "Ivy and Jupiter's Priest," *Homenaje a A. Tovar* (Madrid, 1972), pp. 341–47.

Parke, H.W., *The Oracles of Zeus: Dodona, Olympia, Ammon* (Cambridge, Mass., 1967).

Pascal, C.B., *The Cults of Cisalpine Gaul, Coll. Latomus* 75 (1964).

Pease, A.S., "*M. Tulli Ciceronis De Divinatione*," *Illinois Studies in Language and Literature* 6 (1920), pp. 161–500, 8 (1923), pp. 153–474, repr. Darmstadt, 1963.

Pease, A.S., *M. Tulli Ciceronis De Natura Deorum Libri III*, 2 vols. (Cambridge, Mass., 1955, 1958), repr. Darmstadt, 1968.

Pfiffig, A.J., "Uni-Hera-Astarte," *Oestr. Akad. Wiss. Philos.- hist. Kl. Denkschrift* 88.2 (1965).

Phighi, I.B., *De Ludis Saecularibus Populi Romani Quiritium Libri Sex, Pubblicazioni dell'Università Cattolica di S. Cuore* ser. 5, sci. filol., 35 (1941), repr. Amsterdam, 1965.

Platner, S.B., and Ashby, T., *A Topographical Dictionary of Ancient Rome* (Oxford, 1929).

Poucet, J., "Recherches sur la légende sabine des origines de Rome," *Université de Louvain*

Recueil de Travaux d'Histoire et de Philologie, ser. 4, fasc. 37 (1967).

Poultney, J.W., *The Bronze Tables of Iguvium, Philological Monograph of the Amer. Phil. Assn.* 18.

Pugliese Carratelli, G., "Intorno alle lamine di Pyrgi," *SE* 33 (1965), pp. 221–35.

Pugliese Carratelli, G., "Le stelle di Pyrgi," *Par. Pass.* 20 (1965), pp. 303–305.

Radke, G., *Die Götter Altitaliens, Fontes et Commentationes* 3 (Münster, 1965).

Radke, G., "Punicum," *Gymnasium* 73 (1966), pp. 241–44.

Rix, H., *Das etruskische Cognomen* (Wiesbaden, 1963).

Roscher, W.H. (ed.), *Ausführliches Lexicon der griechischen und römischen Mythologie* vol. 2, pt. 1 (Leipzig, 1890–97).

Rose, H.J., "Two Roman Rites," *CQ* 28 (1934), pp. 156–58.

Rose, H.J., "The 'Oath of Philippus' and the Di Indigetes," *HTR* 30 (1937), pp. 165–81.

Ryberg, I.S., *Rites of the State Religion in Roman Art, Memoirs of the American Academy in Rome* 22 (1955).

Salmon, E.T., *Samnium and the Samnites* (Cambridge, 1967).

Salmon, E.T., *Roman Colonization under the Republic* (Ithaca, 1970).

Schilling, R., *La religion romaine de Venus, BEFAR* 178 (1954).

Scullard, H.H., *The Etruscan Cities and Rome* (Ithaca, 1967).

Shields, E.L., *Juno: A Study in Early Roman Religion, Smith College Studies* 7 (1926).

Skutsch, O., *Studia Enniana* (London, 1968).

Sordi, M., *I rapporti romano-ceriti e l'origine della civitas sine suffragio* (Rome, 1960).

Sydenham, E.A., *Coinage of the Roman Republic* (London, 1952).

Taylor, L.R., "New Light on the History of the Secular Games," *AJP* 55 (1934), pp. 101–120.

Taylor, L.R., *The Voting Districts of the Roman Republic, Papers and Monographs of the American Academy in Rome* 20 (1960).

Taylor, L.R., *Roman Voting Assemblies from the Hannibalic War to the Dictatorship of Caesar* (Ann Arbor, 1966).

Thulin, C., *Die Götter des Martianus Capella und der Bronzeleber von Piacenza, Religionsgeschichtliche Versuche und Vorarbeiten* 3 (1906–1907).

Tibiletti, G., and Barbieri, G., "Lex" in E. De Ruggiero, *Dizionario epigrafico di antichità romane* (Rome, 1957).

Tilly, B., "The Identification of the Numicus," *JRS* 26 (1936), pp. 1–11.

Tilly, B., *Vergil's Latium* (Oxford, 1947).

Trombetti, A., *La lingua etrusca* (Florence, 1928).

Valentini, R., and Zucchetti, G., *Codice topografico della città di Roma*, vol. 2, *R. Istituto Storico Italiano per il medio Evo. Fonti per la storia d'italic d'Italia* 88 (1942).

Vetter, E., *Handbuch der italienischen Dialekte* 1 (Heidelberg, 1953).

Vetter, E., "Di Novensedes, di Indigetes," *IF* 62 (1956), pp. 1–16.

von Domaszewski, A., "Silvanus auf lateinischen Inschriften," *Philologus* 61 (1902), p. 1 ff., *Abhandlungen zur römischen Religion* (Leipzig, 1909), p. 58 ff.

Wagenvoort, H., *Roman Dynamism* (Oxford, 1947).

Walde, A., and Hofmann, J.B., *Lateinisches etymologisches Wörterbuch*, 3rd ed. (Heidelberg, 1938–54).

Warmington, B.H., *Carthage* (Baltimore, 1964).

Weinstock, S., "Martianus Capella and the Cosmic System of the Etruscans," *JRS* 36 (1946), pp. 100–129.

Weinstock, S., "Parca Maurtia und Neuna Fata," *Festschrift... A. Rumpf* (Krefeld, 1952), pp. 151–60.

Weinstock, S., "Two Archaic Inscriptions from Latium," *JRS* 50 (1960), pp. 112–18.

Weinstock, S., *Divus Julius* (Oxford, 1971).

Wissowa, G., *Religion und Kultus der Römer*, 2nd ed. (Munich, 1912).

Index